T0325071

The Cybersecurity Body of Knowledge

Internal Audit and IT Audit

The scope and mandate for internal audit continues to evolve each year, as does the complexity of the business environment and speed of the changing risk landscape in which it must operate.

The fundamental goal of this exciting new series is to produce leading-edge books on critical subjects facing audit executives as well as internal and IT audit practitioners.

Key topics that will be addressed over the coming years include Audit Leadership, Cybersecurity, Strategic Risk Management, Auditing Various IT Activities and Processes, Audit Management, and Operational Auditing.

If you're interested in submitting a proposal for a book to be included in the series, please email Gabriella.Williams@tandf.co.uk

Series Editor:
Dan Swanson

Project Management Capability Assessment: Performing ISO 33000-Based Capability Assessments of Project Management
Peter T. Davis and Barry D. Lewis

Auditor Essentials: 100 Concepts, Tips, Tools, and Techniques for Success
Hernan Murdock

How to Build a Cyber-Resilient Organization
Daniel Shoemaker, Anne Kohnke, and Ken Sigler

Fraud Auditing Using CAATT: A Manual for Auditors and Forensic Accountants to Detect Organizational Fraud
Shaun Aghili

Managing IoT Systems for Institutions and Cities
Chuck Benson

The Audit Value Factor
Daniel Samson

For more information about this series, please visit https://www.crcpress.com/Internal-Audit-and-IT-Audit/book-series/CRCINTAUDITA

The Cybersecurity Body of Knowledge

The ACM/IEEE/AIS/IFIP
Recommendations for a Complete
Curriculum in Cybersecurity

Daniel Shoemaker, Anne Kohnke,
and Ken Sigler

CRC Press
Taylor & Francis Group
Boca Raton London New York

CRC Press is an imprint of the
Taylor & Francis Group, an **informa** business
AN AUERBACH BOOK

CRC Press
Taylor & Francis Group
52 Vanderbilt Avenue,
New York, NY 10017

International Standard Book Number-13: 978-0-367-90094-6 (Hardback)

Visit the Taylor & Francis Web site at
http://www.taylorandfrancis.com

and the CRC Press Web site at
http://www.crcpress.com

Contents

Foreword 1

I have great pleasure in writing this foreword. I have worked with Dan, Anne, and Ken over the past six years as this amazing team has written six books for my book collection initiative. Their newest effort, *The Cybersecurity Body of Knowledge: The ACM/IEEE/AIS/IFIP Recommendations for a Complete Curriculum in Cybersecurity,* brings together a comprehensive understanding of cybersecurity and should be on the book shelf of every professor, student, and practitioner.

Right now, the study of cybersecurity is pretty much in the eye of the beholder. This is the case because the number of interpretations about what ought to be taught is only limited by the number of personal agendas out there in the field.

Through discussion with the team, I've learned that every well-established discipline of scholarship and practice has gone through the process of research, extensive discussions, formation of communities of practice, and thought leadership to continually build the body of knowledge. Over time, diverse voices put forth ideas, concepts, theories, and empirical evidence to advance the thinking, and in every discipline, there comes a time when thought leadership establishes generally accepted standards based on a comprehensive view of the body of knowledge.

I believe that time has come for the discipline of cybersecurity.

Beginning with a narrow focus on computer security, the discipline has advanced tremendously and has accurately become known as a fundamentally computing-based discipline that involves people, information, technology, and processes. Additionally, as the threat environment continues to expand, due to the expanse of global cyber infrastructure, the interdisciplinary nature of the field includes aspects of ethics, law, risk management, human factors, and policy. The growing need to protect not just corporate information and intellectual property but also to maintain national security has created a demand for specialists, across a range of work roles, with the knowledge of the complexities of holistically assuring the security of systems. A vision of proficiency in cybersecurity that aligns with industry needs and involves a broad global audience of stakeholders was needed to provide stability and an understanding of the boundaries of the discipline.

The formation of the CSEC2017 Joint Task Force – involving four major international computing societies: the Association of Computing Machinery (ACM), the IEEE Computer Society (IEEE CS), the Association for Information Systems Special Interest Group on Information Security and Privacy (AIS SIGSEC), and the International Federation for Information Processing Technical Committee on Information Security Education (IFIP WG 11.8) – came together to publish the single commonly accepted guidelines for cybersecurity curriculum (The CSEC2017 Report). The CSEC2017 Report has produced a thought model and structure in which the comprehensive discipline of cybersecurity can be understood. With this understanding, development within academic institutions and industry can prepare a wide range of programs that are grounded in fundamental principles.

This book explains the process by which the CSEC2017 was formulated, its pedigree, and then it discusses the knowledge units of each of the eight knowledge area categories of the field in detail. Upon reading this book, the reader will understand the knowledge that is required as well as a basic understanding of the application and purpose of each of these myriad elements.

I have studied the various chapters and believe the seamless flow of the content will be beneficial to all readers. The extensive use of visuals greatly improves the readability as well as supports a better understanding of the extensive number of knowledge topics that are involved. While knowledge knows no end, dissemination and sharing of knowledge are critical in today's world. I believe this book will help form the foundation of a comprehensive and generally accepted cybersecurity body of knowledge and I congratulate the team on their work and their amazing result.

Dan Swanson
Series Editor

Foreword 2

Cybersecurity is professionalizing. As a field, it has spawned from technical disciplines where it is an increasingly difficult fit, given its increasingly interdisciplinary nature. What started as a one-size-fits-all subject, about mitigating vulnerabilities in information systems, is now expected to cover the range of topics that a Chief Information Security Officer must consider when building an approach to keeping information safe within an organization. This not only includes the technical tools but also things such as policy, procedures, awareness training, audit, compliance, law, and privacy. These subjects clearly go beyond computer science or electrical engineering where students learn to build and apply cybersecurity system components.

Add to this challenge the fact that cybersecurity is evolving quickly. No sooner is a book published than it begins to become out of date! What a challenge for academics and practitioners alike to stay current! And if cybersecurity is becoming a profession like medicine or law, how difficult it becomes to ensure that employers in different parts of the country know what knowledge is in the minds of the cybersecurity expertise they hire. These are employees they are entrusting with the very life blood of their organizations, their information. There is a reason practitioners refer to the "crown jewels" of the company when they identify their most sensitive and valuable data.

With Snowden's and the Manning's raising awareness of how vulnerable an organization's information can be, how big the impacts if compromised, we need to ensure that those we hire to protect it have the knowledge, experience, integrity, and maturity to warrant trust. Hence, the effort to professionalize the field. We're seeing the emergence of codes of conduct, internship programs, certification testing, and standard curricula—all hallmarks of a profession.

Educational standards are at the very heart of any professional discipline. We need to know what those we hire know. Using medicine as an example, we have comfort that no matter what medical school a doctor attends, the basic curriculum is the same and we have board exams and accreditations for verification. Likewise, we need to have the same for cybersecurity, a practice that, if not performed well, could cripple infrastructure, bring down cities, and even cause deaths in the case of medical devices that are increasingly relied upon, yet are exposed online.

My colleagues Daniel Shoemaker, Anne Kohnke, and Ken Sigler have been working on standardization of cybersecurity curriculum for years – first in support of the NSA's efforts to specify what they need in a cybersecurity professional through their NIETP organization which created, working with NIST, the beginnings of educational standards and then through the various evolutions as DHS, professional organizations, certifications have made their contributions.

As the ACM has stepped up to creating cybersecurity education guidelines that invite other countries to help define them, it's time to acknowledge the development of what is becoming a set of educational standards that cybersecurity professionals around the world are acknowledging. With their book, the authors are presenting the case for educational standards as an important part of the emerging profession of cybersecurity.

I remember not too long ago when an HR executive from a large company in my region expressed frustration that advertising for cybersecurity expertise was not enough. You need to know what subdiscipline candidates know and what knowledge base they have in their minds so you can hire appropriately. Since that conversation, NIST/NICE, NSA, DHS, and ACM have wrestled with defining the field. The author's contribution is to synthesize this history and make the case for reliable educational standards that are the foundation of any profession.

Knowing the authors as I do, I can think of no others who could better make this case and also identify the appropriate time – now – to do so. This is an important contribution to the evolution of the cybersecurity profession to the next step – a profession like any other.

This is an exciting time to be in this field. I thank the authors for their efforts.

Barbara Endicott-Popovsky, PhD
Professor and Executive Director,
Center for Information Assurance and Cybersecurity
University of Washington;
Editor in Chief,
Colloquium for Information Systems Security Educators (CISSE) Journal

Author Biographies

Daniel Shoemaker, PhD, is full professor, senior research scientist, and program director at the University of Detroit Mercy's Center for Cyber Security and Intelligence Studies. Dan is a former chair of the Cybersecurity & Information Systems Department and has authored numerous books and journal articles focused on cybersecurity.

Anne Kohnke, PhD, is an associate professor of cybersecurity and the principle investigator of the Center for Academic Excellence in Cyber Defense at the University of Detroit Mercy. Anne's research is focused in cybersecurity, risk management, threat modeling, and mitigating attack vectors.

Ken Sigler is a faculty member of the Computer Information Systems (CIS) program at the Auburn Hills Campus of Oakland Community College in Michigan. Ken's research is in the areas of software management, software assurance, and cybersecurity.

Introduction

The Vital Need for Common Agreement

Every profession is built around formal agreement about the under-lying knowledge of the field. This agreement serves as the point of departure for building an academic discipline. In the case of the discipline of cybersecurity, there has never been a definitive, commonly accepted standard of the critical elements of the field. The purpose of the CSEC2017 Report (referred to as CSEC2017 for the remainder of the book) is to provide an authoritative standard.

The CSEC2017 is built around the assumption that there is a responsibility to specifically articulate what constitutes the field of cybersecurity. The goal of the CSEC2017 is to detail the communal knowledge areas and their constituent knowledge elements. In service of this, the CSEC2017 states and clarifies the separate educational elements of cybersecurity and their interrelationships to each other in professional practice. Each individual knowledge area is different in its focus and aims. Therefore, these disparate knowledge require-ments need to be integrated into a single strategic infrastructure that amounts to a comprehensive definition of the field. The value of a single unified definition is that it provides the depth of understanding necessary to ensure complete, in-depth solutions.

CSEC2017 focuses on the definition of a set of standard knowledge elements rather than the usual teaching and learning issues. In essence, the CSEC 2017 provides a complete conceptual structure containing every knowledge element that is considered to be germane to the study of cybersecurity. The CSEC2017 Report essentially documents and interrelates all of the necessary learning elements into a single common definition of the discipline cybersecurity and is one of the two groundbreaking aspects of this project. The other is that CSEC2017 provides a comprehensive roadmap for teaching and learning holistic cybersecurity.

The latter is important because the lack of a common understanding of the ways in which the diverse elements of the field fit together is one of the major stumbling blocks in building coherent responses to threats. Consequently, the synthesis of the details of the cybersecurity process into a single unified understanding is an invaluable asset for cybersecurity educators.

Defining the Elements of the Field of Cybersecurity: What is CSEC2017?

The CSEC2017 Joint Task Force on Cybersecurity Education (JTF) originated in September 2015 (CSEC-JTF, 2017). The CSEC2017 mission was twofold, "To initiate the processes for (1) developing undergraduate curricular guidance and (2) establish a case for the accreditation of educational programs in the cyber sciences." (CSEC, 2017, p. 10). The recommendations in the report represent fully sanctioned, all-inclusive guidelines about the content and structure of a cybersecurity curriculum. It must be understood that these recommendations are a single conceptual framework for the field. The CSEC2017 document does NOT specify a single monolithic approach, nor is it prescriptive. Instead, the CSEC2017 body of knowledge is meant to be used either completely or in part to develop relevant courses and to modify a broad range of existing programs or course concentrations (CSEC, 2017).

The CSEC2017 delineates the boundaries of the discipline and outlines key dimensions of the curricular structure of the study of cybersecurity. Its aim is, "To develop curricular guidance that is comprehensive enough to support a wide range of program types and to develop curricular guidance that is grounded in fundamental principles that provide stability" (CSEC-JTF, 2017, p. 11). As defined in the CSEC2017, there are eight generic knowledge areas. Taken as a whole, these distinctive areas constitute a common definition of the discipline as well as the learning elements that should be involved in the delivery of an acceptable cybersecurity learning experience.

Organization of the Text

The reader will see how to create a comprehensive cybersecurity teaching program, one that embodies the commonly recognized knowledge elements deemed essential to the field. This book will explain how each of these elements fit together.

The members of the Joint Task Force of major international computing societies identified eight knowledge areas that represent the comprehensive body of knowledge for cybersecurity education (CSEC, 2017). As with any complex design process, the deployment of a fully standard curriculum can only be described through a rational and explicit framework of requirements. The detailed process for creating and deploying those requirements is what is presented in these chapters.

Chapter One: Introduction: Securing Cyberspace Is Everybody's Business This chapter explains the general conditions under which the CSEC2017 was created. It outlines the problems with cybersecurity as we currently understand them. It also presents the background of the CSEC2017 and the role of the Learned Societies in creating it. The goal of this chapter is to give the reader an understanding of the overall strategic concerns associated with cybersecurity practice as well as provide the justification and advantages of a generally accepted common body of knowledge.

Readers will see how the lack of a unified understanding impacts everybody's security. The readers will also understand the reasons why the Learned Societies are so crucial in fostering common agreement in academia. They will see the justification for the actions taken by these societies to ensure a single comprehensive presentation of the elements of the field. Finally, this chapter will outline the eight knowledge elements of the CSEC2017 model.

Chapter Two: The Cybersecurity Body of Knowledge Development and coordination of a curriculum requires a common and coherent point of reference. The overall basis that is outlined in this chapter will give educators a practical understanding of the structure and content of a typical standard curriculum. The goal of this chapter is to provide readers with the ability to create practice-oriented courses on the CSEC2017 model. The reader will learn why a formal, comprehensive body of knowledge, which is aimed at ensuring capable understanding of the elements of the field, is critical to curricular success.

The aim of this chapter is to help the reader understand the role and application of bodies of knowledge in the development of cybersecurity curricula. It will also help the reader understand how bodies of knowledge are used to shape new fields of practice. This chapter will go into depth on the rationale and potential applications of a commonly accepted body of knowledge for cybersecurity. It will also present the knowledge areas of the CSEC2017 in detail. Finally, the constituent elements of each of the knowledge areas will be presented and discussed. Subsequent chapters will discuss how each of these areas fit. The aim here is to provide a rational overview. By the end of this chapter, the reader will understand the typical process for curricular planning, including the necessary learning objectives.

Chapter Three: Knowledge Area One: Data Security The Data Security knowledge area is the perfect area to lead off the body of knowledge. Data Security defines what must be known in order to ensure the security of data assets either at rest, during processing, or in transit (CSEC, 2017). This is a well-accepted and commonly understood part of the current discipline of cybersecurity, and there is no disagreement about its importance in the overall protection of electronic assets. The knowledge elements associated with this protection process include the usual set of commonly acknowledged areas such as basic cryptography concepts, digital forensics concepts, and methods for secure communications, including data integrity and authentication and information storage security (CSEC, 2017).

Thus, this chapter provides an in-depth discussion of Data Security. It will help the reader understand how cryptography is an enabler for assurance. It will show how data integrity and authentication techniques are used to mitigate password attacks. It will discuss the role of access control in preserving Data Security and integrity. It will discuss the communication protocols that offer the best levels of Data Security. It will also consider the importance of cryptanalysis in securing data.

Chapter Four: Knowledge Area Two: Software Security This is another area nobody will find surprising. Software assurance goes back to the very origins of the field. So, it predates any concerns about security. In the 1990s, the methods and techniques in this area focused on creating defect-free code, and the general area of practice was called "software quality assurance" or SQA. Since most of the knowledge, skills, and abilities (KSAs) associated with SQA transfer to the identification of exploitable flaws, the knowledge elements for this area are well defined and commonly accepted as accurate among both academics and business people.

The focus of the CSEC2017 Software Security knowledge units is on common assurance of the security properties of the information and systems that the software protects (CSEC, 2017). Thus, the CSEC2017 recommendations center on such accepted areas of practice as security requirements, design concepts and practice, software implementation and deployment issues, static and dynamic testing, configuration management, and ethics, especially in development, testing, and vulnerability disclosure (CSEC, 2017).

Chapter Five: Knowledge Area Three: Component Security The Component Security knowledge area is perhaps the most novel of the cybersecurity areas in that it is not an element of most of the predecessor bodies of knowledge for cybersecurity. However, it is not surprising to see it here given the inclusion of computer engineering in the issues of cybersecurity assurance. Component Security's body of knowledge focuses on the design, procurement, testing, analysis, and maintenance of the tangible components that are integrated into larger systems (CSEC, 2017).

Thus, the elements of this area include such well-accepted hardware aspects as identification and elimination of vulnerabilities present in system components, component life cycle maintenance and configuration management, secure hardware component design principles, security testing, and reverse engineering. Finally, there is although a healthy dose of supply chain management security knowledge elements due to the industry's commitment to commercial off-the-shelf integration of components.

Chapter Six: Knowledge Area Four: Connection Security   This area is what is colloquially known as, "network security." The security of networks is another quality that is both commonly accepted as well as an essential aspect of good cybersecurity practice. So, it is not surprising to find it featured as an element of the body of knowledge.

Networks and networking have been a fundamental element of the information technology universe since the late 1960s, with ARPANET and other primordial computer communication systems. And networking had reached a high degree of sophistication prior to the advent of the Internet. But the security of networks became a primary concern with the introduction of that groundbreaking technological advancement. The knowledge in this area focuses on the security of the connections between components including both physical and logical connections (CSEC, 2017).

Thus, the CSEC2017 guidelines entail assurance practices for networked systems, networking architecture, and standard secure transmission models, physical component interconnections and interfaces, software component interfaces, and of course, the common types of connection and transmission attacks.

Chapter Seven: Knowledge Area Five: System Security   This knowledge area begins the move off of the technology platform and into the area of standard organizational processes. Hence, the System Security knowledge area focuses primarily on those common organizational practices that ensure the security requirements of systems, which are composed of interconnected components and connections, and the networking software that supports those interconnections (CSEC, 2017).

Accordingly, the knowledge elements in this area embody guidelines that spell out the necessity for a holistic approach to systems, the importance of security policy, as well as organized identification and authentication management processes; this area also contains recommendations for system access control and operational system monitoring processes, as well as the standard recovery, system testing, and system documentation best practices.

Chapter Eight: Knowledge Area Six: Human Security This is a brand-new and very novel element of the body of knowledge. It represents the first serious attempt to provide recommendations with respect to the human attack surface. As we have said, this is terra incognita for the traditional study of cybersecurity, so, although it might not be as mature as areas one through four, it represents a pioneering step in the effort to compile a complete and correct body of knowledge for the field.

The first four knowledge areas comprise what might be considered to be the "usual suspects" in the cybersecurity profession. They are essentially hard, technology focused, elements that encompass generally well-known and commonly accepted axioms regarding the practice of data, software, component, and system assurance. The Human Security area attempts to make benchmark recommendations about the assurance of human behavior and the study of human behavior as it relates to the maintenance of a state of cybersecurity.

Needless to say, this is a new area and one which will probably be susceptible to refinement over a period of time. However, the loss statistics make it clear that the focus on protecting individuals' data and privacy in the context of their role as employees and in their personal lives is an important area of teaching and research (CSEC, 2017). The recommended knowledge elements in the Human Security knowledge area include such areas as identity management, social engineering prevention, assurance of workforce and individual awareness and understanding, assurance of broad-scale social behavioral privacy and security, and the elements of personal data privacy and security protection.

Chapter Nine: Knowledge Area Seven: Organizational Security Organizational security is historically the most well-known and commonly discussed aspect of all of the nontechnical areas. The general content and focus of this area is embodied in the recommendations of the National Institute of Standards and Technology's workforce framework (NIST 800-181) as Knowledge Area Seven, "Oversee and Govern" (Newhouse, 2017).

The Organizational Security area encompasses all of the relevant processes and behaviors for the rational oversight and control of the overall cybersecurity function. This is understandably a very large element of the CSEC2017 model, since those controls embody all of the traditional countermeasures that are associated with the general protection of the organization as a whole. This includes the deployment and oversight of controls to ensure proper monitoring and response to intrusions on the technological attack surface, as well as the entire set of standard behaviors associated with the human attack surface.

The purpose of the knowledge that is embodied in the Organizational Security area is to assure the organization against all relevant cybersecurity threats, as well as manage the inherent risks that are associated with the successful accomplishment of the organization's mission (CSEC, 2017). Consequently, the elements in this area include a detailed set of recommendations for the risk management process, the setting of governance and policy strategies, long- and short-term planning, as well as legal, regulatory, and ethical compliance.

Chapter Ten: Knowledge Area Eight: Societal Security The Societal Security knowledge area is revolutionary, and it reflects the growing awareness of the impact of virtual space on the average person's life. The knowledge items in this category are mostly large societal factors that might, for better or for worse, broadly impact every citizen in our society.

The knowledge elements are essentially still in need of refinement. But their inclusion opens the door to their integration into the overall understanding of how virtual space needs to be channeled into institutional actions that area beneficial to the world community as a whole. This includes thought models for approaching the problems of cybercrime, the legal and ethical dictates associated with good citizenship, as well as social policy, personal privacy, and how that relates to the formal mechanisms of conventional cyberspace (CSEC, 2017).

The specific recommendations promulgated in this area center on the general behaviors to prevent, or alleviate cybercrime, make and enforce laws in cyberspace, ensure ethical thinking when it comes to functioning in cyberspace, as well as the elements of what constitutes proper cyber policies and privacy regulation.

Reader Expectations

This book presents a set of well-defined and commonly accepted knowledge requirements for building recommended curricula in cybersecurity. Therefore, there are no expectations about specialized technical knowledge per se. All readers will learn how to design and develop a commonly sanctioned curriculum in cybersecurity using the holistic recommendations of the CSEC2017 model. After reading this book, the reader will know how to build and maintain a complete, applied curriculum that conforms with the principles of best practice, as well as evolve the curriculum to continue to meet the learning requirements for the field as they evolve. At the end of this book, the reader will be able to:

- Create, sustain, and evolve a holistic cybersecurity curriculum.
- Define and evaluate instructional processes and supporting material.
- Ensure full and complete coverage of all of the essential elements of the discipline of cybersecurity.

References

CSEC, Joint Task Force (JTF) on Cybersecurity Education, "Cybersecurity Curricula 2017, Curriculum Guidelines for Post-Secondary Degree Programs in Cybersecurity, a Report in the Computing Curricula Series," ACM/IEEE-CS/AIS SIGSEC/IFIP WG 11.8, Version 1.0, 31 December 2017.

Newhouse, William, Stephanie Keith, Benjamin Scribner, Greg Witte, "NIST Special Publication 800-181, National Initiative for Cybersecurity Education (NICE) Cybersecurity Workforce Framework," NIST. SP.800-181, August 2017.

1

SECURING CYBERSPACE IS EVERYBODY'S BUSINESS

In this chapter, you will learn the following:

- Why a standard definition of the practice of cybersecurity is important
- How exploitable gaps occur in a real-world cyberdefense
- The importance of teaching cybersecurity as comprehensive process
- The role of professional societies in shaping the discipline of cybersecurity
- The general structure and intent of the CSEC2017 Project
- The practical applications of the CSEC2017 Project.

Introduction: The Current Situation Is Out of Control

It is a well-documented phenomenon that there is a global problem securing cyberspace (Accenture, 2019; Rivero, 2018; Hatchimonji, 2013; Symantec, 2014; Trend-Micro, 2015; PRC, 2017; NIAC, 2018). However, the price of that failure might not be so clear. To use a couple of global concerns to illustrate the problem, first, let's look at the skyrocketing cost of cybercrime. In 2015, cybercrime cost the world $500 billion. By 2018, that expense had escalated sixfold to $3 trillion (Microsoft, 2018). And, by 2021, the price is expected to double again to $6 trillion (Microsoft, 2018). Needless to say, an annual loss that exceeds the combined gross domestic product of Great Britain, Germany, and France combined is going to impact every business in every industrialized country in the world (Figure 1.1).

Additionally, there are advanced persistent threats in cyberspace that target our critical infrastructure, and since the infrastructure underwrites our entire way of life, the prospect of harm to it is a threat to our national survival (NIAC, 2018; Cummins & Pollet, 2009).

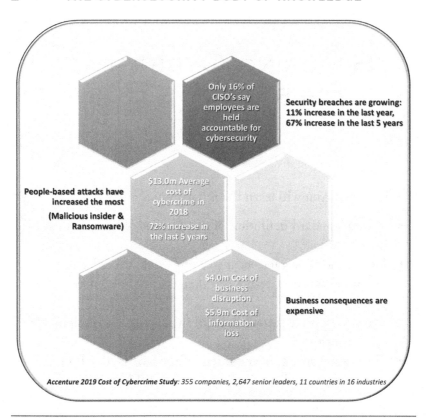

Figure 1.1 Global problem of securing cyberspace.

A potential attack on any major element of our infrastructure is so strategically significant that it has been dubbed as a "Digital Pearl Harbor." The basis for the concern is that much of the infrastructure was designed before the need to protect it was even an issue (NIAC, 2018). So, the automated functions that perform the infrastructure's everyday tasks have no innate resistance to a cyberattack. Still, those components are at risk only if they are remotely accessible (Figure 1.2).

There is an increasing propensity to hook infrastructure components to the Internet for ease of maintenance and operation, which makes the whole architecture almost impossible to defend. This is the reason why the issue of cybersecurity is a serious part of any discussion about our national interest.

What has been our society's response? Unfortunately, the response has been to dither (Brasso, 2016). Specifically, none of the sectors in the United States' national infrastructure domain have developed

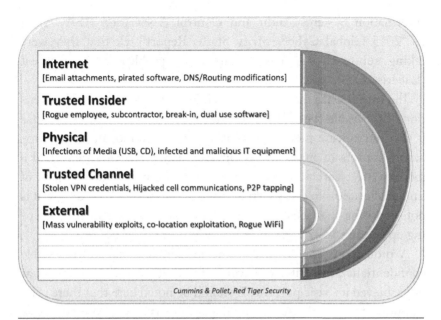

Internet
[Email attachments, pirated software, DNS/Routing modifications]

Trusted Insider
[Rogue employee, subcontractor, break-in, dual use software]

Physical
[Infections of Media (USB, CD), infected and malicious IT equipment]

Trusted Channel
[Stolen VPN credentials, Hijacked cell communications, P2P tapping]

External
[Mass vulnerability exploits, co-location exploitation, Rogue WiFi]

Cummins & Pollet, Red Tiger Security

Figure 1.2   Advanced persistent threat vectors.

an effective strategy or a coherent scheme to protect itself from a concerted cyberattack (NIAC, 2018). And even worse, there is no consistent agreement about what would constitute such an attack (Brasso, 2016). Yet a successful attack on any major element of the national infrastructure could literally end society as we know it (NIAC, 2018).

Consequently, infrastructure cybersecurity now epitomizes the sort of existential threat that nuclear war used to pose. Will such a thing ever happen? In the words of Mike Rogers, the former head of the National Security Agency, "It's not a matter of if, but when!" (NIAC, 2018; Lois, 2015). Thus, it is critically important that we address the significant issues in cyberspace.

The Challenge: How Do You Protect Something that Doesn't Actually Exist?

You would think that every organization's top priority would be the creation of a complete and comprehensive virtual asset protection scheme. However, cybersecurity is treated a lot like the weather; everybody talks about it, but little is done to seriously address it. For example, only 38% of the organizations that were surveyed by

Information Systems Audit and Control Association (ISACA) in its "2015 Global Cybersecurity Status Report" felt that they were taking substantive steps to address the problem of cyberthreat (Laberis, 2016).

The Internet has the same potential impact on society as the invention of moveable type. The difference between these two revolutions is that our culture took three centuries to accommodate to the profound impacts of mass printed information. Whereas, we've had a mere twenty years to adjust to the even more momentous impact of immediate access to every virtual thing in the world. Accordingly, it is not surprising that society's mechanisms have had a hard time keeping up (Figure 1.3).

A protection scheme that is unable to guarantee the reasonable confidentiality, integrity, and availability of its protection objects has not achieved its basic purpose. It should be noted here that there is no exception to this rule. A loss of virtual value is a loss, no matter how the exploit was actually carried out. So, it's a moot point whether it was an insider exploit or an electronic attack. It was still a loss.

The single characteristic by which a cybersecurity effort ought to be judged is its ability to dependably and effectually prevent any type of loss or harm to an organization's virtual assets. In this respect, it is axiomatic that the cybersecurity function is obliged to close off every

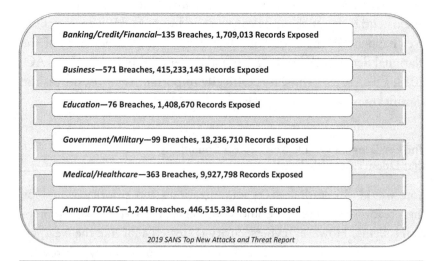

Banking/Credit/Financial–135 Breaches, 1,709,013 Records Exposed

Business—571 Breaches, 415,233,143 Records Exposed

Education—76 Breaches, 1,408,670 Records Exposed

Government/Military—99 Breaches, 18,236,710 Records Exposed

Medical/Healthcare—363 Breaches, 9,927,798 Records Exposed

Annual TOTALS—1,244 Breaches, 446,515,334 Records Exposed

2019 SANS Top New Attacks and Threat Report

Figure 1.3   2018 security breaches.

Top 10 Data Breaches of All Time		
Company	Accounts Hacked	Date of Hack
Yahoo	3 billion	Aug. 2013
Marriott	500 million	2014-2018
Yahoo	500 million	Late 2014
Adult FriendFinder	412 million	Oct. 2016
MySpace	360 million	May 2016
Under Armor	150 million	Feb. 2018
Equifax	145.5 million	July 2017
EBay	145 million	May 2014
Target	110 million	Nov. 2013
Heartland Payment Systems	100+ million	May 2008

Figure 1.4 Top ten security breaches of all time.

potential avenue of attack for all of the virtual assets that it is held accountable for. And ten years of data loss makes it crystal clear that we are getting worse at the task, not better (Figure 1.4).

We Must Re-evaluate Our Assumptions

In 1929, Lieutenant Colonel J.L. Schley wrote in the *Military Engineer*, "It has been said critically that there is a tendency in many armies to spend the peace time studying how to fight the last war." And this has never been truer with the fight to protect cyberspace. On the surface, the justification for our current approach seems simple enough. The virtual world is enabled by computers, which have an explicit set of rules associated with them. These rules are dictated by the unyielding architecture of the machine. Therefore, it seems obvious that we should base our cybersecurity protection paradigms around the well-established scientific principles of computer engineering and networking architecture, which has been the reasoning since the beginning of the field. However, perhaps we have misunderstood the meaning of the term "cybersecurity."

Cybersecurity is a combination of the words cyber, meaning *computer* and *security*. We understand the reason for the cyber part. Virtual information is kept and transmitted electronically by computers so, it seems like common sense to hand the responsibility for cybersecurity to the technical part of the organization. The problem is that *security* is actually its own independent concept and it carries a different set of requirements. Security implies the act of safeguarding something. Cybersecurity, as the term is presently interpreted, does protect some things. For instance, it is well documented that the effective percentage of successful electronic exploits has decreased over the past decade. Even so, it is one thing to protect a virtual asset from unauthorized electronic access, while it is another thing entirely to ensure that the same asset cannot be lost or harmed due to any type of credible exploit or attack.

In this respect, the *security* part of *cybersecurity* expands the protection mission to encompass the responsibility to safeguard every virtual object of value. Thus, cybersecurity's role goes from simply regulating the coming and going of data through a highly restricted point of electronic access, like a firewall, to assuring that the virtual asset cannot be harmed by any foreseeable means. The latter requirement is a much more rigorous test. But it is still an inescapable fact that, a loss of value is a loss no matter what the cause is (Figure 1.5).

55% of organizations do not make *protecting* part of their strategy[1]

550 million the number of phishing emails sent out by a single campaign during 1st Qtr 2018[3]

Largest component of the total cost of a data breach is lost business: **abnormal turnover of customers, reputation losses, diminished goodwill**[5]

3,418,647,753 the total number of records containing personal and other sensitive data compromised between January 2017 and May 2019[2]

34% of organizations see careless/unaware employees as the biggest vulnerability[6]

79% of business leaders say new business models introduce technology vulnerabilities faster than they can be secured[4]

1. EY Global Information Security Survey 2018-19 (GISS); 2. Chronology of Data Breaches, May 2019, https://www.privacyrights.org/data-breaches; 3. DarkReading, 26 April 2018, *New Phishing Attach Targets 550M Email Users Worldwide*; 4. Ninth Annual Cost of Cybercrime Study, AccentureSecurity; 5. Ponemon Institute's 2018 Cost of a Data Breach Study, 18 Sept 2018; 6. EY Global Information Security Survey 2019-19 (GISS)

Figure 1.5   Organizational responses to cybersecurity.

There are two highly credible types of attacks that are unavoidably part of the overall attack surface: human and physical exploits. The willingness of an organization to ignore these plausible lines of attack will preprogram failure into the protection mission. Current research shows that electronic exploits constitute less than one-third of the threat. The rest of the protection problem involves such real-world factors as insider threats and social engineering or even natural complications like fire or flood. So, the question remains, who should be responsible for deploying and coordinating a defense against those types of exploits?

In many organizations, human or physical types of threats are often not included in traditional cyberdefense planning. Most active cyberdefense solutions do not even consider the need to embody tightly integrated, well-defined, and uniformly applied behavioral controls as a fundamental part of the overall cybersecurity process (Laberis, 2016). As a result, well-executed attacks against the non-electronic attack surface are almost certain to succeed. The question is, what is the reason for such a clear disconnect in our planning?

The Adversary Changes Things

The goal of the adversary is to break into the system, not use it. And those adversaries are not constrained by conventional rules of engagement. Besides the traditional task of ensuring that the system operates as intended, system developers and administrators are now expected to ensure that its day-to-day functioning is fully safeguarded from any foreseeable kind of malicious exploitation. In the case of a determined adversary, the scope of the protection perimeter is now opened up to any means necessary to achieve the ends of a wide range of hacker types. If the adversary's aim is to subvert or acquire a virtual asset, then the easiest way to accomplish this would be through the path of least resistance (PRC). As far back as the 1970s, Saltzer and Schroeder codified this as the *Work Factor* principle (Saltzer and Schroeder, 1974). In essence, the adversary will adopt the approach that is the easiest to execute and the most likely to succeed. Sun Tzu characterized this thinking best when he wrote, "Attack weakness not strength." Or in practical terms, the form of the hack will be dictated by the shape of the soft spots in the cyberdefense.

If the organization has constructed a strong electronic defense, a smart adversary will launch anything BUT an electronic attack and the data supports this. In 2006, the predominant percentage of loss was from exploits that could be classified as "electronic" (PRC, 2017). Fast forward and the preponderance of the losses are due to exploits that are classified as "behavioral" (PRC, 2017). This change in tactics illustrates how the adversary has simply shifted their line of attack to accommodate our improved capability in the electronic realm. And since the nontechnical attack surface is so much wider, it is also, most probably, the reason why our loss statistics continue to grow at exponential rates.

From a terminology standpoint, the exploits we have been talking about are nontechnical hacks. Both human-centered and physical types of attacks fall into that category and, as the term implies, nontechnical hacks that do not target the technology directly. Rather than electronic types of approaches, nontechnical hacks increasingly target existing behavioral or physical weaknesses in the organization. Thus, in real-world terms, nontechnical hacks are aimed at the human attack surface. The term *human attack surface* simply denotes every possible way in which intentional behavior that is executed in the physical space could compromise an asset or its confidentiality. Microsoft estimates that by 2020, the human attack surface will encompass 4–6 billion people (Microsoft, 2018).

Because human behavior is distinctive, creative, and unpredictable, there are an infinite number of ways that a nontechnical hack can be executed. The most popular approaches include such familiar exploits as insider and social engineering attacks. But nontechnical impacts can also be the result of humble everyday operational errors like procedural malfunctions and even simple worker negligence (Whatis, 2018).

It is hard to estimate the percent of actual harm that nontechnical hacks represent. Damaging exploits, such as industrial espionage or theft of proprietary trade secrets, are rarely reported, and simple human negligence or inadvertent error tends to get missed or covered up. Therefore, it is impossible to accurately describe the impact of such a set of occurrences. Nevertheless, it is believed that the overall extent of the problem is most certainly far greater than what is currently estimated (Laberis, 2016).

There are two logical reasons why nontechnical hacks go unreported or, for that matter, unnoticed. Both of them illustrate the challenge organizations face when it comes to building a complete and effective cyberdefense. First, companies, and particularly top-level decision makers, simply don't associate human behavior with virtual losses and so the threats that malicious insiders and bumbling employees represent tend to fly under their radar (Laberis, 2016). Nevertheless, nontechnical hacks are now the dominant PRC (2017). And since the adversary is becoming more and more reliant on their use, we will have to learn how to close off all the alternative paths. The ability to identify, classify, and counter nontechnical exploits will have to be amalgamated into every organization's overall understanding and approach to cybersecurity going forward.

Second, human behavior is impossible to accurately predict or effectually monitor. More importantly, an insider is part of the organization; therefore, they are trusted to some extent. Accordingly, it is almost impossible to spot a capable insider who is planning to undertake an attack, and because humans are creative, their harmful actions are almost impossible to assure by automated means (Laberis, 2016). Yet, most of our present-day cyberdefenses are still exclusively oriented toward countering electronic types of attack, which is also reflected in the loss statistics.

At present, 71% of annual losses are due to failures in the physical and human attack domains, while electronic breaches account for roughly 29% (PRC, 2017). Specifically, the leading cause of record loss (36%) over the past decade is attributable to physical exploits (PRC, 2017). A physical exploit is any hands-on theft, harm, or loss. A stolen laptop containing sensitive information is one example. Human behavior is the second leading cause of record loss (35%). Human behavior exploits include such categories as insider theft, social engineering, or human error (PRC, 2017). While the lowest percentage of losses (29%) fall into the area of the classic technology-based attacks, unfortunately, these are often the only kind of attacks factored into an organization's cybersecurity planning.

The Three-Legged Stool

Cyberdefense rests on a three-legged stool: electronic, human, and physical. The practical starting point for good cyberdefense is to begin to assimilate the three important areas into the overall strategic planning function; however, one issue is that the three component domains have traditionally operated independent of each other. So, the question is, how do we start the process? We start by knocking down the stovepipes. Stovepipes, where teams work independently of each other and do not share information, are the reason that credible threats like insider attacks or social engineering need to be called out and addressed in the formal protection planning process (Figure 1.6).

The people who should be involved in constructing the cybersecurity defense may not be aware of the aspects of the problem that they do not touch because of the blind men and the elephant syndrome. In that old fable, six blind men are asked to describe an elephant based on what they are touching. To one, it's a snake, to another it's a wall, and to another it's a tree, etc. But in the end, "Though each was partly in the right, all were entirely wrong."

So, the need to counter threats that arise in other areas is overlooked. Understandably, the job of network security is to secure the network, not necessarily the software applications, just as human resource personnel do not configure firewall rules or restrict access control to servers as part of their mandate. The present stovepiped state of the practice is leveraged by at least three mutually limited views of

Figure 1.6   Blind men and the elephant.

the world, which puts the cybersecurity function into an unavoidably dysfunctional state. Although there are established elements of the field that can capably protect the part of the elephant that they touch, none of the conventional elements are an entirely effective solution in and of itself. And if every practical aspect of the solution is not fully integrated into the response, then the PRC gaps are bound to manifest.

Learning to Play Better with Others

Exploitable gaps are created when the important actors in the cyberdefense process do not collaborate. As we have seen, most of the necessary set of actors are probably unaware of the actual requirement to cooperate. For instance, the failure to lock and monitor the computer room or to thoroughly vet the system manager will always invalidate any elegant security solution. This is because direct access to the machine trumps every other form of countermeasure.

These situations are sources of the types of *exploitable gaps*; however, the design of substantive steps to limit every form of direct physical access to the server, such as locks and employee monitoring and supervision, requires participation of the relevant players from the human resources and physical security areas. Often, these experts are not involved in either the planning or the day-to-day operations of the cybersecurity function.

Every factor has to be considered in order for a cyberdefense to be gap-free. But, because the planning for cybersecurity is often seen as a strictly technological exercise, the organization is not able to deploy the full set of controls necessary to completely and adequately protect its assets from every conceivable source of harm. Accordingly, the challenge is clear. The profession must find ways to ensure that the real-world practice of cybersecurity incorporates a complete, accurate, and highly effective set of well-defined and commonly accepted controls – ones that are capable of closing off every feasible type of adversarial action.

Creating a Holistic Solution

The term *holistic* was adopted to describe a state of comprehensive cybersecurity. Holistic simply means that every type of threat has been identified and countered by a formal control mechanism.

In practical terms, holistic solutions describe organizational situations in which all likely threats have been effectively countered by an actual and fully integrated set of electronic, physical, and human-centered controls and are enabled by a systematic planning process. Therefore, good cybersecurity practice involves strategic architecture and design. The architectural process must consider all reasonable avenues of exploitation and all of the necessary controls and countermeasures are implemented and enforced. The aim of the countermeasures is to ensure a complete and effective cyberdefense. This isn't just a matter of putting together a list of controls. There has to be a specific organizational mechanism in place to rationally integrate every one of these controls into a complete and effective cyberdefense system.

The Importance of Knowing What to Do

We will only be able to implement a holistic solution when we are able to bring all of the essential players together. Since the consolidation of protection responsibilities is likely to incorporate a range of skills and interests, there must be a universal agreement about the elements that constitute correct and effective practice. To be fully effective, the definition must amalgamate all of the essential concepts of cyberdefense into a single unifying practice model; one that has real-world currency.

Best practice is not something that is empirically derived. The term "best practice" simply designates the things that we know as a result of universal lessons learned over time. Best practice is classically embodied in "Bodies of Knowledge" (BOK) which is founded on expert opinions about the best way of doing something. The purpose of the rest of this book is to explain how a common body of knowledge is derived and conveyed, as well as how it can be a difference maker for educators in designing proper curricula and courses.

Enabling Common Understanding

Every profession is built around a common understanding of the appropriate and effective practices of the field. A formal statement of the critical underlying knowledge requirements is the necessary point for building an academic discipline and should serve as the basis for understanding what needs to be studied. The basic knowledge requirements tell the educator and student what they need to know and do, and it helps them understand how all of the elements of their field fit together as they relate to a real-world understanding of the basic responsibilities of the cybersecurity professional.

Up to this point, there has never been a legitimate commonly accepted definition of the critical elements that would constitute the knowledge required to do cybersecurity work. This key missing definition was what motivated the production of the National Institute for Standards and Technology workforce framework (NIST 800-181). NIST prepared the model as a definition of the standard roles in the cybersecurity workforce and is very useful in that respect. It demarcates the limits and job categories of every practical area of work in the profession. It also describes the common knowledge, skill, and ability (KSA) requirements for each area. However, while NIST 800-181 is an excellent first step, its application is still limited to the federal government space.

The government has provided outstanding leadership in the definition of the field. But it has a different role and function than classic institutions of education. As a result, NIST 800-181 still does not represent the essential commonly accepted body of knowledge that educators need to build curricula and courses. Therefore, an officially sanctioned body of knowledge was still the missing link in the formal education process.

Education Is the Key

Education has been the societal entity responsible for embedding new ideas in a culture. Academic scholars conduct research to add to the body of knowledge; however, the practitioner societies (associations) have traditionally developed and documented the essential concepts of the academic fields and their experiences working in organizations. Skilled and experienced practitioners are the entities who are typically most current on the issues that organizations face and the logical people to provide a body of knowledge for cybersecurity. The culmination of the work of the leading cyber associations is the CSEC2017 model, which is discussed in the rest of this text. CSEC2017 should be considered to comprise the single authoritative statement of the knowledge elements that unify the various elements of the field of cybersecurity into a single common vision, and in that respect, CSEC2017 is the first step in defining a stand-alone field of study for cybersecurity.

The Body of Knowledge and Educational Strategy

Along with the coordinated management of the classroom delivery of content, any emerging discipline requires a formally planned and implemented, broad-scale academic strategy. A clear-cut educational approach is the underlying condition that is necessary to impart knowledge in every organized discipline of study from dentistry to mechanic's school. Yet, up to this point, the elements of the field of cybersecurity have not been embodied in any form of all-inclusive strategic direction; particularly where the human attack surface is concerned.

A standard educational delivery approach is made difficult without a communal understanding and acceptance of a credible body of knowledge. All of the participants in the teaching process have to be on the same page in order for the message to be sufficiently well coordinated. So logically, the first requirement for formulating a cogent educational approach is common acknowledgment of what appropriate learning content is for a given study. The requisite knowledge has to be actively identified, catalogued, and disseminated. For example, computer science didn't just show up in college catalogues in one day. It evolved over time as an amalgam of fundamental ideas from the fields of mathematics, electrical engineering, and even philosophy. Subsequently, the official contents of that body of knowledge had to be sanctioned as correct by the relevant practitioners in order to make the study of computer science into a formal educational discipline. Then after that recognition, the body of knowledge had to be formally promulgated to all pertinent educational providers in a systematized fashion.

In academe, the formal mechanism for promulgating BOK are the learned societies that are generally acknowledged as being the legitimate overseers and sanctioners of that particular academic discipline. Every legitimate body of knowledge has to be accepted as accurate by the profession it characterizes and is typically obtained from expert advice about lessons learned in the real world. Professional societies exist and serve as the developers and sanctioners of the fundamental ideas in their respective fields. Thus, it is the professional societies who are responsible for the promulgation and accreditation of a recognized body of knowledge and professional practice. Examples of professional bodies include well-known groups such as:

- The American Medical Association (AMA) for Doctors
- The American Dental Association (ADA) for Dentists
- The American Bar Association (ABA) for Lawyers
- The National Society of Professional Engineers (NSPE) for Engineers

In the case of computer science, interest groups, which are termed "learned societies," have promulgated curricular guidelines for their areas of interest, and each of these societies now sponsors a particular academic discipline. The Association for Computing Machinery, or ACM, sponsors computer science; the Institute of Electrical and Electronic Engineers (IEEE) sponsors software engineering; the Association for Information Systems (AIS) sponsors business information systems; and the International Federation for Information Processing (IFIP) expands the sanctioning of best practice for each of these areas into the international arena (Figure 1.7).

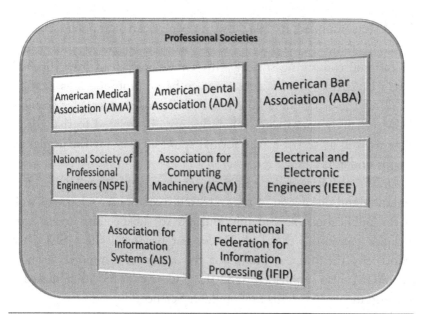

Figure 1.7   Professional associations.

Because computing comprises more than just the science of the computer, over time, other professional and academic interest groups have come together to address the issues in their particular areas. These groups are also involved in establishing guidelines for the BOK as they apply to their specific educational interests. At this present point in time, standardized recommendations for curricula are available for the disciplines of computer science (2013), computer engineering (2016), information systems (2010), information technology (2017), and software engineering (2014) (ACM, 2018).

Cybersecurity as an Academic Study

The four commonly recognized "societies" that sanction the aspects of the field of computing from oldest to newest, are the ACM, the IEEE, the AIS, and the IFIP. Their role is to define the acceptable knowledge for their respective areas of practice as well as maintain standards of accuracy.

The Association for Computing Machinery (ACM)

ACM was founded in 1947 by the American computer scientist Edmund Berkeley. Today, it is the world's largest scientific and educational computing society with a membership of over 100,000 (ISCTE, 2018). ACM is considered to be an umbrella organization for all of the academic and scholarly concerns in computer science. ACM officially coordinates scholarly activities related to that discipline as well as serves as the formal spokesperson for the academic groups under its care.

ACM's activities include holding regular conferences for the presentation and discussion of new research in computer science as well as the publication of academic journals in subspecialty areas. This includes convening the Task Force that produced the CSEC2017 report. As the interest group for the study of computer science, the ACM also published CS2013, "Curriculum Guidelines for Undergraduate Programs in Computer Science."

The International Society of Electrical and Electronic Engineers (IEEE)

As the name implies, IEEE sponsors activities related to the field of electrical and electronic engineering. IEEE actually has its origins in the 1880s, which far predates the computer. However, the interest groups that comprise today's IEEE were not formed into the present entity until 1963. Currently, IEEE has over 395,000 members in 160 countries, and through its global network of geographical units, publications, web services, and conferences, IEEE remains the world's largest technical professional association (IEEE, 2019).

The IEEE is responsible for the development of engineering standards for the computer and electronics industry. IEEE has traditionally been the entity focused on professional application of engineering techniques and tools to improve the software industry. Specifically, relevant to the study of cybersecurity, the IEEE fosters the application of conventional engineering principles and methods for the software industry. As a result, IEEE publishes both undergraduate and graduate curricula for the discipline of software engineering. The discipline was formally sanctioned in 1987 (Ford, 1994). The current IEEE curriculum recommendations for the field of software engineering are SE2014, "Curriculum Guidelines for Undergraduate Degree Programs in Software Engineering" and GSwE2009, "Curriculum Guidelines for Graduate Degree Programs in Software Engineering."

The Association for Information Systems (AIS)

AIS was founded in 1994. It is the professional association that develops and promulgates knowledge and practices related to the management information systems profession. The society itself is mainly an academic association and is comprised of teachers and scholars who foster best practice in the development, implementation, and practical assessment of information systems.

AIS involves participants from more than ninety countries (AISNET, 2018), which represent three regions of the globe: the Americas, Europe and Africa, and Asia-Pacific (AISNET, 2018). The association publishes academic curricula for the study of business information systems, *IS2002, Curriculum Guidelines for Undergraduate Degree Programs in Information Systems*, and the IS2010, *Curriculum Update: Curriculum Guidelines for Undergraduate Degree Programs in Information Systems*. It also publishes *MSIS2006, Model Curriculum and Guidelines for Graduate Degree Programs in Information Systems* (ACM, 2018).

The International Federation for Information Processing (IFIP)

IFIP is a nongovernmental entity responsible for linking the various national information technology associations working in the field of information processing. It serves as the umbrella interest group for all of the national societies in the field of computing. IFIP Technical Committees and Working Groups contribute to, and often lead, progress in the state-of-the-art knowledge and practice in information technology/information processing fields.

IFIP was established in 1960 as an outcome of the first World Computer Congress held in Paris in 1959. It operates under the auspices of UNESCO (IFIP, 2018). IFIP represents IT Societies from over fifty-six countries, spanning five continents with a total membership of over half a million people (IFIP, 2018).

The Importance of Unified Recommendations about Areas of Vital Interest

Occasionally all the societies come together to develop a single unified set of recommendations in the case of a topic of vital mutual interest. The first document of that type was the, *Joint Curricular Recommendations for Computing Curricula* (ACM, CC2005). CC2005 was developed to define the disciplines that were considered to be justifiably a part of the general study of computing. It was an important topic in the late 1990s because the out-of-control proliferation of disciplines that were centered on computer study and were both confusing and dysfunctional in education in general. Hence, CC2005 was significant in that it drew the line around and clarified the academic studies that could be considered to be the components of overall computer education.

After CC2005 was published, it became increasingly evident that a sanctioned definition of the elements of the emerging discipline of cybersecurity was also required. Thus, the societies once more organized a Joint Task Force to formulate the first set of globally accepted curricular recommendations for cybersecurity education (CSEC, 2017). The guideline is entitled the, "Cybersecurity Curricula 2017, curricular volume," or CSEC2017. The aim of CSEC2017 is to be, "The leading resource for comprehensive cybersecurity curricular content for global academic institutions seeking to develop a broad range of cybersecurity offerings at the post-secondary level." (CSEC 2017 Mission Statement, p. 10).

The recommendations of the CSEC2017 body of knowledge provide educators and their students with an authoritative understanding of the complete set of knowledge elements for the field of cybersecurity. The CSEC2017 document is specifically dedicated to providing an authoritative overview of the elements of the field of cybersecurity for a broad array of educational applications. It should be noted that the CSEC2017 thought model is authoritative, in the sense that the computer societies have made the commitment to make them so. Within that thought model, the knowledge elements that are specified for the discipline can be explicitly tailored to the teaching and learning process. Therefore, the CSEC2107 has practical educational application in every curriculum and classroom.

Circumscribing the Field: Background and Intention of CC2005

CSEC2017 is an overview report however, it isn't the first. The first of these types of joint overview reports was published in 2005 by the convened group of sponsoring societies and is called "Computing Curricula 2005," or just CC2005 (ACM, 2005). The goal of CC2005 was to "Provide perspective for those in academia who need to understand what the major computing disciplines are and how the respective undergraduate degree programs compare and complement each other." (ACM, 2005, p. 1).

In general, the contents of CC2005 were intended to summarize the basic similarities and dissimilarities in focus and content of the various curricula that comprise the discipline of computing. The Joint Task Force behind its publication represented. "An unprecedented cooperative effort among the leading computer societies and the major computing disciplines" (ACM, 2005, p. 1).

In order to be thorough and consistent, the Joint Task Force had to inspect and analyze the five discipline-specific curriculum recommendations comprising the ACM Computing Curricula Series (ACM, 2005). This widescale examination was deemed necessary because, "Computing is a broad discipline that crosses the boundaries between mathematics, science, engineering, and business and embraces important competencies that lie at the foundation of professional practice" (ACM, 2005, p. 2). CC 2005 is mainly relevant to the discussion of a common body of knowledge for cybersecurity in that it laid down five underlying purposes that guide the presentation of all forms of computer education content (Figure 1.8).

Shared Identity Is Important: Because of computing's profound impact on society as a whole, there is a responsibility for scholars and practitioners to specifically articulate what computer study is. Therefore, the first aim of CC2005 was to convey the diverse choices of study that are available to students, educators, and their communities. In view of this, the first goal of CC2005 was to articulate the communal identity and purpose of all computer disciplines. This is important to what we are discussing here in that cybersecurity suffers

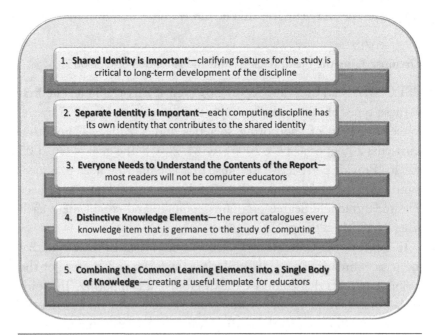

1. **Shared Identity is Important**—clarifying features for the study is critical to long-term development of the discipline

2. **Separate Identity is Important**—each computing discipline has its own identity that contributes to the shared identity

3. **Everyone Needs to Understand the Contents of the Report**—most readers will not be computer educators

4. **Distinctive Knowledge Elements**—the report catalogues every knowledge item that is germane to the study of computing

5. **Combining the Common Learning Elements into a Single Body of Knowledge**—creating a useful template for educators

Figure 1.8   CC2005's five underlying principles of computer education content.

from the problem of diffuse identity. Thus, the role of the societies in clarifying the appropriate features for the study is critical to the long-term development of the field.

Separate Identity Is Important: Each computing discipline has its own identity. Therefore, the second purpose of CC2005 was to acknowledge and clarify the individual identities of each of the component disciplines that contribute to the shared identity of computing. Although there are different views of the field, this does not exclude any one of those views from the overall solution. All education has to have a focus, but the different focuses have to be integrated into a single concept in the larger sense. The value of the individual disciplinary lens is that it provides the depth of understanding necessary to ensure complete mastery of a given essential topic.

Everyone Needs to Understand the Contents of the Report: It was acknowledged that most of the people who read the report would not be computer educators. Thus, the CC2005 report was tailored to address a range of constituencies who might want to understand the contents of a comprehensive academic computing degree. So, it was not technical in any way. Therefore, it must be understood that CC2005 is a social manifesto of sorts. It doesn't so much make recommendations about what needed to be taught in each field, as much as it explained the variation in computer education programs as a whole.

Distinctive Knowledge Elements: The report essentially catalogues every knowledge item that would be germane to the study of computing. This is one of the two groundbreaking aspects of this project and it is the consideration that links CC2005 with CSEC2017. The CC2005 report ignores the usual teaching and learning issues and focuses instead on the definition of a set of standard learning elements. The fact that CC2005 essentially catalogues and presents all of the necessary learning elements for the effective study of computing makes it groundbreaking. It is the focus on the appropriate set of standard elements for the study of cybersecurity that is the chief contribution of CSEC2017.

Combining the Common Learning Elements into a Single Body of Knowledge: The lack of a common understanding of the diverse elements of the practical process of the study of cybersecurity is at the heart of our failure as a society. Thus, the earlier synthesis of the details of computer education into a single vision provides a meaningful and useful template to guide educators and practitioners in the development of complete and correct cybersecurity solutions. In that respect then, the creation of an insightful, consensus-based overview of the computing disciplines is a useful template for the comprehensive set of recommendations for cybersecurity educators that are at the heart of this text.

Defining the Elements of the Discipline of Cybersecurity: CSEC2017

The CSEC2017 Joint Task Force on Cybersecurity Education (JTF) originated in September 2015, and as we have said, the computing societies occasionally create a single initiative to promulgate recommendations in an area of vital interest, as is the case with this particular Joint Task Force report (JTF, 2017). The CSEC2017 mission was twofold, "To initiate the processes for (1) developing undergraduate curricular guidance; and (2) establish a case for the accreditation of educational programs in the cyber sciences." (CSEC, 2017, p. 10). The recommendations in the report represent fully sanctioned, all-inclusive recommendations about the content and structure of an undergraduate cybersecurity curriculum. Additionally, the recommendations represent a single conceptual model for the study of cybersecurity. The CSEC2017 document is specifically not intended to define a single monolithic study nor is it a prescriptive document that is designed to create a lone program type. Instead, the CSEC body of knowledge can be used either completely or in part to develop relevant courses or to modify a broad range of existing programs and course concentrations (CSEC, 2017).

Like CC2005, the CSEC2017 was intended to delineate the boundaries of the discipline. In this case, it outlines key dimensions of the curricular structure of the study of cybersecurity. Its aim is, "To develop curricular guidance that is comprehensive enough to support a wide range of program types and to develop curricular guidance that is grounded in fundamental principles that provide stability" (CSEC, 2017, p. 11). And this is embodied in the CSEC2017 recommendations. As defined in the CSEC2017 report and shown in Figure 1.9, there are eight broad knowledge areas in the curricular framework.

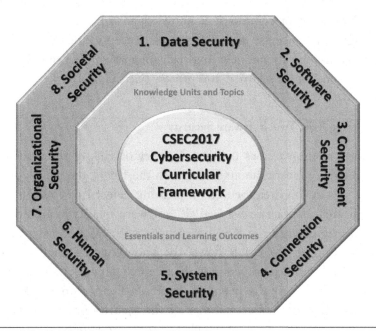

Figure 1.9 Eight knowledge areas of the CSEC2017 report.

The knowledge areas represent the complete body of knowledge within the field. Taken as a set, these distinctive areas constitute a common definition of the discipline as well as the learning elements that should be involved in the delivery of an acceptable cybersecurity learning experience. Each knowledge area will be discussed in much greater depth in the following chapters; however, for the purposes of introduction, the following is an overview of the eight knowledge areas of the CSEC2017 Cybersecurity Curricular Framework (CSEC, 2017).

Knowledge Area One: Data Security

The Data Security knowledge area is the perfect area to lead off with. Data Security defines what needs to be known in order to ensure the security of data assets either at rest, during processing, or in transit (CSEC, 2017). This is a well-accepted and commonly understood part of the current discipline and there is no disagreement about its importance in the overall protection of electronic assets. Chapter 3 focuses on the knowledge elements associated with data security protection to include a set of commonly acknowledged subjects such as basic cryptography concepts, digital forensics concepts, and methods for secure communications including data integrity and authentication, information storage security, and privacy (CSEC, 2017).

Knowledge Area Two: Software Security

Software assurance goes back to the very origins of the discipline and predates concerns about security. In the 1990s, the methods and techniques in this area focused on creating defect-free code and the general area of practice was called "software quality assurance" or SQA. Since most of the KSAs associated with SQA transfer to the identification of exploitable flaws, the knowledge elements for this area are well defined and commonly accepted as correct among both academics and business people. Chapter 4 focuses on the knowledge area regarding the assurance of the security properties of the information and systems of which the software is designed to protect (CSEC, 2017). Thus, the CSEC2017 recommendations center on such accepted areas of practice as security requirements, design concepts and practice, software implementation and deployment issues, static and dynamic testing, configuration management, and ethics, especially in development, testing, and vulnerability disclosure (CSEC, 2017).

Knowledge Area Three: Component Security

Chapter 5 covers the Component Security knowledge area and is somewhat novel in that it is not an element of most of the predecessor BOK for cybersecurity. However, it is not surprising to see it here given the inclusion of computer engineering in the CC2005 set of disciplines. Component Security's body of knowledge focuses on the design, procurement, testing, analysis, and maintenance of the tangible components that are integrated into larger systems (CSEC, 2017). Thus, the elements of this area include such well-accepted hardware aspects as identification and elimination of vulnerabilities present in system components, component life cycle maintenance and configuration management, secure hardware component design principles, security testing, and reverse engineering. Finally, there is a healthy dose of supply chain management security knowledge elements due to the industry's commitment to commercial off-the-shelf integration of components.

Knowledge Area Four: Connection Security

This area is what is colloquially known as *network security* and is discussed in Chapter 6. The security of networks is another quality that is both commonly accepted as well as an essential aspect of good cybersecurity practice. Networks and networking have been a fundamental element of the information technology universe since the late 1960s, with ARPANET and other primordial computer communication systems, as networking had reached a high degree of sophistication prior to the advent of the Internet. But the security of networks became a primary concern with the introduction of that groundbreaking technological advancement. The knowledge in this area focuses on the security of the connections between components including both physical and logical connections (CSEC, 2017). Thus, the recommendations entail assurance practices for networked systems, networking architecture, and standard secure transmission models, physical component interconnections and interfaces, software component interfaces, and of course the common types of connection and transmission attacks.

Knowledge Area Five: System Security

The System Security knowledge area begins the move off of the technology and into the area of standard organizational processes. Chapter 7 focuses on the System Security knowledge area, primarily on those common embedded organizational practices that ensure the articulated security requirements of systems, which are composed of interconnected components and connections, and the networking software that supports those interconnections (CSEC, 2017). Consequently, the knowledge elements in this area embody recommendations that spell out the necessity for a holistic approach to systems, the importance of security policy, as well as organized identification and authentication management processes; this area also contains recommendations for system access control and operational system monitoring processes, as well as the standard recovery, system testing, and system documentation best practices.

Knowledge Area Six: Human Security

This is a brand-new and very novel element of the body of knowledge and is the focus of Chapter 8. The Human Security knowledge area represents the first serious attempt to provide recommendations with respect to the human attack surface. This area is terra incognita in the traditional study of cybersecurity, and although it might not be as mature as areas one through five, it represents a pioneering step in the effort to compile a complete and accurate body of knowledge for the field.

The first five knowledge areas comprise what might be considered essentially hard, technology-focused elements that encompass generally well-known and commonly accepted axioms regarding the practice of data, software, component, and system assurance. The Human Security area attempts to make benchmark recommendations about the assurance and study of human behavior as it relates to the maintenance of a state of cybersecurity. This is a new area and one which will probably be susceptible to refinement over a period of time. However, the loss statistics make it clear that the focus on protecting individuals' data and privacy in the context of their role as employees and in their personal lives is a significant area of teaching and research (CSEC, 2017). The recommended knowledge elements in the Human Security knowledge area include identity management, social engineering prevention, assurance of workforce and individual awareness and understanding, assurance of broad-scale social behavioral privacy and security, and the elements of personal data privacy and security protection.

Knowledge Area Seven: Organizational Security

Organizational security is historically the most well-known and commonly discussed aspect of all of the nontechnical areas and is discussed in Chapter 9. The general content and focus of this area is embodied in the recommendations of the National Institute of Standards and Technology's workforce framework (NIST 800-181) as Knowledge Area Seven, "Oversee and Govern" (Newhouse, 2017). The Organizational Security area encompasses all of the relevant processes and behaviors for the rational oversight and control of the overall cybersecurity function. This is understandably a very large element of the CSEC2017 model since the controls embody all of the traditional countermeasures that are associated with the general protection of the organization as a whole. This includes the deployment and oversight of controls to ensure proper monitoring and response to intrusions on the technological attack surface, as well as the entire set of standard behaviors associated with the human attack surface.

The purpose of the knowledge that is embodied in the Organizational Security area is to assure the organization against all relevant cybersecurity threats, as well as manage the inherent risks associated with the successful accomplishment of the organization's mission (CSEC, 2017). Consequently, the elements in this area include a detailed set of recommendations for the risk management process, the setting of governance and policy strategies, long- and short-term planning, as well as legal, regulatory, and ethical compliance.

Knowledge Area Eight: Societal Security

The Societal Security knowledge area is revolutionary and reflects the growing awareness of the impact of virtual space on the average person's life. Chapter 10 deals with the knowledge items in this category that, for better or worse, broadly impact every citizen in our society. These knowledge elements are essentially still in need of refinement; however, their inclusion opens the door to their integration into the overall understanding of how virtual space needs to be channeled into institutional actions that are beneficial to the global community as a whole. This includes thought models for approaching the problems of cybercrime, the legal and ethical dictates associated with good citizenship, as well as social policy, personal privacy, and how that relates to the formal mechanisms of conventional cyberspace (CSEC, 2017). The specific recommendations promulgated in this area center on the general behaviors to prevent or alleviate cybercrime, make and enforce laws in cyberspace, ensure ethical thinking when it comes to functioning in cyberspace, as well as the elements of what constitutes proper cyber policies and privacy regulation.

Real-World Utilization of the CSEC2017 Body of Knowledge

As a matter of practical application, the range of requisite skill sets comprising the discipline of cybersecurity span the gamut from the technical to the procedural. As we have discussed, there have always been familiar technical areas that are part of the everyday study of cybersecurity. However, there are also related processes and behavioral aspects of the field that have been beautifully captured in the CSEC2017 body of knowledge. This specific set of eight highly integrated knowledge areas are all required to underwrite the strategic and operational practice of the profession of cybersecurity.

Therefore, the practical instantiation of a formal cybersecurity study should incorporate an inclusive range of elements, all of which are designed to impart the requisite technical and behavioral knowledge. Besides the ability to design effective strategic and procedural controls, the behavioral learning elements also call out the critical thinking and analysis capabilities necessary to conceptualize effective and practical real-world cybersecurity systems (CSEC, 2017). There are also requisite skills implicit in cybersecurity work, which includes the ability to function well in teams, communicate effectively with nontechnical audiences, and understand the wide range of resourcing aspects of projects (CSEC, 2017).

Finally, because cybersecurity impacts everybody, it is also necessary that cybersecurity professionals are able to work effectively within a wide range of cultural circumstances. Specifically, the U.S. Chief Human Capital Officers Council (CHCO) has developed a list of nontechnical competencies that should be considered to be part of the cybersecurity skill set. As shown in Figure 1.10, the list includes the following skill sets (CSEC, 2017, p. 78):

- Accountability
- Attention to detail
- Resilience
- Conflict management
- Reasoning
- Verbal and written communication
- Teamwork.

Figure 1.10 Cybersecurity skill set competencies.

It should be noted that the CSEC2017 report makes it clear that adaptability is the key behavioral quality that every practitioner will need to exhibit. In essence, the cybersecurity professional must be able to easily accommodate to changes to, "Environmental conditions and situational contexts" (CSEC, 2017, p. 79). Accordingly, that capability is particularly essential to the CSEC because given the rate of technological growth, it will be necessary for every cybersecurity professional to know how to use emerging technologies as well as embrace the inevitable change that will occur (CSEC, 2017).

CSEC2017 Framework Areas of Application

Finally, the CSEC2017 provides a particularly useful recommendation about the academic areas of study, called the *application areas*, where the practical application of cybersecurity knowledge is important (CESC, 2017, p. 80). The application areas are a practical way for the developers of the CSEC2017 to associate the embedded competencies of their model with potential real-world career applications. The application areas themselves define the depth of coverage associated with each of the core ideas in the CSEC2017 (CSEC, 2017). It allows individuals to associate the CSEC2017 recommendations with the existing workforce models that will be thoroughly discussed in the next chapter.

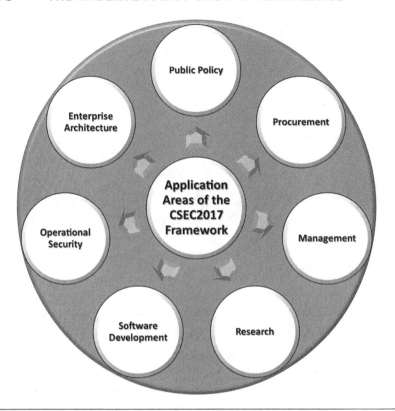

Figure 1.11 Application areas of the CSEC2017 framework.

As shown in Figure 1.11, the seven application areas included in the CSEC2017 Report are (CESC, 2017, pp. 80–81) as follows:

Public Policy: Decision makers must pass laws, develop regulations, and set policies that affect the development, deployment, and use of information technology; regulators will control the applications of these mandates; and relevant public and private officials will develop de facto public policies that will impact cybersecurity solutions. These individuals need to be capable of understanding what a cybersecurity protection system is capable of accomplishing and what it can't do. This also means that decision makers must understand every aspect of the cost of security in both budgetary and human terms (CESC, 2017, p. 80).

Procurement: Those who acquire information technology, and who hire the people who will work with it, must understand the inherent risks of supply chains as well as both the business continuity and risk management implications. The responsibility is to know what is required of the constituent people, systems, infrastructure, procedures, and processes in a cybersecurity solution in order to provide the desired level of security (CESC, 2017, p. 80).

Management: Managers need to work with issues associated with threat and concomitant risk. They must understand that compliance and business continuity issues are factors in their day-to-day oversight. Managers must make certain that the people who are using the systems that fall under their areas of accountability are properly authorized. Also, managers must be well versed in the ins and outs of effective identity and authorization management. Technological evolution will require that those managers understand the purpose of tests and reviews and all other forms of assurance. Finally, managers need to have a basic understanding of both incident management and accident recovery (CESC, 2017, p. 81).

Research: Scholars who are dedicated to advancing knowledge in the field of cybersecurity must understand the purpose and application of the fundamental principles of the field. Those include such well-known aspects as access control and trust management. The actual requirement for scholars and researchers will vary widely depending on the specific focus of their study. But in all respects, their research will be based on a well-defined and commonly accepted understanding of the field (CESC, 2017, p. 81).

Software Development: All individuals directly associated with the system development, maintenance, and the acquisition needs of the software process need to understand the basic life cycle concepts of good software engineering. This includes the life cycle areas of requirements specification, design, coding, and assurance. They also must understand that these factors are often controlled by laws, regulations, business plans, and organizational factors (CESC, 2017, p. 81).

Operational Security: It is essential that day-to-day cybersecurity practitioners are familiar with the fundamentals of security operations. Additionally, system administrators, system security officers, and all other information security personnel must understand how to translate requirements into procedures and configurations. Finally, cybersecurity workers need to understand the basics of system maintenance (CESC, 2017, p. 81).

Enterprise Architecture: Last but not the least, because the enterprise architecture has a direct impact on the security of the infrastructure, enterprise architects, designers, and planners must be familiar and capably work with the policy, procurement, management, and operations application knowledge specified in the CESC (2017, p. 80).

Thirty Review Questions: Introduction to the CSEC Standard

1. Why is cybercrime an important societal issue?
2. What are the two specific reasons why our national infrastructure is vulnerable?
3. What is the single logical criterion for judging the success of a cybersecurity effort?
4. Why is it important to understand the difference between "cyber" and "security?"
5. What is an "attack surface?"
6. Besides electronic, what other two areas of security comprise the attack surface?
7. How does the adversary change the demands on IT's traditional assumptions?
8. What is a "nontechnical hack?"
9. What causes "exploitable gaps?"
10. What does a "holistic" solution to cybersecurity contain?
11. Why is it difficult to create a unified vision of the essential concepts of cybersecurity?
12. What must be defined to ensure a unified understanding of the elements of the field?
13. What is the role of standard bodies in underwriting this understanding?
14. Why is education the key to a fully capable practice of cybersecurity?
15. What is a unified body of knowledge? Why is it necessary for the education process?

16. What is the role of the "learned societies" in creating BOK?
17. How is an academic study created? What other fields require BOK?
18. What are the four societies that guide the practice of computing?
19. Why are joint recommendations from those societies important?
20. What are the eight commonly accepted domains in the body of knowledge of cybersecurity?
21. Why is there a gamut of skill sets involved in the practice of cybersecurity?
22. What are the three common organizational areas that must work together?
23. What are the strategic abilities that are required to conceptualize effective controls?
24. What are the affective skills implicit in cybersecurity work?
25. Why is cultural understanding important to cybersecurity work?
26. List the seven nontechnical competencies associated with cybersecurity work.
27. Which one of these areas is the key behavioral quality that every practitioner will need?
28. What is the purpose of the application areas in CSEC2017?
29. What do the application areas define?
30. What are the seven application areas and why are they important?

You Might Also Like to Read

- Bonney, Bill, Gary Hayslip, and Matt Stamper, *CISO Desk Reference Guide*, CISO DRG Joint Venture Publishing, San Diego, CA, 2019.
- Brooks, Charles J., Christopher Grow, and Philip Craig, *Cybersecurity Essentials*, 1st Edition, Sybex, London, 2018.
- Friedman, Allan and Peter W. Singer, *Cybersecurity and Cyberwar: What Everyone Needs to Know*, Oxford University Press, Oxford, 2014.
- Gregory, Peter H., *CISM Certified Information Security Manager All-in-One Exam Guide*, 1st Edition, McGraw-Hill Education, New York, 2018.

- Harris, Shon and Fernando Maymi, *CISSP All-in-One Exam Guide*, 8th Edition, McGraw-Hill Education, New York, 2018.
- Hasib, Mansur, *Cybersecurity Leadership: Powering the Modern Organization*, 3rd Edition, Amazon Publishing, Seattle, DC, 2014.
- Shoemaker, Daniel and Wm. Arthur Conklin, *Cybersecurity: The Essential Body of Knowledge*, Cengage Learning, Boston, MA, 2011.
- Shoemaker, Daniel, Anne Kohnke, and Kenneth Sigler, *A Guide to the National Initiative for Cybersecurity Education (NICE) Cybersecurity Workforce Framework (2.0) (Internal Audit and IT Audit)*, Auerbach Publications, Boston, MA, 2016.
- Stallings, William, *Effective Cybersecurity: A Guide to Using Best Practices and Standards*, Addison-Wesley, Boston, MA, 2018.
- Zinatullin, Leron, *The Psychology of Information Security: Resolving Conflicts between Security Compliance and Human Behaviour*, IT Governance Publishing, Ely, Cambridgeshire, UK, 2016.

Chapter Summary

- The development of the Internet is the most significant advance in technology since the invention of moveable type. We need to adjust to the impacts of that change.
- The sole characteristic by which a cybersecurity effort should be judged is whether it is able to effectively prevent loss or harm to the assets that are under its protection.
- The presence of the adversary imposes a different set of demands on the protection process.
- The most logical way to subvert a cybersecurity defense is through the PRC. An approach that does not target the technology directly is a called nontechnical hack.
- A nontechnical hack is an action that targets behavioral weaknesses, rather than electronic ones.
- The human attack surface comprises every possible way that human behavior might compromise an asset or breach confidentiality.

- Because nontechnical hacks are rarely defended against, they have become the PRC.
- A complete cyberdefense rests on a three-legged stool; electronic, human, and physical controls.
- The generic term "holistic" was been adopted to describe a state where every aspect of threat has been considered and countered.
- Every profession is built around common understanding of the proper practices of the profession.
- An officially sanctioned universal body of knowledge is the foundation of every new educational endeavor.
- Formal authorization of a body of knowledge is always the responsibility of the group that is acknowledged to be the overseer and sanctioner of the academic study.
- The recommendations of the CSEC2017 body of knowledge provide educators and their students with an authoritative understanding of the complete set of knowledge elements for the field of cybersecurity.
- These recommendations represent on a single conceptual model for the study of cybersecurity. There are eight generic knowledge areas. Data Security, Software Security, Component Security, Connection Security, System Security, Human Security, Organizational Security, and Societal Security.

Keywords

Architecture – the design and implementation of an underlying framework of processes

Best Practice – a set of lessons learned validated for successful execution of a given task

Controls – a discrete set of human or electronic behaviors set to produce a given outcome

Critical Asset – a function or object that is so central to an operation that it cannot be lost

Cybersecurity – assurance of confidentiality, integrity, and availability of information

Infrastructure – a collection of large components arrayed in a logical structure in order to accomplish a given purpose

Reliability – proven capability to perform a designated purpose over time

Strategic Planning – the process of developing long-term plans of action aimed at furthering and enhancing organizational goals

References

Accenture Security, "Ninth Annual Cost of Cybercrime Study", 2019. www.accenture.com/_acnmedia/PDF-99/Accenture-Cost-Cyber-Crime-Infographic.pdf#zoom=50, accessed October 29, 2019.

Association for Computing Machinery (ACM), "Curricula Recommendations", 2018. www.acm.org/education/curricula-recommendations, accessed 18 December.

Association for Information Systems, "About AIS", 2018. https://aisnet.org/page/AboutAIS, accessed December 2018.

Brasso, Bret, "Cyber Attacks against Critical Infrastructure Are No Longer Just Theories", Fire-Eye, 29 April 2016. www.fireeye.com/blog/executive-perspective/2016/04/cyber_attacks_agains.html, accessed December 2016.

CSEC2017, Joint Task Force (JTF) on Cybersecurity Education, "Cybersecurity Curricula 2017, Curriculum Guidelines for Post-Secondary Degree Programs in Cybersecurity, a Report in the Computing Curricula Series", ACM/IEEE-CS/AIS SIGSEC/IFIP WG 11.8, Version 1.0, 31 December 2017.

Cummins, J., and Pollet, J., All Hazards Approach for Assessing Readiness of Critical Infrastructure. 2009 IEEE Conference on Technologies for Homeland Security, Boston, MA.

Ford, Gary, "A Progress Report on Undergraduate Software Engineering Education", Software Engineering Institute, CMU/SEI Report Number: CMU/SEI-94-TR-011, May 1994.

Hatchimonji, Grant, "Survey Results Reveal Both IT Pros' Greatest Fears and Apparent Needs", CSO Online, 18 September 2013. www.csoonline.com/article/2133933/strategic-planning-erm/survey-results-reveal-both-it-pros--greatest-fears-and-apparent-needs.html, accessed January 2017.

Institute of Electrical and Electronics Engineers (IEEE), 2019. www.ieee.org/about/index.html, accessed October 29, 2019.

International Federation for Information Processing (IFIP), "About IFIP", 2018. www.ifip.org/index.php?option=com_content&task=view&id=124&Itemid=439, accessed December 2018.

ISCTE, University of Lisbon, 2018. http://iscte.hosting.acm.org/, accessed October 29, 2019.

Joint Task Force for Computing Curricula, "Curricula 2005, The Overview Report", The Association for Computing Machinery (ACM), The Association for Information Systems (AIS) The Computer Society (IEEE-CS), 30 September 2005.

Laberis, Bill, "20 Eye-Opening Cybercrime Statistics", Security Intelligence, IBM, 2016. https://securityintelligence.com/20-eye-opening-cybercrime-statistics/, accessed October 29, 2019.

Lois, Jason E., "It Can Happen to You: Know the Anatomy of a Cyber Intrusion", Navy Cyber Defense Operations Command (NCDOC), Story Number: NNS151019-05, 2015, Release Date: 19 October 2015.

Microsoft Security Team, "The Emerging Era of Cyber Defense and Cybercrime", 2018. https://cloudblogs.microsoft.com/microsoftse-cure/2016/01/27/the-emerging-era-of-cyber-defense-and-cybercrime/, 27 January 2016.

National Infrastructure Advisory Council (NIAC), "Surviving a Catastrophic Power Outage", Department of Homeland Security, 11 December 2018.

Newhouse, William, Stephanie Keith, Benjamin Scribner, and Greg Witte, "NIST Special Publication 800-181, National Initiative for Cybersecurity Education (NICE) Cybersecurity Workforce Framework", NIST. SP.800-181, August 2017.

Privacy Rights Clearinghouse, *A Chronology of Data Breaches*, PRC, San Diego, CA, 2017.

Rivero, Nicolas, "The Biggest Data Breaches of All Time, Ranked", Quartz, 2018. Downloaded from https://qz.com/1480809/the-biggest-data-breaches-of-all-time-ranked/.

Saltzer, Jerome H. and Michael D. Schroeder, The protection of information in computer systems, *Communications of the ACM*, 17, 388–402, 1974.

Symantec, "A Manifesto for Cyber Resilience", 2014.

TechTarget, "Human Attack Surface", Whatis.com, 2018.

2
THE CYBERSECURITY
BODY OF KNOWLEDGE

In this chapter, you will learn the following:

- The background and application of bodies of knowledge
- The importance of bodies of knowledge in shaping new fields
- How bodies of knowledge effect the development of curricula
- The rationale and potential applications of the body of knowledge for cybersecurity
- The knowledge areas of the CSEC2017
- The constituent elements of each of the knowledge areas in the CSEC2017.

Bodies of Knowledge Are Essential Tools in Educational Settings

A standard body of knowledge is an important tool in every educational setting because the teaching of any major academic subject entails a wide variety of complex factors that must be integrated and presented to the student. Teaching cybersecurity is particularly challenging in that it is a crosscutting field. In essence, the subject matter that comprises cybersecurity extends across the breadth of knowledge from computer engineering through management and law and even intelligence and military science. Thus, an explicit statement of the critical knowledge skill and ability requirements for the evolving discipline of cybersecurity is an important next step in underwriting the teaching and learning process.

As we said in Chapter 1, one key factor is the joint recognition of the CSEC2017 Framework as a standard model for cybersecurity education. This is a critical condition for success because the correctness of teaching any form of new discipline is often in the eye of the beholder. Hence, the existence of a well-defined and commonly accepted standard model of best practice is a very useful start for defining the curricula and research agendas. It is also the reason why a universally understood and commonly accepted knowledge framework represents the indispensable foundation for ensuring that all of the necessary bases will get addressed in the teaching and learning process. A standard model of the knowledge elements of the field also provides a practical basis for validating the correctness of any subsequent additions. In the case of a subject that is as new and constantly evolving as *cybersecurity*, this stable point of reference is an important factor.

Bodies of Knowledge

From a practical perspective, a commonly accepted body of knowledge is the first logical evolutionary step in building a discipline. A standard model of the body of knowledge documents a highly integrated collection of elements that represent expert advice. As we said, bodies of knowledge are the single, authoritative point of reference which can then be used to validate and sanction any curricular content that is deemed appropriate. This aggregation, by definition, represents the commonly acknowledged elements of the field. Thus, the rational structure of the body of knowledge will categorize a complete array of elements for a particular field of application. Moreover, the description is essential to the coherent development and evolution of the shared concepts of the field.

Expert bodies of knowledge are composed of a unified set of generic knowledge units. Those units are the complete set of entities that a practicing professional needs to know. Expert bodies of knowledge also specify the associated skills and abilities that might be required to guarantee a minimum level of capability in each member of the profession. So, in essence, the basis of a body of knowledge in expert advice provides a fully validated roadmap of the things educators who are seeking guidance on what to include in the curricular and course content of the field they are teaching.

The CSEC2017 body of knowledge encompasses the full range of conventional learning requirements for the real-world understanding of the cybersecurity process – from high-level governance concepts like policy and procedure all the way through the technical nuances of digital signing and encryption. The underlying curricular objectives, which flesh out that body of knowledge, make the individual concepts for each of these areas tangible and, therefore, easier to understand and accept. The ability to nurture an integrated understanding and acceptance of the conceptual elements of the field might be one of the more important attributes of the CSEC2017 body of knowledge. This is because all learning requires motivation, and it is difficult to be motivated to study something that has not been suitably and authoritatively defined.

One of the most important features of any body of knowledge is that it provides the structure for practical course delivery. In effect, the contents of the body of knowledge can serve as a template for creating a comprehensive and practical set of courses. The framework gives curricular planners, who are responsible for the design, and the educators, who must deliver the actual content, a detailed top-down assembly of well-defined and commonly accepted content topics. These topics define the professional practice of cybersecurity, and they are essentially validated by the expert advice that is conveyed through the recommendations of the model.

Through expert advice, an academic program can be confident that it is presenting the learning elements and experiences that will allow graduates to be successful after graduation. The expertise that is embodied in the CSEC2017's expert advice also allows students to leverage their individual capabilities into an appropriate professional skill set. Those capabilities will ensure competent practice in their chosen area of cybersecurity work. The model also provides a common yardstick for all of the various external stakeholders to judge that the curriculum it has adopted is sufficient and correct.

Bodies of knowledge also provide a common benchmark for learners to decide which curricular offerings are directly relevant to their particular area of professional interest. In this respect, the body of knowledge provides a common roadmap for developing, implementing, and measuring the effectiveness of a cybersecurity program. An expert-driven, commonly accepted model of the process, like the CSEC2017, warrants that the knowledge items that are presented in a program's curriculum are legitimate and accurate and can be properly applied within the context of real-world challenges. Accordingly, the CSEC2017's standard body of knowledges becomes the stable foundation on which a fully validated and comprehensive program in cybersecurity can be built.

Making Cybersecurity Teaching Real

Since all real-world curricula are individual to the organization, the recommendations of any particular body of knowledge have to be tailored to fit the institution in which it is offered. The adaptation of a formal model into a substantive program of study implies a process by which the generic topics that are specified in that model are presented in a specific classroom setting. Accordingly, the act of translating a body of knowledge into a day-to-day system of knowledge delivery is the quintessential first step in enacting the real-world cybersecurity teaching and learning process. The outcome of the curriculum/course tailoring process is a detailed description of each requisite learning objective as it applies within the larger context of the standard body of knowledge. The learning elements are specified at a level of detail that is sufficient to guide the presentation of cybersecurity content at all curricular levels within a given academic setting.

So, in essence, the detailed descriptions of the CSEC2017's learning objectives become a structured statement of all of the actions the student will need to master in order to attain the desired level of cybersecurity competence for a given situation. The systematic top-down documentation of the teaching content makes the outcomes of the learning process predictable across all of the curricular levels. The teaching process will then execute a conventional, substantive instructional delivery activity, which is designed to achieve the specific learning goals for that particular topic.

The top-down mapping of content from an expert model is an important aspect in the systematic delivery of any type of formal education due to the requisite learning being part of a disciplinary process. The actions embodied in the disciplinary processes must be consistent in order to endure a desired and repeatable outcome. The mapping provides the checklist that ensures that the disciplinary outcomes represent the expected and desired set of learned behaviors. Disciplinary outcomes can be defined at every level in the teaching and learning process, from K-12 all the way up to doctoral study. Therefore, if the disciplinary outcomes can be mapped back to the expert advice contained in the CSEC2017 model, then it can be assumed that the resultant cybersecurity curriculum will represent the sort of professional capabilities that are essential to the pragmatic performance of the educational process.

Additionally, the outcomes of a teaching process that are built around a set of well-defined disciplinary practices can be studied, and the ongoing lessons learned can then be utilized to ensure the continuous improvement and refinement of the learning experience. Consequently, future curricular topics and issues can be developed, and outcomes can be fine-tuned in the ongoing process of addressing stakeholder needs. Therefore, in addition to delivering validated content, a body of knowledge can also be highly useful as a means for continuous improvement and the ongoing refinement of the study of cybersecurity.

Validating Curricular Concepts

As we saw in the previous chapter, the constantly shifting landscape of threat has been a universal and pervasive reality since the foundation of the field. The ongoing phenomenon of constant change is an innate aspect of the technological universe. In many respects, dynamic evolution is the single characteristic that defines technology. Accordingly, the emergence of an unequivocal new understanding of the elements of the field, like the CSEC2017, provides a stable landmark for the development and refinement of educational programs. The stable point of reference that the CSEC2017 knowledge areas provide is the baseline that can be used to create new courses and fit them into existing curricula. This is particularly the case for integrating the knowledge areas that represent the softer aspects of cybersecurity such as organizational management and human behavior-based threats.

Naturally, there are a few core concepts, or principles, that are commonly accepted as central to the cybersecurity curriculum. That acceptance is underwritten both by logic and real-world practice. The core concepts represent the fundamental elements of knowledge in a cybersecurity education program and they must be present in order for a learning experience to be considered truly accurate. The core concepts comprise the universal basis of the discipline and their presence is implicit in any effective vision of the field of cybersecurity.

Examples of these core concepts would be such aspects of computing as system assurance, enterprise network security, and secure software development practice.

Technological knowledge is a fact of life in the teaching of any form of cybersecurity practice and that type of learning is both dynamic and evolving. At the same time, technical knowledge is a traditional part of any type of computer education program and its relevance and the linkages associated with it are generally well understood. There are also new, and to some extent, foreign knowledge elements that are potentially part of the puzzle and must be judged for their relevance, or usefulness in the total learning package. And one challenge is that because these concepts represent emerging perspectives, their relevance might not be so clear within the field of cybersecurity. Yet, because these newer softer areas are the places that are currently experiencing the greatest number of successful attacks, they must be embodied in a single common understanding.

Accordingly, it is extremely important that the knowledge associated with human behavior is properly understood and appropriately integrated with the technical know-how that has always been a given element of the field. The structure of the CSEC2017 is the basis for the assessment.

The recommendations of the CSEC2017 offer a valid basis for testing each emerging idea, or new phenomenon, that might potentially be included in a course of study in any subject area and the resultant practical implications can be assessed and authorized on that basis. This is the way a curriculum for a field evolves, and it is the reason why the existence of a single point of reference is so essential to the development of an effective discipline. It should go without saying that this validation process is necessary in order for educators to be confident that what they are teaching reflects the correct concept or approach to the discipline.

The dynamic and somewhat disputed nature of the appropriate content of the body of knowledge in cybersecurity is also the reason why a single universally sanctioned model of the process, such as the CSEC2017, was an eventual necessity. And the fact that the CSEC2017 has been sanctioned by all of the relevant societies establishes it as the sole authoritative point of reference in which to build a curriculum.

Because educators have to understand the recommendations in order to take the concrete steps to develop curricula and courses, the discussion in this chapter is aimed at helping the reader understand how the various perspectives in the field have developed into a single statement of knowledge for the discipline of cybersecurity. You will see that there are numerous crosscutting elements in the CSEC2017 body of knowledge and that many of the differences that exist in the actual definition of the field lie in the fact that these elements are viewed from different perspectives depending where the individual, who is doing the viewing, sits. The highly integrated set of eight knowledge *areas* and *units* in the CSEC2017 framework, as shown in Figure 2.1, go a long way toward providing a complete and comprehensive understanding of the field as well as where the knowledge should be specifically applied.

Applying the CSEC2017

As we presented in the Chapter 1, the CSEC2017 was promulgated by the sponsoring societies in order to establish the basis for a discipline of cybersecurity. This was achieved by publishing a fully documented collection of recommendations about the distinct knowledge elements of the field. In essence, the architecture of the CSEC2017 comprises a fully sanctioned body of academic knowledge which can reliably underwrite the evolution of authorized curricula and courses for the field. The detailed specification of knowledge ensures that the delivery of cybersecurity education is uniform in approach across disciplines. It also ensures that the contents of curricula are built on a suitable and appropriate understanding of the body of commonly accepted best practice. Finally, this document serves to maintain explicitly documented linkages between a given area of study and all of the appropriate knowledge for the profession.

The linkages that are presented in the standard underwrite effective understanding of the necessary intercommunication linkages between academic areas of study, as well as a suitable degree of insight into how each of these various knowledge units fit within the overall execution of the cybersecurity process. This detailed understanding supports economy of effort. The current problem for conventional curriculum planners is that the knowledge requirements for cybersecurity are too extensive to fit within a single academic field of study, which creates a practical problem of time and space.

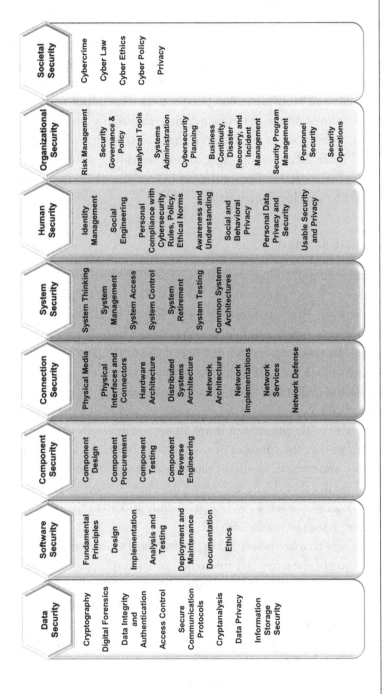

Figure 2.1   The cybersecurity body of knowledge.

Academic disciplines at any level are constrained by the realities of the traditional educational delivery model. In essence, there is only so much time in a given day and only a defined number of days in a given term. So, there are practical limits to what can be taught within the restrictions of a conventional academic degree program. Much more importantly, academic programs themselves have different disciplinary lenses, in the sense that the strictly linear, mathematical orientation of a computer science program is going to differ in its particulars and focus from the practical and applied focus of a business information system curriculum (Figure 2.2). As we said in Chapter 1, those differences were codified in the computer society's joint CC2005 model as five disciplinary lenses (ACM, 2005):

1. Computer Engineering – which is a subset field of electrical engineering
2. Computer Science – which is a mathematically based study of the machine
3. Software Engineering – which is an application-based study of the software life cycle

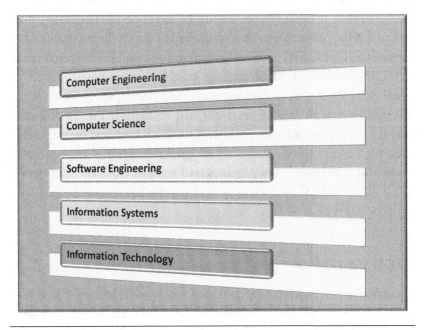

Figure 2.2 The five disciplinary lenses used in the development of the CC2005 model.

4. Information Systems – which is a business-oriented study of information support
5. Information Technology – which is a hands-on study of information technology use.

Each of these traditional academic fields is well established in the academic firmament, and like any other traditional collection of like-minded people, their practitioners all have their own specific point of view about the way their brand of education ought to be delivered.

In essence, each of the programs among the sponsoring societies represents an aspect of the overall profession of cybersecurity, and the curriculum of each of these disciplinary lenses embodies a consciously and deliberately created subset of the whole body of knowledge for the profession. A well-defined and commonly accepted understanding of the disciplinary lens of that particular curriculum allows curriculum designers to concentrate their course delivery on only those practical knowledge elements that support the particular role and perspective their program of study has chosen to occupy in the overall cybersecurity education scheme.

Designed to be crosscutting, the CSEC2017 body of knowledge affords curriculum designers the flexibility to provide instruction through many different types of disciplinary lenses. Logically, it is expected that a curriculum that is developed under the recommendations of the CSEC2017 will include all of the essential elements from each knowledge area. However, the specific learning outcomes, the actual delivery of the knowledge units, and the depth to which each unit will be covered will differ. That will be both by the disciplinary lens, e.g., computer science versus information systems, and also the level, e.g., community college versus graduate study. Consequently, it was also anticipated that adopters will spend a different number of hours on the CSEC2017 topics based on their disciplinary lens and institutional type.

The CSEC2017 Model

A curriculum structure that is based on a well-defined disciplinary model is a perfectly reasonable and acceptable way to achieve the general purposes of professional computer education. In effect, the framework bundles the educational content that is essential for success in a given field of study into specific categories. The categories can be used as a point of reference to define the learning necessary to achieve the specific purposes and in-depth performance criteria of any given real-world area of application. Cybersecurity is an applied profession. Its students are expected to fit within the existing cybersecurity workforce.

Therefore, educators must be cognizant of the precise way in which their particular curricular requirements fit within the explicit structure of that workforce. Since cybersecurity work involves a range of diverse knowledge requirements, the thought model that underlies and supports any given set of professional recommendations has to be clear about how the content that is developed for any given program of study will be utilized in the real world.

Because the CSEC2017's knowledge requirements tend to be crosscutting, the model was specifically designed to clarify, in an intellectually valid fashion, how its knowledge elements will interrelate with each other, as well as how each of the disciplinary lenses would utilize the specific elements in the delivery of curricular content. The outcome of that clarification process would be a practical understanding of how the contents of the CSEC2017 model can be used to structure a program of cybersecurity study within each of the participating disciplines.

The relationship and priority of a given knowledge element within the overall framework of that curriculum is the critical part of the puzzle. In essence, the model makes it possible for individual curriculum and course designers in each discipline to document and clarify, within the overall conceptual framework of the CSEC2017, all of the particular content elements and practical crosscutting linkages for their specific area of focus.

The eight knowledge areas are the fundamental conceptual building blocks of the CSEC2017. Taken together, these knowledge areas represent a sanctioned framework for the complete body of knowledge for the field of cybersecurity. Of the eight knowledge areas, five of them are largely technical and three of them are mostly behavioral in focus, as shown in Figure 2.3. The knowledge itemized in each of these individual areas represents the concepts that every student will have to master in order to be considered fully proficient in the

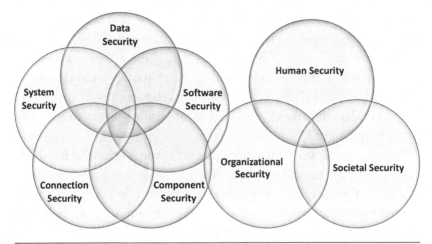

Figure 2.3 The Technical and Behavioral knowledge areas of the cybersecurity body of knowledge.

subject matter. The requirement for general mastery is implicit in the body of knowledge itself, no matter what the actual disciplinary lens of the individual student might be.

Each knowledge area contains explicitly itemized knowledge *units* that serve to clarify the focus and intent of the area. These knowledge units differentiate the eight knowledge areas in that taken together, these units describe the typical knowledge elements for each area. Each knowledge unit contains an itemized set of learning objectives. These objectives comprise the particular knowledge, skill, and ability (KSA) characteristics that are a part of that aspect of the discipline. Furthermore, the CSEC2017 assumes that these knowledge elements will change over time, as the field evolves.

Each of the essential KSAs for a given area describes what the learner will need to be able to know or do at the conclusion of educational process. Thus, each CSEC2017 area can be viewed as an itemization of the entire range of knowledge elements, skills, and abilities that the learner is expected to have mastered in order to be considered capable in a given topic.

The CSEC2017 is structured under the assumption that the fundamental ideas that are specified for any individual knowledge area will be embodied as appropriate in each cybersecurity curriculum. The depth of the coverage is dictated by the disciplinary lens of the given academic program. For example, it would be expected that the cryptographic topics in Data Security would be presented differently in a computer science program, than they would be in an information technology program. Nonetheless, the final outcome of that presentation would be that both types of students would be fully conversant in the topic at an acceptable level of depth for their particular specialty.

The elements of cybersecurity are both broad and necessarily crosscutting. So, the aggregate knowledge for a given topic is not likely to be provided in a single course or study unit. In that respect, the designers of the CSEC2017 do not intend for the knowledge units, which underlie each of the model's knowledge areas, to be mutually exclusive. Thus, the designers clearly state that a number of the knowledge units are deliberately recurring in more than one knowledge area. In essence, the content of each individual knowledge unit is presented in a way that assumes that there are crosscutting applications or interdisciplinary aspects that need to be considered in the content delivery. Therefore, it should be expected that most real-world cybersecurity courses will contain knowledge units that have appeared in some form, or another, in other courses.

In its practical implementation, the fact that many elements are repeated means that the curriculum designer will have to embed explicit linkages or hooks for each tangible instance that points to other instances. The purpose of these links is to indicate the additional areas in the curriculum where that instance might appear. The hooks allow the student to inter-associate the particular learning experience that they are undertaking with the aspects of knowledge that they have already acquired in other courses.

The role of the instructor in delivering the CSEC2017 sanctioned content is to ensure that the student is able to make the necessary connection between the knowledge units as they appear in the subject matter in different courses. For instance, software assurance knowledge units are important topics in the Software Security knowledge area. At the same time, software assurance is also a vital part of the Organizational Security areas. The actual detail of the knowledge units might be different. But the underlying relevance should be explicated for both cases. Therefore, learning items like the application and outcomes of static tests need to be explained in the context of both application instances.

The student's ability to aggregate individual instances of a knowledge into a complete, fundamental concept of the intents and purposes of the cybersecurity body of knowledge is an essential part of the teaching goals regardless of the disciplinary lens. The main necessity is that the explicit linkages to those other instances will allow the student to assemble a comprehensive personal vision of the topic under study.

The CSEC2017 Organization

The CSEC2017 thought model embodies an organizational architecture that is intended to allow each individual learner to integrate the knowledge from each of the eight knowledge areas in such a way that the outcome will produce an in-depth and comprehensive vision of the cybersecurity process for their particular disciplinary lens. As shown in Figure 2.4, the CSEC2017 thought model incorporates six crosscutting concepts (ACM, 2019, p. 22):

1. *Confidentiality*: Rules that limit access to data and information to authorized persons
2. *Integrity*: Assurance that the data and information are accurate and trustworthy

Figure 2.4 Six crosscutting concepts of the CSEC2017 framework.

3. *Availability*: The data, information, and system are accessible
4. *Risk*: The likely potential for gain or loss
5. *Adversarial Thinking*: Consideration of potential actions against the desired result
6. *Systems Thinking*: Trading off constraints to enable assured operations.

These concepts have different applications depending on the computing discipline. CC2005 model documents five distinctively different computer disciplines (ACM, 2005). These fields all revolve around some aspect of the computer. But they take considerably divergent curricular views. On one end of the spectrum are the mathematical disciplines, computer engineering, and computer science. In the middle is the more applied discipline of software engineering, and on the other end are the wholly applied business disciplines of information systems and information technology. The computer underlies all of these fields and so the focus and content of the cybersecurity body of knowledge is applicable to each. However, the rigor and depth of the application of the knowledge elements will vary based on the purpose and intentions of the field. That depth of application is the disciplinary lens.

The CSEC2017 is very direct in stating that, "The disciplinary lens drives the approach, depth of content, and learning outcomes resulting from the interplay among the topics, essential and crosscutting concepts." (ACM, 2019, p. 22). For instance, the coverage of insider theft in the context of Human Security will be different for students in a mathematically based computer science-type cybersecurity program than it will be for those in a business process-based information systems-type cybersecurity program. Thus, curriculum designers for these two different computer fields will, quite legitimately, instantiate the same topic differently. That will be both in terms of teaching approach and course materials.

The topics which a curriculum designer must actually select are specified in the CSEC2017. However, the specific course content that delivers those topics is left to the individual who is developing the curriculum. The assumption is reasonable in that only the individual who knows the instructional objectives for that particular program is capable of deciding how the content is presented. However, the focus for a generic topic, like insider theft, will still remain the point of reference in the detailed design process. For instance, the educators who design the insider threat section in a computer science course are likely to focus on automated methods for heuristically detecting anomalous behavior among system users or staff, whereas an information system curriculum would be more likely to focus on how to conduct auditing and inspection processes and training experiences that would allow the organization to identify and counter an individual who is thinking about going off the rails. In both cases, the topic of insider threat is covered. Still, the coverage is determined by the disciplinary lens of the faculty and students.

The CSEC2017 Implementation Process

As outlined in Chapter 1, there are eight explicitly defined knowledge areas in the CSEC2017. Each of these is discrete, in that they represent a distinct knowledge and skill set that can be cross related to professional activities described in the National Institute of Standards and Technology's NICE Workforce Framework (Newhouse et al., 2017). As a point of reference, the knowledge area headings of the CSEC2017 are as follows:

1. Knowledge Area One – **Data Security**
2. Knowledge Area Two – **Software Security**
3. Knowledge Area Three – **Component Security**
4. Knowledge Area Four – **Connection Security**
5. Knowledge Area Five – **System Security**
6. Knowledge Area Six – **Human Security**
7. Knowledge Area Seven – **Organizational Security**
8. Knowledge Area Eight – **Societal Security**.

The CSEC2017 is structured top down by knowledge area, knowledge units, and then topics. As shown in Figure 2.5 and Figure 2.6, each area contains essential knowledge units that are explicitly identified with the knowledge topics that are characteristic of that area. The essential concepts are crosscutting in that they may either appear as a specific knowledge unit or as an integral set of elements in a range of knowledge areas. Taken together, the eight knowledge areas constitute a comprehensive description of the knowledge skills and abilities

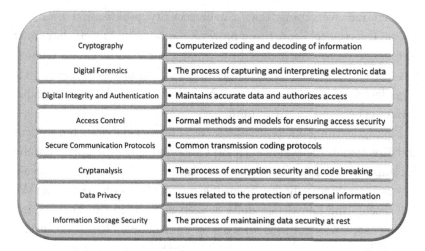

Figure 2.5   The Data Security knowledge units.

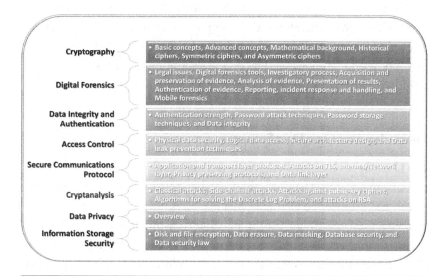

Figure 2.6   The knowledge units and topics of the Data Security knowledge area.

that a professional would have to master in order to do cybersecurity work.

The multiple number of knowledge units that underlie each knowledge area represent an integrated grouping of subject matter topics, which encompass the required curricular content for each of the knowledge areas. Taken as a whole, the content of the underlying knowledge units defines a base level of proficiency for that particular knowledge area. As a complete set, these knowledge units characterize everything that a cybersecurity professional needs to know. The concepts constitute professional practice in that they must be touched on to some extent by every student to some extent regardless of the disciplinary lens of the program. Accordingly, the knowledge described in these units must be fully presented by every suitably correct cybersecurity curriculum.

Finally, learning outcomes that serve to further elaborate the content and direction of each knowledge unit are provided at the bottom of the decomposition ladder. These describe the outcomes that will be necessary to unambiguously document mastery of the knowledge unit. We will discuss the knowledge units of each of these in the final section of this chapter. The aim is to give you an overview of the constituent knowledge of each area, rather than provide detailed advice about the teaching and learning process associated with each category. It perhaps goes without saying that some of these areas are conceptually broader than others and, therefore, the component knowledge is extensive. In every case, we will broadly itemize the recommended content for each knowledge area as well as provide some rationale for why it was included. The rest of the book chapters will explain each area in depth.

Knowledge Area One: Data Security

The **Data Security** knowledge area is a logical place to lead off the process of categorizing the discipline of cybersecurity since Data Security entails the knowledge elements that are essential to the purpose of the computer; secure storage, processing, and transmission of computerized information. Securing these areas has always been the classic mission of the information assurance function. Therefore, the CSEC2017 views the protection requirements as being based around a set of well-known and fundamental information protection principles. The principles have been part of old-style computing for a long time and they are generally well known and commonly acknowledged as being components of the generic profession of information assurance (Figure 2.5).

1. Cryptography – involves the computerized encoding and decoding of information
2. Digital Forensics – the process of capturing and interpreting electronic data

3. Data Integrity and Authentication – maintains accurate data and authorizes access
4. Access Control – the formal methods and models for ensuring access security
5. Secure Communication Protocols – the common transmission coding protocols
6. Cryptanalysis – the process of encryption security and code breaking
7. Data Privacy – overviews the issues related to protection of personal information
8. Information Storage Security – the process of maintaining Data Security at rest.

Each of these individual knowledge units is accompanied by a listing of topics as shown in Figure 2.6. The topics provide guidance for an individual course knowledge unit presentation or cross-curricular content solution that will satisfy the learning requirements for that particular knowledge element (all from ACM, 2019).

Cryptography – This is one of the most fundamental topic areas in cybersecurity. It covers basic cryptographic concepts including data integrity, non-repudiation, ciphertext/plaintext, secret key (symmetric), cryptography, and public key (asymmetric) cryptography. It also includes the concepts for information-theoretic security and computational security as they apply to data protection.

Digital Forensics – This topic includes the definition and categorization of forensics inquiry processes and digital forensic tools. It provides a generic description of the types of tools, legal issues, legal authority, legal processes, and preservation of digital evidence associated with data capture. It also includes the forensic investigation process as it applies to the acquisition and preservation of evidence, analysis of evidence, and chain of custody. Finally, there is a description of the forensic incident response and reporting process.

Data Integrity and Authentication – This topic includes the topics related to the authentication process and the assurance of authentication strength. It discusses the classic password attack methods and the related storage techniques for passwords as well as the classic message authentication processes, which underwrite the assurance of data integrity.

Access Control – In simple terms, this is the access control knowledge element. This includes such large and extensive topics as physical Data Security, logical data access control models, secure architectural design, and data leak prevention techniques.

Secure Communication Protocols – These examine the standard protocol topics that are characteristic of the Open Standard Interface (OSI) Model's application and transport layer. It also includes topics that are related to the data link layer. Finally, it examines the more exotic privacy-preserving protocols such as terms of reference (TOR).

Cryptanalysis – It focuses on classical cryptologic attacks such as brute force as well as the range of side channel exploits such as power consumption or timing attacks. It also looks at more sophisticated areas of attack such as cypher attacks and attacks against algorithms or specific encryption methods, for instance Rivest-Shamir_Adleman (RSA).

Data Privacy – Topics in this area examine the various laws and regulations related to privacy as well as the legal and ethical implications of privacy laws and the methods for ensuring privacy in the real world. This is an example of a crosscutting topic in that these knowledge units appear in a number of other knowledge areas in the CSEC2017 including Societal Security and Organizational Security.

Information Storage Security – This knowledge unit encompasses primarily database security topics including the legal and ethical implications. But it also comprises data masking methods as well as classic large-scale data management topics such as information auditing and secure access authentication techniques.

Knowledge Area Two: Software Security

The **Software Security** knowledge area focuses on the development and utilization of software that will exhibit fundamental properties of good design, secure and efficient processing, effective performance, and reliable and stable operation. The CSEC2017 views the Software Security knowledge units as being characteristic of the principles and practices that are normally associated with good software engineering. Those principles and practices were first codified in the software

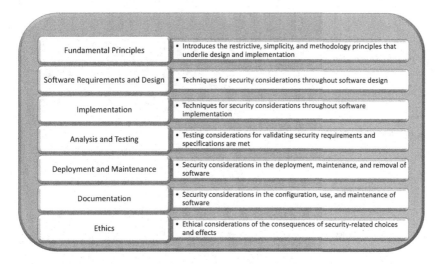

Figure 2.7 The Software Security knowledge units.

engineering body of knowledge (SWEBOK) in 2004, and they have been generally well known and well accepted since that time. The CSEC2017 embodies six essential elements, shown in Figure 2.7, five of which look like traditional waterfall stages (ACM, 2019):

1. Fundamental Principles – introduces the restrictive, simplicity, and methodology principles that underlie design and implementation
2. Security Requirements and Design – techniques for security considerations throughout software design
3. Implementation – techniques for security considerations throughout software implementation
4. Analysis and Testing – testing considerations for validating security requirements and specifications are met
5. Deployment and Maintenance – security considerations in the deployment, maintenance, and removal of software
6. Documentation – security considerations in the configuration, use, and maintenance of software
7. Ethics – ethical considerations of the consequences of security-related choices and effects.

The knowledge units in the Software Security knowledge area comprise the fundamental principles and practices of good software engineering development, operation, maintenance, and acquisition.

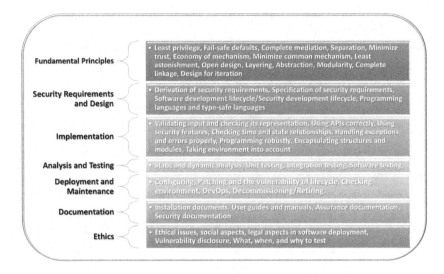

Figure 2.8   The knowledge units and topics of the Software Security knowledge area.

Each of the individual knowledge units is accompanied by a listing of topics as shown in Figure 2.8. The topics provide guidance for an individual course knowledge unit presentation or cross-curricular content solution that will satisfy the learning requirements for that particular knowledge element (all from ACM, 2019).

Fundamental Principles – This catch-all category states the conceptual and practical requirements that are associated with software work, which includes the Saltzer and Schroeder (1974) principles of least privilege, open design, and abstraction. Topics also include the classic waterfall stages of security requirements and their role in design as well as implementation and coding issues. On the back end of the process are the static and dynamic testing knowledge units along with the methods for configuration management and patching. There is also a section of this unit that is devoted to ethics, especially in development, testing, and vulnerability disclosure.

Security Requirements and Design – This knowledge unit describes the various techniques that can be utilized to build security in. The topics itemize the secure specification and design methods that apply throughout the requirements and design stages of the life cycle. This includes how to derive and specify security requirements, secure design and development throughout the software life cycle, and secure programming and programming languages.

Implementation – This knowledge unit entails the standard best practice processes for thinking about and incorporating the necessary security considerations throughout the concrete process of programming/implementing the software, which include methods for validation of input and checking for accuracy, as well as correct implementation and use of application programming interface (API) and security features. Topics include methods for properly encapsulating structures and modules, checking for accurate run time and proper state relationships, ensuring the proper handling of exceptions and errors, and how to consider program operating environment in order to program robustly.

Static and Dynamic Analysis – This unit introduces classic software assurance knowledge as it applies to confirming that the software meets all explicit and implicit security requirements as specified. This topic describes the wide range of methods for accomplishing these purposes, including how to structure and execute an effective static and dynamic analysis testing process, including the restrictions of each. This topic describes how to test the software as a whole and place unit and integration testing in a proper framework. It describes how to test the software components as they are integrated. It also underwrites programming in the large in that it examines the mechanisms for performing static and dynamic tests on enterprise software systems. Finally, this unit embodies topics that are related to assessing general robustness in system operation including whether unstated and undocumented features are present.

Maintenance – This is the topic area where configuration management best practice is presented and discussed. The knowledge in this unit encompasses considerations for the use of software following its acceptance into service. This includes methods for secure deployment, maintenance, and eventual decommissioning and removal of software systems. The topics comprise methods for secure software system installation and operation. It also details the methods for change management as they apply to security assurance, including vulnerability reporting, remediation and assurance of the change, and patch distribution. It also touches on methods for automating and monitoring the process. Finally, this knowledge unit contains topics that outline how to perform secure retirement activities, including how to remove an old system without causing security problems.

Documentation – This knowledge unit describes an essential but often overlooked area of Software Security. It outlines the methods and practices that can be used to ensure that awareness of security-related issues and considerations is formally embedded in the software life cycle process. This includes how to create and operate a configuration management documentation process as well as how to maintain security-related reports, manuals, design documents, and security-related documentation.

Ethics – This knowledge unit introduces ethical considerations in the software development and use life cycle. The aim is to ensure that the consequences of security-related choices and effects are understood including ethical issues in software development, such as reuse. It also looks at societal factors as they relate to software including the penalties of insecure coding practices and the legal ramifications of liability and regulatory compliance, including legal and ethical concerns related to disclosure.

Knowledge Area Three: Component Security

The **Component Security** knowledge area embodies fundamental assurance practices that are associated with the interconnection of components and their use within larger systems that are built from constituent parts. Therefore, the overall security process starts at the component level. Knowledge units, shown in Figure 2.9, center on the assurance of processes for component development, or acquisition, as

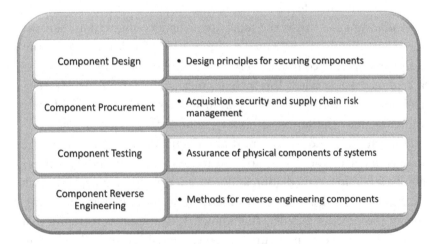

Component Design	• Design principles for securing components
Component Procurement	• Acquisition security and supply chain risk management
Component Testing	• Assurance of physical components of systems
Component Reverse Engineering	• Methods for reverse engineering components

Figure 2.9 The Component Security knowledge units.

well as the secure sustainment of all of the discrete components that are integrated into a larger system entity. Therefore, this knowledge area focuses primarily on the security aspects of design, construction, procurement, testing, and analysis of embedded system components. This includes formal practices for ensuring complete and proper design, development, acquisition, and testing of the integrated component set. The following four knowledge units comprise the Component Security knowledge area (all from ACM, 2019).

1. Component Design – design principles for securing components
2. Component Procurement – acquisition security and supply chain risk management
3. Component Testing – assurance of physical components of systems
4. Component Reverse Engineering – methods for reverse engineering components.

Each of the individual knowledge units is accompanied by a listing of topics and shown in Figure 2.10.

Component Design – This knowledge unit introduces classic design concepts for the long-term assurance of the components of a larger system entity and includes an itemization of potential threats that might arise during the component design process such as theft of

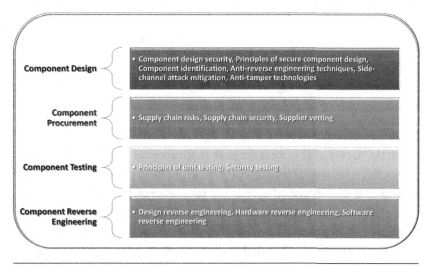

Figure 2.10   The knowledge units and topics of the Component Security knowledge area.

intellectual property, tampering, and counterfeits. This also includes such large topics as, security policy, strategic system design, assurance of trust, risk analysis and mitigation, and basic design principles such as simplicity and layering. It also includes best practices such as component identification and defensive techniques such as obfuscation of design and anti-theft measures.

Component Procurement – This knowledge unit entails all of the knowledge related to effective supply chain risk management practice and includes understanding security threats to both hardware and software during the acquisition process as well as strategies for assurance of physical security of components during the procurement process. Finally, this area contains knowledge units that are specifically focused on supplier vetting, including topics such as supplier certification and the credentialing of trusted foundries.

Component Testing – This knowledge unit centers on the practices for component testing and assurance. This is another strongly crosscutting concept that appears in a number of places throughout the CSEC2017. For this knowledge area, the focus is on the tools and techniques for assuring the security properties of a component. The aim is to test the security properties of a component to explicitly assure its functional correctness.

Component Reverse Engineering – This knowledge unit examines the tools and techniques used to reproduce the design and functionality of a product given incomplete knowledge of its discrete components and construction. That includes both hardware and software reverse engineering. The aim is to be able to explain how a given component might impact the security of the overall system.

Knowledge Area Four: Connection Security

The **Connection Security** knowledge area is perhaps the most classic of the CSEC2017 areas in that it focuses on the security of the connections between components including both physical and logical. It is critical that every cybersecurity professional have a basic knowledge of digital communications and networking and how components in a network interact. Therefore, the contents in this area are among the most extensively detailed and presented subject matter topics among the knowledge units covered by the CSEC2017. Because the

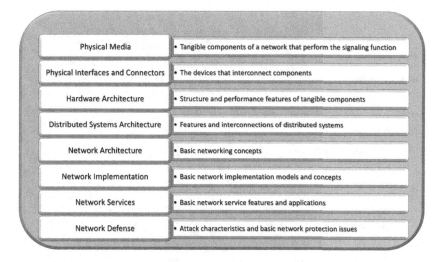

Physical Media	• Tangible components of a network that perform the signaling function
Physical Interfaces and Connectors	• The devices that interconnect components
Hardware Architecture	• Structure and performance features of tangible components
Distributed Systems Architecture	• Features and interconnections of distributed systems
Network Architecture	• Basic networking concepts
Network Implementation	• Basic network implementation models and concepts
Network Services	• Basic network service features and applications
Network Defense	• Attack characteristics and basic network protection issues

Figure 2.11   The Connection Security knowledge units.

knowledge units in this area represent the basic purpose of computing machinery, they are also among the most extensively crosscutting
(Figure 2.11). Knowledge units within this knowledge area are as follows (ACM, 2019):

1. Physical Media – tangible components of a network that perform the signaling function
2. Physical Interface and Connecters – the devices that interconnect components
3. Hardware Architecture – structure and performance features
   of tangible components
4. Distributed Systems Architecture – features and interconnections of distributed systems
5. Network Architecture – basic networking concepts
6. Network Implementations – basic network implementation
   models and concepts
7. Network Services – basic network service features and
   applications
8. Network Defense – attack characteristics and basic network
   protection issues.

Each of the individual knowledge units is accompanied by a listing of
topics as shown in Figure 2.12.

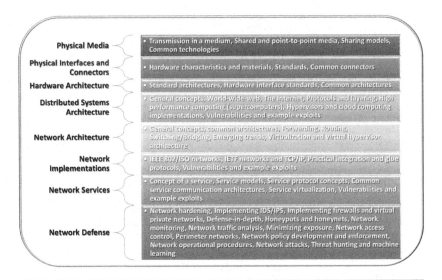

Figure 2.12   The knowledge units and topics of the Connection Security knowledge area.

Physical Media – This is a very large area, and so the label might be a little deceptive. Essentially, this knowledge unit involves the topics that are associated with the components used for physical signaling and the transmission of electronic signals. These are general concepts, and they are best discussed in a historical context. Therefore, the topics are presented in an evolutionary order including systems, architecture, models, standards, and connection attacks.

Physical Interface and Connecters – This topic describes the characteristics of the hardware items that interconnect components. This is an important topic in that students need to understand the differences between the various connectors, their capabilities, and performance issues. Because standardization is an essential element of component interconnection, it is also critical for the student to be fully conversant in the appropriate standardizations for common network technologies.

Hardware Architecture – This knowledge unit focuses on the hardware that comprises the network. The aim is to help the student understand the classic hardware components of a network as well as understand and work with the advantages and disadvantages of various standard hardware architectures including such items as adding plug-and-play functionality within the base architecture without changing its overall structure.

Distributed Systems Architecture – This is understandably a very large area, and the focus in this area is on similarities, differences in architectural solutions, and why design choices are made. This unit contains the knowledge units that describe the distributed systems in concept and explains how they are interconnected. The unit overviews the various architectures for communicating between processes and people including both local area communication all the way up to the World Wide Web. Attack vectors and surfaces are examined in the light of inherent potential vulnerabilities.

Network Architecture – The items in this unit comprise fundamental networking knowledge. These classic elements are an essential foundation for further study of topologies and transmission characteristics. The basics of standard packet transmission and virtuality are the key concepts. Network architecture concepts are usually illustrated by reference to specific implementations. Nevertheless, it should be made clear that any particular network example is only one of a range of possible solutions.

Network Implementations – This is a very real-world oriented knowledge unit and focuses on the various technologies that characterize the networking process. It should be emphasized that vulnerabilities are exploited in implementations. This is the knowledge unit that does the intensive presentation of international standards as well as the Transmission Control Protocol/Internet Protocol (TCP/IP) universe. It is supported by explicit examples from the technologies that are part of the program focus. This will be different depending on the disciplinary lens.

Network Services – This knowledge unit characterizes the various standard models for connectivity. This is another one of the areas that is crosscutting and can be explored at many levels. The aim is to have the student understand that all of the models that are presented can be implemented in different architectures. This topic looks at specific network services and how their protocols are implemented, e.g., Hypertext Transfer Protocol (HTTP), Simple Network Management Protocol (SNMP), or Hypertext Transfer Protocol Secure (HTTPS).

Network Defense – This knowledge unit explores the existing ideas about how to protect a network. The emphasis is on itemizing and exploring all of the known connection vulnerabilities. Defense in depth and other network protection strategies as well as the various attack patterns and common mitigations are presented here. The aim is to prepare a student to counter every viable form of attack.

Knowledge Area Five: System Security

The **System Security** knowledge area embodies the security thinking with respect to systems. It is crosscutting in that all systems have components (KA 3), require connections (KA 4), and make use of software (KA 2). Therefore, the steps to ensure the security of a system require a unified vision of the components, connections, and software that comprises it. This requires a holistic understanding of the system. Figure 2.13 lists the seven knowledge units that comprise the System Security knowledge area:

1. System Thinking – the ability to view the system in a holistic fashion
2. System Management – secure management of system operation and resources
3. System Access – ensuring regulated and controlled use of system resources
4. System Control – ensuring reliable control of access
5. System Retirement – decommissioning a system in a secure manner

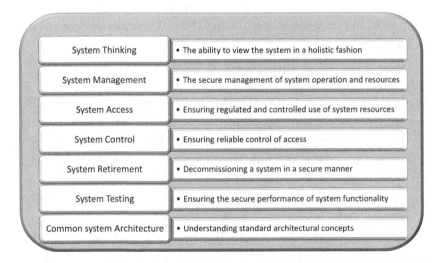

Figure 2.13   The System Security knowledge units.

6. System Testing – ensuring the secure performance of system functionality

7. Common System Architecture – understanding standard architectural concepts.

Each of the individual knowledge units is accompanied by a listing of topics as shown in Figure 2.14.

System Thinking – Systems are a collection of interconnected components, and in this respect, every component has a purpose and the interactions between components are designed to produce a desired outcome with the maximum degree of efficiency. Understanding how that all works is the aim of this knowledge area. This topic puts system engineering into context within the cybersecurity purpose. Topics include risk management in a holistic setting for both general and special purpose systems.

System Management – This knowledge unit focuses on the secure management of the system. It looks at various professional models for overall secure management of systems in the documenting, policy-making, operation and maintenance, and commissioning/decommissioning of systems. This area also raises the prospect of insider threat, which is a strongly crosscutting theme within the CSEC2017.

System Access – This knowledge unit looks at the general topic of access control from a system's perspective. Access control is a

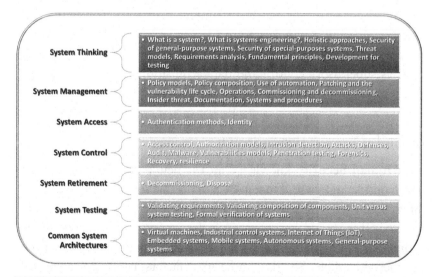

Figure 2.14 The knowledge units and topics of the System Security knowledge area.

crosscutting theme in the CSEC2017. However, its application in its particulars is dependent on the context. This provides the system view. Topics include methods for identification and authentication.

System Control – Where System Access focuses on authentication, this knowledge unit focuses on authorization. Thus, System Control is the area where the topics that are related to enforcing explicit control over access rights and recognition of response to attacks occur. Therefore, there is a long list of topics related to detection and mitigation of threat in this area including, intrusion detection, malware detection, audit, penetration testing, and forensics.

System Retirement – The point where the system is decommissioned is a vulnerability if there are no procedures in place to ensure that this is done securely. Therefore, this knowledge unit provides topics related to the secure decommissioning and disposal of systems such as impact analysis and wiping.

System Testing – This area is analogous to the secure software testing knowledge unit, and therefore, it is crosscutting. It deals primarily with methods and models for assurance that the system requirements have been properly verified and validated and that the components of the system are functioning properly. The topics in this area embody the knowledge related to classic testing and assurance.

Common System Architectures – Systems are aggregations of components assembled for a purpose. Common architectural models exist because those purposes can be common. Therefore, this knowledge unit examines all topics related to specific architectures of functions such as virtual machines that are in common use. That includes such areas as supervisory control and data acquisition (SCADA), mobile, and autonomous systems.

Knowledge Area Six: Human Security

The **Human Security** knowledge area is new and still evolving. The main consideration with Human Security is that it embodies an entirely different challenge than has usually been posed for the study of cybersecurity. This should be noted since the component elements of the entire body of knowledge are systematic, in that they are meant to work together as a whole. So, Human Security factors have to be integrated into the learning experience in order to achieve a holistic understanding.

The primary focus of this area is on the protection of individual data and the assurance of privacy rights within both the business operation as well in the personal life of each citizen. This implies a strict focus on human behavior as it relates to cybersecurity. Thus, the aim of this area is to ensure the confidentiality, integrity, and availability of individual data within both organizational and a personal use context. Shown in Figure 2.15, the following seven knowledge units comprise the Human Security knowledge area:

1. Identity Management – assurance of identity of individuals seeking access
2. Social Engineering – exploits aimed at tricking victims into surrendering sensitive data
3. Personal Compliance – willingness to follow a defined set of rules of behavior
4. Awareness and Understanding – general grasp of issues related to cybersecurity
5. Social and Behavioral Privacy – privacy as it relates to individuals in the social context
6. Personal Data Privacy – privacy issues related to individuals in the personal context
7. Usability and Security – assurance of ease of use to encourage secure behavior.

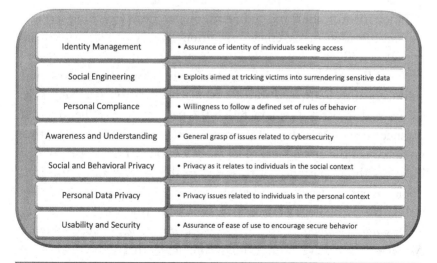

Figure 2.15   The Human Security knowledge units.

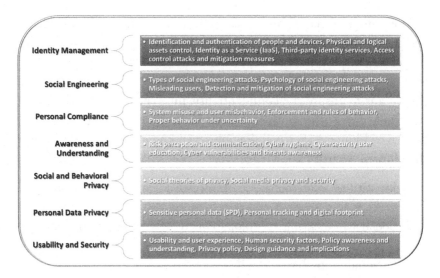

Figure 2.16 The knowledge units and topics of the Human Security knowledge area.

Each of the individual knowledge units is accompanied by a listing of topics as shown in Figure 2.16.

Identity Management – This topic represents the individual user side of the classic area of access control. Because access and rights are granted based on the identity of the person or process requesting access, getting identity right is an important area of cybersecurity. And because the identity of the request will determine the access granted, many of the topics in this knowledge unit revolve around common identification and authorization practices, including services for identification management. Additionally, classic identity threats as well as mitigations are included as topics in this area.

Social Engineering – Social engineering is perhaps the greatest and least frequently addressed threat in the cybersecurity universe. There are no real statistics to characterize the percent of loss due to social engineering scams such as phishing and pretexting but the fact is that up to 35% of the annual record loss is due to behavioral causes, which indicates the importance of this area in the cybersecurity universe. Topics focus on types and methods of social engineering attack as well as the psychology of deception as a countermeasure.

Personal Compliance with Cybersecurity Rules, Policy, Ethical Norms – There have been studies conducted that indicate that up to 90% of the overall problem is attributable to simple human error and noncompliance with rules. So, rather than a malicious nation-state, we may be "done in" by nothing more than an unawareness or unwillingness to follow the rules. Thus, topics in this area have to do with formulation and enforcement of rules of behavior in the workplace aimed at preventing system misuse or user misbehavior. That includes educating users in ways to make the right choice in the face of uncertainty.

Awareness and Understanding – This is the necessary companion piece to the item above. In simple terms, users have to be fully aware of the consequences of their behavior in order to make proper choices. This can only be underwritten by formal awareness and training activities. Thus, topics in this area center on methods to ensure proper cyber hygiene, user awareness, and training and awareness of the consequences of actions in virtual space.

Social and Behavioral Privacy – The virtual revolution has more or less ensured that individual privacy is a lost commodity in our society. Between the actions of social media, big data, and the ignorance of our citizens in general, what we assume to be our personal privacy is actually a commodity in multiple data warehouses around the globe. The concept of privacy within society at large is essentially a theoretical issue, and so the topic areas in this knowledge unit are related to ensuring understanding the role of such large-scale social phenomena as social media and the economies of the data harvesting industry.

Personal Data Privacy and Security – This is the other side of the coin from the big data question above. People in general are unaware of the implications and impacts of their personal information, and this ignorance makes them vulnerable. The cybersecurity process is obligated to ensuring that individuals are sufficiently cognizant of the threats represented by how they create and share personal information, and how they are able to protect themselves. Thus, topics in this area touch on types of personal information and how it is used to track and influence the individual owner of that data. The focus is on method rather than theory, and the outcome needs to be individuals who know how to protect themselves.

Usable Security and Privacy – Much of the problem with cybersecurity comes from the fact that it can be rather inconvenient. People do not use long complex passwords, simply because they are hard to remember. People frequently do not utilize security best practice because it is just "one more thing for them to do." Therefore, the Saltzer and Schroeder (1974) principle of "usability" becomes a significant factor in whether we are willing to protect ourselves. This is a planning and deployment challenge as much as it is one of simple awareness. Therefore, topics in this area focus on issues related to proper usability design, human factors in design, and use and best use policy. These are major operational/application issues with widescale significance in the overall assurance of personal and organizational cybersecurity.

Knowledge Area Seven: Organizational Security

While Human Security focuses on the individual, the **Organizational Security** knowledge area focuses on the organization as a whole. Its focus is large scale and strategic rather than individual. Therefore, the knowledge units in this area are oriented toward cybersecurity threat identification and mitigation and the management of broad risk. All of this is in service of and dictated by the organizational purpose. Organizations are composed of stakeholders, and those stakeholder's needs are individual. Therefore, the knowledge units in the Organizational Security area are, by necessity, aimed at satisfying a range of potential constituent needs. As a result, each of these knowledge units is huge in terms of its scope and content (Figure 2.17).

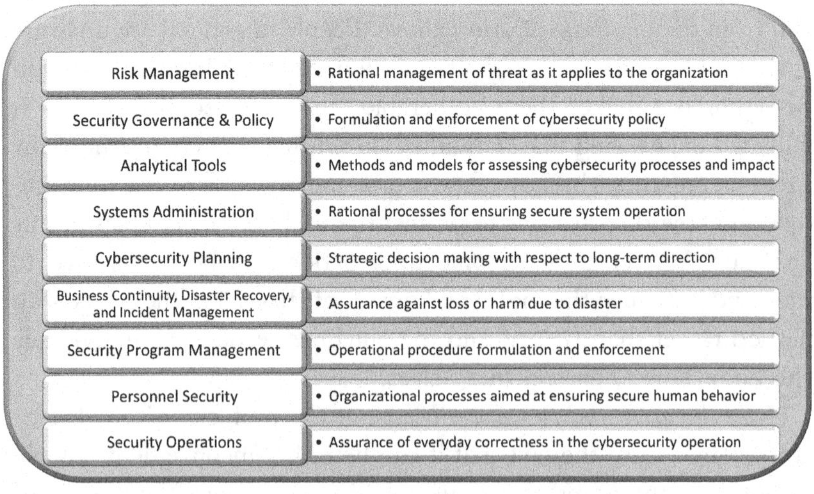

Risk Management	• Rational management of threat as it applies to the organization
Security Governance & Policy	• Formulation and enforcement of cybersecurity policy
Analytical Tools	• Methods and models for assessing cybersecurity processes and impact
Systems Administration	• Rational processes for ensuring secure system operation
Cybersecurity Planning	• Strategic decision making with respect to long-term direction
Business Continuity, Disaster Recovery, and Incident Management	• Assurance against loss or harm due to disaster
Security Program Management	• Operational procedure formulation and enforcement
Personnel Security	• Organizational processes aimed at ensuring secure human behavior
Security Operations	• Assurance of everyday correctness in the cybersecurity operation

Figure 2.17 The Organizational Security knowledge units.

Specifically, the nine knowledge units in the Organizational Security knowledge area are as follows (ACM, 2019):

1. Risk Management – rational management of threat as it applies to the organization
2. Security Governance and Policy – formulation and enforcement of cybersecurity policy
3. Analytical Tools – methods and models for assessing cybersecurity processes and impact
4. Systems Administration – rational processes for ensuring secure system operation
5. Cybersecurity Planning – strategic decision-making with respect to long-term direction
6. Business Continuity and Recovery – assurance against loss or harm due to disaster
7. Security Program Management – operational procedure formulation and enforcement
8. Personnel Security – organizational processes aimed at ensuring secure human behavior
9. Security Operations – assurance of everyday correctness in the cybersecurity operation.

Each of the individual knowledge units is accompanied by a listing of topics as shown in Figure 2.18.

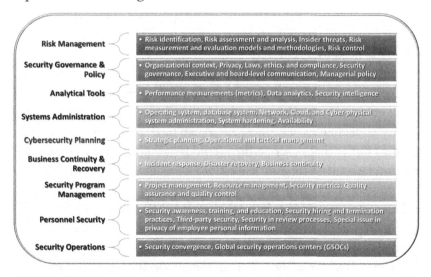

Figure 2.18 The knowledge units and topics of the Organizational Security knowledge area.

Risk Management – Because threat and risk are fundamental elements of the cybersecurity equation, risk management crosscuts all of the knowledge areas. It is located here because risk management is the responsibility of the organization as a whole. The knowledge units in this area all relate to the process of identifying and mitigating risks to organizational information assets including such topics as: asset identification, threat modeling and assessment, risk and impact analysis, insider threat, risk measurement, and risk control methodologies.

Security Governance and Policy – Because it's a fundamental aspect of practical control, cybersecurity policy and governance is another strongly crosscutting knowledge area. Governance is the responsibility of the senior management, and it is implemented by strategic planning. Without a unified set of strategic policies and their applied governance processes, it would be impossible for an organization to oversee and manage its constituent elements. Every aspect of cybersecurity development planning, organizational risk management, and daily operational assurance is carried out by means of the policies, plans, programs, and budgetary controls established to ensure their proper functioning, and organizational context is a critical factor. Topics in this area focus on policy and procedure compliance with all applicable standards, laws, and regulations for privacy and security governance. These are important topics given the regulatory environment and laws such as Health Insurance Portability and Accountability Act (HIPAA) and Sarbanes–Oxley. Also, topics related to organizational communication up and down the chain or command need to be covered.

Analytical Tools – Classic empirical approaches are one of the most reliable ways of identifying and mitigating threats in the cybersecurity environment. The general term used to describe this type of activity is data analytics. Thus, the Analytical Tools knowledge unit contains topics that describe the methods and performance measures that can be used to monitor operations and support decision-making with respect to cyberthreats. This includes such topic items as types and classifications of Analytic Tools, how these tools work, and the relationship between analytic software and tools and forensics and sources of security information such as InfraGard.

Systems Administration – This is the single function that ensures continuous and effective day-to-day operation of the security response.

The orientation of this knowledge area is toward the existing system infrastructure, primarily the technical system infrastructure. Therefore, this knowledge area implicitly assumes prerequisite knowledge of computer systems and network administration, network and database administration, and more recently, cloud administration.

It also includes knowledge of how to securely manage the physical infrastructure of the system as well as overall risk management for the physical system. As we have seen, this knowledge area is often divorced from classic system management and so the two knowledge units in this area must be closely coordinated.

Cybersecurity Planning – This is the knowledge unit that focuses on the long-range strategic planning of the organization's cybersecurity strategy. It has implementation and resource allocation overtones, and therefore, topics such as strategic positioning, organizational strength, weakness, opportunities, and threats analysis; and process alignment with business goals and objectives appear here. This might sound a bit high level, but the knowledge in this unit is important, since one of the primary criticisms of cybersecurity operations, as they currently exist, is that they are divorced from considerations of the goals of the business.

Business Continuity, Disaster Recovery, and Incident Management – This used to be called "backup" back in the day. However, given that organization date is integral to the survival of most businesses; the information and its processing equipment must be protected from any disastrous eventuality. The continuity of the organization in the wake of major events is the goal of this knowledge unit. Consequently, this knowledge area is based around strategic contingency planning activities that center on all "what-if" scenarios relevant to any significant threat. If the disaster occurs, then disaster recovery planning addresses the recovery of information and systems in the event of a disaster. This area also includes tactical response planning with respect to all conceivable incidents as well as the classic backup and recovery functions. The aim of all three of these planning activities is to ensure the planned availability of essential resources in the case of a foreseen emergency.

Security Program Management – This is the classic project management area that crosscuts almost every aspect of security assurance. It details current practices in project resource management as it relates to cybersecurity. Security Program Management embodies the project management body of knowledge, and therefore, it covers the traditional skills, tools, and techniques related to ensuring that the security project satisfies its stated requirements. Topics are typical of good project resource management: scoping and scope management, time and cost management, quality management, human resource and risk management, and procurement management. Finally, this area contains crosscutting advice concerning the use of security metrics for strategic, tactical, and operational planning, as well as security program performance evaluation.

Personnel Security – As we've seen, this area accounts for a large percentage of the overall record loss, and so, it is a critical element of the field. It is also crosscutting in that all of the other areas involve people and is particularly related to Human Security. This knowledge area is based around education and training as a positive means of ensuring adherence to the organizational rules of behavior. However, it also includes topics related to hiring, termination, and third-party security practices. It includes topics relevant to security reviews and vetting and continuous assurance of personal trust. This area also includes practices to secure the personal information of employees and other stakeholders.

Security Operations – As we have seen, much of the problem with cybersecurity rests in the area of overall organizational coordination of the effort. The knowledge units in this important topic area involve the means of maintaining control and traceability over all components integrated into the cybersecurity operation. It includes assignment and oversight of fully integrated managerial accountability in the three areas of cybersecurity functionality: electronic, personnel, and physical. It also includes topics related to getting and maintaining a global threat awareness by means of a formally established global security operations center.

Knowledge Area Eight: Societal Security

Societal Security is a new area of thought in cybersecurity. Until recently, all of the thinking with respect to the form and function of the field of cybersecurity has been concentrated in the immediate area of electronic protection. This final knowledge area considers

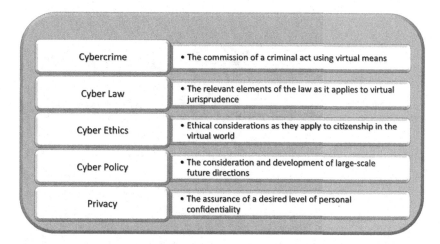

Figure 2.19   The Societal Security knowledge units.

cybersecurity as an entity that functions within our society as a whole. Thus, the topics in this area comprise larger social entities such as social policy, personal privacy, cybercrime, cyberlaw, and ethics and how the key concepts of this knowledge area related to each other. Shown in Figure 2.19, the five knowledge units of the Societal Security knowledge area entail the following:

1. Cybercrime – the commission of a criminal act using virtual means
2. Cyber Law – the relevant elements of the law as it applies to virtual jurisprudence
3. Cyber Ethics – ethical considerations as they apply to citizenship in the virtual world
4. Cyber Policy – the consideration and development of large-scale future directions
5. Privacy – the assurance of a desired level of personal confidentiality.

Each of the individual knowledge units is accompanied by a listing of topics as shown in Figure 2.20.

Cybercrime – As we saw in the Chapter 1, cybercrime is an area that might represent the single greatest threat to society as a whole. Therefore, cybercrime topics are extremely significant considerations in the body of knowledge. The knowledge units aim to ensure practical understanding of the scope, cost, and legal issues that relate to

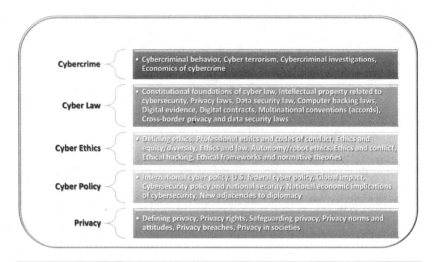

Figure 2.20 The knowledge units and topics of the Organizational Security knowledge area.

virtual crime. Topics include legal, economic, and ethical aspects of cybercrime enforcement.

Cyber Law – This knowledge unit is specifically focused on the law and legal systems. The aim is to ensure comprehensive knowledge of the tricky legal and ethical issues that are uniquely related to cyberspace. This includes consideration of laws in cyber-based legal cases in all potential jurisdictions. It also includes the law enforcement problems associated with these jurisdictional boundaries. Topics include applicable legal legislation and an understanding of the development of precedent within the legal environment as well as societal perspectives and ethical frameworks as they relate to cybersecurity.

Cyber Policy – Like every other knowledge unit in this knowledge area, cyber policy is crosscutting. However, because most of the conceptualization and deployment of a cybersecurity response hinges on proper policy, this might be the most significant crosscutting element of all.

The general intention of this unit is to present cyber policy issues as they relate to national and international actions in that domain. This includes such topics as cyber hacking and cyber war as instruments of state policy as well as a means of economic competition among individuals, organizations, and nations.

Privacy – This final element is as generally crosscutting as the others. However, since privacy is more a quality than an actual area of study, the aim or this particular knowledge unit is to convey all of the challenges to personal and organizational privacy as they relate to cyberspace.

The topics relate to the various trade-offs associated with providing too much access versus too little and has been known as the Goldilocks principle, "Not too much, not too little, just right." Because privacy at the corporate level is related to protection of confidential information, some topics also consider the company's duties and responsibilities with respect to the collection, storage, and handling of corporate and personal data. This can include the concepts of appropriate use as well as protection of information.

Twenty Review Questions: The Cybersecurity Body of Knowledge

1. Why is the community's joint recognition the key factor for a body of knowledge?
2. What does sanctioning the outcomes of a new body of knowledge accomplish?
3. Why is a single point of reference important?
4. Why is tailoring an important concept when it comes to bodies of knowledge?
5. What are curricular core concepts? How do they differ from any other concepts?
6. What is a "Learned Society" and why are they important to a profession?
7. What are crosscutting elements and why do they make cybersecurity confusing?
8. What is the role of "linkages" in applying a body of knowledge?
9. What is a disciplinary lens and how does it impact teaching cybersecurity?
10. Why does institutional type matter in the definition of cybersecurity content?
11. What is a disciplinary model?
12. Why do crosscutting elements need to be clarified? Where does this clarification apply?
13. Why is there a requirement for general mastery of the entire eight knowledge areas?
14. How does change factor into the development/addition of knowledge units?

15. How do depth of coverage and disciplinary lens relate?
16. What is the role of the instructor when it comes to crosscutting elements?
17. How is the thought model an organizational architecture?
18. How do rigor and depth apply to the disciplinary lens?
19. Why is each individual instance of a cybersecurity curriculum individual?
20. What role do the six crosscutting concepts play in the definition of learning outcomes?

You Might Also Like to Read

- Greene, Sari, *Security Program and Policies: Principles and Practices*, 2nd Edition, Pearson, London, 2014.
- Patterson, Wayne and Cynthia E. Winston-Proctor, *Behavioral Cybersecurity: Applications of Personality Psychology and Computer Science*, 1st Edition, CRC Press, Boca Raton, FL, 2019.
- Peltier, Thomas R., *Information Security Policies and Procedures: A Practitioner's Reference*, 2nd Edition, Auerbach, Boca Raton, FL, 2004.
- Russo, Mark A., *The National Cybersecurity (NCF) Framework 1.1: For Businesses*, Amazon Publishing, Seattle, WA, 2018.
- Santos, Omar, *Developing Cybersecurity Programs and Policies (Pearson IT Cybersecurity Curriculum (ITCC))*, 3rd Edition, Pearson, London, 2018.
- Shrobe, Howard, David L. Shrier, and Alex Pentland (Editors), *New Solutions for Cybersecurity*, The MIT Press, Cambridge, MA, 2018.

Chapter Summary

- An explicit statement of the essential knowledge skill and ability requirements for a discipline such as cybersecurity is an important tool in the teaching and learning process.
- Bodies of knowledge are a single, tangible point of reference that can be used to authenticate and sanction any curricular content that is deemed appropriate for the field.

- The key factor is joint recognition of the CSEC2017 as a standard model of the elements of the field.
- The foundation of a body of knowledge in expert advice allows a group of educators, who want expert guidance about the necessary curricular and course content, a validated roadmap of the field.
- Bodies of knowledges also provide a common benchmark for curricular offerings that can be directly related to a given area of professional practice.
- Bodies of knowledge structure for practical course delivery.
- Using expert advice, an academic program can install a full set of learning elements and experiences that they can be certain will allow graduates to be successful after graduation.
- The recommendations of any particular body of knowledge have to be tailored to fit the institution that is offering it.
- The outcome of the curriculum/course tailoring process is a detailed description of each requisite learning objective as it applies within the larger context of the standard body of knowledge.
- The CSEC2017 is a baseline that can be used to create new courses and integrate them into existing curricula.
- The sanctioning of the CSEC2017 by all of the relevant societies sets it up as the single authoritative point of reference to build a curriculum on.
- There are numerous crosscutting elements in the CSEC2017 body of knowledge and that many of the elements are viewed through differing disciplinary lenses.
- The CSEC2017's detailed specification of knowledge serves to ensure that the delivery of cybersecurity education is uniform in approach across disciplines.
- The CSEC2017 model was specifically designed to clarify, in an intellectually valid fashion, how its knowledge elements will integrate with each other, as well as how each of the disciplinary lenses would utilize the specific elements in the delivery of curricular content.
- The eight knowledge areas are the fundamental conceptual building blocks of the CSEC2017. Taken together, these

knowledge areas represent a sanctioned framework for the complete body of knowledge for the field of cybersecurity.

- Each knowledge area contains explicitly itemized knowledge units that serve to clarify the focus and intent of the area.
- The CSEC2017 is structured under the assumption that the fundamental ideas that are specified for any individual knowledge area will be embodied as appropriate in each cybersecurity curriculum.
- The depth of the coverage is dictated by the disciplinary lens of the given academic program.
- The role of the instructor in delivering the CSEC2017 model is to ensure that the student is able to make the necessary connections between the knowledge units as they are appear in the subject matter in different courses.
- The CSEC2017 thought model includes six crosscutting concepts: Confidentiality, Integrity, Availability, Risk, Adversarial Thinking, and Systems Thinking.
- The knowledge area headings of the CSEC2017 are Data Security, Software Security, Component Security, Connection Security, System Security, Human Security, Organizational Security, and Societal Security.
- The multiple number of knowledge units that underlie each knowledge area constitute an integrated grouping of subject matter topics, which encompass the required curricular content for each of the knowledge areas.

Keywords

Architecture – the design and implementation of an underlying framework of processes

Best Practice – a set of lessons learned validated for successful execution of a given task

Body of Knowledge – integrated characterization of the elements of a complete field of study

Conceptual Model – a collection of conceptual components arrayed in a logical structure in order to convey a large-scale idea

Curriculum Planning – the process of developing a teaching process that achieves a desired set of long-term learning goals

Disciplinary Lens – the particular curricular perspective of a given computing study

Knowledge Area – a primary constituent element of the body of knowledge

Knowledge Item – a discrete set of human, or electronic behaviors, set to produce a given outcome

Learning Objective – a specifically stated desired outcome of a teaching process

Tailoring – modification of a standard item to reflect the particular curricular application.

References

Joint Task Force for Computing Curricula, "Curricula 2005, the Overview Report", The Association for Computing Machinery (ACM), the Association for Information Systems (AIS), and the Computer Society (IEEE-CS), 30 September 2005.

Joint Task Force (JTF) on Cybersecurity Education, "Cybersecurity Curricula 2017, Curriculum Guidelines for Post-Secondary Degree Programs in Cybersecurity, a Report in the Computing Curricula Series", ACM/ IEEE-CS/AIS SIGSEC/IFIP WG 11.8, Version 1.0, 31 December 2019.

Newhouse, William, Stephanie Keith, Benjamin Scribner, and Greg Witte, "NIST Special Publication 800-181, National Initiative for Cybersecurity Education (NICE) Cybersecurity Workforce Framework", NIST. SP.800-181, August 2017.

Saltzer, Jerome H. and Michael D. Schroeder, The protection of information in computer systems, *Communications of the ACM*, 17, 7, 1974.

3
Data Security

In this chapter, you will learn the following:

- How cryptography is an enabler for Data Security
- How data integrity and authentication techniques are used to mitigate password attacks
- The role of access control in preserving Data Security and secure architecture
- The communication protocols that offer the best levels of Data Security
- The importance of cryptanalysis in Data Security
- How data privacy is factored into the overall understanding of Data Security
- The techniques of data sanitation for proper disposal of data after its useful life.

Surviving in a Digital Era

If you are currently using your smartphone, you are actually generating reams of valuable information in which technology companies can mine for insights, sell to advertisers, and use to optimize their products. The media offer stories on nearly a daily basis. For instance, the Cambridge Analytica scandal, which involved a third-party Facebook app that harvested data for use in political campaigns, went well beyond the scope of the 270,000 users who initially consented to its terms of service. Incidents such as this highlight the vulnerability of consumer data in this digital age. And it is easy to forget about those risks while tapping out messages to friends or scrolling endlessly through the web. The ready availability of online access has radically reduced the presumption of privacy in our daily lives. Studies highlight this digital privacy paradox, in which people express concerns over their privacy but then act in ways that undermine these beliefs.

At the same time, as organizations embark on digital transformation, there is a pressing need for enterprise data privacy and protection. New data privacy laws and the growing enforcement of existing regulations challenge organizations. Meanwhile, organizations face rapid data growth and proliferation across the enterprise. Organizations have more data, more use cases, and more locations than ever before. Yet surprisingly, many of those same organizations don't even have a Data Security plan in place.

A data breach is an unauthorized disclosure of information that compromises the security, confidentiality, or integrity of personally identifiable information (PII). And these data breaches continue to dominate both business and IT news, with bigger and uglier attacks on data being regularly announced. How bad is this problem? The Privacy Rights Clearinghouse (www.privacyrights.org/data-breach) keeps track of every data breach that is reported. According to their research, more than 11.5 billion database records have been breached between January 2005 and the time of this writing in early 2019 – over the course of over 8,800 separate data breach events. Can we put a price tag on all of that unprotected and lost data? We can certainly try. Studies have shown that organizations that had experienced a data breach concluded that the average security breach can cost anywhere between $90 and $305 per lost database record. But coming up with a precise figure can be difficult because of the additional, extenuating circumstances surrounding data breaches. The cost needs to factor in such details as the expenses of legal fees, call centers, lost employee productivity, regulatory fines, customer losses, stock losses, and the nebulous cost of bad publicity.

The obvious conclusion is that data breaches are costly, even at the low end of $90 per record. Consider a typical data breach case. On November 27, 2018, AccuDoc Solutions, Inc. reported an incident in which their network server was hacked. According to the Privacy Rights Clearinghouse, the total number of records involved was 2,652,540. So, what did that cost? At the low end, the cost is $238.7 million, but at the high end, it balloons to over $809 million. Those numbers in and of themselves are enough to make any Chief Information Security Officer (CISO) loose a night or two of sleep.

Data is necessary. Without data, an organization has no record of transactions. Data supports the ability to serve customers and make managerial decisions. In modern times, every organization within every private or public sector relies on information and communications technology (ICT) systems, and those systems rely on data to produce the information necessary to operate effectively. Therefore, Data Security is a critical aspect of cybersecurity.

A generic definition of Data Security is: the policies and procedures associated with protecting data in transmission, in processing, and at rest (storage). Many public and private organizations now use a guideline developed by the National Institute of Standards and technology (NIST) entitled the *Framework for Improving Critical Infrastructure Cybersecurity* (CSF) as a basis for identifying security policy that leads to the implementation of security controls. The CSF defines Data Security as: "Information and records (data) are managed consistent with the organization's risk strategy to protect the confidentiality, integrity, and availability of information." (NIST, 2019). The value that organizations place on data is the factor that motivates attackers to steal or corrupt it. Thus, an effective Data Security program will protect its integrity and value. The remaining sections of this chapter present the eight knowledge units that CSEC2017 defines as necessary components to achieve adequate Data Security practices.

The CSEC2017 Data Security Knowledge Units

As the name implies, the Data Security domain encompasses five large constructs that specify the knowledge elements associated with the secure data and its use. Examining these concepts in combination, there is strong evidence that the CSEC2017 emphasizes the interdisciplinary nature of the process of achieving true confidentiality, integrity, and availability. Too often, data is only associated with information processing, and that tends to limit its scope to just ICT functions. However, Data Security spans the gamut well beyond the capability of controls placed within ICT functions, and also includes the disciplines of computer science, criminal justice, and to a large extent business management; since once of the primary goals of collecting, processing, and storing data is to achieve business requirements. Thus, the areas that fall under the purview of Data Security comprise a wide range of relevant data functions including: cryptography, forensics, data integrity and authentication, access control, cryptanalysis, secure communication protocols, data privacy, and information storage security. Shown in Figure 3.1, there are eight massive areas in the Data Security knowledge area:

1. *Cryptography* – methods for obfuscation
2. *Digital Forensics* – methods for analyzing incidents
3. *Data Integrity and Authentication* – methods for ensuring correctness
4. *Access Control* – authentication and authorization
5. *Secure Communication Protocols* – methods for ensuring message transfer
6. *Cryptanalysis* – codebreaking
7. *Data Privacy* – methods for ensuring confidentiality
8. *Information Storage Security* – methods for ensuring data at rest.

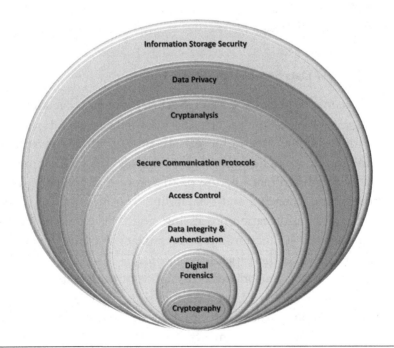

Figure 3.1   The Data Security knowledge units.

Knowledge Unit One: Cryptography

Cryptography is a term that comes from the Greek words meaning *hidden writing*. Theoretically, it is the process of changing the structure of data so that it is secure and cannot be accessed by unauthorized individuals. This process is accomplished by scrambling the data in such a way that only the intended recipients can access it. When cryptography is applied, the process of changing the original data into a scrambled message is called encryption. When the receiver retrieves the data, the reverse process called decryption is performed in order to change the data back to its original form. In order to speak the "language" of cryptography, three key terms must be understood: (1) *Plaintext* – is unencrypted data in its original format that eventually will be used as input for encryption or is the output of decryption, (2) *Ciphertext* – is the scrambled and unreadable output of the encryption process, and (3) *Cleartext* – is readable (unencrypted) data that is transmitted or stored without any cryptography processes applied to it (Figure 3.2).

At a high level of abstraction, the cryptographic process entails the plaintext data as input to a cryptographic algorithm (also called a cipher). That algorithm is an obfuscation function that is based on a binary mathematical formula intended to encrypt the data. A *key* is a

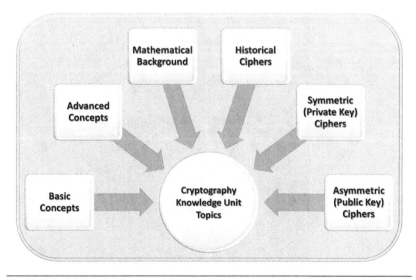

Figure 3.2 The cryptography knowledge unit topics.

binary mathematical value entered into the algorithm to produce the ciphertext. This can be analogized using the lock on the front door of your home representing what we are referring to as the algorithm and the key that you insert into that lock representing the binary key used in the encryption process. When the ciphertext is to be returned to plaintext, the reverse process occurs with a decryption algorithm and key.

Basic Concepts

This topic provides an overview of the concepts, methods, and tools of the actual cryptographic process. This first CSEC2017 topic is a direct response of the complicated nature of cryptography and provides a basis for further expansion of each concept. In doing so, it introduces encryption and decryption (similar to how it was explained in the preceding section).

As shown in Figure 3.3, one of the underlying messages that must be delivered through this topic is that cryptography can support the following four basic protections: (1) *Confidentiality*. Cryptography can protect the confidentiality of data by ensuring that only those that are authorized can view it. When confidential information is transmitted across the network or stored in a database, its contents can be

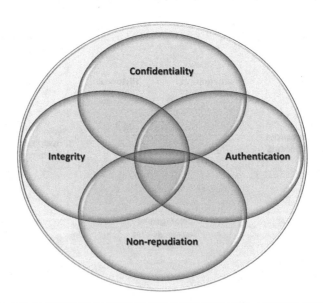

Figure 3.3 Four protections of cryptography.

encrypted, which allows only authorized individuals who have the key to see it. (2) *Integrity*. Cryptography can protect the integrity of data by ensuring that the information is correct and no unauthorized person or malicious software has altered that data. Because ciphertext requires that a key must be used to open the data before it can be changed, cryptography can ensure that the only way encrypted data can be interpreted is through access to that key. (3) *Authentication*. The authentication of the sender can be verified through cryptography by adding an additional layer of security called a digital signature to already encrypted data. (4) *Non-repudiation*. Cryptography can enforce non-repudiation. *Repudiation* is defined as denial; non-repudiation is the inability to deny. In ICT, non-repudiation is the process of proving that a user performed an action, such as sending an email message. Non-repudiation prevents an individual from fraudulently reneging on an action.

A distinction must also be made between the two primary forms of cryptography. The original cryptographic techniques for encrypting and decrypting data are known as symmetric cryptography. Symmetric cryptographic algorithms use the same single key to encrypt and decrypt data. Both the sender and receiver use the identical algorithm and same key to encrypt or decrypt the data. It is, therefore, essential that the key be kept private (confidential), because if an attacker obtained the key, the encrypted data would, thus, be vulnerable. For this reason, symmetric encryption is also called *private key cryptography*.

Asymmetric cryptography is a completely different approach from symmetric cryptography. Asymmetric cryptography is also known as *public key cryptography*. Asymmetric encryption algorithms use two keys instead of only one. These keys are mathematically related and are called the public and the private key. The public key is known to everyone and can be freely distributed, while the private key is known only to the individual to whom it belongs. There are several important principles that distinguish asymmetric cryptography from symmetric cryptography, they are: (1) *Key pairs*. Symmetric cryptography uses only one key, while asymmetric cryptography requires a pair of keys and (2) *Public key*. These are designed to be public and do not need to be protected. They can be freely given to anyone or even posted on the Internet, thus, eliminating extra processing necessary for securely transmitting the key from sender to receiver. (3) *Private key.* It is always kept confidential and never shared. Asymmetric cryptography keys can work in both directions. Data encrypted with a public key can be decrypted with the corresponding private key. In the same way, data encrypted with a private key can be decrypted with its public key.

The basic conceptual assumptions of cryptography include the expectation that perfect secrecy can be achieved. For years computer scientists have attempted to develop an algorithm that is capable of perfect secrecy and computationally secure. One such algorithm is the one-time pad. Its implementation starts with a random sequence of letters for the standard text (which is the key in this case). Suppose, e.g., organizations use RQBOPS as the standard text, assuming these are six letters chosen completely at random, and suppose the message is the same, such as ATTACK. Then encryption algorithm employs a shifting methodology to alter the plain text, based on the position in the alphabet of the corresponding letter in the random text string. Thus, the resulting ciphertext would be RJUORC. The strength of the one-time pad comes from identical key length to the plaintext and the length of the key applied.

Advanced Concepts

This topic encompasses the advanced concepts that influence good cryptographic security. It includes such advanced protocols as zero knowledge proofs, secret key sharing techniques, as well as the techniques that facilitate secure multiparty computation. In a time where there is an increase in cases where communication between two distrusting parties exist, a detailed exploration of commitment and oblivious transfer is imperative. As is the nature of all areas of cybersecurity, the field of cryptography continues to evolve. This topic area provides the capacity for recent developments in the field such as obfuscation, quantum cryptography, and Kirchoff-Law-Johnson_Noise secure key (KLJN) scheme to be explored.

Mathematical Background

Most encryption is based heavily on number theory, with heavy emphasis on abstract algebra. Additionally, other subjects should be understood well; probability (including basic combinatorics), information theory, and asymptotic analysis of algorithms. To be proficient in cryptography also requires knowledge in areas on math such as Fermat's little theorem, Euler's theorem (based on totient), Euclid's algorithm for greatest common denominators (specifically Euclid's extended algorithm to generate multiplicative inverses), Carmichael numbers, Fermat primality test, Miller–Rabin primality test, modular exponentiation, and discrete logarithms.

Those that chose to extend their knowledge of cryptography past the intermediate level will need exposure to finite fields (specifically Galois fields), polynomial rings, elliptic curves, etc. This discussion of math capability is not intended to limit the mathematical knowledge necessary. Rather, each advanced cryptographic technique is unique in the form of math necessary for its application. For example, NUTRUEncrypt is based on lattices/shortest vector problem solving, and the McEliece cryptosystem is based on Goppa codes. However, number theory, finite math, and discrete logs are a prerequisite to understanding the advanced math necessary to perform the techniques of the more complex cryptographic algorithms.

Historical Ciphers

The current day capabilities of cryptography cannot be appreciated unless a history of ciphers is introduced and understood. The first known evidence of the use of cryptography was found in an inscription carved around 1900 BC, in the main chamber of the tomb of the noble king of Egypt. The scribe used unusual symbols in several places within the tomb to send a message. The purpose was not to hide the message but perhaps to change its form in a way which would make it appear dignified. Though the inscription was not a form of secret writing, but it incorporated some sort of transformation of the original text and is the oldest known text to do so.

Fast forward to around 100 BC, Julius Caesar was known to use a form of encryption to convey secret messages to his army generals posted in the war front. This was known as Caesar cipher and is perhaps the most mentioned historic cipher in academics labeled as a substitution cipher, where each character of the plain text is substituted by another character to form the cipher text. The variant used by Caesar was a shift by three cipher. Each character was shifted by three places, so the character "A" was replaced by "D," "B" was replaced by "E," and so on. The characters would wrap around at the end, so "X" would be replaced by "A." Similar to the shift by 3 cipher, a more recent day cipher called ROT13 rotates each letter by 13 rather than 3, as shown in Figure 3.4.

It is easy to see that such ciphers depend on the secrecy how they were encoded rather than an encryption key. Once the system is known, these encrypted messages can easily be decrypted. In fact, a substitution cipher can simply be broken by the frequency of letters in the text data.

During the 16th century, Blaise de Vigenere designed a cipher that was supposedly the first cipher which used an encryption key. In one of his ciphers, the encryption key was repeated multiple times spanning the entire message, and then the cipher text was produced by adding the message character with the key character and applying the mathematical modulus operation. As with the Caesar cipher, Vigenere's cipher can also easily be broken; however, Vigenere's cipher brought the very idea of introducing encryption keys into the picture, though it was poorly executed. Comparing this to Caesar cipher, the secrecy of the message depends on the secrecy of the encryption key, rather than the secrecy of the system.

At the start of the 19th century, everything became electric. Edward Hugh Hebern designed an electromechanical device which was called the Hebern rotor machine. It uses a single rotor, in which the secret key is embedded in a rotating disc. The key encoded a substitution

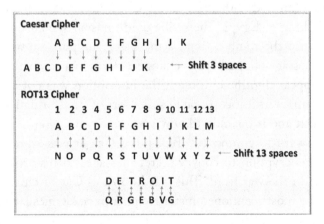

Figure 3.4 Caesar and ROT13 cipher examples.

table, and each key press from the keyboard resulted in the output of cipher text. This also rotated the disc by one notch and a different table would then be used for the next plain text character. This was again broken by using letter frequencies.

The Enigma machine was invented by German engineer Arthur Scherbius at the end of World War I and was heavily used by the German forces during the World War II. The Enigma machine used three or four or even more rotors. The rotors rotate at different rates as you type on the keyboard and output appropriate letters of cipher text. In this case, the key was the initial setting of the rotors. The Enigma machine was eventually broken by British cryptographers and became obsolete. The lack of efficiency from substitution ciphers led to developments by IBM in the 1970s to provide a technology that provided a more secure means for transferring data, thus, leading to the emergence of symmetric ciphers.

Symmetric (Private Key) Ciphers

Most symmetric algorithms use either what is called a block cipher or a stream cipher. They are both symmetric, so they both use the same key to encrypt or decrypt data. However, they divide data in different ways. A block cipher encrypts data in specific-sized blocks, such as 64-bit blocks or 128-bit blocks. The block cipher divides large amounts of data into these blocks and then encrypts each individual block separately. Stream ciphers encrypt data as a stream of bits or bytes rather than dividing it into blocks.

In general, stream ciphers are more efficient than block ciphers when the size of the data is unknown or sent in a continuous stream, such as when streaming audio and video over a network. Block ciphers are more efficient when the size of the data is known, such as when encrypting a file or a specific-sized database field. An important principle when using a stream cipher is that encryption keys should never be reused (such as the key that is used with the one-time pad previously discussed). If a key is reused, it is easier for an attacker to crack.

An example of a stream cipher symmetric algorithm that has been used to provide wireless encryption is Rivest Cipher 4 (RC4). Wired Equivalent Privacy (WEP) uses RC4 stream cipher for symmetric encryption. RC4 is a secure algorithm when it's implemented correctly, but WEP did not follow the important stream cipher principle of never reusing keys. If wireless systems generate enough traffic, WEP reuses keys for RC4. Attackers in turn realize that they can use packet injection techniques to increase the number of packets on a wireless network, detect the duplicate keys, and in turn crack the encryption. Nevertheless, when implemented correctly, RC4 has long been known as a strong cipher. For many years, it has been the recommended encryption mechanism in Secure Sockets Layer (SSL) and Transport Layer Security (TLS). SSL and TLS encrypt Hypertext Transfer Protocol Secure (HTTPS) connections on the Internet.

Alternatively, block cipher algorithms have demonstrated a greater depth of adoption throughout the IT industry for many years. In the early 1970s, IBM needed to answer to demands of their customers for some form of encryption. With that, they assembled a team called the "crypto group" headed by Horst Feistel. The group designed a cipher called Lucifer that had a key length of 128 bits. In 1973, the U.S. Government (through the National Bureau of Standards, now NIST) put out a request for proposals for a block cipher which would become a national standard. Lucifer was eventually adopted, and the name changed to DES or the Data Encryption Standard (using 56-bit key lengths). In the years that followed, the DES algorithm was determined to be insecure. The main problem with DES was the small size of the encryption key. As computing power increased, it became easy to use a form of attack called brute force to determine all of the different combinations of the keys in an effort to obtain a possible plain text message.

In 1997, NIST again put out a request for proposal for a new block cipher. It received fifty submissions, and in 2000, it adopted a more secure algorithm called AES or the Advanced Encryption Standard. AES is preferred because of a three-step process of mathematical functionality that is applied to every block of 128 bits of plain text. More significant to this algorithm's strength is that it can accept key sizes ranging from 128 to 256 bits. Depending upon the designated key size used, determine how many times the second step of the process repeats.

Asymmetric (Public Key) Ciphers

A different approach from symmetric cryptography takes advantage of asymmetric cryptographic algorithms, also known as public key algorithms. Asymmetric encryption uses two keys rather than one. These keys are mathematically related and are called the public and the private keys. The public key is made public and can be freely distributed, while the private key is known only to the system that created it. When the originator wants to send secure data to a recipient, they use the recipient's public key to encrypt the data. The recipient then uses their own private key to decrypt it. The common asymmetric cryptographic algorithms include RSA, elliptic curve cryptography (ECC), Digital Signature Algorithm (DSA), and several that have a specific purpose for facilitating key exchange.

The asymmetric algorithm RSA was published in 1977 (about the same time as the DES symmetric algorithm was adopted). RSA is the most common asymmetric cryptography algorithm and is known for its simplicity. RSA derives its security from the difficulty of factoring large integers that are the product of two large prime numbers. The two prime numbers, p and q, are generated using the Rabin–Miller primality test algorithm. A modulus, n, is calculated by multiplying p and q. This number is used by both the public and private keys and provides the link between them. Its length, usually expressed in bits, is called the key length. Once the keys have been generated using RSA, they are used as described above to encrypt and decrypt the data.

ECC first gained popularity in the mid-1980s. ECC distinguishes itself in that, instead of using large prime numbers as with RSA, it uses sloping curves. An elliptic curve is a function drawn on an X–Y axis as a curved line that can pass through the x and y axis at several different coordinate points. By adding the values of two points on the curve, a third point on the curve can be derived. With ECC, users share one elliptic curve and one point on the curve. One user chooses a secret random number and computes a public key based on a point on the curve; the other user does the same. Once the public keys have been established, data can be exchanged because the shared public keys can generate a private key on an elliptic curve as well.

One question that often arises is, how the recipient can identify that data was sent by the expected originator. Asymmetric cryptography also can be used to provide proofs. Because the recipient's public key is widely available, anyone could use it to encrypt the document. An attacker could have created a fictitious document, encrypted it with the recipient's public key, and then sent it on, while pretending to be the expected originator. The public key can verify that no one read or changed the document in transport, but it cannot verify the sender. That becomes an issue.

Proof can be provided with asymmetric cryptography, however, by creating a digital signature, which is simply an electronic verification of the sender. The DSA is a U.S. federal government standard for digital signatures. DSA was developed by NIST in 1991 for use in their own Digital Signature Standard (DSS). In turn, they have made the algorithm available worldwide royalty-free. The basis for a digital signature rests on the ability of asymmetric keys to work in both directions (a public key can encrypt data that can be decrypted with a private key, and the private key can encrypt a data that can be decrypted by the public key.

In order to understand how DSA implements digital signatures, you must first have background in message hash algorithms. Message hashes are a means by which integrity of data is ensured by applying an identical mathematical function to data on both the originator and receiver side. The hash algorithm generates what is called a digest that acts as a "fingerprint" of the data that can be matched on both the originator and recipient side. The digest is encrypted using DSA and the originator's private key to create a digital signature, before sending the encrypted data and digital signature to the recipient. The recipient then uses the public key of the originator to decrypt the data and digital signature. Upon successful decryption, the recipient will know that the data came from the expected originator because it was the originator's public key that was necessary through the decryption process.

While asymmetric cryptography allows two users to send encrypted messages using separate public and private keys, it does leave problem unresolved. That problem centers around the ability to exchange keys between the originator and the recipient. One solution is to make the exchange outside of the normal communication channels, but there have been developments in cryptography that make the process of key exchange more efficient and effective including: *Diffie–Hellman (DH)* – requires the originator and the receiver of the data to each agree upon a large prime number and related integer. Those two numbers can be made public, yet both parties, through mathematical computations and exchanges of intermediate values, can separately create the same key, *Diffie–Hellman Ephemeral (DHE)* – differentiates itself from DH by using different keys called ephemeral keys (which are temporary keys used only once and then discarded), and *Elliptic Curve Diffie–Hellman (ECDH)* – which uses ECC instead of prime numbers in its computation.

Knowledge Unit Two: Digital Forensics

The Internet, combined with the rapid expansion of computer technologies, has created new operational environments for criminals. Criminal behavior and activities that would not otherwise be conceivable without the use of computer technologies have proliferated into a range of criminal crimes. This combination of computer use, the Internet, and related technologies in the commission of a crime is called *cybercrime*. One important difference between traditional crime and cybercrime is that cybercrime has no physical or geographic boundaries due to the global nature of the Internet and 24/7 access to people and organizations worldwide.

Cybercrime has many facets from defrauding individuals using email to obtaining credentials and financial information, to theft of proprietary information and trade secrets from businesses. Additional types of cybercrime include cyberterrorism, cyberextortion, cybervandalism, cyberstalking, cyberbullying, and even cyber prostitution (Maras, 2015). From a legal perspective, computers must either be the *target* of the crime or *used as a tool* to commit the crime. Examples of crimes in which a computer is a target include hacking (unauthorized access) into a computer system; launching a denial of service (DoS) or distributed denial of service (DDoS) attacks; emailing malware with embedded viruses, worms, and spyware. Examples of crimes in which the computer is used as a tool to commit the crime include phishing (posing as a legitimate entity to deceive individuals and steal credentials to gain access to valuable information/assets), cyberharassment, illegal prescription drug sales, and embezzlement. The proliferation of the variety of cybercrime has created a great need for effective legislation and enforcement processes. The challenge is to be able to anticipate and think ahead on how cybercriminals will exploit new victims and engage in illicit activities.

The global share of households with a computer has increased from 27.6% in 2005 to 48.3% in 2018, and as of April 2019, 56.1% of the world's population has Internet access (Statista, 2019a). This translates into 4.38 billion worldwide Internet users, which is a significant number for criminals to potentially target (Miniwatts, 2019). With the widespread adoption of computers in homes, businesses, and government agencies, digital evidence has proliferated resulting in the demand for digital forensics investigators to lawfully collect evidence for use in solving crimes and prosecuting offenders.

The generic digital forensics process can be broken down into a number of distinct stages, such as: *Preparation for evidence collection* – the collection of any digital information must follow recognized and accepted forensic procedures so that it may be used as evidence in any legal or disciplinary proceedings. It is essential to understand the nature of the case and be prepared to seize not only computers but smart TVs, gaming systems, network components, tablets, secure digital (SD) cards, mobile phones, and any other electronic device that may have essential data. The protection of all devices must be ensured if transporting them to a forensics lab or if the suspect is physically nearby and can potentially destroy any evidence.

Given the complexity of these challenges, digital forensics is a critical and multifaceted discipline within the field of cybersecurity. As shown in Figure 3.5, the topics in this knowledge unit reflect that imperative: (1) Introduction, (2) Legal issues, (3) Digital forensics tools,

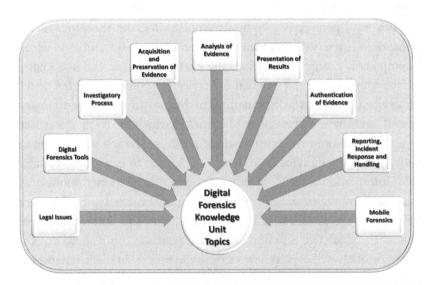

Figure 3.5   Digital forensics knowledge unit topics.

(4) Investigatory processes, (5) Acquisition and preservation of evidence, (6) Analysis of evidence, (7) Presentation of results, (8) Authentication of evidence, (9) Incident handling, and (10) Mobile forensics.

Introduction

The field of computer forensics, which is now typically called *digital forensics*, has developed significantly over the years. Even the definition of digital forensics continues to evolve. Starting out as a branch of forensic science focusing on securing and analyzing digital information stored on a computer for use as evidence in civil, criminal, or administrative cases, it has expanded to include mobile phone forensics, network forensics, video forensics, research, incident response, and a host of others (Nelson et al., 2019). The NIST defines *digital forensics* as 'the application of science to the identification, collection, examination, and analysis of data while preserving the integrity of the information and maintaining a strict chain of custody for the data (Kent et al., 2006). Typically, investigating digital devices includes collecting data securely, examining suspect data to determine details such as origin and content, presenting digital information to courts, and applying laws to digital device practices (Nelson et al., 2019). To be an effective digital forensics investigator, you need to have broad knowledge of a variety of devices, their operating systems, hardware and software applications, legal (case law, search warrants, legal processes and procedures, chain of custody, etc.), computer networks, incident response, not to mention all of the digital forensics software and hardware tools used during investigations.

Legal Issues

In addition to knowing the technical tools of the digital forensics trade, investigators should be aware of how decisions made at the federal and local levels may impact their ability to acquire evidence in criminal, civil, and private/corporate investigations. Digital evidence is essentially the same as any other evidence in that it is information collected with the goal of placing people and events within timeframes that would establish causality for criminal activities and the proliferation and pervasiveness of personal electronic devices hold increasingly significant levels of valuable data that can definitively produce evidence to strongly challenge reasonable doubt.

Legal authority can also be obtained in the form of a *Foreign Intelligence Surveillance Act of 1978* (FISA) warrant. An application is made to the Foreign Intelligence Surveillance Court, an eleven-member tribunal of federal judges, and a warrant is issued to wiretap someone suspected of spying with or for a foreign government entity. Although the proceedings are secret, established rules and data collection procedures are expected to be followed. More common warrants, conducted at the local level, are *Title III of the Omnibus Crime Control and Safe Street Act of 1968 warrants* and are used to intercept communications between private citizens over the telephone, Internet, email, etc. Title III applications for a surveillance order must include a statement of the alleged offence, a listing of the facilities from which the communications will be intercepted with specific description, the identity of the target individual(s), statement of necessity, and the period of time for which the interception is to be maintained. Additionally, investigators must follow a rigid protocol in the interception of the communication. If the investigators fail to follow rigid procedures or it turns out that probable cause did not exist to begin with, all data collected via wiretap can be suppressed.

Digital Forensics Tools

Digital forensics tools are constantly being designed, developed, patched, updated, and discontinued, so it is important to evaluate what types of investigations will be conducted to wisely choose among the specialized tools. There are tools designed to perform specific tasks and are divided into two categories: hardware forensics and software forensics. Some tools are portable to allow the investigator to collect evidence at the scene of the crime where others require a more extensive lab environment. Some tools are specialized to perform a single task whereas others are designed to perform a variety of tasks. Figure 3.6 provides an overview of tools and their function used in the digital forensics field. More detail on digital forensics tools is covered later in this chapter.

Function	Description	Tool
Write blockers	Write-blockers are used to protect evidence on storage devices by preventing data from being written and changed on the evidence drive. There are hardware and software write-blockers.	PDBlock from Digital Intelligence; Dsi USB Write Blocker; CRU WeibeTech WriteBlocker; Tableau Forensic SATA/IDE, PCIe, USB 3.0 Bridges
Data History	To understand if data was stolen, moved, or accessed, an investigator needs to view what actions were taken by a user and what event occurred on the machine. Other tools parse USB information from the Windows registry to list all USB drives that were plugged into the machine.	USB Historian; LastActivityView; PlainSight Live CD based on Knoppix Linux distro
Acquisition: Disk Imaging	The first task in a digital forensic investigation is to make a copy of the original drive(s). It is critical to preserve the original drive to prevent damage or corruption in the data acquisition stage of a digital forensics investigation.	Software suites: Paladin Forensic Suite; FTK Imager; Magnet AXIOM. Hardware devices include: Tableau TD2, Logicube Talon; Image MASSter Solo-4 Forensic
Verification and Validation	Using a hashing algorithm during data acquisition allows for the verification that the original data has not changed and that copies are of the same unchanged data or image. The National Institute of Software and Technology has designed the *National Software Reference Library* (NSRL) to collect software and compute file profiles for use in digital investigations. The comprehensive lists of digital signatures and known file hashes for operating systems, images, and applications can be downloaded from NIST IT Laboratory-Software and Systems Division.	EnCase; FTK Imager; DEFT; NIST's NSRL
Extraction and Analysis	After acquisition, an investigator needs to recover and analyze data for the collection of clues. Tools for data extraction need to support activities to include viewing data, conducting keyword searches and filters to recover relevant data, decompressing and uncompressing data, record carving (in Europe it's called salvaging), decrypting, extracting digital artefacts from volatile memory (RAM) dumps, and bookmarking or tagging.	The Sleuth Kit (+Autopsy); FTK Imager; Xplico (open source); bulk_extractor; Simple Carver Suite; DataLifter; OS Forensics; 7Zip; WinZip; pzip; Volatility; ExifTool; Free Hex Editor Neo; FireEye RedLine; HxD
Incident Response	Tools to gather contextual information in incident response scenarios such as a process list, scheduled tasks, or Shim Cache also need to support Expert Witness Format (E01), Advanced Forensic Format (AFF), and RAW (dd) evidence formats. Other activities include generating timelines from system logs, examining the recycle bin, password cracking utility, and scanning for malware.	CrowdStrike CrowdResponse; SANS SIFT; The Sleuth Kit (+Autopsy); Linus 'dd'; DEFT; HELIX3 Free

Figure 3.6 Digital forensics tools.

Due to the critical need to ensure the reliability of computer forensics tools, the Computer Forensics Tool Testing Program (CFTT), developed by NIST, established a methodology for testing software, procedures, criteria, and hardware used in the digital forensics field. Use of forensics tools must produce consistent, accurate, and objective test results. Significant legal decisions are often drawn from these test results and can adversely impact court cases if proven to be faulty. A helpful online database called the *Computer Forensics Tools & Techniques Catalog* allows practitioners to search and find tools and techniques to meet their specific technical needs (CFTT, 2019).

Investigatory Processes

Public criminal investigations, conducted by law enforcement and government agencies, are initiated by the state and the burden of proof to prove that the individual guilty beyond a reasonable doubt is the responsibility of the state. As computers and mobile devices are increasingly used in criminal cases, digital forensics investigators are called in to collect evidence for use to solve crimes. Evidence collection can occur through the use of inspections, searches and seizures, and subpoenas. Searches are restricted by the *Fourth Amendment* to the United States Constitution (Figure 3.7).

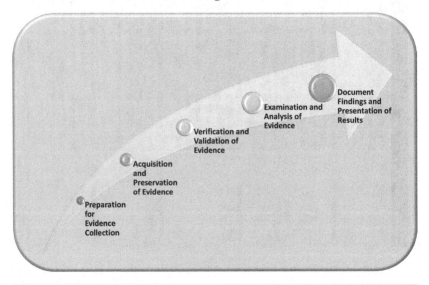

Figure 3.7　The digital forensics investigatory process.

Digital forensics investigators must have a *search warrant* to enter and conduct a search of a person, location, or vehicle for evidence of a crime and to confiscate or seize any evidence found. Search warrants must specify the location where the search will be conducted and name the objects or materials that may be evidence of a crime at that location. Once a judge or magistrate signs the order to authorize a search, the most common practice during a search is the seizure of collected evidence (computers, mobile devices, laptops, USB drives, external hard drives, etc.). Evidence is often taken off-site to a forensic lab for a search of the contents and subsequent analysis as the forensics process can be very time consuming. One of the most important steps in a digital forensic investigation is the preparation that is done before a search and seizure of evidence. Identifying the nature of the case starts with understanding whether the investigation involves the private or public sector.

Private-sector investigations involve employee issues such as email harassment, abusing Internet privileges, and policy violations on company-issued devices. Public-sector law enforcement cases involve issues such as drug trafficking, homicide, and child pornography. The nature of the case will dictate how to proceed and the types of forensics tools needed during the investigation. The more information about the location of the forensics investigation site, the better the chances that the evidence can be gathered effectively. The ability to seize computers and digital devices from the scene of the crime or incident and take them back to a lab environment for further processing is ideal.

Removing computers from a private-sector organization is not always prudent in that it can cause irreparable harm to the business. The acquisition times for larger terabyte hard drives may take several hours so you need to be prepared in the event the data collection must occur on-site. Understanding environmental and safety issues in cases involving a drug bust of a methamphetamine lab or a terrorist attack using chemical, biological, or nuclear contaminants is also critical. Working with a hazardous materials (HAZMAT) team to recover evidence may include carefully decontaminating digital components so as to not destroy any digital evidence needed in the investigation.

Acquisition and Preservation of Digital Evidence

Acquisition and preservation of evidence is a fundamental factor in all forensic activities, and if evidence is not collected and preserved in a sound manner, it will have no value in any criminal or civil proceedings. Acquisition of evidence is the stage where investigators duplicate hard drives and other media storage devices including RAM using forensically sound tools. Tested and known procedures, which are accepted by the jurisdictions in which a case is brought, must be considered at all stages of the investigation.

The first step in the acquisition phase is to determine whether the target device is powered on or off, in hibernation, or sleep mode. Due to the volatility of random access memory (RAM), if the device is powered off, it should be left powered off; however, if it is on, a professional judgment call will need to be made as to what to do next. Some government agencies teach investigators to "pull the plug"; however, things to keep in mind when approaching a live device are as follows: (1) Loss of essential network activity records may occur if power is abruptly terminated. (2) Data could become corrupt through covert means (by the owner of the computer) such as self-destruct mechanisms. (3) If left powered on, suspects may be able to remotely wipe the contents of hard drives. (4) If left powered on, ensure power cords are located so that batteries are not depleted before the device can be examined.

It is recommended to keep a journal and document everything in this phase to help establish a *chain of custody* and provide context and additional explanation for the findings. Establishing a chain of custody is especially important when evidence is required to be shown in a court of law, and meticulous documentation can show the sequence of custody, control, transfer, analysis, and disposition of all collected evidence. Credibility only exists when a chain of custody can be substantiated (tracked, logged, protected) proving that there was no tampering or corruption of the evidence found at the crime scene.

Data acquisition and preservation: this knowledge unit involves making a copy of any storage media that is considered evidence. Once the target device(s) have been seized, a forensic image or copy of the original drive is conducted. There are two types of acquisitions: static and live acquisitions. *Static acquisitions* are typically conducted on seized devices. Depending on the size of the hard drive, duplicating an entire drive is time consuming and not always feasible to conduct on-site. A *live acquisition* is conducted in the event the drive is encrypted, powered on, and a password or passphrase is available.

Acquisition methods include the following types: the first is disk to image; which is the most common method of acquisition. In this process, a duplicate of the entire physical hard drive is created to make a bit-by-bit copy of the source drive using a hash algorithm such as Message Digest 5 (MD5) and Secure Hash Algorithm (SHA-1) values to create a unique digital footprint to certify its authenticity. Hash algorithms are discussed in the *Authentication of Evidence* section below. *Disk-to-disk copy* – is created due to incompatibilities or hardware or software errors on older drives.

The second approach is logical data copy, which captures specific files or file types of interest to the case when the event time is limited or when the entire drive does not need to be examined. This is also used when obtaining a live copy of a disk partition in the event of drive encryption. The third is sparse data copy; which is used to collect fragments of unallocated (deleted) data, specific email files such as an .ost or .pst file, or only specific records from a storage area network (SAN) that are configured to store petabytes or even exabytes of data.

Acquisition methods are determined by several factors such as how much time is available to conduct the acquisition, the size of the source drive(s), whether the devices can be retained and transported to a lab or an acquisition must be made on-site, whether the data is encrypted, and a live acquisition is feasible. As previously outlined, there are several tools that can be used for data acquisition; however, they all follow the same basic *imaging procedure*: (1) Document the chain of custody process for the target drive, (2) remove the source (evidence) hard drive from the suspect's computer, (3) connect the evidence drive to the write-blocker device, adjusting jumpers as needed for integrated drive electronics (IDE) drives (does not apply to serial advanced technology attachment (SATA) or USB drives), (4) create a storage work folder on the target drive, and then (5) run the data acquisition tool to create a disk-to-image file – each tool has their own graphical user interface (GUI) interface to perform this function.

In digital forensics, the *order of volatility* signifies the order, from least to most easily lost, in which evidence is available to be acquired. Data written to RAM and in running processes exist for only milliseconds and is easily lost when the power is interrupted, whereas data on hard drives, USB, and SD drives are stored for much longer periods of time. Flash memory storage devices such as USB, cell phones, and solid-state hard drives must also be acquired immediately due to a feature called wear leveling. Wear leveling is a process where the memory cells in flash memory storage devices shift or rotate data from one memory cell to another to ensure that all the cells on the device wear evenly. Depending on the manufacturer's design, memory cells are designed to perform only 10,000–100,000 reads/writes, and when they reach their limit, they no longer retain data.

Thus, making a full forensic copy as soon as possible is critical. Tape and disk-to-disk backups may be configured to be written over a period of 1–3 days or only after a week which is something to keep in mind if a data acquisition is imperative within a certain time period of an incident. Examples of the least volatile types of data are computer printouts and DVDs shown in Figure 3.8.

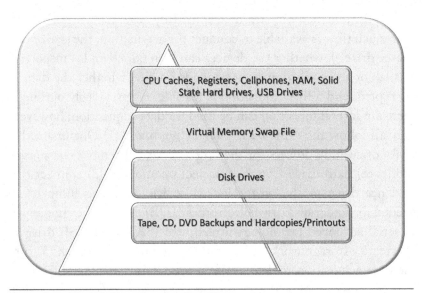

Figure 3.8 The digital forensics order of volatility.

Analysis of Evidence

Any information related to a criminal or civil incident that is stored or transmitted in digital form is considered digital evidence and is treated as a tangible object in a court of law. In the United States, the Scientific Working Groups on Digital Evidence and Imaging Technology (SWGDE/SWGIT) developed guidelines and recommendations for the capture, storage, processing analysis, transmission, and output of images for their application in the criminal justice system (SWGIT, 2010). Where to look for digital evidence at the scene of an incident can vary widely.

Sources of digital evidence can be found in such diverse places as: (1) Computer-generated records include data that the system maintains or generated from an algorithm or process. Examples are system log files, proxy sever logs, and hash files computed from MD5 and SHA-1 tools. (2) Computer-stored records are created by end users and saved on a device. (3) Flash memory cards such as SD and microSD cards found in cell phones, digital cameras, computers, laptops, tablets, etc. (4) Mobile phones including subscriber identity module (SIM) cards, billing records from cellular providers.

Metadata provides detailed information about files to include clues such as date last accessed, hash values, date last modified, and file size. When a suspect tries to obscure their activities or hide evidence by tampering with metadata, inconsistencies arise across various metadata points and can reveal that the files have been altered. Log files are created by network devices such as routers, switches, firewalls, and intrusion detection systems; operating systems; third party software applications, etc., that document system activities and generate records in chronological order. Depending on the amount of activity, log files can grow quite large in a short amount of time and need to be managed.

Finally, in order to ensure successful file recovery, forensic investigators must understand and know how to identify all of the partitions created and possibly hidden on a hard drive, the file system selected when the hard drive was formatted (NTFS, HFS+, Ext4), the operating systems (Windows, Mac OSX, Linux) installed on the partitions, and familiarity with each operating system to know where to find the metadata to aid in the collection of evidence. Metadata is stored in

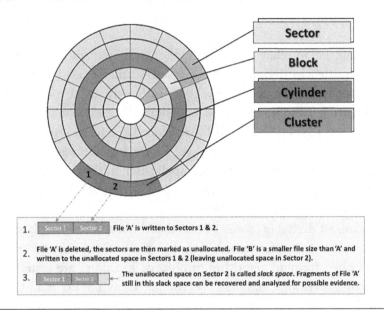

Figure 3.9   Data stored on hard drive in tracks and slack space.

the actual file system selected and includes additional elements such as the names and hierarchy of folders and files, the physical address of where the file is stored on the hard drive, file owner user id, permissions, and file types.

Figure 3.9 shows how data is stored on a hard drive and how slack space can be used to hide possible evidence.

Presentation of Results

To present the results of a digital civil or criminal investigation, forensics case requires clear and concise reports of all relevant information with sufficient detail to describe a process that is both repeatable and defensible. Different reports may include an affidavit to support the issuance of an arrest or search warrant, a forensic report consisting of facts from findings, one that presents evidence for the purpose of supporting further investigation, a report that is admissible in court or at an administrative hearing, a report that is used for a probable cause hearing, a motion hearing in a civil or criminal case, evidence in a grand jury hearing, or in the case of a corporate employee misconduct case – a report that will be used as a basis for disciplinary action.

The audience for forensics reports is wide ranging and may include law enforcement, attorneys, judges, juries, human resources, executives, forensics experts, etc., and is ideally divided into sections that are tailored to the varying groups and their knowledge level of technical jargon. For example, it is important that reports be written in language that a layperson can understand with technical details and terms reserved for specific sections and clearly marked as such. If a particular audience has no technical knowledge, part of the report should include informative information such as definitions and explanations to help readers understand the technical contents.

The U.S. Federal Rules of Evidence governs the admissibility of evidence in federal courts such as proof of facts and expert opinions. Expert testimony must be based on scientific technique and generally acceptable as reliable in the relevant scientific community. Qualifying expert witnesses must have personal knowledge of the crime or specialized knowledge resulting from experience and education and possess the skills required to authenticate or refute information that is being presented in a case.

Authentication of Evidence

The provable integrity of data is critical when that data is presented in court; therefore, validating digital evidence is one of the most critical aspects of the investigation. Tools such as hexadecimal editors and hashing algorithms allow for the matching of contents and files from acquisition copies of digital evidence.

Examination and analysis of evidence – tools that have been tested and accepted by the courts as providing information in a true form and capable of being reproduced by other sources are used during this phase. Examinations of evidence should be carried out on an image of the original material and conducted in a comprehensive and thorough manner with the goal of determining what occurred regarding the events leading up to and during an incident and drawing accurate conclusions. To ensure the results can be recreated by another investigator, observations and findings should be thoroughly documented.

Hashing algorithms such as MD5 and SHA-1 are used to verify that a dataset or a copied image from a hard drive has not been altered or corrupted during the evidence acquisition and analysis process of the

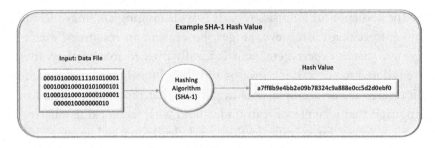

Figure 3.10   Example hash algorithm output.

digital forensics investigation. Hash values are also helpful to validate specific files or sectors to ensure whether the data fragments match the contents of known files such as illegal child pornography files.

When a hash algorithm is used, a string of numbers is computed for a file and any change to that file will result in a change to the hash value. Figure 3.10 shows a hash value for a file.

Reporting, Incident Response, and Handling

The authors of the NIST's *Computer Security Incident Handling Guide* make a distinction between "events" and "computer security incidents." They define *events* as "any observable occurrence in a system or network" (Cichonski et al., 2012). Notice how this does not necessarily mean malicious activity or a security breach. However, they define a *computer security incident* as "a violation or imminent threat of violation of computer security policies, acceptable use policies, or standard security practices" (Cichonski et al, 2012). When incidents occur, it is critical to respond as quickly and effectively as possible. This requires previous planning and the establishment of an incident response and handling process, shown in Figure 3.11. The sooner an incident is detected and analyzed, the possibility of loss, disruption of services, or theft of information can be mitigated.

The process of incident response includes many pre- and post-activities and a streamlined process such as the creation of a detailed communication plan that includes contact information for all team members within and outside of the organization (primary and backup contacts) such as law enforcement, incident response teams, and escalation management chain.

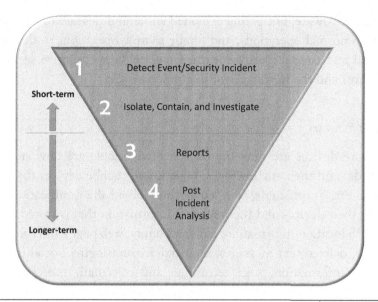

Figure 3.11 Digital forensics incident response process.

Incident reporting mechanisms that will be used during incidents to include secure reporting messaging systems to anonymously report incidents; an issue reporting and tracking system; a war room for central communication and coordination; a secure storage facility for security evidence and sensitive materials which will conform to a rigorous chain of custody; digital forensic workstations and tools to create disk images, preserve log files, and all relevant incident data; evidence gathering accessories such as notebooks for continuous detailed documentation, cameras, audio recorders, chain of custody forms, evidence storage bags, tags, and bins; physical access to all necessary rooms where networking equipment is located; and finally, the implementation of user awareness and training programs, malware prevention, network security, and risk assessments.

Post-incident handling activities include the following: identify and confirm that a security incident actually occurred and requires immediate follow-up, rapid initial assessment, and containment documentation of the scope of the security incident; acquisition of the facts and relevant information, adherence to preplanned and documented communication, and escalation plan manage the perception of the incident both internally and externally to the business, work to eradicate components of the incident such as disabling user accounts, deleting malware, mitigating exploited vulnerabilities and restore systems to normal operations, and finally resume operations to the new normal and conduct lessons learned meeting(s) to improve security measures and the incident handling process itself.

Mobile Forensics

As more devices are now Internet-enabled, people are now storing more data on their smartphones, tablets, and mobile devices than on computers. Surprisingly, few people think about the ramifications of losing their devices and the wealth of information that is stored such as: GPS location information, email accounts, web pages and browser history, deleted text messages, financial account logins, social media account information, voice recordings and voicemail, and chat sessions, instant messaging logs.

The main concerns when confiscating mobile devices are loss of power, synchronization with cloud services, and remote wiping. Depending on the timing of the warrant or subpoena, seizure might be relevant as messages received on the mobile device after seizure may not be admissible in court. System data is stored in electronically erasable programmable read-only memory (EEPROM), which enables the phones to be reprogrammed without having to physically access the memory chips. Isolating the device from incoming signals and broadcasting will prevent the device from being remotely wiped. However, it is important to note that isolating and keeping devices on puts them into roaming mode which will accelerate battery drainage.

Investigating mobile devices is a particular challenge due to the abundance of makes, models, operating systems, and installed versions and how rapidly new handsets flood the market. The hardware consists of a microprocessor, RAM, read-only memory (ROM), a radio module, a digital signal processor, microphone and speaker, LCD display, Bluetooth, Wi-Fi, and hardware interfaces such as GPS devices, cameras, keypads, and removable memory cards. Many basic phones have a proprietary operating system; however, smartphones generally use scaled down versions of the same operating systems that run on computers and include the Android OS, based on the Linux operating system, iOS for Apple devices, Windows mobile, and others with a small segment of the market share such as Nokia's Symbian,

Research In Motion's Blackberry OS, and Java ME. Most mobile operating systems are tied to specific hardware with little flexibility and the operating system determines what artifacts are created and how they are stored on the devices.

Knowledge Unit Three: Data Integrity and Authentication

It is probably safe to assume that data within an IT system that is incorrect or not in the expected format is literally useless to the organization. The ability to ensure that data has not been modified is known as data integrity. However, there is a caveat that needs to be kept in mind when we use this term. Database administrators look at integrity from the perspective of structural integrity, which ensures that the database access is not compromised.

The Data Integrity knowledge area includes ensuring data integrity through the use of hash functions, which is a cryptographic technique used to fingerprint the data prior to its storage or transmission. By matching the fingerprint as the data is retrieved from storage or received through transmission, we can be assured of the integrity of the data. Further, integrity can also be achieved if only authorized individuals or systems are given access to the data. In order to verify that authorized parties are attempting to access the data, one of several authentication mechanisms can be used to confirm identity. Shown in Figure 3.12, there are four large knowledge units in the data integrity area: (1) *Authentication Strength*, (2) *Password Attack Techniques*, (3) *Password Storage Techniques*, and (4) *Data Integrity*.

Authentication Strength

In today's prolific age of security threats, those being introduced to the field of cybersecurity must understand that passwords alone do not provide the adequate level of authentication to protect large-scale IT systems. Organizations are forced to use multiple levels of authentication to ensure that only authorized users gain access. Thus, they have emerged the concept of multifactor authentication (MFA). NIST SP 800–63 Rev 3 "Digital Identity Guidelines" describes MFA as a characteristic of an authentication system or an authenticator that requires more than one authentication factor for successful

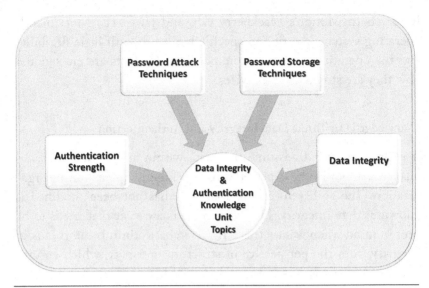

Figure 3.12 Data integrity and authentication knowledge unit topics.

authentication. MFA can be performed using a single authenticator that provides more than one factor or by a combination of authenticators that provide different factors.

The three authentication factors are: (1) something you know (e.g., passwords), (2) something you have (e.g., cryptographic tokens used with cryptographic devices), and (3) something you are (e.g., Biometrics) and shown in Figure 3.13. With MFA, the key requirement is using more than one of the factors listed above during the authentication process. For example, when authenticating to an application, a user identifies him or herself with username, then is prompted for a password, and an SMS one-time passcode on a mobile

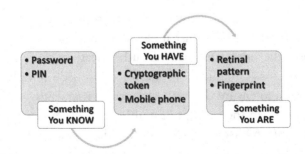

Figure 3.13 Multifactor authentication.

phone. The password is something the person knows, and the SMS passcode is something the person has (via the phone).

While the obvious reason for MFA is that it adds additional layers of security, there is one key point. Each organization is different and, therefore, will have unique needs. The right MFA solution should strike a balance between added security and user convenience, versus a one-size-fits-all solution that may not work for the organization. This highlights the point that while the nature of this topic from the CSEC2017 perspective is technical, a background in building authentication policy based on business requirements is imperative.

Password Attacks

In most IT environments, a user logging in would be asked to identify themself. This is normally done by entering identifier usually known as the username, such as JKozmugic. But because anyone could enter this username, the next step is for the user to authenticate by proving that they are who they say they are. The most common form of authentication has been and continues to be a password. However, despite their popularity, passwords provide only weak protection.

Many people believe that passwords are compromised by guessing: an attacker enters different passwords at the login prompt until they guess the right password and is admitted access. This is called an online attack. However, this approach is not used because it is impractical. Instead of randomly guessing a password, attackers use far more sophisticated methods. Attacks that can be used to discover a password include social engineering (phishing, shoulder surfing, or dumpster diving). But these attacks have their limitations, such as the need to physically access a user's computer or watch the user enter a password.

Instead, most password attacks are in the form of an offline attack. When a password is first created, a one-way hash algorithm creates a message digest (or hash) of the password. This digest is then stored instead of the original plaintext password. When a user attempts to log in, they enter their password and another digest is created from it. This is then compared against the stored digest, and if they match, the user is authenticated.

In an offline attack, the file of password digests is stolen and put onto the attacker's computer. In turn, they can then attempt to discover the passwords by comparing the stolen digests with their own digests that they have created. Several offline password attack techniques attempt to match an attacker's known password digest with stolen digests. It is important to be aware of these attacks so that protective measures can be put into place and to create passwords that are least vulnerable to discoverability. These attacks include: **brute force** – every possible combination of letters, numbers, and characters is used to create digests that can be matched against those in the stolen digest file, **dictionary** – the attacker creates a digest of common dictionary word as candidate and then compares them against those in a stolen digest file, **rainbow tables** – make password attacks easier by developing a large pre-created dataset of candidate digests, after which those datasets (tables) are matched to the stolen digest file.

While it is easy to imagine an attacker manually performing these and any number of other forms of password attacks, clearly, that would be impractical. A quick search on the Internet will demonstrate the ease in which password attack tools can be downloaded and utilized. Realistically, new approaches for cracking passwords and new tools for using those approaches are developed as quickly as security solutions to protect against each form of attack that are discovered. Innovative techniques for protecting against password attacks continue to be a priority in any security curriculum.

Password Storage Techniques

To the user of an authenticated system, the process of authenticating, using a password, to a system is transparent. An ideal choice of password must be chosen, entered into the system, and then remembered each time the access is desired. To provide adequate protection of the passwords used to authenticate the task for the organization storing the password is a bit more daunting.

As mentioned in the discussion of data integrity and offline attacks, when the user selects a password, a hash algorithm is used to create and store (generally in an authentication server) a digest that is later compared, when the user later attempts access using that password. It follows, then, that the strength of that digest serves as a basis for the strength of the storage capabilities provided by the authentication server. Each of the techniques used to create the digest must be understood in order to evaluate the appropriateness of a specific technique for the security level desired of password storage.

Cryptographic hash functions include Secure Hash Algorithm 256 (SHA 256) or Secure Hash Algorithm 3 (SHA 3) and are defined as one of the most secure ways to protect digital information (when used in combination with one of the other techniques described below). The strength of either of these algorithms stems from the technique used to generate the hash. SHA 3 is the last to be approved and adopted by NIST, largely due to its low number of possible collisions (the same digest created for two different input sources). The number of possible combinations of letters and numbers produced by SHA can be analogized as exceeding the number grains of sand on earth. That makes guessing the data hidden within the hash virtually impossible.

Salting employs a "salt," which is simply an added layer of password security in which a random string is added to the plaintext password before it is hashed. This technique provides two significant benefits. One, dictionary attacks and brute force become much more difficult due to the longer string that must be determined. Two, multiple users can pick the same password with the random salt serving as the variation between them.

Key stretching uses algorithms such as scrypt, bcrypt, or PBKDF2; the idea of key stretching is to put the input through a larger number of successive mathematical iterations. Theoretically, if more iterations are required to create the password digest, the more interactions would be required by an attacker to crack the password.

Data Integrity

The most common technique for ensuring data integrity is a form of cryptographic algorithm sometimes referred to as one-way hash algorithm. As noted above, hash algorithm creates a unique "digital fingerprint" of a set of data. This process is called hashing, and the fingerprint produced is a digest (sometimes called a message digest or hash) that represents the contents.

It is important to note that, although hashing is for cryptography, its purpose is not to create ciphertext that can later be decrypted. Rather, the purpose of hashing is to be one directional in that its digest cannot be reversed to reveal the original set of data (as is the case with symmetric and asymmetric algorithms). For example, when 11 is multiplied by 33 the result is 363. If someone attempted to determine the two numbers used to create the number 363, it would not be possible to work backward and derive the original numbers with absolute certainty because there are too many mathematical operations that could have been used to derive that number. The point is that the number 363 represents or has significance to the other two corresponding numbers (11 and 33).

A hashing algorithm is considered secure if it has these characteristics: **Fixed size** – the length of the data should not matter. Each digest should always be the identical size; **Unique** – each set of data (whether the difference is one character or one thousand characters) will produce a different digest; **Original** – you should not be able to work backward by creating a dataset that will produce a desired digest.

The value of hashing to data integrity comes from the ability to verify that the original contents of an item have not been changed. This is accomplished by generating the digest and storing or transmitting it with data. Upon receipt, the digest is regenerated against the data in the identical fashion. A match indicates that no tampering has occurred to the data. Recall from our discussion earlier in the chapter that message digests are also used as part of the Public Key Infrastructure (PKI) as the means from which digital signatures are established.

Significant to the conversation of this CSEC2017 knowledge unit are the Hashed Message Authentication Code (HMAC) and Cipher Block Chaining–Message Authentication Code (CBC–MAC) because both use hashing to authenticate the sender. They do this by using both a hash function and a secret cryptographic key. An *MAC* combines the original message with a shared secret key that only the sender and receiver know. A hash function is then applied to both the key and the message, and for added security, they are hashed in separate steps. When the receiver gets the HMAC or CBC–MAC, it then creates its own to compare with what was sent: if they match, then it knows that the MAC came from the sender (because only the sender has the secret key), thus authenticating the sender of the message.

Knowledge Unit Four: Access Control

This knowledge unit introduces the specific access control techniques that are associated with Data Security. It describes the tools and techniques that are employed to protect the physical components that contain data. It also makes the explicit provision for characterizing the approaches that will be used in order to ensure the logical data access upon conclusive evidence of user authorization. It demonstrates the artifacts that are necessary in accomplishing secure architecture design. Finally, with the growing number of data breaches occurring internationally, preventive techniques are introduced. That is the specific means of ensuring overall functional correctness in the design.

Most cybersecurity curricula approach the discussion of access control only from the perspective of understanding approaches to define system level access. While topics such as physical security and architectural design are normally introduced, they are not brought into perspective about providing a combined approach to controlling who or what has access to system components containing data. CSEC2017 makes the point that access control should be characterized from a larger scope of concepts that together provide a framework that can be used to ensure that proper policies are created to define procedures for data access at all system levels. Given this proviso and shown in Figure 3.14, there are

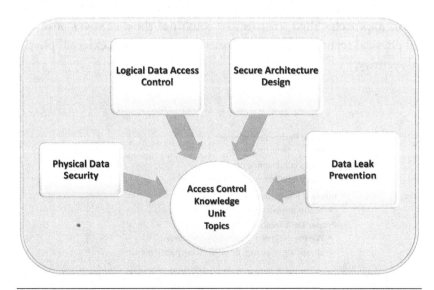

Figure 3.14   The access control knowledge unit topics.

four plainly appropriate knowledge units in the Access Control knowledge area: (1) *Physical Data Security*, (2) *Logical Data Access Control*, (3) *Secure Architecture Design*, and (4) *Data Leak Prevention*.

Physical Data Security

Too often we look at securing access only from a logical perspective. There is a tendency to overlook the physical nature of gaining access to data. Preventing an attacker from physically accessing any device or part of an IT system is as important as preventing the attacker from accessing it remotely through a network. CSEC2017 characterizes physical security to include external perimeter defenses, internal physical access security, and proper data destruction as shown in Figure 3.15.

External perimeter defenses are designed to restrict access to the areas (such as data centers) where system devices containing valuable data are located. This type of defense includes human beings acting as security guards, video surveillance cameras, barriers (such as fences or walls), and motion detection devices.

While external defenses prevent access into a facility, an additional layer of physical access control must be in place inside the facility. The most common approach to use is to secure high data content areas of a facility using standard door locks or key cards. One other internal access approach called "man-traps" combines the incentives of internal physical security with objectives achieved through external physical security.

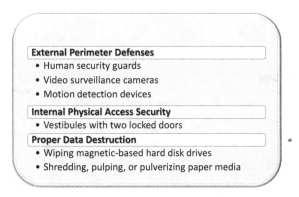

External Perimeter Defenses
- Human security guards
- Video surveillance cameras
- Motion detection devices

Internal Physical Access Security
- Vestibules with two locked doors

Proper Data Destruction
- Wiping magnetic-based hard disk drives
- Shredding, pulping, or pulverizing paper media

Figure 3.15   Physical Data Security.

Before electronic security was even a possibility, vestibules with two locked doors were used to control access to sensitive areas. To enter you would need to show some form of credentials to a security guard, who would then open the first door to a small room (a vestibule) and ask you to enter and wait until your credentials could be checked. If the credentials were approved, the second door would be unlocked; if the credentials were not approved, you would be trapped in the vestibule (a *mantrap*).

Another aspect of physical security consists of how organizations destroy data once it is no longer needed. Because data is not tangible, destroying it involves destroying the media that the data is stored. First and foremost, that media should never just haphazardly be thrown away in a dumpster, recycle bin, or trash can. Paper media can be destroyed by burning, shredding, pulping, or pulverizing. Data in electronic form should never be erased simply by using the operating system "delete" command. Instead, data sanitation tools are available (some for free) that can securely remove data. The most popular technique is called wiping; where the data is overwritten with zeros or random data. Data on magnetic-based hard disk drives must be degaussed which permanently destroys the entire drive by removing the magnetic field.

Logical Data Access Control

As its name implies, access control is granting or denying approval to use specific resources; it is controlling access. While physical access control consists of fencing, hardware door locks, and mantraps to limit contact with devices, in a similar way, logical access control consists of technology restrictions that limit users on digital devices from accessing data. Access control has a set of associated terminology used to describe its actions. There are also standard access control models that are used to help enforce access control.

Access control models are often referred to as access control models, methods, modes, techniques, or types. They are used by security administrators for access control but are not created or installed. Rather, these models are already part of the software and hardware components of the system.

There are several models that are popular in industry today, shown in Figure 3.16: Discretionary Access Control, Mandatory Access Control,

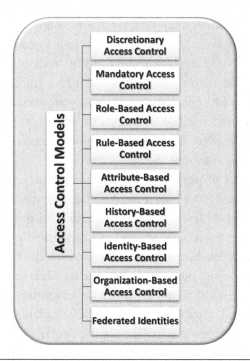

Figure 3.16   Access control models.

Role-Based Access Control, Rule-Based Access Control, and Attribute-Based Access Control. However, CSEC2017 also recommends that curriculum contain introduction to History-Based Access Control, Identity-Based Access Control, Organization-Based Access Control, and Federated Identities.

While knowledge of password storage and retrieval is necessary for adequate implementation of any of models just mentioned, it is necessary to emphasize that each model is unique in how it is in the information provided on access control lists and their configuration through group policy.

Secure Architecture Design

Architectural design decides how each of the system requirement, which has been identified in the security specification, will be implemented. This process then establishes an explicit and consistent architecture for the protection of the information within the system. The goal of this process is to incorporate every one of the identified requirements into a logical design that will guide the construction of the eventual result. Architectural design dictates a practical, real-world solution for each individual requirement and then validates that a satisfactory representation of the entire set of requirement set has been attained. In order to perform secure architecture design, CSEC2017 recommends conceptual and practical knowledge of the principles of secure architecture, in combination with knowledge of information protective measures that can be placed into functional information systems.

The aim of architectural design is to translate every item in the requirement set to an analogous design element. Those components are then further explicated in a detailed design process. Aside from capturing the functional security requirements of the system, this process also performs the top-level design for the security of the systems external and internal interfaces, as well as for any prospective databases. Finally, the specific artifacts created through this process must be fully and completely documented.

Data Leak Prevention

The final topic of the CSEC2017 access control knowledge unit addresses the capabilities that must be available to protect all of the data flowing in and out of the organization, ensuring that it does not fall into the wrong hands. One way of securing data and in turn preventing leaks is through data loss prevention (DLP). DLP is a combination of security tools that an organization uses to inventory data that is critical to the organization and ensure that it is protected. Beyond inventory, this type of protection includes monitoring the usage of the data and how it is accessed. Regardless of the suite of tools used, the goal of DLP is to protect data from users that have not been given the appropriate authorization. This is accomplished by doing an examination of the data as it resides in three common data states: data at rest, data in process, and data in transit. Tagging procedures are used for data that is considered critical to the organization or needs to be confidential. Thus, an attempt to access the data to disclose it to an unauthorized individual will be prevented. Two of the most common uses of DLP are monitoring emails through a mail gateway and blocking the copying of files to a USB flash drive, a technique known as USB blocking.

Most DLP systems use a technique called content inspection in combination with index matching. Content inspection identifies the security level of the data, who is requesting it, where the data is stored, when it was requested, and where it is going. Through index matching, data identified as requiring protection are analyzed by the DLP system, and complex computations are conducted based on the analysis. From that point on, if even a small part of the data is leaked, the DLP system can establish immediate recognition.

Knowledge Unit Five: Secure Communication Protocols

This knowledge unit describes the implications of network protocols and network security to the capabilities designed for Data Security. Network security has been a huge concern in the cybersecurity field due to the interconnected devices across the world. It has become very important in our lives because the Internet continues to evolve, and computer networks grow dramatically. The fundamentals of network protocols give you a better understanding how the network is structured and how data is being transmitted. In this knowledge unit, CSEC2017 considers each layer of the Transmission Control Protocol/Internet Protocol (TCP/IP) stack and identifies criteria within each layer that are most important to acknowledge.

The TCP/IP standard is a layered set of protocols that are fundamental communication for data communication over the Internet and it consists of two core protocols, the TCP and the IP. The TCP/IP was developed in the Unix operating system in 1989. The purpose was to have computers communicate in a simple way and transmit information across the network. For example, a user interacts with an application and TCP is responsible for sending the message to the destination host. After the TCP sends the message, it returns an IP header which includes the location and the IP address destination. As cybersecurity and the need for data protection have evolved, consideration must be given to each layer of the TCP/IP stack to provide assurance that appropriate Data Security measures are deployed to protect communication using each of the protocols on a given layer. This topic is thoroughly presented in the Connection Security knowledge area. However, given the crosscutting nature of the field of cybersecurity, its relevance to Data Security must also be examined here.

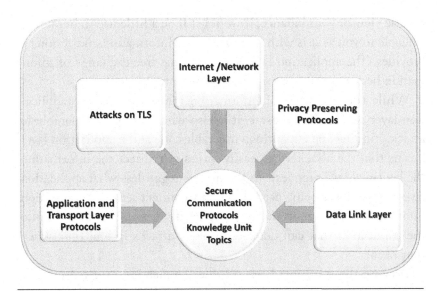

Figure 3.17 The secure communication protocols knowledge unit topics.

Shown in Figure 3.17, there are five relevant areas in the Secure Communication Protocols knowledge area. These are (1) *Application and Transport Level Protocols*, (2) *Attacks on TLS*, (3) *Internet Network Layer*, (4) *Privacy Preserving Protocols*, and (5) *Data Link Layer*.

Application and Transport Layer Protocols

CSEC2017 discusses these protocols and all of the layers of the Open Standard Interface (OSI) and TCP/IP stack in the Connection Security knowledge area. As such, we will be discussing them in that context in a later chapter. However, it is important to understand the impact that each of the protocols has within the scope of Data Security.

What makes the protocols at the application layer so valuable is the information they access. If you go onto your desktop computer, go to your bank's website and provide your username and password, you expect to be able to view your balance, transfer funds, deposit money, and anything else related to online banking. However, for this to take place, the browser needs to communicate with and receive data that is stored by your bank. The information stored by your bank travels through layers of communication protocols, until it reaches the application layer. If your online banking session could only give you a static view of your balance, it would still be a little useful but not as valuable to you as it is with all of the other information and actions it provides. The application layer facilitates the free exchange of information between the user and some other entity.

While this exchange of information is what makes the application layer so valuable to users, it is also what makes it vulnerable to attack. Finding and exploiting vulnerable code at the application layer means that the attacker can easily access or redirect the information the legitimate user requests to themselves regardless what application layer protocol was being used. In order to protect sensitive application information, it is important to have security measures built right into the application that can detect and block attacks in real time when they occur.

Because the transport layer provides connection-oriented or connectionless services for transporting application layer services between networks, it too is important to the discussion of Data Security. Protocols at this layer can be used to protect the data in a single communication session between two hosts. The biggest concern is that IP information is added at the network layer. As such, the transport layer controls cannot protect it. To help protect HTTP traffic, the TLS standard is usually used. The drawback is that the use of TLS requires each application to support that standard. Although unlike application layer protocols, which involve extensive customization of the application, transport layer controls such as TLS are much transparent because they do not need to understand the application's functions or characteristics. Although using TLS may require modifying some applications, TLS is a well-tested protocol that has several implementations that have been added to many applications, so it is a relatively low-risk option compared to adding protection at the application layer.

Attacks on Transport Layer Security

The major attacks on TLS continue to mount and frustrate security professionals, there have been several major attacks on TLS, including attacks on its most commonly used ciphers and modes of operation. But those security professionals expected to protect data must continue to be educated in the newest categories of TLS attacks in order to develop protective alternatives. However, as organizations get better about encrypting network traffic to protect data from potential attacks or exposure, online attackers are also getting smarter at their SSL/TLS attempts to hide their malicious activities. The growth in SSL/TLS usage includes both legitimate and malicious activities, as criminals rely on valid SSL certificates to distribute their content.

Internet/Network Layer

The responsibilities of the protocols at this layer are to route packets across networks. IP is the fundamental network layer protocol for TCP/IP. Other commonly used protocols at the network layer are Internet Control Message Protocol (ICMP) and Internet Group Management Protocol (IGMP).

The protocols existing at this layer can be applied to all applications; thus, they are not application-specific and, therefore, a threat to the security of data. Some IT environments utilize network layer standards such as Internet Protocol Security (IPsec) provide a much better solution than transport or application layer controls because of the difficulties in adding controls to individual applications. Network layer standards also provide a way for security professionals to enforce specific security policies. Additionally, since IP header information (such as IP addresses) is added to the packet at this layer, the security measures can be taken to protect both the data within the packets and the IP information.

Privacy Preserving Protocols

There are several protocols that make it harder for eavesdroppers to trace end-to-end communications such as mix networks, the Tor browser, and the encrypted messaging service developed by the Signal Foundation. Originally published in a 1979 paper, the concept of Mix Networks was introduced. The mix networks routing protocol breaks the link between the source and destination of requests by using proxy servers to mix and shuffle messages from multiple senders and send them out randomly to the next destination. So instead of the sender knowing the network destination at the time of the request, mix networks only know the node that it immediately received the message from and the next immediate destination address. The idea here is to make it harder to make the network resistant to malicious mix nodes.

The Tor Project, originally named "The Onion Router," hence the acronym Tor, is an open-source software application that includes a browser, instant messaging, and other communication forms designed to protect the personal privacy of its users and keeps their Internet activities confidential. The user's location and usage is encrypted and essentially concealed from anyone conducting network surveillance or traffic analysis. Although Tor protects a user's privacy, it does not hide online services from determining when Tor is being used to access their sites. Some websites restrict usage of Tor and require special permission to access content.

Data Link Layer

The data link layer handles communications on the physical network components. For years, the most widely known protocol has been Ethernet. However, with the emergence of wireless communication (and associated protocols) over the past twenty years, an even greater threat to Data Security at this layer has emerged.

Data link layer security measures are applied to all communications on a specific physical link, such as a dedicated circuit between two buildings or a dial-up modem connection to an Internet Service Provider (ISP). Because the data link layer is below the network layer, security measures at this layer can protect both data and IP information. Compared to those at the other layers, data link layer security is relatively simple, which makes it easier to implement; also, security applied at this layer also supports other network layer protocols besides IP. Data link layer protocols have been used for many years primarily to provide additional protection for specific physical links that should not be trusted. To support the increase of wireless communication, CSEC2017 recommends introduction to technologies such as Point-to-Point Protocol (PPP) and RADIUS.

Knowledge Unit Six: Cryptanalysis

In an earlier section of this knowledge area, CSEC2017 recommended a basic and advanced conceptual knowledge of cryptography.

Emphasized was the importance of being able to apply understanding of symmetric and asymmetric techniques. We also discussed that in both major forms of cryptography an algorithm (often called a cipher) is used encrypt and decrypt the data. For a security professional to adequately protect data using cryptography, they must have the capability to understand which cipher is going to provide the greatest level of sustainability (Figure 3.18).

In *any* area of cybersecurity, it is vital that the individual implementing security controls be able to think like an attacker. In attempting to interpret data that has been encrypted, the attacker is going to use a practice known as cryptanalysis. The science behind cryptanalysis is largely the ability to "break" a cipher using one of several different algorithms, in an effort to uncover the plaintext equivalent of encrypted data previously converted to ciphertext. This section of CSEC2017 recommends introduction to each major category of cryptographic attacks, including: classical attacks, side-channel attacks, attacks on private key (symmetric) ciphers, attacks on public key (asymmetric) ciphers, algorithms for solving discrete log problems, and attacks on RSA. Knowledge of each form of attack will provide the security professional the knowledge they need to use the most appropriate cipher, gauged against the value and risk imposed upon the data for which it protects. Given this, there are six knowledge

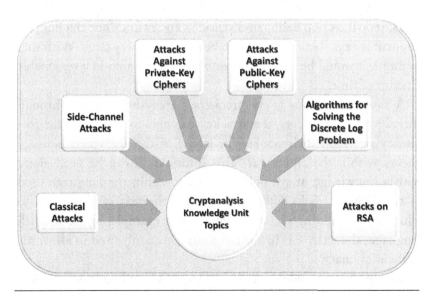

Figure 3.18   The cryptanalysis knowledge unit topics.

units within the Cryptanalysis Knowledge Unit: (1) *Classical Attacks*, (2) *Side-Channel Attacks*, (3) *Attacks Against Private Key Ciphers*, (4) *Attacks Against Public Key Ciphers*, (5) *Solutions to the Discrete Log Problem*, and (6) *Attacks on RSA*.

Classical Attacks

Even though the first developed ciphers, such as substitution ciphers, were thought to be safe from attack, different techniques have been developed to easily find the key of the cipher and, therefore, can decrypt the entire ciphertext. These techniques date back to the 1950s, when attacks were devised to decipher data encrypted using the Enigma machine. While that form of cryptography is rarely used anymore, it serves as an example of classical approaches that have been popular for many years. Several other possible methods to break more recent substitution ciphers include brute force, frequency analysis, and the birthday paradox.

Brute force is the simplest to understand and implement out of all algorithms used to break substitution ciphers. This technique is possible since most cryptographic techniques use a specific key length allowing for all possible keys to be checked until the correct one is found. Even though it may seem that the brute-force method is a reasonable way of trying to break simple substitution ciphers, in most cases, it will end up being an unfeasible algorithm since the number of possible keys that might need to be checked is very large. With that in mind, it would be nearly impossible to do a search in a reasonable amount of time.

A faster algorithm is the frequency analysis method. Through this algorithmic process, the attacker attempts to determine the frequency at which each symbol (or letter) of the encrypted message occurs within the ciphertext. This information can be used along with a knowledge of symbol frequencies within the language used in the cipher to help determine which ciphertext symbol maps to which corresponding plaintext symbol. For example, in the English language, the letter e is by far the most commonly used in all words of the dictionary.

The birthday-paradox attack is generally used to crack hashed ciphers, is generally used for password attacks, and answers to the need for knowledge of probability and statistics to effectively perform cryptanalysis. This type of attack is based on the fact that in a room of 183 people, there would be a 50% chance of one of them sharing your birthday. However, if you wanted a 50% chance of finding any two people who had matching birthdays, you would surprisingly only need twenty-three people in the room. For hashed ciphers, this means that it is much easier to find any two matches if you don't care which two they are. It is possible to precompute hashes for a given password length to determine if any collisions occur.

Side-Channel Attacks

A side-channel attack is a form of reverse engineering (a topic we will discuss in a later chapter) and requires background knowledge of electronics. However, this form of attack utilizes information gained from analysis of system component or product behavior. Examples of these attacks include timing attacks, power consumption attacks, and differential fault analysis (often known as leaks). In each case, data is exposed that can be exploited. What side-channel attacks have in common is that each monitors electronic transmissions and other aspects of performance and then, using statistical analysis, draws conclusions about operating the part of the system containing the data in order to secretly obtain the access.

All side-channel attacks intentionally look for data that is unblocked or improperly shielded. Therefore, there are two approaches that can be used to prevent the attack. The first is to find the vulnerability within the system and eliminate it. The second is to make an attempt to break the connection between a discovered vulnerability and any protected data.

Attacks against Private Key Ciphers

In this topic, CSEC2017 delineates the first of two major categories of cryptanalysis in which emphasis is placed on knowledge of attacks that can be imposed on private key (symmetric) ciphers. As described earlier in the chapter, the most popular cipher used in symmetric cryptography is DES. The type of attacks on these early forms of cryptographic algorithm is called "known plaintext."

During known-plaintext attacks, the attacker has access to the ciphertext and its corresponding plaintext. Their goal is to guess the secret key (or a number of secret keys) or to develop an algorithm which would allow them to decrypt any further messages. This gives the attacker much bigger possibilities to break the cipher than just by performing ciphertext only attacks (similar to those we described in previous sections of this chapter).

Known-plaintext attacks are most effective when they are used against the simplest kinds of ciphers. For example, applying them against simple substitution ciphers allowing the attacker to break them almost immediately. Originally, they were used for attacking the ciphers used during the World War II, on attempts made by the British to attack the Enigma ciphers. Today, the most common forms of attack are the differential, linear, and meet-in-the-middle attacks.

Attacks against Public Key Ciphers

This topic focuses on the cryptanalysis algorithms that have been developed with the specific intention of cracking public key ciphers. It should be noted forthright that the most popular form of public key cipher is RSA. However, because of the exclusive nature of RSA, the CSEC2017 guideline separates that from the required knowledge base of public key attacks in general.

Regardless, all public key algorithms are based on factoring in one form or another. The problem of finding nontrivial factors of a positive composite integer is known as the integer factorization problem. The integer factorization problem is widely believed to be difficult to interpret. There are few, if any, polynomial time algorithms that solve the problem for a large proportion of possible inputs. That in part is why this mathematical approach has been used in the field of cryptography. Note that factoring is obviously not always hard, but a hard instance of the problem can be easily created, by simply multiplying two large chosen prime numbers.

Several factoring methods exist, and each has its own significance in terms of the degree of complexity that is integrated into the algorithm. Three popular factoring methods widely used in public key ciphers today are: Pollards p-1, quadratic sieve, and number field sieve.

Algorithms for Solving the Discrete Log Problem

In designing public key cryptosystems, two problems dominate the designs: the integer factorization problem (as we discussed in the past section) and the discrete logarithm problem. Both techniques are still major mathematical approaches used in public key cryptanalysis, today.

In general, we reduce the complexity of a problem by storing a square root of the prime number used. For example, given a prime number 14,947, we only need to store 123 values. Unfortunately, as our prime numbers get larger, the amount of computer memory we need increases. And so discrete logs continue to be a hard task for a computer. If someone uses a 512-bit prime number, we will need to store an astronomical amount of values in a table used to compute the logarithm. Imagine the number of values required for 2,048-bit prime numbers. Regrettably, the growth of quantum computers has made this line of thinking much more clouded, since they do not struggle as much with discrete logarithms and will be able to crack them in a reasonable amount of time.

Discrete logs are the mathematical approach from which elliptic curves are based. While CSEC2017 makes no mention of elliptic curve algorithms in the recommendations for cryptanalysis, they have proven to be a strong cryptosystem using elliptic curves and discrete logarithms. Additionally, other cryptosystems that utilize discrete logs include: Pohlig–Hellman, Baby Step/Giant Step, and Pollards rho method.

Attacks on RSA

In 1978, Rivest, Shamir, and Adleman introduced the RSA public key cryptosystem. RSA is deployed in many commercial systems and is used to provide privacy and to ensure authenticity of digital data. This form of cryptography mainly relies on the difficulty of factoring carefully chosen large integers (an aspect of cryptanalysis the CSEC2017 emphasizes in this knowledge unit). After this breakthrough, other public key cryptosystems were proposed to produce alternatives to RSA, some of which are still in existence today.

There are numerous mathematical attacks on RSA. They can basically be classified into three categories independent of the protocol in use for encryption or digital signature: (1) Attacks exploiting the polynomial structure of RSA, (2) attacks based on its homomorphic nature, and (3) attacks resulting from a bad choice of parameters.

The first category of attacks relies on the polynomial structure of RSA. Since Lucas sequences (integer sequences named after the mathematician) can be expressed in terms of Dickson polynomials, all of these attacks can be straightforwardly adapted. Using division polynomials, the second type of attacks does not extend so easily to Lucas sequences because of their non-homomorphic nature. Therefore, they are much more resistant. However, multiplicative attacks can sometimes be rewritten in order to be applied to RSA-based systems. The last category of attacks does not really result from a weakness of RSA but rather from a bad implementation. Parameters have to be carefully chosen when used with the algorithm. Unfortunately, there is no general recipe to mitigate this kind of attack beyond a careful choice of parameters.

Knowledge Unit Seven: Data Privacy

Earlier in this chapter and throughout many parts of *any* book on cybersecurity, we are reminded that confidentiality remains one of the major objectives that we aim to achieve through the implementation of numerous risk mitigation measures. Such measures may not necessarily relate just to the confidentiality of data but also other areas including Human Security, Organizational Security, and Societal Security. Clearly, synonymous to the meaning of confidentiality is the word "privacy" (which is context that CSEC2017 puts the topic into within their guideline). Because of the implications of privacy throughout many facets of cybersecurity, you will see similar discussions within several of the CSEC2017 knowledge areas. Here, our focus is on privacy of data.

It is a common understanding that at the core of cybersecurity, the goal is to keep sensitive data away from the people that can use that data to cause harm to either individuals or organizations. Further, it is not unusual for cybersecurity to be characterized and associated with the phrase "theft prevention." Likewise, it is not unusual for the techniques for preventing data from being stolen to be identified by an organization as a primary objective of their information security program. Theft of organizational data can include stealing intellectual property business information, such as R&D documentation for a new product or a list of customers that competitors would be eager to acquire.

On an individual level, personal data theft usually involves someone's personal data such as credit card numbers that are in turn used to purchase upward to thousands of dollars of merchandise online before the victim is even aware the number has been stolen. Another form of personal data theft is identity theft, where the victim's personal information, such as social security number is stolen and then used to impersonate the victim, normally for financial gain.

The topics outlined by the CSEC2017 guideline emphasize that while security is often viewed as keeping sensitive data away from attackers, it is also important to keep private data from leaking into the hands of *any* unauthorized persons, whether they are seeking the data or not. That can transpire through inadvertent data leaks, or through mistrust of content put on social media, or the creative techniques that an attacker employs through social engineering. The message that must be emphasized is to know where the data resides, know who has access, and don't trust anyone.

Practicing data privacy and security involves understanding what privacy is and its risks, as well as practical steps in keeping data safe.

An informal definition of privacy includes that it is a condition of being free from public attention to the degree that you determine. Put differently, privacy is freedom from attention, observation, or interference, based on your discretion. Privacy is the right to be left alone to the level that you choose.

Until recent technology trends emerged, any individual or organization was able to choose the level of privacy that they desired. Those who wanted to have very open and public exposure could freely provide information to others. While those that wanted to be very quiet or even unknown could limit what information was disseminated. In short, both of those wanting a public exposure and those wanting to remain private could choose to do so by controlling information about themselves. However, times have changed.

Today, the level of control once enjoyed is no longer possible. Data is collected on literally every action and transaction that is performed. This includes data collected through a wide range of technologies and techniques, the web pages you browse, online and in-person purchases, employment information, family data, prison records, surveys that get filled out after visiting certain websites. There is information out there about the activities individuals perform such as the choice of movies streamed through the Internet, the location signals emitted by a cell phone, and even the path of walking as recorded by a surveillance camera. This data is then aggregated by data brokers. These brokers then sell the data to interested third parties such as marketers or even governments.

In addition to the need to keep data secure to prevent theft, there is also a need to keep data private and secure for legal and compliance issues, in order to follow the requirements of legislation, rules and regulations, specified standards, or the terms of a contract. Depending upon the industry from which an organization performs business, several federal and state laws have been enacted to protect the privacy of electronic data, and businesses that fail to protect data they possess may face serious financial penalties. Shown in Figure 3.19,

Figure 3.19 Government regulatory laws for the protection of data.

one of these laws include the Health Insurance Portability and Accountability Act of 1996 (HIPAA), the Sarbanes–Oxley Act of 2002 (SOX), the Gramm–Leach–Bliley Act (GLBA), the Payment Card Industry–Data Security Standard (PCI-DSS), and various state notification and security laws. Some of the legal and compliance issues relate to data retention or how long data must be kept and how it is to be secured. This is the single topic in the privacy knowledge unit.

Knowledge Unit Eight: Information Storage Security

Based on the discussions we have presented of the first seven knowledge units of Data Security, it may seem that CSEC2017 has focused recommendations for understanding of topics that aim to provide security mechanisms for data in transit and data in process. There is a third facet of Data Security, data at rest, which has received little attention. The guideline does not exclude the importance of conceptual understanding of how to protect or properly remove data in storage. Rather, that area of Data Security is so important that the guideline separated it into its own unit.

Data at rest is data that is not actively moving from device to device or network to network such as data stored on a hard drive, laptop, flash drive, or archived/stored in some other way. Data protection at rest aims to secure inactive data stored on any device or network. While data at rest is sometimes considered to be less vulnerable than data in transit, attackers often find data at rest a more valuable target than data in motion. The risk profile for data at rest depends on the security measures that are in place to provide the proper level of security of the data in residing in storage or being disposed.

There are multiple approaches to protecting data at rest, although most of the attention is directed toward using one of several encryption techniques. While the guideline recommends knowledge of both data and file encryption, other topics in this unit include data erasure, data masking, and Data Security. While Data Security law does have implications toward how an organization stores and removes data, the guideline addresses legal considerations more thoroughly in recommendations prescribed for data privacy and is further discussed in the Organizational Security knowledge area.

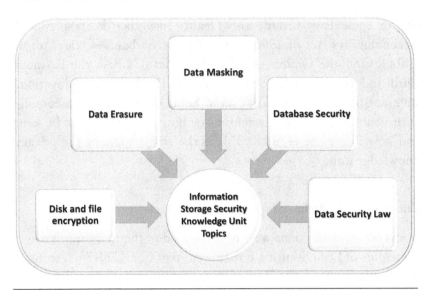

Figure 3.20   The information storage security knowledge unit topics.

Shown in Figure 3.20, there are five topics in this unit: (1) *Disk and File Encryption*, (2) *Data Erasure*, (3) *Data Masking*, (4) *Database Security*, and (5) *Data Security Law*.

Disk and File Encryption

In most of the discussions we have had in this chapter related to encryption, there was an assumption being made that the techniques explained must be developed and implemented manually. That is not always the case. Encryption can be implemented through cryptographic software running on a system so that it can be applied to individual files by using the software to encrypt and decrypt each file. The encryption also can be performed on a larger scale through the file system or by encrypting the entire disk drive.

Encryption software can be used to encrypt or decrypt files one by one. However, that can often times be a very time-consuming process. As an alternative, protecting groups of files, such as all files in a specific folder, can take advantage of the operating system's file system. Protecting individual files or multiple files through file system cryptography can be performed using software such as Pretty Good Privacy or features that are now build directly into the operating system. One popular operating system feature used to protect organizational data on individual Windows-based workstations is BitLocker (which provides full disk encryption). BitLocker encrypts the entire system volume, including the Windows registry and any temporary files that might hold confidential information. Full disk encryption prevents attackers from accessing data by booting from another operating system or placing the hard drive in another computer.

One problem with software encryption is that, similar to applications, it can be subject to attacks to exploit its vulnerabilities. As a result, many organizations are turning to a more secure option, cryptography embedded directly into the hardware. Hardware encryption cannot be exploited like software encryption. Hardware encryption emerged as a means for protecting data on USB devices and later evolved to include capabilities for encrypting standard hard drives. More sophisticated hardware encryption options include self-encrypting drives, the trusted platform module (which is a chip providing cryptographic services inserted onto the motherboard), and the hardware security model providing cryptography directly within the computer's processor.

Data Erasure

Unlike the early days of computer systems where data was simply stored on punch cards and in the rare case some other form of legacy electronic media, the modern storage environment is rapidly evolving. Data may pass through multiple organizations, systems, and storage media in its lifetime. The pervasive nature of data propagation is only increasing as the Internet and data storage systems move toward a distributed cloud-based architecture. As a result, more organizations than ever are responsible for effective disposal of media and the potential is substantial for residual sensitive data to be collected and retained on the media. This responsibility is not limited to those organizations that are the originators or final resting places of sensitive data but also intermediaries who transiently store or process the information along the way. The efficient and effective management of information from inception through disposition is the responsibility of all those who have handled the data. The application of sophisticated access controls and encryption helps reduce the likelihood that an attacker can gain direct access to sensitive information. As a result, attackers attempting to obtain sensitive information may seek to focus their efforts on alternative access means such as retrieving residual data on media that has left an organization exposed to data theft, without enough sanitization effort having been applied. Consequently, the application of effective sanitization techniques and tracking of storage media are critical aspects of ensuring that sensitive data is effectively protected by an organization against unauthorized disclosure.

Protection of information is paramount. That information may be on paper, optical, electronic, or magnetic media. An organization may choose to dispose of media through internal or external transfer or by recycling it in accordance with applicable laws and regulations if the media are obsolete or no longer usable. Even internal transfers require increased scrutiny, as legal and ethical obligations make it more important than ever to protect data such as PII. No matter what the final intended destination of the media is, it is important that the organization ensure that no easily reconstructible residual representation of the data is stored on the media after it has left the control of the organization or is no longer going to be protected at the confidentiality categorization of the data stored on the media.

Sanitization refers to a process that renders access to target data on the media infeasible for a given level of effort. Perhaps the most valuable resource to the knowledge of the topic comes from NIST SP 800-88 "Guidelines for Media Sanitization" which defines three methodologies for media: Clear applies logical techniques to sanitize data in all user-addressable storage locations for protection against simple noninvasive data recovery techniques; typically applied through the standard read and write commands to the storage device, such as by rewriting with a new value or using a menu option to reset the device to the factory state (where rewriting is not supported). Purge applies physical or logical techniques that render target data recovery infeasible using state-of-the art laboratories. A common form of purging used for magnetic media sanitization is electromagnetic degaussing, whereby a dedicated degaussing device produces a buildup of electrical energy to create a magnetic field that removes the data from the device when discharged. Destroy renders target data recovery infeasible using state-of-the-art laboratory techniques and results in the subsequent inability to use the media for storage. Industry-tested and accepted methodologies of secure data destruction include crushing, shredding, and disintegration, but even these secure end-of-life solutions require thoughtful security considerations.

NIST 800-88 was developed to protect the privacy and interests of organizations and individuals. The guideline provides an outline of appropriate procedures for secure data sanitization that both protects PII and confidential information while reducing organizational liability. Determining proper policies is realized by fully understanding the guidelines, following the sanitization and disposition decision flow, implementing data sanitization best practices, and engaging in ongoing training and scheduled maintenance.

Data Masking

Data masking is the process of protecting sensitive information in non-production databases from inappropriate visibility. It ensures that sensitive data is replaced with realistic but not real data. The goal is that sensitive PII is not available outside of the authorized environment. PCI-DSS is perhaps the largest regulatory driver of data masking in database systems because it requires that the payment card number be obscured on printed receipts.

Data masking can be done while deploying test environments so that copies created to support application development and testing do not expose sensitive data. Valid production data is replaced with useable but incorrect or obfuscated data by using one of several masking techniques. After masking, the test data is usable just like the production data but the content of the data, as it appears in the production environment, is secure. Another form of data masking applies directly to production data, such that the data is accurate in the database but masked upon retrieval and display.

Database Security

Much of the critical data that organizations store is accessible through Database Management Systems (DBMS). The process of maintaining the confidentiality, integrity, and availability of the data managed by a DBMS is known as database security. Database security is accomplished by applying a wide range of managerial, physical, and technical controls consistent with the priorities defined in the risk management plan. Managerial controls include policies, procedures, and governance. Technical controls include access control and authentication (as we discussed earlier in the chapter), auditing, application security, backup and recovery, encryption, and integrity processes. The challenge for most security professionals is, in order for Data Security to be implemented properly, a substantial amount of mathematical and analytical algorithms must be used.

Data Security Law

Data security includes topics such as the protection of digital privacy; the collection, use, and handling of personal data; the protection from unauthorized access; and the secure disposal of data. With no formal legislation of data security at the federal level, the United States relies on a patchwork of piecemeal federal level laws, competing state level laws, and numerous enforcement organizations. The regulations and laws are often sector-specific or focus on specific types of data (e.g., health, financial), sometimes creating overlapping and contradictory protections.

At the federal level, the Cable Communications Policy Act of 1984 stipulates the privacy protection of subscriber information. The Children's Online Privacy Protection Act (COPPA) prohibits the online collection of any information for children who are under 13 years of age. The Health Insurance Portability and Accountability Act (HIPAA) Privacy Rule protects individual's medical records and other personal health information. The Family Educational Rights and Privacy Act (FERPA) governs educational institutions from disclosing personally identifiable information in education records. The Video Privacy Protection Act (VPPA) protects the wrongful disclosure of online streaming, sale records, or videotape rentals. The Driver's Privacy Protection Act of 1994 (DPPA) governs the privacy and disclosure of personal information gathered.

Hundreds of bills that address cybersecurity, privacy, and data breaches are currently pending at the state level (Brumfield, 2019) however, one of the most comprehensive laws is the California Consumer Privacy Act (CCPA) that gives the state's consumers greater control over their own personal data. The Nevada Senate Bill 220 Online Privacy Law requires an opt-out provision regarding to the sale of personal information by businesses. The Maine Act to Protect the

Privacy of Online Consumer Information prohibits broadband ISPs from using, disclosing, selling, or permitting access to the personal information of their subscribers. Examples of other state laws include:

- New York Stop Hacks and Improve Electronic Data Security (SHIELD) Act
- New Jersey—An Act concerning disclosure of breaches of security and amending P.L.2005, c.226 (S. 51)
- Oregon Consumer Information Protection Act (OCIPA)
- Massachusetts Bill H.4806—an act that stipulates consumer protections from security breaches

In 2016, the European Parliament adopted The General Data Protection Regulation (GDPR), which applies to organizations that collect data on citizens of all 28 European Union (EU) member states. This strict new standard requires that organizations must provide a reasonable level of protection for personal data. Additional law related topics will be further discussed in Chapter 9, Organizational Security.

Chapter Review Questions

1. What is cryptography, and what is its purpose in cybersecurity?
2. What are the advantages of asymmetric cryptography over symmetric cryptography?
3. What are digital signatures, and why are they important within the principles of cryptography?
4. How is a substitution cipher similar or different to a shift cipher?
5. Why are stream cipher algorithms slower than block cipher algorithms?
6. How can the elliptic curve be used to facilitate the creation of public and private keys?
7. Why was the DES symmetric algorithm considered to be weak compared to others that were later developed?
8. What are the broad knowledge areas in which a digital forensics investigator must have in order to be effective?
9. What is the process that is generally followed when collecting data during a digital forensic investigation?
10. What types of artifacts are considered as digital forensics evidence?

11. What are some of the tools used during a digital forensics investigation and what do they accomplish?
12. Why is preserving the chain of digital evidence necessary in prosecuting cybercrimes?
13. Why do investigators need a search warrant?
14. Under what circumstances can an investigator collect evidence without a warrant?
15. What is the procedure to acquire an image of a suspect's hard drive?
16. What are the types of sources of digital evidence that can be found at a crime site?
17. What is a hash file and why is it used?
18. What is data integrity? How is the term different in the database context compared to the cybersecurity context?
19. What are the three characteristics necessary to make a hash function secure?
20. What are three types of offline password attacks?
21. What are the three factors that NIST suggests existing within MFA?
22. What is external physical security and describe why it is important?
23. What is internal physical security and describe how it differentiates from external physical security?
24. What is the purpose of access control models?
25. What is DLP and how does it prevent data leaks?
26. What is the purpose of the TCP/IP protocol stack?
27. How do the protocols at the application layer make data vulnerable?
28. What is TLS and how does it affect the ability to keep data secure?
29. Why is the lack of application-specific protocols at the network layer, a threat to Data Security?
30. What is the purpose of the data link layer protocols?
31. What is the purpose of cryptanalysis within the scope of cybersecurity?
32. How do brute-force attacks differ from frequency-based attacks?
33. Describe the general intention of a side-channel attack?

34. Describe how differential and linear attacks differ from classical substitute cipher attacks.
35. What is the benefit that exists in most public key algorithms being based on factoring?
36. What is meant by the phrase data at rest?
37. Distinguish between disk and file encryption techniques as a visible information storage solution.
38. Describe the three NIST SP 800-88 methods for data sanitation.
39. What is the goal of data masking in ensuring the protection of personal information?
40. What role does access control and authentication play in the overall scope of database security?
41. What is data integrity? How is the term different in the database context compared to the cybersecurity context?
42. How are the results of a hash function different from encryption?
43. What are the three characteristics necessary to make a hash function secure?
44. What are three types of offline password attacks?

You Might Also Like to Read

- Aumasson, Jean-Philippe, *Serious Cryptography a Practical Introduction to Modern Encryption*, 1st Edition, No Starch Press, San Francisco, CA, 2010.
- Britz, Marjie T. *Computer Forensics and Cyber Crime an Introduction*, 3rd Edition, Pearson, Boston, MA, 2013.
- Casey, Eoghan, *Digital Evidence and Computer Crime: Forensic Science, Computers and the Internet*, Academic Press, Waltham, MA, 2011.
- Chapple, Mike, *Access Control, Authentication, and Public Key Infrastructure*, Jones & Bartlett, Burlington, MA, 2013.
- Dooley, John, *History of Cryptography and Cryptanalysis: Codes, Ciphers, and their Algorithms*, Springer, Berlin, 2019.
- Elbirt, Adam J., *Understanding and Applying Cryptography and Data Security*, 1st Edition, CRC Press, Boca Raton, FL, 2009.

- Hayes, Darren R. *A Practical Guide to Computer Forensics Investigations*, Pearson Education, Indianapolis, IN, 2015.
- Hoerl, Manual, *Secure Communication Protocols*, CreateSpace Publishing, Scotts Valley, CA, 2015.
- Luttgens, Jason T., Matthew Pepe, and Kevin Mandia, *Incident Response and Computer Forensics*, 3rd Edition, McGraw Hill Education, New York, 2014.
- Maras, Marie-Helen, *Computer Forensics: Cybercriminals, Laws, and Evidence*, 2nd Edition, Jones & Bartlett Learning, Burlington, MA, 2015.
- Miller, Phillip, *TCP/IP: The Ultimate Protocol Guide: Volume 2: Applications, Access and Data Security*, Brown Walker Press, Boca Raton, FL, 2009.
- Morrissey, Sean, *iOS Forensic Analysis: for iPhone, iPad, and iPod Touch*, Apress, New York, 2010.
- Paar, Christof and Pelzl Jan, *Understanding Cryptography a Textbook for Students and Practitioners*, 1st Edition, Springer, Berlin, 2017.
- Simpson, Gina, *Data Security and Cryptography*, Willford Press, Forest Hills, NY, 2019.
- Stamp, Mark, *Applied Cryptanalysis: Breaking Ciphers in the Real World*, Wiley-IEEE Press, Hoboken, NJ, 2007.

Chapter Summary

- Data Security is the process of keeping predetermined confidential or personal information private.
- Data Security involves implementing one or more methodologies aimed at keeping data safe.
- The practice of cryptography makes data in a computer system or on a storage media, illegible and meaningless.
- As a result of a strong dependency on algorithms as a means for protecting data applying adequate techniques for Data Security requires a strong mathematical background to the level of linear and differential equations.
- The strength of cryptography in protecting data is primarily centered on the algorithm used and the length of key used as input to that algorithm.

- Cryptanalysis is based on knowledge of the attacks used to interpret encrypted data and how the algorithm is "broken" in order to view the original data content.
- Digital signatures utilize a cryptographic technique called hashing and authenticate the sender of the encrypted data.
- Through Data Security integrity is preserved, while loss and corruption are prevented.
- When data is processed, it is normally changed in some way. Integrity describes the correctness of that change.
- Safeguards are needed to ensure that data has integrity by detecting mistakes or any malicious change to the data.
- The most obvious choice for protecting data is to keep it locked in a predetermined room.
- Data can be protected electronically by employing one of several forms of access control, which limits the availability of data to only individuals or systems that have been previously determined as a viable user of the data.
- Data moves from one location to another through the application of a set of rules called protocols. Appropriate use of each protocol will ensure that data is constantly secure when in transit.
- Once a physical location for data storage is identified, that facility should use safeguards such as: lock and key, biometrics, ID card scanning, or alarm systems as a means for allowing entry to only authorized individuals.
- Cryptography was originally designed to support data in transit. However, technology has evolved to the extent that personal data can be encrypted as a protective mechanism while it is being stored.
- Data should never be disposed of while still readable on electronic media. Many physical and electronic techniques exist, which allow for proper purging of data residing on devices that have exhausted their useful life.

Learning Objectives for the Data Security Knowledge Area

Mastery of the requisite learning outcomes for the Data Security knowledge area will be established through the student's ability to paraphrase and explicate the key contents of the knowledge units within this knowledge area (Bloom Levels Two and Three). In addition, the student will exhibit specific behaviors that demonstrate a capability to utilize the relevant concepts in common practical application. Specifically, the student will be able to paraphrase and explain the following twelve knowledge elements (CSEC, 2017):

1. Describe the purpose of cryptography and list the ways it is used in data communications.
2. Describe the following terms: cipher, cryptanalysis, cryptographic algorithm, and cryptology, and describe the two basic methods (ciphers) for transforming plaintext in ciphertext.
3. Explain how Public Key Infrastructure supports digital signing and encryption and discuss the limitations/vulnerabilities.
4. Discuss the dangers of inventing one's own cryptographic methods.
5. Describe which cryptographic protocols, tools, and techniques are appropriate for a given situation.
6. Explain the goals of end-to-end Data Security.
7. Describe what a digital investigation is, the sources of digital evidence, and the limitations of forensics.
8. Compare and contrast variety of forensics tools.
9. Explain the concepts of authentication, authorization, access control, and data integrity.
10. Explain the various authentication techniques and their strengths and weaknesses.
11. Explain the various possible attacks on passwords.
12. Describe the various techniques for data erasure.

Keywords

Cryptography – assurance that data cannot be read by unauthorized parties.

Forensics – the application of science to questions that are of interest to the legal profession.

Data Integrity and Authentication – practices that ensure that data is correct and verifying the identity of the people or systems accessing the data.

Access Control – application of principles that define the level of authorization to data.

Secure Communication Protocols – technical measures aimed toward secure transmission of data.

Cryptanalysis – techniques designed to break or better understand the capabilities of cryptographic algorithms.

Data Privacy – assurance of a fundamental right to digital privacy in virtual space.

Information Storage Security – fundamental principles that underlie and motivate effective and secure data storage and removal.

References

Brabant, Malcolm, Microchipping Humans Wields Great Promise, but Does it Pose Greater Risk? PBS News Hour, 2019. Accessed from www.pbs.org/newshour/show/human-microchipping-sparks-debate-over-privacy-exploitation, January 2019.

Brumfield, Cynthia. 11 New State Privacy and Security Laws Explained: Is Your Business Ready? CSO Communications, https://www.csoonline.com/article/3429608/11-new-state-privacy-and-security-laws-explained-is-your-business-ready.2019. html, accessed January 29, 2020.

Cichonski, Paul, Thomas Millar, Tim Grance, and Karen Scarfone, *Computer Security Incident Handling Guide: Recommendations of the National Institute of Standards and Technology*, Special Publication 800-61, Revision 2, National Institute of Standards and Technology, Gaithersburg, MD, 2012.

Kent, Karen, Suzanne Chevalier, Timothy Grance, and Hung Dang, *Guide to Integrating Forensic Techniques into Incident Response*, NIST Special Publication 800-86, National Institute of Standards and Technology, Gaithersburg, MD, 2006.

Maras, Marie-Helen, *Computer Forensics: Cybercriminals, Laws, and Evidence*, 2nd Edition, Jones & Bartlet Learning, Burlington, MA, 2015.

Miniwatts Marketing Group. Internet World Stats: Usage and Population Statistics, 2019. Accessed from www.internetworldstats.com/stats.htm, June 2019.

Nelson, Bill, Amelia Phillips, and Christopher Steuart, *Guide to Computer Forensics and Investigations*, 6th Edition, Cengage, Boston, MA, 2019.

NIST, CFTT: Computer Forensics Tools and Techniques Catalog, 2019. Accessed from https://toolcatalog.nist.gov/, January 2019.

Statista, Share of Households with a Computer at Home Worldwide from 2005 to 2018, 2019a. Accessed from www.statista.com/statistics/748551/worldwide-households-with-computer/, June 2019.

Statista, Number of Sent and Received e-mails per Day Worldwide from 2017 to 2023 (in Billions), 2019b. Accessed from www.statista.com/statistics/456500/daily-number-of-e-mails-worldwide/, June 2019.

SWGIT, Overview of SWGIT and the Use of Imaging Technology in the Criminal Justice System, 2010. Accessed from www.crime-scene-investigator.net/overview-of-swgit-and-the-use-of-imaging-technology-in-the-criminal-justice-system.html, June 2019.

4
SOFTWARE SECURITY

In this chapter, you will learn the following:

- The Software Security fundamental design principles
- How to apply least privilege to software functionality
- The concept of open design and abstraction
- The importance of security requirements and the roles they play in design
- Implementation issues that can affect the security of software
- Similarities and differences of static and dynamic analysis
- The affect that proper configuration and patching have on overall security of software
- Ethical issues in the development, testing, and vulnerability disclosure of software.

Building Pathways toward Software Security

Browsing through any IT security periodical, it is likely that you will come across several Software Security-related stories, from malware attacks that abuse a gullible user to install malicious software to widespread worm outbreaks that leverage software vulnerabilities to automatically spread from one system to another. Although the question still arises in why Software Security so difficult? The answer is complicated.

Both protection against and exploitation of security vulnerabilities crosscut through all layers of abstraction and involve human factors, usability, performance, system abstractions, and economic concerns. While attackers may target the weakest link, defenders must address all possible attack vectors. A single flaw is enough for an attacker to compromise a system while the defender must consider any feasible attack according to a given threat model.

It is important for students to have an appreciation that security and especially Software Security concerns affect all areas of our life.

We interact with complex interconnected software systems on a regular basis. Bugs or defects in these systems allow unauthorized access to our data or escalate their privileges such as installing malware. With such a high degree of impact, a user who uses software to make safe and critical decision must be particularly cautious. Additionally, to manage software, people across several layers of an organization must work together: managers, administrators, developers, and security researchers. A manager will decide on how much money to invest into a security solution or what security product to buy. Administrators must carefully reason about who gets which privileges. Developers must design and build secure software systems to protect the integrity, confidentiality, and availability of data given a specific access policy. Security researchers must be able to identify flaws and propose mitigations against weaknesses, vulnerabilities, or systematic attack vectors.

In practice, Software Security is the development and enforcement of policies through defense mechanisms over data and resources. Therefore, a knowledge base and appreciation that Software Security policies specify *what* we want to enforce and the defense mechanisms specify *how* we enforce the policy (i.e., an implementation/instance of a policy) becomes a vital requisite for understanding the underlying practices of Software Security. For example, Data Execution Prevention is a mechanism that enforces a Code Integrity Policy by guaranteeing each page of physical memory in a process address space is either writable or executable but never both. Through defined curricula, students must understand that *Software Security* is the area of security that focuses on testing, evaluating, improving, enforcing, and proving the *security* of software.

The CSEC2017 Software Security Knowledge Units

To form a common basis of understanding and to set the scene for Software Security, the CSEC2017 Software Security knowledge area focuses on the skills needed to develop and use software that in turn provide the necessary mechanisms to adequately protect the information that it produces and the system from which it resides. In large part, the overall security in IT system and data that it stores and manages is dependent on the security of both system and application software. Further, the security of software is dependent on the degree to which requirements meet software needs and how well the software is designed implemented, tested, procured, and maintained.

The knowledge area first introduces and defines basic Software Security principles. Once a foundation is built, emphasis is placed on security policy and mechanisms within each of the phases of the software life cycle (including supporting processes such as documentation, configuration management, and quality assurance). Finally, a discussion of integrating ethical behavior into secure software processes is provided, reminding us that in all facets of cybersecurity, the goal is to promote confidentiality, integrity, and availability, but we must continue to pursue security based on ethical behaviors established and standardized by the organization from which the software resides. The seven knowledge units in this knowledge area reflect the following (Figure 4.1):

- *Fundamental Principles* – basic concepts of secure software development
- *Design* – principles for architecture and design as they apply to security
- *Implementation* – principles of programming and integration as they apply to security

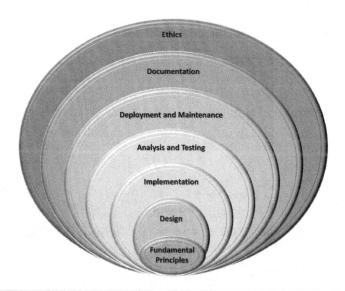

Figure 4.1 The Software Security knowledge units.

- *Analysis and Testing* – standard methods and models for assuring the build
- *Deployment and Maintenance* – principles of program acceptance and sustainment
- *Documentation* – principles for making the software visible and understandable
- *Ethics* – principles for ethical operation of the software.

Knowledge Unit One: Fundamental Principles

As the perception of security as a key artifact of quality software development has evolved, the understanding of what goes into the developing secure software has become a common expectation of many organizations. The challenge is in the learning curve. Most developers understand the activities and tasks associated with the software development life cycle (SDLC) but lack the years of lessons learned of underlying Software Security principles that affect each phase of development. In an effort to bridge this gap, the Fundamental Principles knowledge unit presents a set of practices derived from real-world experience that can help guide software developers in building more secure software (Figure 4.2).

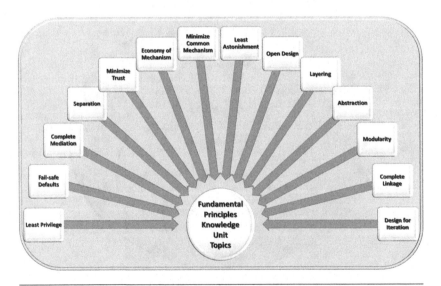

Figure 4.2 The Fundamental Principles knowledge unit topics.

Many of the principles introduced in this section of CSEC2017 are derived from the work of Jerome Saltzer and Michael Schroeder who were the first researchers to develop and communicate a set of high-level security principles in the context of protection mechanisms that serve as the foundation needed for designing and implementing secure software systems. These principles define effective practices that apply primarily to the decisions made regarding the architecture of software decisions. Further, they are necessary regardless of the platform or language of the software. You will notice that the principles, which do not necessarily guarantee security, at times may have an effect of the design of software that appears to be in opposition to each other, so appropriate trade-offs must be made. Software developers, whether they are developing new software, performing maintenance, or assessing existing software, should always apply these design principles as a guide and yardstick for making their software more secure.

CSEC2017 presents several principles, many from Saltzer and Schroeder's original work and a couple of others from other leaders in the Software Security space. What is important is that no two software systems are the same. There are no universal recipes for building each of the principles into the design of software. However, they help organizations make decisions in new situations using proven experience and industry best practice. By considering several principles, you can derive a greater degree of control over the requirements for Software Security and make more informed implementation decisions. In essence, the principles in this knowledge unit can and should be used to develop a definitive set of policies, standards, baselines, procedures, and guidelines that are integrated into and drive an organization's secure software development process. The following are the 14 basic concepts that underlie Software Security.

Least Privilege

One of the most fundamental concepts in security is *least privilege*. In the case of software, least privilege means that a user or interconnected system should have only the necessary rights and privileges to perform its current task with no additional rights and privileges. Limiting privileges limits the amount of harm that can be caused, thus limiting software exposure to damage. If it is required that different levels of security be assigned for separate tasks, it is better to switch security levels, rather than run all the time at a higher level of privilege.

Another issue that falls under the least privilege concept is the security context in which a software runs. All programs, scripts, and batch files run under the security context of a specific user on an operating system (OS). Thus, execution will be performed based on the specific permissions of the user. The infamous Sendmail exploit takes advantage of this design issue. Sendmail needs root-level access to accomplish much of its functionality, and hence, the entire program is run as root by a user. If the software was compromised after it had entered root access state, the attacker could obtain a root-level shell. The crux of this issue is that software should execute only in the security context that is needed for it to perform its duties successfully.

Fail-Safe Defaults

It is given that all systems will experience failures. The fail-safe design principle characterizes the importance that when a system experiences a failure, it should fail to a safe state. One form of implementation is to use the concept of explicit deny. Any function that is not specifically authorized is denied by default. When a system enters a failure state, the attributes associated with security, confidentiality, integrity, and availability need to be appropriately maintained. Availability is the attribute that tends to cause the greatest design difficulties. Ensuring that the design includes elements to degrade gracefully and return to normal operation through the shortest path assists in maintaining the resilience of the system. During design, it is important to consider the path associated with potential failure modes and how this path can be moderated to maintain system stability and control under failure conditions.

Complete Mediation

The principle of complete mediation states that when authorization is verified with respect to an object and an action, this verification occurs every time access is requested to that object. The system must be designed so that the authorization system is never circumvented, even with multiple, repeated accesses. Modern OSs and IT systems with properly configured authentication systems are very difficult to compromise directly, with most routes to compromise involving the bypassing of a critical system such as authentication. With this in mind, it is important during design to examine potential bypass situations and prevent them from becoming instantiated.

Separation of Duties

Another fundamental approach to security is separation of duties. Separation of duties ensures that for any given task, more than one individual needs to be involved. The critical path of tasks is split into multiple items, which are then spread across more than a single entity. By implementing a task in this manner, no single individual can abuse the system. A simple example might be a system where one individual is required to place an order and a separate person is needed to authorize the purchase.

While separation of duties is often learned within the context of system design, CSEC2017 frames the concept in that the same principles must be designed into a system. Software components enforce separation of duties when they require multiple conditions to be met before a task is considered complete. These multiple conditions can then be managed separately to enforce the checks and balances required by the system.

Minimize Trust

Care must be taken when interpreting this design principle. Later in this chapter, a discussion will ensue related to the need to designing software in such a way that all inputs are validated. This concept differs from what is under discussion, here. Security measures include people, operations, and technology, shown in Figure 4.3. Where technology is used, hardware, firmware, and software should be designed and implemented so that a minimum number of system elements need to be trusted in order to maintain the desired level of security. Equally important is to minimize the amount of software and hardware expected to provide the most secure functions for the system (as we discuss in the next topic).

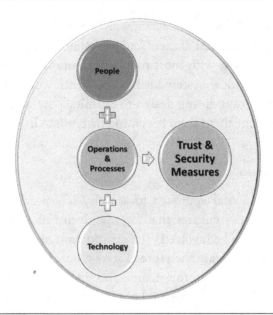

Figure 4.3 Trust and security measures.

The easiest approach to trust minimization is to assume that all external interconnected systems are insecure. Mechanisms should be in place such that the trust between systems is earned. But what is important, here, is that there should be a presumption that the security measures of an external system are different than those of a trusted internal system and design the System Security features accordingly.

Economy of Mechanism

This topic emphasizes the importance to keep the design of secure software as simple and small as possible. This well-known principle applies to any aspect of a system, but it deserves emphasis in a discussion of Software Security because design and implementation errors that result in unwanted access paths will not be noticed during normal use (since normal use usually does not include attempts to utilize improper access paths). As a result, techniques such as line-by-line inspection of software and physical examination of hardware that implements security mechanisms are necessary. For such techniques to be successful, a small and simple design is essential.

Minimize Common Mechanism

The message delivered through minimization of common mechanism (often referred to as "least common mechanism") is that a design method should prevent the inadvertent sharing of information. Having multiple processes share common mechanisms leads to a potential information pathway between users or processes. Having a mechanism that services a wide range of users or processes places a more significant burden on the design of that process to keep all pathways separate. When presented with a choice between a single process that operates on a range of supervisory and subordinate-level objects and/or a specialized process tailored to each, choosing the separate process is the better choice.

The concepts of least common mechanism and leveraging existing components can place a designer at a conflicting crossroad. One concept advocates reuse and the other separation. The choice is a case of determining the correct balance associated with the risk from each.

Least Astonishment

This topic (sometimes referred to as "psychological acceptability") emphasizes that users are a key part of software and its security. To include a user in the security of a system requires that the security aspects be designed so that they are least amount of complexity (the least astonishment) to the user. When a user is presented with a security system that appears to obstruct their productivity, the result will be the user working around the security aspects of the system. For instance, if a system prohibits the emailing of certain types of attachments, the user can encrypt the attachment, masking it from security, and perform the prohibited action anyway.

Ease of use tends to trump many functional aspects. The design of security in software systems needs to be transparent to the user, just like air – invisible, yet always there, serving the need. This places a burden on the designers; security is a critical functional element, yet one that should impose no burden on the user.

Open Design

CSEC2017 also recommends the introduction of security through obscurity. This approach has not been effective in the actual protection of the object within object-oriented software systems. Security through obscurity may make someone work harder to accomplish a task, but it does not provide actual security. This approach has been used in software to hide objects, like keys and passwords, buried in the source code. Reverse engineering and differential code analysis have proven more effective at discovering these secrets, eliminating this form of security.

The concept of open design states that the security of a system must be independent of the form of the security design. In essence, the algorithm that is used will be open and accessible and the security must not be dependent upon the design but rather on an element such as a key. Modern cryptography has employed this principle effectively; security depends upon the secrecy of the key, not the secrecy of the algorithm being employed.

Layering

This topic is the first of three that CSEC2017 recommends focusing on the design principles of modularization. However, a basis must be built first, by introducing the concept of Separation of Concern (SOC). Simply put, don't make one software component do a bunch of unrelated things. For example, the software component that sends information to another computer shouldn't be involved with helping the user select the information to be sent.

It all starts with design. A common practice is to design the software by decomposing the main goal into sub-goals and those sub-goals into sub-sub-goals and keep going until you can't decompose any longer, shown in Figure 4.4. Then start implementing yourself back up that chain, assigning each decomposed sub-goal to a class or a module or a function or whatever is the lowest level of granularity your language supports. Continue implementing backup of the chain of goals until you satisfy the top-level goal.

The SOCs comes in by keeping the connections between unrelated goals to the minimum, preferably none. As you do the design

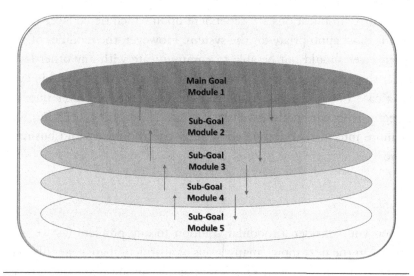

Figure 4.4 Layering for optimal software organization.

decomposition, from time to time you will find you have what might be considered an overseer goal that controls multiple sub-goals. It's at that point that the concerns converge. But because you have one overseer and the sub-goals don't talk to each other directly, the control and interaction become localized and simplified.

Based on the understanding of SOC, students can now approach an understanding of layering as several different layers defined, each performing tasks that progressively become closer to the machine instruction set. At the outer layer, the modules perform user interface operations. At the inner layer, components perform OS interfacing. Intermediate layers provide utility services and application software functions. These architectural styles are only a small subset of those available. Once requirements engineering uncovers the characteristics and constraints of the system to be built, the architectural style and/or combination of styles that best fits those characteristics and constraints can be chosen. For example, the application layer is often broken down into other layers that are expressed in terms of tiers. The most common tier architecture is called "n-tier" to denote modules existing on the client side, and a scalable number of servers (such as web, application, and database servers) hosting modules services support just the functionality of that server-side component.

Security implications are dependent upon which tiered layer structure is most appropriate for the system. However, the modules of any given layer should not be able to communicate with any other layer other than the one above or below. Put differently, there should never be a case in which the modules of the user interface layer interact directly with the modules of the database layer, thus, utilizing one or more intermediary layers containing control objects and business logic.

Abstraction

When you consider a modular solution to any problem (as we will discuss in the next topic), many levels of abstraction are generally evident. At the highest level of abstraction, a solution is stated in broad terms using the language of the problem environment. At lower levels of abstraction, a more detailed description of the solution is provided. Problem-oriented criteria are combined with implementation-oriented criteria in order to clearly state a solution. Finally, at the lowest level of abstraction, the solution is stated in a manner that can be directly implemented. As different levels of abstraction are developed, developers work to create both procedural and data abstractions. A procedural abstraction refers to a sequence of instructions that have a specific and limited function. The name of a procedural abstraction implies these functions, but specific details are not provided. For example, a procedural abstraction would be the word open for a door. Open implies a long sequence of procedural steps. Depending upon how an individual opens a door would dictate how many and which steps would be taken. A data abstraction is a named collection of data that describes a data object. In the context of the procedural abstraction open, we can define a data abstraction called door. Like any data object, the data abstraction for door would include a set of specific attributes that describe the door. The main idea is that the procedural abstraction open would make use of information contained in the attributes of the data abstraction door.

An important security characteristic about the relationship between procedural and data abstraction is that the procedural and data elements are completely hidden within each layer of abstraction; leaving only the interface between each layer exposed. Among other things, this allows changes to be made at each layer without affecting the components of other layers (unless there is a need to modify the means by which the layers interact).

Modularity

Modularity is the most common application of SOCs. Software is divided into separately named and addressable components, sometimes called modules, which are integrated to satisfy problem requirements. Many software developers will have difficulty arguing that modularity is perhaps the single artifact of software that allows it to be intellectually manageable. Very early forms of software development saw monolithic approaches to building software in which a large program may be composed of a single module. Such practices used for the complex software built today would be easily grasped by a software engineer. The number of control paths, span of reference, number of variables, and overall complexity would make understanding the flow of the processing close to impossible. A newer and more widely accepted approach is to break the design into many modules, hoping to make understanding easier and, as a consequence, reduce the cost required to build the software.

Recalling our discussion of SOCs and abstraction, it is possible to conclude that if you subdivide software indefinitely, the effort required to develop it will become relatively small. Unfortunately, other forces come into play, causing this conclusion to be (sadly) invalid. The effort (cost) to develop an individual software module does decrease as the total number of modules increases. Given the same set of requirements, more modules mean smaller individual size. However, as the number of modules grows, the effort (cost) associated with integrating the modules also grows. As the effort cost increases, so too does the cost of the entire software.

You modularize a design (and the resulting software) so that development can be more easily planned; software increments can be defined and delivered; changes can be more easily accommodated; testing and debugging can be conducted more efficiently, and long-term maintenance can be conducted without serious side effects. The net result, when each of these criteria become a priority in the design process, is software that provides a greater depth of overall security.

Complete Linkage

In the standard context of software engineering, it is suggested that when a software product is completely developed and about to be deployed, the unit, integration, volume, and system test cases that have been performed were developed based on the prescribed criteria defined in the design specification and the design specification developed based on requirements identified within the software requirements specification (SRS). Students should be guided toward understanding that by adding security into the mix of functional and nonfunctional requirements, the same linkage must exist to ensure proper security measures have been considered, designed, and implemented. The most appropriate process for gaining this assurance is through qualification testing.

The general outcome of qualification testing is to provide a definitive answer to two questions. First, does the software meet the requirements specified in the SRS? The process of answering this question is known as verification. The second is, do the requirements and the resulting software meet the intended quality needs of the acquiring organization? The process of answering this question is known as validation.

Through a series of previously documented test cases (separate from those described above) and structured audits, the primary purpose of software qualification testing is to demonstrate compliance with levels of design, performance, security, and quality specified for the software. The tests are also intended to demonstrate that the system meets or exceeds the requirements of the acquiring organization.

The scope and detail of qualification requirements should be tailored to the design and complexity of the software being evaluated. The qualification test procedure is intended to discover defects or security vulnerabilities in design and system operation that could make the software stop working.

The tests must be designed not only to evaluate compliance with the software requirement specification but with the requirements of the acquiring organization and its own standards and legal obligations as well. The testing includes selective in-depth examination of the software, the inspection and evaluation of documentation, and optional tests that verify performance and function under normal and abnormal conditions.

Design for Iteration

Students should understand that in software engineering changes to software are inevitable. Those changes can occur through the progression of iteration approaches to software development or through the maintenance phase of the life cycle for existing software. Such changes can be as simple as modifying an interface to simplify its usage or as complex as correcting major functionality that provides interfaces to other software or even systems of supply chain partners. Regardless of the purpose and extent of the changes, the design specification for the initial software outlay and each successive iteration must consider that changes to the software can have a dramatic effect on security. With that in mind, the design specification must constantly be matched to the security requirements of the software in order to provide consistency for the security of the existing software environment.

Knowledge Unit Two: Design

The construction of secure of secure system or application infrastructure begins with requirements and becomes built in if designed as part of the design phase of the secure development life cycle. Designing in the security requirements allows the coding and implementation phases to create a more robust and secure software product (Figure 4.5).

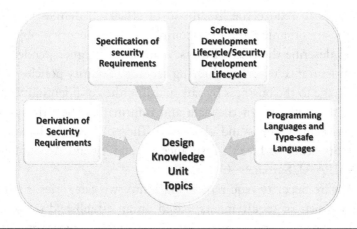

Figure 4.5   The Design knowledge unit topics.

What needs to be emphasized, however, is the context from which CSEC2017 recommends design topics. Those familiar with the traditional software life cycles know that requirements are elicited and specified prior to the design phase in which those requirements are constructed to implementable solutions. The guideline approaches this knowledge unit from the perspective the design of software doesn't start after requirements are identified. Rather, to build secure software, vulnerabilities must be identified and protective measures considered from the point at which the need for software is established and carried forward throughout the entire development process. Thus, there are four major topics in the Design knowledge unit: *Derivation of security requirements*, *Specification of security requirements*, *Software development life cycle/Security development life cycle*, and *Programming languages and type-safe languages*.

Derivation of Security Requirements

The CSEC2017 guideline leads this topic off with an extremely vital perception. That is, Software Security requirements must be derived based on business, mission, and other objectives. This is an important point and one that should not be taken lightly. Before a discussion of Software Security requirements can take place, there is value in understanding the principles associated with implementation of organization-wide security policy.

Security policy allows an organization to set security practices and procedures to reduce the likelihood of attack. It defines rules that regulate an organization in accomplishing its security objectives. Policies describe the roles of users, managers, designers, coders, and quality assurance team in achieving security. Security policies reduce the damage to the business by safeguarding the confidentiality, availability, and integrity of the data and information. Security policies identify security needs and objectives. The policies may include the regulatory acts like Health Insurance Portability and Accountability Act (HIPAA), Sarbanes–Oxley, etc.

Software Security requirements fall into two categories. First category consists of requirements, based on an established set of policies, for the software's security functions (such as cryptographic and user authentication functions). This is followed by Software Security requirements for the software's own security properties and consistently secure behaviors.

Since software development follows a series of processes (the blueprint), it is of paramount importance that security requirements are determined alongside the functional and business requirements. In other words, consider Software Security requirements to be an integral part of the blueprint itself and involve a security professional. Performing a Software Security requirements analysis requires a good understanding of security principles and their applicability in the design specification. This in turn makes this activity the foundation of creating secure software. As shown in Figure 4.6, the tasks within the security requirements elicitation process include the following:

- *Conducting interviews with stakeholders*: The goal is to engage stakeholders at the beginning of the design process so that they not only understand their business or functional needs but also are able to map Software Security requirements (including privacy and intellectual property protection).
- *Identifying applicable policies and standards*: Identify and conduct reviews of security policies and standards, as well as map applicable security controls to functional specifications so that software development takes into consideration the established policies and standards.

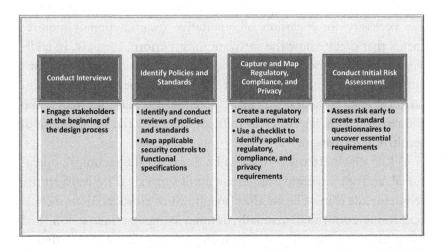

Figure 4.6 The security requirements elicitation process.

- *Capturing and mapping regulatory, compliance, and privacy considerations*: During this activity, the approach is to create a regulatory compliance matrix and use the same as a checklist to identify applicable regulatory (legal), compliance, as well as privacy requirements.
- *Conducting initial risk assessment*: Assessing risk early on can help create standard questionnaires which can uncover the essential requirements of confidentiality, integrity, and availability.

Specification of Security Requirements

Student must be introduced to the point that once technical, operational, and administrative security requirements have been identified, they must be documented in a specification commonly referred to as a software requirements specification (SRS). This specification provides details that will become important for issuing a request for proposals, formulating the security design for the software, and eventual development of test cases used for validation and verification. Additionally, it serves as a communicative resource for reiterating the identified security requirements to the stakeholders.

There are several industry standards that outline the contents of an SRS, and each stipulate that it must contain a valid set of functional and qualitative requirements. Additionally, each emphasizes the necessity for inclusion of qualitative (nonfunctional) requirements that dictate how the software must perform securely. In addition to performance requirements, the specification standard each emphasize the need to document methods of operation and maintenance, environmental influence, potential for personal injury, and the requirements necessary to mitigate the potential compromise of sensitive information.

While much attention tends to be drawn to the technical, operational, and administrative requirements of software, Physical Security requirements cannot be an afterthought. Such considerations include operations performed manually, human–computer interaction, and physical constraints that may limit the software in some way that in term will put security in jeopardy.

Software Development Life Cycle/Security Development Life Cycle

This topic of CSEC2017 recommends understanding of the SDLC and security life cycle as a series of steps, or phases, that provide a framework for developing and securing software while managing it through its entire life cycle. Although there's no specific technique or single way to develop applications and software components, it is important that there be understanding of established methodologies that organizations use and models they follow to address different challenges and goals. These methodologies and models typically revolve around a standard, such as ISO/IEC 12207, which establishes guidelines for the development, acquisition, and configuration of software systems. As shown in Figure 4.7, the most frequently used software development models include the following:

- *Waterfall*: This technique applies a traditional approach to software development. Development teams complete an entire phase of the project before moving on to the next step or phase. As a result, business results are delivered at a single stage rather than in an iterative framework.

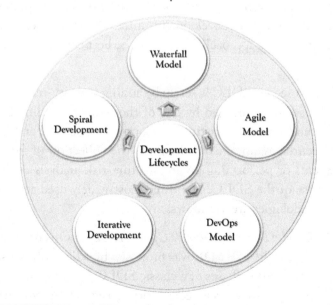

Figure 4.7 Software development life cycle models.

- *Agile*: Adaptive planning, evolutionary development, fast delivery, continuous improvement, and a highly rapid and flexible response to external factors are all key components of an Agile approach. Developers rely on a highly collaborative, cross-functional framework – with a clear set of principles and objectives – to speed development processes.
- *DevOps*: This technique combines "development" and "operations" functions in order to build a framework focused on collaboration and communication. It aims to automate processes and introduce an environment focused on continuous development. Learn how Veracode enables DevOps.
- *Iterative Development*: As the name implies, iterative software development focuses on an incremental approach to coding. The approach revolves around shorter development cycles that typically tackle smaller pieces of development. It also incorporates repeated cycles: an initialization step, an iteration step, and a project control list. Iterative development is typically used for large projects.
- *Spiral Development*: This framework incorporates different models based on what works best in a given development process or situation. As a result, it may rely on waterfall, Agile, or DevOps for different components or projects that fit under the same software development initiative. Spiral uses a risk-based analysis approach to identify the best choice for a given situation.

Simply put, a secure SDLC is set up by adding security-related activities (such as those proposed by one of the industry leading security maturity models) to an existing development process. For example, writing security requirements alongside the collection of functional requirements or performing an architecture risk analysis during the design phase of the SDLC. The three most widely used security life cycle methodologies are as follows:

- *MS Security Development Life Cycle (MS SDL)*: One of the first of its kind, the MS SDL was proposed by Microsoft in association with the phases of a classic SDLC.
- *NIST SP 800-160*: Provides security considerations within the SDLC. Standards were developed by the National Institute

of Standards and Technology to be observed by U.S. federal agencies.

• *OWASP CLASP* (*Comprehensive, Lightweight Application Security Process*): Simple to implement and based on the MS SDL. It also maps the security activities to roles in an organization.

Programming Languages and Type-Safe Languages

Too often incorrect conclusions are made that insecure software is only the fault of a software engineer programming application to the extent that security requirements are missed and thus vulnerabilities within the application become apparent. While in some cases failure to implement security requirements does justify the extent of vulnerabilities within applications, CSEC2017 recommends emphasis on the vulnerabilities that are embedded within each of the programming languages that could be used for development. It would not be an exaggeration to state that there is no programming language that is completely secure. In an effort to foster awareness of known programming language vulnerabilities and a defined set of rules for eliminating those vulnerabilities, the Software Engineering Institute (SEI) has developed a set a coding standards, for many of the most widely used languages, that software engineers can use to mitigate the risks imposed within the built-in components of the language.

Secure coding standards are language-specific rules and recommended practices that provide for secure programming. It is one thing to describe sources of vulnerabilities and errors in programs; it is another matter to prescribe forms that, when implemented, will preclude the specific sets of vulnerabilities and exploitable conditions found in typical code.

Application programming can be considered a form of manufacturing. Requirements are turned into value-added product at the end of a series of business processes. Controlling these processes and making them repeatable is one of the objectives of a secure development life cycle. One of the tools an organization can use to achieve this objective is the adoption of an enterprise-specific set of secure coding standards.

Organizations should adopt the use of a secure application development framework as part of their secure development life cycle process. Because secure coding guidelines have been published for most common languages, adoption of these practices is an important part of secure coding standards in an enterprise. Adapting and adopting industry best practices are also important elements in the secure development life cycle.

One common problem in many programs results from poor error trapping and handling. This is a problem that can benefit from an enterprise rule where all exceptions and errors are trapped by the generating function and then handled in such a manner so as not to divulge internal information to external users.

CSEC2017 also recommends awareness that utilizing the most appropriate language will also circumvent security issues. If possible, type-safe programming languages (such as Java, C#, Python, or Ruby) should be used. Type safety is the extent to which a programming language prevents errors resulting from different data types in a program. Type safety can be enforced either statically at compile time or dynamically at runtime to prevent errors. Type safety is linked to memory safety. Type-safe code will not inadvertently access arbitrary locations of memory outside the expected memory range. Type safety defines all variables, and this typing defines the memory lengths. One of the results of this definition is that type-safe programming resolves many memory-related issues automatically.

Knowledge Unit Three: Implementation

The implementation, or coding, phase of secure software development is the straightforward application of secure coding practices in a programming language to achieve design objectives. The use of approved languages, functions, and libraries is paramount, with the removal of deprecated functions and recoding of legacy code as required. The use of static program checkers to find common errors is intended to ensure coding standards are maintained (Figure 4.8).

Important to note is that the CSEC2017 recommendations do not include introduction to programming skills. Rather, the assumption is made that the student already has introductory or intermediate-level programming background and the topics presented suggest the

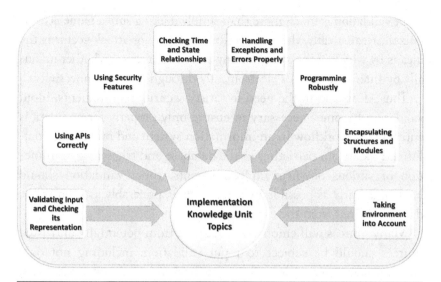

Figure 4.8 Implementation knowledge unit topics.

means by which those skills can be used to code system or application software securely. There are seven highly logical topics in the Implementation knowledge unit: (1) *Validating input and checking its representation*, (2) *Using APIs correctly*, (3) *Using security features*, (4) *Handling exceptions and errors properly*, (5) *Programming robustly*, (6) *Encapsulating structures and modules*, and (7) *Taking environment into account*.

Validating Input and Checking Its Representation

While CSEC2017 recommends the introduction of input validation only within the context of implementation, it should be emphasized that the most vulnerable part of software is the functionality in which any input is accepted. With that in mind, it follows that this topic is likely to arise in many other conceptual discussions related to secure software development.

From the early days of software engineering, when most business applications were housed on mainframes and coded in COBOL, programmers were taught to validate input. In those early days of business computing, supply chain interconnectivity was less prominent and the validation was limited to making sure that the user formatted a date of birth (DOB) correctly. As secure software has become a priority, input validation is much more than simply making sure a name is capitalized. Realistically, the most common source for attack vector is the means by which input can enter any software product (whether manually by Internet clients or electronically through system connectivity).

Thus, if we add in the need to satisfy security requirements, input validation becomes necessary to ensure only properly formed data is entering the workflow in an information system and preventing malformed data from persisting in the database and triggering malfunction of various downstream components. Input validation should happen as early as possible in the data flow, preferably as soon as the data is received from the external party.

Many sources will emphasize that data from potentially untrusted sources should be subject to input validation, including not only Internet-facing web clients but also backend feeds over extranets, from suppliers, partners, vendors, or regulators, each of which may be compromised on their own and start sending malformed data. We recommend emphasis that ALL input be validated regardless of the level of trust that has already been established with the external party.

Another form of input validation that should be introduced is called bounds checking. The objective of validating arrays and buffers is to ensure that only the amount and range of data originally allocated for the storage location is what resides in memory. A popular form of attack called "buffer bashing" will cause memory locations adjacent to an array or buffer to be maliciously filled program control information that will intentionally point to injected code putting your system at risk. Array bounds checking and buffer overflow validation techniques are the most common approach for ensuring such memory management is being performed legitimately.

Using API's Correctly

Interconnection between internal and external software systems is a vital aspect of understanding software principles. However, CSEC2017 suggests that a student attempting to understand secure software is likely not going to be aware of the purpose of application programming interfaces (APIs). Therefore, introduction to software interfaces will be necessary before further discussion about secure interfaces can be entertained.

APIs define how software components are connected to and interacted with. Modern software development is done in a modular fashion, using APIs to connect the functionality of the various modules. APIs are significant in that they represent entry points into software. The attack surface analysis and threat model should identify the APIs that could be attacked and the mitigation plans to limit the risk. Third-party APIs that are being included as part of the application should also be examined and errors or issues be mitigated as part of the SDL process. Older, weak, and deprecated APIs should be identified and not allowed into the final application.

On all interface inputs into your application, it is important to have the appropriate level of authentication. It is also important to audit the external interactions for any privileged operations performed via an interface.

Using Security Features

As can be seen by the topics under discussion in this knowledge unit and other resources available that are related to software implementation, there is a tremendous amount of security features that should be built into software in order to make it truly secure. Secure software curricula would do well to introduce as many security features as possible. In this topic, CSEC2017 emphasizes just two features students must have knowledge: use of cryptographic randomness and proper procedures for restricting process privileges.

In Chapter 3, we discussed the importance of cryptography as a means for protecting sensitive data throughout its entire life cycle (including as it is being created and/or processed). We discussed that only approved cryptographic libraries should be used and that attention should be made to the type of algorithms used and key length. One additional area of cryptography that should be of particular concern to software developers relates to the random number function. In short, the pseudorandom function that is built into most libraries may appear random and have statistically random properties, but it is not sufficiently random for cryptographic use. Cryptographically sufficient random number functions are available in approved cryptographic libraries and should be used for all cryptographic random calculations.

Returning to the discussion of the design principle "Least Privilege" introduced earlier in the chapter, that discussion was within the context of users being given the least amount of privileges necessary within system or application software to perform their role. Students must also be introduced to least privilege from a process perspective. Most processes (or objects) within a software system relay on the functionality of other processes and the capabilities of communication between them. As much as users must be assigned specific access levels, so too do the processes within software. As one process requests communication with another, appropriate authority must be verified and authentication functionality performed.

Checking Time and State Relationships

In a day when at any moment software can be exploited, it follows that we can no longer assume that processes are completed at the expected time, performed on the correct data, and that each process is completed as expected. CSEC2017 recommends that curricula emphasize "checks and balances" be coded directly into the software to ensure that what requirements of the software are accomplished. In the case where one process must complete before another begins, e.g., instructions can be coded into the second process that confirm proper conformance to required functionality of the first, before further processing is performed.

Handling Exceptions and Errors Properly

In this topic, CSEC2017 emphasizes that no application is perfect, and given enough time, they will all experience failure. How an application detects and handles failures is important to a security professionals knowledge base. Some errors are user driven; some can be unexpected consequences or programmatic errors. The challenge is in how the application responds when an error occurs. This is referred to as error handling. The specific coding aspect of error handling is referred to as exception management.

When errors are detected and processed by an application, it is important for the correct processes to be initiated. If logging of critical information is a proper course of action, one must take care not to expose sensitive information such as personally identifiable information (PII) in the log entries. If information is being sent to the screen or terminal, then again, one must take care as to what is displayed. Disclosing paths, locations, passwords, user ids, or any of a myriad of other information that would be useful to an adversary should be avoided.

Exception management is the programmatic response to the occurrence of an exception during the operation of a program. Properly coded for exceptions are handled by special functions in code referred to as exception handlers. Exception handlers can be designed to specifically address known exceptions and handle them according to pre-established business rules.

There are some broad classes of exceptions that are routinely trapped and handled by software. Arithmetic overflows are a prime example. Properly coded for, trapped, and handled with business logic, this type of error can be handled inside software itself. Determining appropriate recovery values from arithmetic errors is something that the application is well positioned to do and something that the OS is not.

Part of the development of an application should be an examination of the ways in which the application could fail and also the correct ways to address those failures. This is a means of defensive programming, for if the exceptions are not trapped and handled by the application, they will be handled by the OS. The OS does not have the embedded knowledge necessary to properly handle the exceptions.

Exceptions are typically not security issues; however, unhandled exceptions can become security issues. If the application properly handles an exception, then ultimately through logging of the condition and later correction by the development team, rare, random issues can be detected and fixed over the course of versions. Exceptions that are unhandled by the application or left to the OS to handle are the ones where issues such as privilege escalation typically occur.

Programming Robustly

There is a big difference between the approach taken by a software developer and that taken by someone attacking the software. A developer typically approaches programming based on what it is intended to do. In other words, they are coding the software to perform specific tasks based on functional requirements identified in software requirements and design specifications. An attacker, on the other hand, is more interested in what an application can be made to do and operates on the principle that "any action not specifically denied, is allowed." To address this, programmers cannot sure assume that the functionality they are building is truly secure. Rather, they must be defensive in their programming. Put differently, rather than assuming that the software being developed won't be exploited, assume that there is always a chance it will.

Programming robustly requires that programmers take into consideration all of the topics that have been discussed in this knowledge unit. Specifically, CSEC2017 recommends that the following additional concepts be added into Software Security curricula, shown in Figure 4.9:

- If programming at the system level, only memory that has been allocated should be deallocated.
- All variables (regardless of their purpose) should be initialized. Some programming languages provide the initialization by default. The best practice is not to assume the compiler will default the correct value into a variable. Programmers must hard code the initial values directly into the code.
- Ensure that behaviors that are utilized within code are appropriately defined.

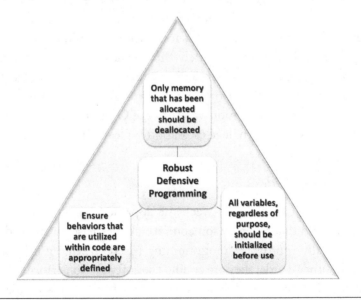

Figure 4.9 Robust defensive programming concepts.

Encapsulating Structures and Modules

CSEC2017 recognizes that students within a security curriculum will likely have little, if any, programming background (much less have an understanding of object-oriented technology). Before introducing any of the topics in this knowledge unit, a conceptual introduction to or review of object-oriented programming is imperative.

In many instances, there is value in beginning the introduction with an explanation of the structured top-down approach to programming. In understanding the structured approach, students will gain the conceptual knowledge of breaking program functionality into individual modularized tasks that are called upon during the operation of the program at which time the task must be completed.

Object-oriented programming is also modularized; however, the functionality of the program is performed by taking advantage of data and modularized behaviors (called methods) encapsulated (or hidden) within each instance of an object. Object-oriented programs operate through the capability of exchanging messages created and processed using the encapsulated data and methods. Emphasis must be placed on designing object-oriented programs in such a way that authorization and authentication must be performed before any message exchanges between objects at any layer of the software system.

Taking Environment into Account

One of the fundamental practices that has been used since the early days of programming is to type information that the software will use each time it executes directly into the code. This is known as hard coding. CSEC2017 recognizes that one problem that has evolved over the years is that software engineers have become much more relaxed in what they hard code into source code; to the extent that sensitive data is being exposed to anyone that can gain access to the program source.

Students must understand that hard-coding passwords, encryption keys, and other sensitive data into programs has several serious drawbacks. First, it makes them difficult to change. Yes, a program update can change them, but this is a messy way of managing secret data. But most importantly, they will not stay secret. With some simple techniques, hackers can reverse-engineer code and, through a series of analysis steps, determine the location and value of the secret key. This has happened to some large firms with serious consequences in a very public forum. This is easy to check for during code walkthroughs and should never be allowed in code.

Knowledge Unit Four: Analysis and Testing

In the conventional sense, as modules are coded by the development team, they progress through a series of individual and integrative tests to validate and verify functional requirements have been satisfied and that the code is error free. In this knowledge unit, CSEC2017 makes recommendations for inclusion of introductory material to the common testing techniques that have been a vital task within software engineering for many years (Figure 4.10).

However, when coding is being performed, tools and techniques can also be used to assist in the assessment at the security level. Code can be analyzed, either statically or dynamically to find weaknesses and vulnerabilities. Coming out of a security curriculum, students should understand that code analysis can be performed at virtually any level of development, from unit level to subsystem to system to complete application. The higher the level, the greater the test space and more complex the analysis. When the analysis is done by teams of humans reading the code, typically at the smaller unit level, it is

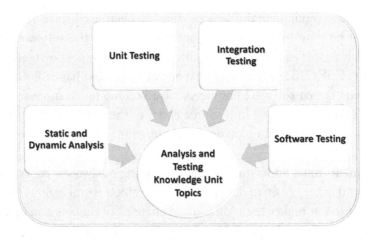

Figure 4.10   Analysis and Testing knowledge unit topics.

referred to as code reviews. Code analysis should be done at every level of development, because the sooner that weaknesses and vulnerabilities are discovered, the easier they are to fix. Issues found in design are cheaper to fix than those found in coding, which are cheaper than those found in final testing, and all of these are cheaper than fixing errors once the software has been deployed. There are four clearly relevant topics in the Analysis and Testing knowledge unit: (1) *Static and dynamic analysis*, (2) *Unit testing*, (3) *Integration testing*, and (4) *Software testing*.

Static and Dynamic Analysis

Static code analysis is performed by examining the code without being executed. This analysis can be performed on both source and object code bases. The term source code is typically used to designate the high-level language code, although technically, source code is the original code base in any form, from high language to machine code. Static analysis can be performed by humans or tools, with humans, the analysis is limited to the high-level language, while tools can be used against virtually any form of code base. For that reason, static code analysis is frequently performed using automated tools. These tools are given a variety of names but are commonly called source code analyzers. Sometimes, extra phrases, such as binary scanners or byte code scanners, are used to differentiate the tools. Static tools use a variety of mechanisms to search for weaknesses and vulnerabilities. Automated tools can provide advantages when checking syntax, approved function/library calls, and examining rules and semantics associated with logic and calls. They can catch elements a human might overlook.

Dynamic analysis is performed while the software is executed, either on a target or emulated system. The system is provided specific test inputs designed to produce predetermined forms of behavior. Dynamic analysis can be particularly important on embedded systems, where a high degree of operational autonomy is expected.

Dynamic analysis requires specialized automation to perform each specific test. There are dynamic test suites designed to monitor operations for programs that have high degrees of parallel functions. Security testing features within those suites include thread-checking routines to ensure multicore processors and software are managing threads correctly. Additionally, there are also programs designed to detect other security vulnerabilities such as race conditions and memory addressing errors.

Unit Testing

Unit testing focuses verification efforts on the smallest unit of software design, the software component, or module. Using the design specification as a guide, important control paths are tested to uncover errors within the boundary of the module. Generally, the developer is attempting to match the error-free functionality of the module to what has been defined in the specification. It is through unit testing that the developer will also perform such analysis as appropriate access to the process, input validation, and array out-of-bounds checking. The unit test focuses on the internal processing logic and data structures within the specific module.

In the context of security, the student should be made aware that through unit testing, the module interface is tested to ensure that information properly flows into and out of the program unit under test. Local data structures are examined to ensure that data stored temporarily maintains its integrity during all steps of execution. All independent paths through the process are tested to ensure that all statements in a module have been executed at least once. Boundary conditions are tested to ensure that the module operates properly at boundaries established to limit or restrict processing. And finally, all error-handling paths are tested.

Integration Testing

A student in a cybersecurity program might ask the seemingly legitimate question once all modules have been unit tested: "If they all work individually, why do you doubt that they'll work when we put them together?" The problem, of course, is "putting them together" is interfacing (which CSEC2017 strongly emphasizes as a viable vulnerability within software). Data can be lost across an interface; one component can have an inadvertent, adverse effect on another; subfunctions, when combined, may not produce the desired major function; individually acceptable imprecision may be magnified to unacceptable levels; global data structures can present problems. Sadly, the list goes on and on.

Integration testing is a systematic technique for constructing a secure software architecture while at the same time conducting tests to uncover errors associated with interfacing. The objective is to take unit-tested software components and build a program structure that has been dictated by design and exhibit the desired level of security risk tolerance.

Software Testing

While CSEC2017 refers to this topic as "software testing," the more common term used in software circles is "validation testing." In validation testing it begins at the culmination of integration testing, at which point individual software components have been thoroughly tested, the software is completely assembled as a package, and all modularized security and interfacing errors have been uncovered and corrected. At the validation or system level, the distinction between different software categories disappears. Testing focuses on user-visible actions and user-recognizable output from the system. Put differently, the main focus is on providing a completely tested, quality software product that meets the security requirements for the software project and conforms to all established Organizational Security policies.

Knowledge Unit Five: Deployment and Maintenance

A review of the Software Security design principles that were discussed earlier in this chapter provides an example of a misconception software engineers have regarding securing software artifacts. That is, there is tremendous emphasis on building security into software during the requirements analysis, design, and implementation phases of the SDLC, with very little consideration given to the need to carry forward a priority for security into deployment (which isn't necessarily a defined phase of the life cycle but is rolled into the activities of implementation), in addition to operations and maintenance life cycle phases. This knowledge unit makes a direct assertion that Software Security curricula should include the important security implications within the scope of deployment, operations, and maintenance (Figure 4.11).

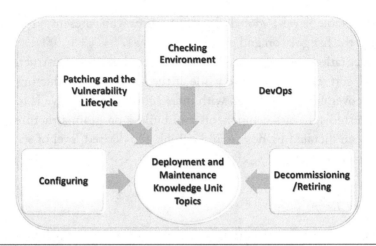

Figure 4.11   Deployment and Maintenance knowledge unit topics.

The main objective of the software deployment activity is to ensure that the software is embedded in the existing systems in an approved state of correctness and that the necessary strategic planning is done to ensure operational effectiveness. In essence, deployment is part of a short, practical, transitionary phase of the life cycle. Nevertheless, because they set the tone for operational use, the tasks performed have long-term implications for the overall success of the functionality of the software and the system from which it is embedded.

The purpose of the deployment activity is to embed a product that meets the agreed-upon requirements into the target environment. In order to execute this process effectively, it is necessary to develop a strategy and criteria for appropriate installation and configuration. These criteria must allow the stakeholders in the system, normally the customer and supplier, to demonstrate compliance with the software requirements specified in the contract. The product is then configured within the target environment and deployed for use. Its readiness for use in its intended environment is assured by tests and reviews. This is all done based on a plan that the stakeholders have prepared in advance of the deployment activity. Once the software is deployed, the operations and maintenance phases of the life cycle are engaged.

As the name implies, the purpose of the software operations phase is to securely "operate" the software product in its deployed environment. Essentially, this means that there is a major focus on the assurance of product effectiveness, as well as product support for the user community. Additionally, since the operations process almost always involves attention to the hardware, the operational activities it applies to software assurance should also be applied to hardware. Because the operations process is an ongoing organizational function, it too requires a strategy to guide its everyday execution. That strategy centers on getting a standard definition of the terms, conditions, and criteria that will be used to judge the quality of the execution of the product within its intended environment.

The operations phase involves a diverse set of activities, which are performed across the entire organization. Therefore, an appropriate set of standard guidelines and work instructions, which include standard security practices, should be developed and publicized to guide the execution of the intended software and system functionality. The overall goal is to define and establish a stable, routine set of activities and tasks to ensure the proper secure operation of each system, software product, or software service within the organization.

The main purpose of the software maintenance phase is to provide cost-effective modifications and operational support for each of the software artifacts within the organization. Additionally, maintenance provides ad hoc services for the organization's stakeholders, including such activities as training or operating a help desk. In real-world practice, maintenance goes hand in hand with the operations phase. For that reason, today, the two phases are commonly referred in combination as "sustainability." Normally, the maintenance phase involves those activities and tasks that are typically undertaken by the organizational entity that has been designated to fulfill this role. However, since maintenance is also likely to entail other organizational processes, specifically development, it must be understood that the maintenance operation should never function as a stand-alone element of the organization.

In general, maintenance is composed of planning, control, and assurance and communication activities. In effect, the maintenance process originates from a user-generated request to change, modify, or enhance an existing system, software product, or service. The goal of maintenance is to control those changes in such a way that the integrity and quality of the product are preserved. In practice, the execution of the maintenance process itself is concerned primarily with the consistent documentation and tracking of information about the artifact. In conjunction with the routine practices of everyday housekeeping, the maintainer may also be required to perform activities that would normally be associated with development.

CSEC2017 considers deployment, operations, and maintenance to be vital components to security curricula. To that extent, it is recommended that students be provided introduction to: secure software configuration, patch management and implications of the vulnerability life cycle, secure software environment assurance, concepts of DevOps, and secure software decommission and retirement. Thus, shown in Figure 4.11, there are five logical elements to the Sustainment knowledge area: (1) Configuring, (2) Patching and the vulnerability life cycle, (3) Checking environment, (4) DevOps, and (5) Decommissioning/retiring.

Configuring

This topic can mean many different things depending upon what context it is put into with regard to the overall secure software deployment process. We would argue that the CSEC2017 authors of this knowledge area intended for security curricula to contain material related to providing the proper configuration of software, according to defined requirements, as it is being installed. Another term that can be used within this context is "bootstrapping." Performing the practice of bootstrapping to any product or process implies a set of operations that will both properly launch intended functionality and ensure its correctness.

Considering the technical aspects of deployment of software, bootstrapping tends to entail any one-shot process that ensures the correctness of the initial configuration. That includes setting the proper defaults and execution parameters, as well as ensuring the accuracy and correctness of the security features in the operational product. Examples of this would be the configuration of the reference monitor settings in the OS to ensure the desired level of access control and the definition of privacy, security, and public key infrastructure management settings to ensure effective protection of information.

Patching and the Vulnerability Life Cycle

Oftentimes the activation of the processes within software maintenance is necessary to fix vulnerabilities or bugs that result from patches that have been created by vendors and installed into applications. There are numerous methods of delivery and packaging of patches from a vendor, and each patch can be labeled as either a patch, hot fix, or result of quick fix engineering (QFE). The important point that CSEC2017 makes in its recommendation isn't in the naming but in what the patch changes in the software. Because patches are issued as a form of repair, the questions that need to be understood before blindly applying them in production are, "What does the patch repair?" and "Is it necessary to do so in production?"

Students should be made aware that patch release schedules vary, from immediate to regularly scheduled events per a previously determined calendar date. A good example relates to how Microsoft releases patches on what has been coined "Patch Tuesday." Frequently, patches are packaged together upon release, making the operational implementation easier to implement. However, there are times when large groups of patches are bundled together into larger delivery mechanisms called service packs. Service packs primarily exist to simplify new installations, bringing them up to date with current release levels with less effort than applying the myriad of individual patches.

One of the challenges associated with the patching of software is in the regression testing of the patch against all of the different configurations of software to ensure that a fix for one problem does not create other problems. In short, regression testing examines changes to one change for how that change will affect other software components. Although most software users rely upon the vendor to perform regression tests before releasing patches in order to ensure that what they receive provides the value needed, software vendors are handicapped in their ability to completely perform this task. Only the end users can completely model the software in the enterprise as deployed, making the final level of regression testing one that should be done prior to introducing the patch into the production environment.

Checking Environment

A topic that tends to get little attention within Software Security curricula but is worth much more is the environment from which the software will operate. Software is deployed in an enterprise environment where its functional processes are rarely performed in isolation. Organizations will have standards as to deployment platforms, Linux, Microsoft Windows, specific types and versions of database servers, web servers, and other infrastructure components. A new software system may provide new functionality but would do so by interacting with existing software or system components, such as connections to users, parts databases, and customer records. It is for this reason that a set of operational requirements is built around the idea that a new or expanded system must interact with the existing systems over existing channels and protocols.

As software is deployed, it must remain consistent with operational requirements that define an environment that best suits its maintainability, data access, and access to needed services. Ultimately, at the finest level of detail, the functional requirements that relate to system deployment will be detailed for use. An example is the use of a database and web server. Organizational and industry standards will drive many of the selections. Although there are many different database and web servers in the marketplace, most enterprises have already selected an enterprise standard, sometimes by type of data or usage. Understanding and conforming to all the requisite infrastructure requirements are necessary to allow seamless interconnectivity and security throughout the enterprise infrastructure.

DevOps

The word "DevOps" is a combination of "development" and "operations" but it represents a set of security ideas and practices much larger than those two terms alone or together. CSEC2017 recommends DevOps be included within security curriculum because it does include security, collaborative ways of working, data analytics, and other vital aspects that are pertinent to the maintenance and operation of software?

The principles of DevOps provide practices intended to speed up the processes in which a maintenance project (like a new software feature, a request for enhancement, or a bug fix) goes from development to deployment in a production environment where it can provide value to the user. An important emphasis that should be made is that these approaches require that developers and operations teams have the capacity to communicate frequently and approach their work with empathy for their peers. Scalability and flexible provisioning are also necessary. With DevOps, those that need power the most, get it through self-service and automation technologies. Developers work closely with IT operations to speed software builds, tests, and releases without sacrificing reliability and security.

Decommissioning and Retiring

The purpose of the software decommissioning and retiring process is to safely terminate the existence of a system or a software entity. This process is an important component of security because of magnetic remanence. In simple terms, old systems retain their information even if they have been put on the shelf. So, it is necessary to remove from service all software and hardware products in a way that ensures that all of the information that is contained therein has been secured. Also, the decision to perform a retirement process will, by definition, cease the active support of the product by the organization. So, at the same time the information is being secured, decommissioning and retirement will guide the safe deactivation, disassembly, and removal of all elements of the affected product. The process then transitions the functions performed by the retired system to a final condition of deactivation and leaves the remaining elements of the environment in an acceptable state of operation.

Students should be made aware that, like all formal IT processes, the process of decommission and retirement is conducted according to a plan. As shown in Figure 4.12, the plan defines schedules, actions, and resources that (1) terminate the delivery of software services; (2) transform the system into, or retain it in, a socially and physically acceptable state; and (3) take account of the health, safety, security, and privacy applicable to actions performed according to the plan and to the long-term condition of resulting physical material and information.

Additionally, constraints are defined as the basis for carrying out the planned activities. Therefore, a strategy is defined and documented

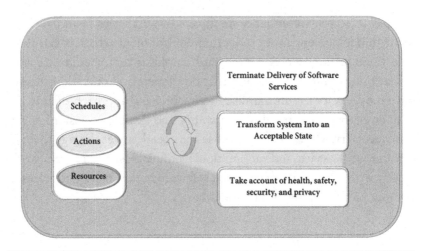

Figure 4.12 Software decommission and retirement process.

as a first step in the process. This plan stipulates the steps that will be taken by the operations and maintenance organizations to remove active support.

Once the plan is in place, it can be executed. The main point of this plan is to ensure an efficient transition into retirement. Therefore, users must be given sufficient timely notification of the plans and activities for the retirement of the affected product. These notifications must include such things as a description of any replacement or upgrade to the product, with its date of availability, as well as a statement of why the product will no longer be supported. Alternatively, a description of other support options, once support has been dropped, can also be provided.

Knowledge Unit Six: Documentation

No doubt that there is agreement for communication to be a vital artifact to the deployment and sustainment of a quality software product. Academia has ensured that point was made clear early and often. Until the emergence of the Agile approach to system and software development, life cycle methodologies provided activities that resulted in the development of plans and specifications which, among other things, provided appropriate directives for the ensuing phase of the life cycle. Speaking from the context of the traditional waterfall methodology as an example, the major byproduct of the project management phase was a project management plan which provides direction for all of the managed aspects of the project. In the software analysis phase, a requirement specification is written to define the functional and nonfunctional requirements of the software. Today, such a specification also takes into consideration the security that must be built into the software artifact. The software specification is in turn used during the design phase of the life cycle which has as its byproduct a design specification intended to describe how the functional and nonfunctional requirements are to be met. The development team is then able to utilize the design spec during the implementation phase of the life cycle to develop a software quality assurance (SQA) plan, software test plan, maintenance plan, and properly code the software artifact. The point is that the methodologies contained built-in documentation/communication mechanisms that provided guidance for each successive phase of the life cycle (Figure 4.13).

Where the call for documentation within the SDLC has been traditionally weak has been in the operations and deployment phases. This lack of communicative capability is even more concerning with the continued adoption of the Agile methodology within industry (which focuses on expeditious delivery of software artifacts as compared to documentation and, in many cases, quality), and the ever-increasing urgency for communicating the mechanisms necessary to

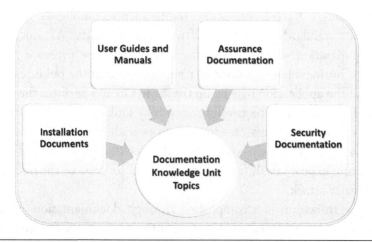

Figure 4.13 Documentation knowledge unit topics.

integrate security into the development, delivery, and use of software within organizational IT systems.

CSEC2017 recognizes the deficiency of documentation within later phases of the software life cycle methodologies used in industry today. And, while the authors of this knowledge area of the guideline recognize the importance of introducing students to all document artifacts of the entire software life cycle, within security curricula, they also put emphasis on introduction of security implication within the scope of installation documentation, and user guides and manuals, while at the same time draw attention to the necessity for software assurance documentation, and a deeper understanding of the need for building software that meets the criteria of an established security policy framework. There are four simple components in this highly practical knowledge unit: (1) *Installation documents*, (2) *User guides and manuals*, (3) *Assurance documentation* and the necessary, (4) *Security documentation*.

Installation Documents

One of the most common obstacles regarding securely deploying software is the lack of standardization of configuration of identical software within the organization infrastructure. This lack of a consistent configuration is a problem that arises when similar technologies are used in different ways by different lines of business and the same software functionality must be able to operate within this diverse array of technology. Each business unit has its own technologists applying different standards to similar software functionality. Assume, e.g., an organization with physical stores and an online presence. Both lines of business have an inventory application that the public cannot access. The application may be on the same OS and perform the same basic functions. Yet the configuration may look completely different if two different groups of administrators maintain the application. Software that is poorly configured or lacks standardization of configuration exposes itself (and all connected resources) to the potential of security attack.

Standardization is accomplished through documentation. While there may be no way to avoid implementing the same software product (or at a minimum similar functionality) upon a diverse technology within an IT infrastructure, organizations can alleviate much of the risk imposed within distributed technological infrastructures through the development of software installation manuals.

Because every organization technology infrastructure is unique, there is no formal definition for the structure of or specific content of an installation manual. However, the software development team must have the knowledge of what type of system the software will be installed upon, and knowledge of the interconnection of technological components on that system, in order to provide the documentation necessary to configure the newly developed software in a manner that will provide the necessary functionality and communication across the technologies of that system, in addition to the configurations that will be required in order put the software into compliance with established Organizational Security policy.

User Guides and Manuals

In just about any book you read on the topic of cybersecurity, there will be emphasis on the software vulnerabilities existing as a result of misuse use of the product. Too often the end user is not given proper instruction on how to use the software and keep the information that the software accepts as input, processes, stores, or produces as output secure. There are various means by which proper use of the software can be communicated, and traditional academia is partially to blame for the minimal value put into this communication. Most software courses stop short of providing students the techniques they need to communicate proper and secure use of the software and its functionality. This is usually done through user guides and manuals.

Students should understand and participate in exercises that help them understand that the user manual should be written using nontechnical terminology and should include the key features and functions of the software system. The manual should explain how the user must securely operate the software and provide sufficient detail and plain language so that all levels of users can easily understand how to use the product.

During the software development process, it is up to the project team to determine the approach taken to present the information and the media that will be most effective for the user community.

CSEC2017 makes an excellent recommendation that tutorials and "cheat sheets" be used as an alternative to the elaborate textbook style instruction approach.

As shown in Figure 4.14, we recommend the following best practices be introduced within curricula as a means for developing user manuals that make security a priority in software usage:

- *Collaborate* – The user manual should be developed in collaboration with all project team members and stakeholders.
- *Determine and Include* – The creation of the user manual should not stop short of providing all the pertinent details necessary to utilize all functionality effectively and securely. It should also provide the necessary steps to take when presented with warnings and error messages.
- *Design* – All content should have the same look and feel, regardless if you are presenting the material in an online format or in print.
- *Approve* – Characteristic to every other facet of the SDLC approval is necessary before the user manual is implemented.

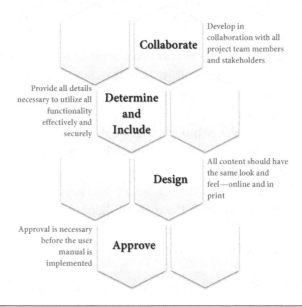

Figure 4.14   Best practices for developing user manuals.

Assurance Documentation

In this topic, CSEC2017 suggests introduction to documentation that focuses on how correctness of the software was established and what correctness means. Essentially what is under discussion is how validation and verification (which was described earlier in the chapter) are performed through a defined SQA life cycle process.

The purpose of the SQA process is to ensure that software products and processes comply with predefined provisions and plans. Put differently, the purpose of SQA is to monitor software development and related functions and bring any deviations to management's attention. SQA is based on a strategy and a plan that maintains software quality; identifies and records any problems conforming to requirements; and verifies that products, processes, and activities adhere to applicable standards, procedures, and requirements.

The two aspects of the quality assurance process are product assurance and process assurance, although the first of these aspects, assurance of the product, is the basis of this CSEC2017 topic.

Because quality assurance is primarily an oversight and coordination activity, the first requirement is to confirm that plans for implementing the activity of SQA are fully documented, mutually consistent, and executed as required by the contract.

When correctness of the plans has been ensured, the organization should have a formalized assurance process that ensures correctness in terms of the flow of products that result from these plans. A key characteristic of the documentation produced through an SQA process is that it must be assured that they comply with contractual requirements and their expressed plans. In anticipation of delivery of the software, the product must fully satisfy all contractual requirements and be acceptable to the organization or business unit from which the software was requested.

Security Documentation

At the code of required security documentation for software development and use is the existence of an Organizational Security policy framework. Security policies are really a collection of several documents. They generally start with a set of principles that communicate common rules across the organization. It is these principles that established governance practices use to interpret more detailed policies. Principles are expressed in simple language. An example may be an expression of risk appetite by employing the "need to know" approach to the granting of access. From these security principles flow security policies that detail how the principles are put into practice.

When combined, these policy documents outline the controls, actions, and processes to be performed by an organization. An example is the requirement that a customer provide a receipt when returning an item to a retail store for a refund. That may be a simple example of a policy, but essentially, it places a control on the return process. In the same vein, security policies require placement of controls in processes specific to the information system (such as software development). Security policies discuss the types of controls needed but not how to build the controls. For example, a security policy may state that some data can be accessed only from one particular software component. How the security control would be built to prevent other forms of access, e.g., would not appear in the policy.

Security policies should cover every threat to the system from which software resides. They should include protecting people, information, and physical assets. Policies should also include rules of behavior such as acceptable use policies. The policies must also set rules for users, define consequences of violations, and minimize risk to the organization. Enforcement will depend on the clarity of roles and responsibilities defined in policies. Remember, you need to hold people accountable for policies. When it's unclear who is accountable, a policy becomes unenforceable. Other documents in the policy framework provide additional support.

Once policies have been established and controls implemented to enforce them, software engineers can more effectively build security into software residing on the system. They do so by including within the functional and nonfunctional requirements of the SRS that criteria that will be necessary to make the software compliant with the relevant policies within the framework. It follows that those requirements would then be part of the overall design, implementation, and sustainment of the software system.

Knowledge Unit Seven: Ethics

Ethics is often characterized as moral principles that govern a person's behavior. No doubt it is a critical part of any sound cybersecurity defense strategy. Without clear ethical standards and rules, cybersecurity professionals are almost indistinguishable from the black-hat criminals from which they are trying to protect systems and data. One of the difficulties the IT industry has is that ethics can be subjective, influenced by an individual's background, culture, education, personality, and other factors. Some white-hat hackers, e.g., have no problem casually testing their phone company's billing platform for vulnerabilities. By poking holes in the phone providers' security infrastructure, they believe they are legitimately contributing to the common good of cybersecurity. Others might regard these activities as criminal, or at least unethical, well-intentioned or not (Figure 4.15).

The study of cybersecurity ethics, which encompasses a wide range of approaches and schools of thought, does not offer a simple solution to the many complex ethical dilemmas IT professionals, Chief Information Security Officers (CISOs), and organizations face every day. In this quickly changing technology-filled world, we tend to focus on developing individuals' cybersecurity knowledge and talent and putting them on the front line as quickly as possible. In that frame of mind, we often forget to consider how new students or new

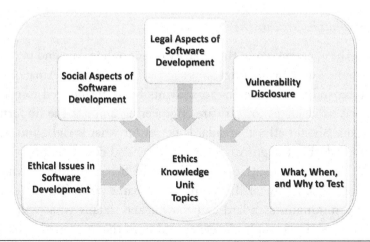

Figure 4.15 Ethics knowledge unit topics.

cyber professionals could potentially abuse these abilities on the job or in the wild. Lacking context on cybersecurity ethics, individuals must defer to their personal moral beliefs. This leads to good decisions as often as it leads to mistakes.

How can educators infuse the highest of cybersecurity ethical standards and intrinsic values? If a cybersecurity curriculum has not already done so, strong consideration should be made to introducing ethical practice policy, guidelines, and/or code of conduct. As changes to the cybersecurity landscape continue to change, so will the ethical behaviors that must be evident by cyber professionals as much as curricula changes to introduce new technology. Cybersecurity educators must continue to evaluate evolving ethical cybersecurity behaviors for protecting that technology, by introducing new ethical standards and guidelines as they evolve.

The CSEC2017 Software Security knowledge area is the only one within the curriculum guideline that includes a specific knowledge unit dedicated to ethics, although many of the topics suggested for introduction are echoed in other knowledge areas throughout the guideline. As would be expected, the focus, here, is on the ethical behaviors related to the processes in software development. There are five basic elements in the software Ethics knowledge unit: (1) Ethical issues in software development, (2) Social aspects of software development, (3) Legal aspects of software development, (4) Vulnerability disclosure, and (5) What, when, and why to test.

Ethical Issues in Software Development

Given the concerns about the security of our online data and personal information used by organizations such as Facebook and Amazon, we must expand those concerns to students being introduced to cybersecurity, as it relates to software engineering and ask the important question: Should ethical standards be set for what is right and what is wrong during the process of engineering and developing new software? The dilemma surfaces in making the determination of what is legal and what is ethical. These are not the same thing. The law establishes a minimum standard of behavior and details what will happen if you fail to comply. As we eluded to in the introduction to this knowledge unit, ethics is about what is right and proper when viewed from an ethical perspective: what are the potential consequences of your action; do you have a duty to stakeholders; and what are your ethical obligations to them.

To a large extent, these questions are unanswered perhaps because the software industry is still in an infant stage compared to more mature industries. Likewise, it doesn't seem as though those involved with the software industry care very much about ethical standards. For example, many software engineers have taken on a practice of software reuse. For years, the cliché "don't reinvent the wheel" has been used through software circles. That catchy statement is simply meant to encourage software engineers not to recode software components that may exist in other applications. While that practice works well when reusing software within the single organization, the issue of ethical standard violation comes into question when source code from licensed software developed by a separate software organization is reused. Considering the popularity of open source software, students need to appreciate the value of software reuse but must be made aware of when ethical lines of behavior are being crossed.

To clarify the fine line between ethical and nonethical behavior in software development, the Institute of Electrical and Electronics Engineers and the Association of Computing Machinery (IEEE-CS/ACM Joint Task Force on Software Engineering Ethics and Professional Practice) developed the International Standard for Professional Software Development and Ethical Practice (often known as the IEEE-CS/ACM Code of Ethics). The statement addresses eight principles that define the public interest obligation of software engineers: acting in the best interest of clients and the employer, the need for integrity, independence, and professional judgment; the need to follow an ethical approach to the management of software development and maintenance; and to promote an ethical approach to the practice of the profession.

CSEC2017 recommends the introduction of the Code of Ethics because there is obvious benefit from an ethical decision-making process standpoint to deal with issues, such as those mentioned earlier, that arise in the practice of the software and cybersecurity profession. In other words, how can they effectively deal with ethical dilemmas.

Social Aspects of Software Development

Software development has shifted from simply a technical process to an exercise of social morality. In the same way, crash testing has become a mandated part of automotive manufacturing, there is a social obligation for security to become a part of the SDLC from the point of project inception.

As with vehicle safety, Software Security is often an added cost for organizations that have not yet implemented basic security hygiene. Some organizational executives may be tempted to ignore the need for security, thus passing the cost and risk of insecure software on to consumers. Similar to unsafe cars affecting more than just the car owner, insecure software can affect third parties through distributed denial of service (DDoS) attacks and provide the ability for attackers to use insecure computers to exploit systems anonymously.

Within a cybersecurity curriculum, it must be reinforced that software developers and security professionals not just influence but are responsible for challenging this temptation. The good news for organizations is that it is less expensive and more effective for them to maintain a high standard of security for their products and services by integrating security earlier in the development life cycle, than it is to approach security with a sense of ignorance.

At a minimum, organizations need to make sure that the software they develop adheres to industry standards for security on release and that it is easy to issue patches as new vulnerabilities arise. An excellent approach in providing this level of understanding to students new to this practice is introduction to the OWASP Top 10, which provides a good baseline of the most common and dangerous vulnerabilities currently existing in software.

Legal Aspects of Software Development

There is likely no argument that most commercial and proprietary software contains serious flaws and defects, some of which are exploitable as vulnerabilities. This has always been the case, because it has been impossible to fully test software, and while flaws/defects can reduced substantially through the use of SQA processes, it is safe to say that software is never really free of flaws, either overlooked during development or intentionally left uncorrected at time of shipment.

Over the last four decades, there have been numerous advances in software technology associated with the presence of computers (first mainframes, then personal computers, and now mobile devices) and computer networks; the digital automation of once-mechanical controls for physical systems and processes; growing concerns over Information Warfare; the rise of hacking, malware, and computer crime; the open source movement; cloud computing; and now the new buzz of the Internet of Things. With each advance, software has increased in size, complexity, exposure, and criticality with a strong dependence on humans for software correctness, reliability, and security.

Aside from specialized software houses that focus on developing real-time embedded software systems, the software industry has never shown interest in self-regulation and has resisted external regulation of the software component characteristics of quality, safety, or security. Governments have also been unwilling to regulate the software industry out of fear of slowing industry. The point being made is that in the absence of regulation, any customer who falls victim to the catastrophic results of software faults and failures has only one recourse: the courts.

Beyond the language contained within software licensing agreements, there has been much debate within government, the courts, the industry, and academia about how the law applies to software faults and bugs. The urgency of debate increases with the continued threat that those defects can lead to exploitable security vulnerabilities. It for that reason CSEC2017 recommends that the debate continue through academic discussions that take place related to software ethics.

Vulnerability Disclosure

Another ethical topic that should be included within cybersecurity curriculum is how to approach software vulnerability disclosures. The abundance of bugs within software programs presents great opportunities for no fault disclosure, but many organizations are still skeptical of hackers' motivations and very wary of those bugs being an open invitation to be hacked.

The ongoing battle between cybercriminals and trying to defend against them is still too large for internal security teams to handle on their own. And realistically, most open source components remain unpatched once they are built into software. Organizations need outside help, but to get it, they need to encourage white-hat hackers to research without fear of repercussion. One practice that has been used by websites, organizations and other software developers are to reap the value of bug bounty programs, which allow individuals to get recognition and compensation for reporting bugs, especially those pertaining to exploits and vulnerabilities. However, such programs often do not go far enough to protect their participants; they tend to be too narrow in scope, and restrictive legal disclaimers may prevent the participant white-hat hackers from looking as thoroughly as they could or reporting everything they find. This may contribute to the volume of known but undisclosed vulnerabilities, which are likely in use by a large number of applications used every day.

The IT industry needs to embrace "coordinated disclosure" as a standard practice. Such a practice should encourage the vulnerability researcher and the software development team work together on corrective measures and collaborate on disclosing vulnerabilities. The key is for individuals to share what vulnerabilities they find, as compared to not sharing their insights at all. Relaxing disclosure restrictions will lead not only to more secure software but to greater information sharing, which builds a more cohesive community of developers, internal security teams, and independent security researchers. This kind of community is critical as we work toward the common goal of securing software.

What, When, and Why to Test

In an earlier knowledge unit of this chapter, we discussed the types of testing that must be performed on software in order to provide security assurance. Recall that we emphasized that at the core of software testing lies a conceptual characteristic of the SDLC called Verification and Validation (V&V). Verification, we said, ensures that the developed software meets the requirements set forth by the SRS. Alternatively, validation ensures that the software meets the needs of the acquirer and is delivered at an appropriate level of quality. Neither of those two characteristics can be accomplished, however, without the support of a well-defined SQA process that includes the development of a test plan containing test cases that ensure the security of each function of the software product.

In the presence of a well-defined process, ethical issues related to what, when, and why to test become less apparent. However, in the development of test cases, quality assurance teams are often faced with the questions such as... How much is too much? And, is there time to test the software adequately? While these dilemmas are not new to software testing, they become more critical in the scope of assuring the development process has produced secure software functionality.

Over the past couple of decades, the software industry has experienced a shift in popularity of development methodology. The traditional waterfall, which provided ample time to adequately test the quality of software, has recently given way to the much more expeditious Agile methodology. The manifesto for the Agile methodology emphasizes rapid development and less emphasis on quality. As such, test teams are put into the predicament of deciding whether to bring identified flaws to the attention of the developers or stay silent in an attempt to get the software product to the acquirer as quickly as possible. As the software industry continues steer toward development using the Agile methodology, more automated tools are being developed to support the testing process. However, the capabilities of those tools to adequately identify security vulnerabilities are still in question. Further, whether or not to report known flaws cannot be resolved simply by implementing, into the testing and quality assurance process, the use of automation. As such, ethical testing continues to be a topic that requires discussion both within the software industry and as part of Software Security curricula.

Twenty Review Questions for This Chapter

1. How does the least privilege principle protect the overall security of software?
2. Why should Software Security measures be kept simple? Are we making sacrifices by doing so?
3. Why is it important to develop software that validates access between objects?
4. What is meant by the principle of open design?
5. Explain the importance of considering security policies while eliciting software requirements.

6. Describe the difference between functional and nonfunctional security requirements.
7. What is meant by the term buffer bashing?
8. What are APIs and what significance do they have in coding software securely?
9. What is the value of encapsulation of objects in coding software securely?
10. Describe the difference between standard software testing and security analysis.
11. What is the value of encapsulation of objects in coding software securely?
12. Do you agree or disagree with the trend for operations and maintenance to be a combined life cycle phase? Why do you take that position?
13. Explain the value of automation to the activities of operations. Provide some examples of when it could be utilized.
14. What factors should be considered in secure configuration of software?
15. Explain how installation manuals contribute to IT infrastructure standardization.
16. Describe four best practices that should be applied in the development of user manuals.
17. What is the value of security policies within the scope of software development?
18. What is the purpose of the SQA process?
19. What are some examples of moral behaviors that can be exhibited during the software development process?
20. Explain how the software industry has helped to reduce the fine line between ethical and nonethical behavior.

You Might Also Like to Read

- Arthur, Conklin and Shoemaker Daniel, *CSSLP Certification All-in-One Exam Guide*, 2nd Edition, McGraw Hill, New York, 2019.
- Daniel, Shoemaker and Sigler Ken, *Cybersecurity: Engineering a Secure Information Technology Organization*, Cengage Learning, Boston, MA, 2014.

- Grembi, Jason, *Secure Software Development: A Secure Programmers Guide*, Cengage Learning, Boston, MA, 2008.
- McGraw, Gary, *Software Security: Building Security In*, Addison-Wesley Professional, Boston, MA, 2006.
- Nancy, Mead and Carol Woody, *Cyber Security Engineering: A Practical Approach for Systems and Software Assurance (SEI Series in Software Engineering)*, Addison-Wesley Professional, Boston, MA, 2016.

Chapter Summary

- To effectively implement Software Security takes the collaborated effort of managers, administrators, developers, and security researchers.
- Security of software is dependent upon how well requirements meet security needs and how those requirements are designed, implemented, and maintained.
- There is a decisive link between Software Security and a quality development process. Successful progression through that process is dependent upon core security design principles.
- In order to design a secure software product, security requirements must be based on the organizations mission, vision, and objectives.
- A secure SDLC can only be effectively established if security activities are added to an already existing managed life cycle process.
- While many security vulnerabilities are created due to improper software design, each programming language also contains embedded vulnerabilities that must be considered during the design phase in order to reduce the attack surface.
- Secure implementation requires the use of the most current programming languages, functions, and libraries tested using static program checkers to find common errors to ensure coding standards are maintained.
- Standard software testing utilizes a variety of techniques to verify and validate each module as it is developed. In order to test for security vulnerabilities, those standard techniques must include successful static and dynamic analysis.

- During the deployment, operations, and maintenance phases of the software life cycle security professionals must ensure software configuration consistent with established baselines, ongoing risk-free operability through and established DevOps process, and maintain the software as changes to the organizations risk environment evolve.
- Despite popular belief within current industry software development methodologies, documentation throughout the life cycle (including deployment and operation) continues to be vital for communicating proper configuration, use, testing, and security of a software product.

Any professional performing activities within a process of the software life cycle has an ethical obligation to behave in a manner consistent with the industry standards and policies set forth by the organization.

Learning Objectives for the Component Security Knowledge Area

Mastery of the requisite learning outcomes for the Data Security knowledge area will be established through the student's ability to paraphrase and explicate the key contents of the knowledge units within this knowledge area (Bloom Levels Two and Three). In addition, the student will exhibit specific behaviors that demonstrate a capability to utilize the relevant concepts in common practical application. Specifically, the student will be able to paraphrase and explain the following twenty-two knowledge elements (CSEC, 2019):

1. Discuss the implications of relying on open design or the secrecy of design for security.
2. List the three principles of security.
3. Describe why each principle is important to security.
4. Identify the needed design principle.
5. Explain why security requirements are important.
6. Identify common attack vectors.
7. Describe the importance of writing secure and robust programs.
8. Describe the concept of privacy including PII.
9. Explain why input validation and data sanitization are necessary.

10. Explain the difference between pseudorandom numbers and random numbers.
11. Differentiate between secure coding and patching and explain the advantage of using secure coding techniques.
12. Describe a buffer overflow and why it is a potential security problem.
13. Explain the difference between static and dynamic analysis.
14. Discuss a problem that static analysis cannot reveal.
15. Discuss a problem that dynamic analysis cannot reveal.
16. Discuss the need to update software to fix security vulnerabilities.
17. Explain the need to test software after an update but before the patch is distributed.
18. Explain the importance of correctly configuring software.
19. Explain the concept that because you can do it, it doesn't mean you should do it.
20. Discuss the ethical issues in disclosing vulnerabilities.
21. Discuss the ethics of thorough testing.
22. Identify the ethical effects and impacts of design decisions.

Keywords

Agile Methodology – a software development methodology that features requirements and solutions evolving through a collaboration of the customer and cross-functional organizational teams.

Application Program Interface – a set of software functions, communication protocols, and tools that allow software components to interconnect through cross-function communication.

Bootstrapping – a set of operations that will both properly launch intended functionality and ensure its correctness.

Exception Handling – functionality within software that provides the capability for continued processing or exiting safely in the event of a critical error.

Hard Coding – the practice of including data directly in the source code in order for it to be included within the processing each time a software function is executed. For the purpose of cybersecurity, this is not recommended.

Quick Fix Engineering – the practice of identifying a bug or fault in software and writing code that provides a satisfactory but not necessarily optimal solution.

Software Decommissioning – the process of removing software from operation.

Software Quality Assurance – a software life cycle process containing a set of activities that aim to ensure quality of the software artifact being developed.

Sustainability – A common term used recently to represent the combination of activities that exist within the software operations and maintenance phases of the software life cycle.

Type-Safe Language – a feature within programming languages that assigns the proper data type to data stored within a program, databases, and memory locations in an effort to prevent errors or unexpected program behavior.

Validation – is a process that uses testing to ensure that the needs of a system or software have been met at a desired level of quality.

Verification – is a process that uses testing to ensure that the defined requirements of a system or software have been met.

Waterfall Methodology – a software development methodology that breaks down the project activities into a set of sequential phases. Each phase must be completed in its entirety before the next one begins.

Reference

Joint Task Force (JTF) on Cybersecurity Education, "Cybersecurity Curricula 2017, Curriculum Guidelines for Post-Secondary Degree Programs in Cybersecurity, a Report in the Computing Curricula Series", ACM/IEEE-CS/AIS SIGSEC/IFIP WG 11.8, Version 1.0, 31 December 2019.

5

COMPONENT SECURITY

In this chapter, you will learn the following:

- The practical role and relationship of design concepts in Component Security
- The threat issues that impact component design
- The design principles and practices associated with secure components
- The principles and practices that are part of supply chain risk management
- The knowledge elements associated with recognized design concepts
- The knowledge elements of secure component design
- The knowledge elements associated with ensuring trusted sourced components
- The knowledge elements associated with component testing and assurance
- The knowledge elements associated with the practice of reverse engineering.

It All Starts with the Components

All digital things are conglomerations of components and those components implement every conceivable function. The functions underwrite a society that is radically different from the world in which any person over the age of forty grew up in. Twenty years ago, you couldn't bank online or buy stocks. You couldn't play online games or interact with people via a mass virtual medium like Facebook or Minecraft. You couldn't utilize a mobile device to communicate with people in cyberspace or even more farfetched, remotely communicate with your household appliances. Now all of that is possible and new advances in virtual space are appearing at an exponential rate.

213

And the architecture of digital components of this cybersecurity issue is becoming increasingly complex and, as a result, much more vulnerable. Moreover, as new functionality is added to the growing list of component capabilities, the out-of-control growth of "things" poses new problems for our society. This is a valid concern because our way of life is almost totally dependent on the security of the components of our digital technology.

The CSEC2017s *Component Security* knowledge area introduces the necessary process considerations, design concepts, and common development ideas for a curriculum that is devoted to ensuring trust in digital components. Moreover, the reality that an entire knowledge area is devoted to Component Security also represents a departure from current curricular models. In this, the focus on components expands general cybersecurity education into the hardware realm. Thus, this new area also offers a necessary and proper adaptation to the genuine problems that are associated with complex component architectures.

Component Security is essentially a design issue. That is, good design practice is the one common factor that ensures the necessary security of a component architecture. The design and implementation of component architectures is a significant activity, one that involves many tasks across the organization. Hence, rational planning and the systematic coordination of the overall design process are a vital part of ensuring the success of the resultant architecture.

First of all, every good process starts with a management plan. So, it must be understood that the strategic planning and management of the design effort is not a trivial add-on activity – it is central to Component Security. The management activities in the Component Security process are the control element that ensure all of the necessary common actions are properly executed during the creation of the design artifact.

Like any effort where resources are committed, the starting point is the design project plan. This plan specifies the major requisite activities in the overall design process as well as their resource requirements. The plan provides the organization's specific view about what has to be done in order to satisfy product design goals. In addition, the plan also provides an itemization of the specific organizational resources to be allocated to accomplish those goals. Besides resources, the plan also specifies the review activities that will be taken and the necessary accountabilities to ensure strict management control. No two design activities are ever the same, and consequently, each individual design process has to be considered to be different in its particulars. These differences may be large or small, but because they always exist, every organization must explicitly specify the process, concepts, methods, and tools that will be utilized in the creation of the desired component architecture.

The design process itself is highly conceptual in nature as well as labor intensive. The everyday performance of an intricate set of tasks always requires a substantive operational management process. That operational control is established by the design project plan. Once the general shape and resourcing of the design effort has been established, each of the inherent best practices that must be carried out in order to ensure a capable and effective design is fully documented and integrated into a collective design document. The document outlines a logical set of rationally interacting behavioral and technical control objectives, which are designed to achieve a defined outcome in the overall process. In practical application, these controls are typically expressed as a consistent set of best practice recommendations for the execution of the design work.

Component architecture is fundamentally a process concern. Simply put, the choices that are made about how any given set of components is arrayed and then subsequently maintained is a conscious one that will determine the success or failure of the eventual product. The assumption is that if the choices are properly and correctly made, then any threats associated with component performance can be viewed as mitigated or reduced to an acceptable level.

One issue that quickly stands out is that digital architectures are incredibly diverse so there is no single common method for component design. Instead, the component design process relies on proper understanding of the digital artifact's functional requirements. In practical terms, this means that a correct representation of the essential real-world requirements that a given architecture must fulfill is needed to guide the design and development process. The basic premise of digital component design is that the elements of a given functional object have to be characterized to a level of detail that ensures that all constituent elements of that object are fully understood and are correctly interacting.

Because this requires precise description of real-world things, that type of design method is probably most commonly associated with the profession of engineering. Consequently, the formal practices that are utilized to communicate the physical and logical requirements of a given entity are similarly precise, logical, and empirically stated.

The only general methodology that all design activities have in common is functional decomposition. This approach is a traditional conceptual modeling technique that achieves satisfactory understanding of the design space by means of a set of progressively refined views taken of the design object. Essentially, this is a case of peeling back the onion. Each of these views characterizes the object in increasingly more detailed terms. In the end, the process will have broken the design object down to a level where every requisite behavior or functional property, as well as the necessary interrelationships, is fully understood and can be documented as a set of well-defined behaviors. In common terminology, the complete set of these individual discrete behaviors or modules is termed an "architecture."

The *process* view is the entry point to understanding. This first stage takes a look at the object at the highest level of abstraction. The process view specifies how the various stages and activities of the architectural design and development process will be performed and then interconnected. This is normally termed a "logical" representation of the object.

The next level catalogues all of the discrete operations that the object will perform, as well as their interrelationship within the eventual architecture. In common terms, this is normally called a *design* view. This is the first of the actual architectural conceptualization steps in that the major components of the design object are identified and characterized in terms of their discrete behavioral requirements. The functional objects associated with meeting those specific requirements are derived from that understanding.

The next level down is the *module* view. This refinement displays and interrelates the discrete functional elements of the design object. Each of the resulting modules comprises a detailed behavioral aspect of the overall architecture, and this is essentially what is developed and assembled into the final product.

In the end, there is also the necessary *physical* level view. This is the vision of the tangible artifact. The physical view comprises the concrete tangible arrangement of the concrete elements of the design.

This is often known as a schematic view and it is what guides the actual construction of the artifact.

The CSEC2017 Component Security Knowledge Units

As the name implies, the Component Security domain encompasses four large strategic processes; these specify the knowledge elements associated with the secure development, acquisition, and assurance of digital products at all levels of design and use. The aim of the knowledge elements in the Component Security domain is to provide an in-depth specification of the contents and interrelationships of each of the relevant knowledge units associated with the secure design, development, and assurance of component architectures.

Accordingly, the areas that fall under the purview of Component Security mostly involve secure engineering and acquisition of the physical and virtual components of the virtual product. This includes such obviously pertinent large-scale activities as life cycle design, commercial off-the-shelf (COTS) acquisition, life cycle validation and verification procedures, and the unique engineering activities that are associated with finding out how a product is made, and then using that information to reproduce the product. The latter activity is usually for nefarious purposes. This knowledge unit is commonly called "reverse engineering." Shown in Figure 5.1, the CSEC2017 knowledge unit areas are as follows:

1. *Component Design* – the life cycle conceptual design consideration as it relates to the creation of components and component architecture.
2. *Component Procurement* – the assurance of trusted sourced components and current and proposed best practices related to the secure acquisition of digital items via supply chains.
3. *Component Testing* – fundamental life cycle principles that underlie the assurance of the quality and security of component and product architectures.
4. *Component Reverse Engineering* – the practices related to the extraction of knowledge about the structure and operation of an existing product for the purpose of either reproducing the product or exploiting it.

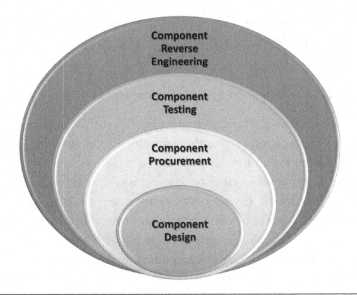

Figure 5.1 The Component Security knowledge units.

As previously mentioned, the Component Security process must take place within a formal life cycle management framework. It probably goes without saying that any technical process needs to be managed, and unfortunately, that sometimes doesn't happen, particularly in detailed design work. While ad hoc or top-down approaches might successfully address the functional requirements of the particular project, a lack of perspective constrains the situational awareness to a point where it is almost impossible to recognize the larger security concerns. Therefore, it is important to execute the component design process within a standard life cycle management model. Besides the actual design work specifications, the model must also specify a completion schedule and the individual(s) responsible for performing each activity and task.

Life cycle management is critical to ensuring security in any domain of application because a well-defined process ensures a stable base for the performance of commonly accepted best practices. The best practices dictate how the designers will think about the production of any given design and the necessary assurance concerns that are associated with that artifact. Naturally, those assurance concerns must be directly referenced to known threats. Thus, the best practices are needed to ensure that the subsequent design work is carried out using the approved set of standards, methods, tools, and computer languages.

Knowledge Unit One: Component Design

In order to create a proper digital component design, the designers draw up a tangible graphic model that conveys the complete picture of the tangible architecture of the entity. That model describes each of the various components that comprise the entity as well as their exact interrelationship. Obviously, the description of these components must be expressed in such a way that they can be directly referenced to the specified real-world needs that motivated the design in the first place. Thus, design processes are iterative in the sense that the depiction of the architecture and its components is successively refined to a point where there can be no possibility of misunderstanding of either the elements of the product or the interrelationship of its overall set of components. Once that design is perfected, it can be transitioned into the development phase for implementation (Figure 5.2).

The real-world form of the design is the direct result of a complete specification of the discrete functional and qualitative requirements. That specification includes an explicit statement of all of the necessary performance behaviors and physical characteristics that must be embedded in each component. The specification of requirements is developed in reference to a full understanding of the environmental conditions under which the component is expected to operate. In addition, the specification itemizes all of the internal and external interfaces, as well as the qualification criteria for the build. These criteria must be defined during the planning and design stage because

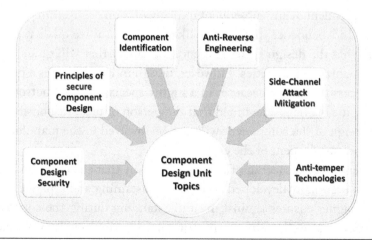

Figure 5.2 The Component Design knowledge unit topics.

they will eventually be used in the downstream performance and qualification testing facets of the process.

Once a complete understanding is achieved of what's required, the designer conceptualizes and documents a complete and consistent top-level architecture. That top-level view itemizes and arranges all of the basic components and relationships in the planned architecture into a coherent set of "things." The goal of the top-level architectural development process is to amalgamate all of the formally documented performance requirements into a complete and detailed rendering of the overall product. That rendering then serves as a comprehensive road map of how the designer proposes to meet product requirements in that particular instance.

A comprehensive, top-level view allows the designer to think about all of the relevant implementation and sustainment issues. The designer develops and documents an unambiguous description of all of the relevant components that will be required. That includes their interrelationships and the explicit interfaces between external entities and any given component, as well as between all of the internal components of the proposed architecture. This helps the designer identify any potential security threats in the operational environment, as well as mitigate the likelihood of harm or compromise of the architecture. The final product of this phase of the process is full and complete characterization of all pertinent traceability, testability, and feasibility requirements of the build.

A top-level view also allows the designer to ensure that the design is independent of any subsequent implementation or sustainment concerns. Independence might seem like an anti-intuitive quality, in the sense that the design is the reference document that will guide all of the downstream activities. However, design independence is a practical necessity. That is because, in a highly specialized and outsourced world, it can't be just assumed that the person or team responsible for the design of the component will also be involved in the manufacturing and sustainment of the entity.

Therefore, approaching the design in a way that ensures that whatever is eventually developed is fully self-sustaining and separate from the designer ensures against misunderstanding during the construction phase, as well as the exasperating need to continually "walk back and forth" to determine what the designer "really meant." This is an especially relevant consideration where the designers and the implementers could be located on different continents and it is the general cause of a lot of security vulnerabilities.

Along with a top-level description of the artifact, it is also important to specify how it will be tested and assured. Testing and assurance are perhaps the most critical aspect of the security function, at least for any given set of components. The specification of the exact testing and qualification requirements for each component in the top-level design permits a much greater level of assurance control over the quality and security of the product. Ultimately, all of the components in every architecture must be evaluated to confirm that they have effectively implemented the functions they are meant to provide. More importantly, it must be demonstrated that whatever potential threats that were identified in the environment have been addressed with provenly effective mitigations.

The top-level design activity is really an organizational process, not a technical one. In essence, the top-level view provides the connection between stakeholder requirements and the concrete realization. Therefore, the general statement of design intent must be understandable at the stakeholder level. At the stakeholder level, every single documented requirement should be clearly traceable to an analogous component in the design. The resulting component set is then individually documented by the design.

Component Design Security

This topic itemizes the concepts, methods, and tools of the actual process of Component Security design. This first CSEC2017 topic is a direct response to the threat environment surrounding components, in that it considers ways that the designer can counter threats to design artifacts. It employs such techniques as multiple decomposition views and detailed design schematics. It also addresses the need to protect designs from societal concerns such as intellectual property theft, reverse engineering, tampering, side channel analysis, and counterfeiting.

Component design security applies sound scientific and engineering principles to the identification of vulnerabilities and the minimization or containment of the risks that might be associated with these vulnerabilities. In general, this activity involves the integration of product architectural design with cybersecurity best practices. It also implies the incorporation of explicit security elements into the evolving component design as well as the subsequent product baselines. Shown in Figure 5.3, the common best practices that are normally associated with this integration process are as follows:

Perform Criticality Analyses by Phase: In this step, the designer evaluates the artifact purpose, identifies the component functions, and produces an initial component architecture that is sufficient to satisfy all mission critical functions. Following that, the designer refines the critical function list to a point where it is possible to characterize all of the critical system components as well as the associated subcomponents of the overall product, e.g., the hardware, software, and firmware. The list of identified components and subcomponents is then refined into a documented set of design elements. The designer then reviews that list in order to ensure the complete and satisfactory coverage of the component array. This is then submitted to the configuration management process to ensure a stable status.

Operations and Sustainment: The designer reviews the final list of critical product components and subcomponents in order to ensure that the life cycle through which they will be developed and maintained has the proper potential integrity. To do this,

Figure 5.3   Component design best practices.

the designer assesses the process risks and determines the necessary mitigation approaches. The aim is to minimize process vulnerabilities and design weaknesses. Where there is a threat, the designer identifies specific countermeasures and mitigations. That analysis is driven by a practical set of cost/benefit trade-offs, which are meant to ensure affordability.

In general, the security threats that are identified in these two phases boil down to a couple of universal areas of concern. The first of these is that malicious logic might be installed on a hardware or software component at some point in the development process. Malicious logic is embedded in order to fulfill some specific purpose. Therefore, the assurance that a component is free of malicious code should be a high priority.

Embedding a malicious object is always a hostile act. Therefore, malicious objects are by definition not part of the delivered functionality. Since it is difficult enough to ensure the quality and security of the desired functions of the component, it is asking for a lot to expect that any functions that should not be present, like a hardware Trojan, should also be identified and eliminated. This problem is addressed by rigorous testing and inspection. The decision to embed a piece of malicious logic in a product is intentional. Therefore, the object is by definition concealed. The most effective way to root out such an object is to maintain strict oversight testing and reviews over the design, development, and implementation of the component.

The other general threat is the installation of counterfeit components. Counterfeits execute product functions as intended. However, they are dangerous because they are not the same as the actual part. So, at a minimum, a counterfeit threatens product integrity. Generally, the reason for using a counterfeit is to save money. As a result, counterfeits embody quality or security shortcuts that can fail in many ways. The other option is to supply a feature that the developer is otherwise incapable of providing. That inability raises all kinds of overall integrity issues. Therefore, the potential to embed counterfeits at any point in the design must be directly mitigated.

Since they function like the original part, it is often hard to spot a counterfeit in a large array of components. Therefore, it is critical that the product developer understand the technical provenance of any component by carefully inspecting everything that is integrated into the build. In order to ensure this, the developer must have direct knowledge of all of the downstream suppliers and fully assess all of their business and technical practices. This assessment must take place prior to engaging in any design activity.

Principles of Secure Component Design

This topic encompasses the generic concepts that influence good component design. It includes such topics as security policy, as well as the process features that are part of good component design. General principles include the basic concepts of trusted computing, risk mitigation, and defense in depth. It also includes a set of general architectural design rules that every detailed design process has in common. In essence, shown in Figure 5.4, every design process must incorporate some aspect of each of these underlying principles (note – this is alphabetical order, not priority):

> *Abstraction*: which is the means that is employed to break the design object down into successively smaller and more manageable pieces. Abstraction is accomplished by suppressing

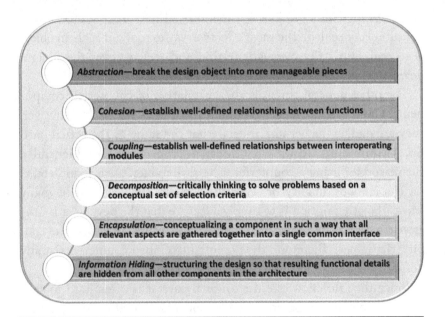

Figure 5.4 General architectural design principles.

the unnecessary details and emphasizing the relevant or most important ones.

Cohesion: which is the practice of establishing well-defined relationships between functions or procedures within each of the single modules within the component architecture. The aim is to ensure that each module is highly cohesive.

Coupling: which is the practice of establishing well-defined relationships between two or more interoperating modules. The relationships are normally based on the passing of signals or data. The aim is to make each individual module as independently self-sustaining as possible.

Decomposition: which is sometimes referred to as "critical thinking." This describes the age-old practice of solving the problem by breaking it into its constituent parts based on a conceptual set of selection criteria.

Encapsulation: which is also known as "polymorphism." This is the practice of conceptualizing a component in such a way that all relevant aspects of the function, including data, are gathered together into a single unit behind a single common interface. This enacts the concept of modularity.

Information Hiding: this involves structuring the design in such a way that all of the resulting functional details of a component are hidden from all other components in the architecture. The aim is to ensure that the failure of one module does not cascade to another.

In addition to fundamental concepts, shown in Figure 5.5, there are also twelve specific design qualities that have to be kept in mind when a designer sets about creating a component architecture. These are as follows:

1. Context
2. Composition
3. Correctness
4. Dependencies
5. Information hiding
6. Design patterns
7. Interfaces
8. Structure

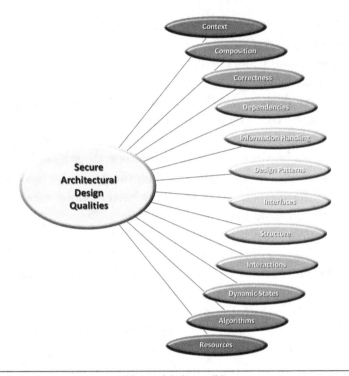

Figure 5.5 Secure component architectural design qualities.

9. Interactions
10. Dynamic states
11. Algorithms
12. Resources.

The first of these considerations is **context**. Context simply views the component in terms of the discrete set of services that it needs to provide. Thus, context has to be viewed as a heterogeneous collection of user requirements, which taken together constitute the essential functionality of the product. The perspective that the designer needs to take in thinking about context is how each of the known individuals or stakeholders intends to make use of the product.

The next consideration is **composition**. This identifies the logical components of the product. The designer has to identify all of the elements that must exist within the architecture in order to achieve its functional purpose. Once the entire component set is identified, then the roles of each of those elements in achieving the fundamental ends of the product must be identified and prioritized for implementation purposes.

The **correctness** consideration is the first one of these qualities that is an essential part of security assurance. Essentially, the architecture is composed of parts. The question is whether the parts have been accurately identified and described and that their portrayal is at a uniform and consistent level of description. If this is not done correctly, then there is the potential for logical gaps or holes in the implementation. These can lead to exploitation. The presence of gaps is often a downstream consideration at the testing and review stage. However, the conceptual model is the best place to identify anomalies and inconsistencies.

Components are arrayed in order to produce an intended outcome. That array will necessarily entail interdependencies among components. Therefore, there is a **dependency** consideration that is built into every design exercise. Nevertheless, the aim of good design practice is to capture the proper relationship between each component in terms of their purpose and interaction. Since many attacks are through unknown, or improperly defended interdependencies, the interdependency quality is an essential part of good cybersecurity practice.

All digital products process **information** in some form. Thus, the assurance of proper storage and exchange of that information is a critical piece of good design. The specific consideration of the information elements of the product generally hinges on the design of the database system as well as the functionality that manages how information is processed. However, this is the specific area where considerations of confidentiality, integrity, and availability take place.

Design activity is leveraged by the existence of commonalities in the design process. Those common **patterns** are an essential part of good design practice because they eliminate a lot of the unnecessary steps in the process. Obviously, the ability to reuse a design concept at a different level, or apply a common architectural style, or framework template in the overall process of product development saves time and effort that can be better spent dealing with things that don't already have built-in solutions. Thus, design patterns and their application in professional design work are an essential thing to know.

Component interfaces are a critical part of any design. Thus, every potential **interface** in the design object needs to be identified and considered in the creation of the formal architecture. From this consideration, every detail of the external and internal interfaces can be thought through both in terms of proper alignment as well as the potential vulnerabilities.

Every architecture comprises a **structure**. That structure is real, in the sense that it involves an identifiable set of discrete components arranged to fulfill a given purpose. In the strictest sense, that structure is the tangible representation of the product. Therefore, structure is a critical feature in both implementing and sustaining the product as well as securing it. Thus, the proper documentation of the internal functions and organization of that structure becomes a primary aspect of the overall security assurance process.

All of the components in an architecture interact either directly or indirectly. The sum of that **interaction** comprises the overall product functionality and purpose. Thus, the how and why of the discrete interactions within the overall product architecture have to be known and mapped in order to ensure both proper understanding of the operation of the product as well as to understand the unique mechanisms that should be considered in designing sufficient protection for the product.

The active **states** of a design are critically important to document. That is because at its basic level of operation, a product is nothing more than the sum of the modes, states, transitions, and preprogrammed responses that have been built into it. Thus, the consideration and itemization of the specific dynamic states of the product can also serve as the basis for studying potential modes of attack. Thus, dynamic states are a very important consideration in the realm of cybersecurity.

All state changes and component interactions are preprogrammed to be executed based on a rational set of logical steps. The documentation of the underlying **algorithmic** logic is one way to unequivocally describe how the product will operate. Thus, the comprehensive description of the internal details and logic of each component is a particularly important part of detailing the assurance requirements of the product as a whole.

Finally, all designs involve the utilization of **resources**. Therefore, resource considerations are an inevitable part of the product design process. This applies to the business considerations, both in terms of cost benefit and also in terms of strategic prioritization. However, because cybersecurity is resource intensive, the consideration of resource requirements also involves decisions about whether to go forward with the entire project.

Component Identification

The point of this unit will be made again in the section on procurement. It must be understood that counterfeit components are an extreme security threat in any commercial off-the-shelf (COTS) or other type of products. Thus, the set of suggested CSEC2017 topics, including such considerations as watermarking, fingerprinting, metering, encrypted IDs, and physical unclonable functions, are important security measures. The ability to individually mark and then indisputably associate a component to its source is also a means of preventing intellectual property theft.

All of these notions are important elements of the security problem because component arrays and architectures are complex. They are also difficult to tell apart in their particulars. Therefore, Component Security control begins with the labeling of each software and hardware item using a unique and impossible to remove identifier. Those identifiers can include complex watermarks, on images, unique fingerprint labels, and any other mark that is not physically duplicable. Components are often grouped into logical baselines for greater control of the inventory of using these labels.

The point of this activity is to maintain explicit control over an inventory of things by uniquely identifying the components of a build, as well as differentiating its versions. This requires full and complete understanding of the status of each component as it is integrated into products. That is accomplished by explicitly identifying each component or module in a given entity and then placing surreptitious unduplicatable markings on each of those elements in order to ensure tracking and control.

The ability to create an unduplicatable identifier is the key to this process. That is because the identifier is the element that allows for all of the subsequent documentation and tracking of the item. Thus, a baseline composed of components, all having verifiable product identifiers, provides the basis for trust. The aim of the identification process is not simply to prevent intellectual property theft but to ensure that the precise status of a given component, module, product, or system is known at all times based on knowledge of the unique elements.

Anti-reverse Engineering Techniques

As we will see later in this chapter, reverse engineering is a legitimate threat to product security. It allows competitors to understand the underlying structure of products for the purpose of competitive intelligence. It also allows any individual who is capable of reverse engineering to steal intellectual property. Therefore, techniques that make components and their implementations difficult to reverse engineer are a critical part of the body of knowledge for Component Security.

In general, these techniques center on the steps that are taken to obfuscate and/or mask a component design. Obfuscation involves the act of deliberately inserting aspects or elements in a component, or code module, which makes the product difficult for an adversary to understand. That includes such ruses as label obfuscation, which amounts to using meaningless or deceptive terminology for labels; code confusion, which includes writing code in a deceptive, or nonconventional way; and steganography, which is the process of presenting an obfuscated item in a form that either can't be read or is not seen as meaningful. All of these techniques use some form of deception in order to hide the actual intent and form of the component.

Masking is best understood as redaction. Essentially, an aspect of the component is deliberately hidden or eliminated from any form of conventional viewing. The point of reverse engineering is to obtain an understanding of the architecture and components of the target technology. If parts of that technology are either hidden from view, or obfuscated, then it is impossible to achieve full knowledge. That is the aim of masking. Shown in Figure 5.6, common techniques for masking include the following:

- Encryption – redacted elements are encrypted
- Obfuscation – redacted elements are obfuscated by deception
- Perturbation – inputs are modified but elements produce the same output
- Exclusion – specific critical elements are hidden
- Hashing – obfuscates a critical element by a mathematical process.

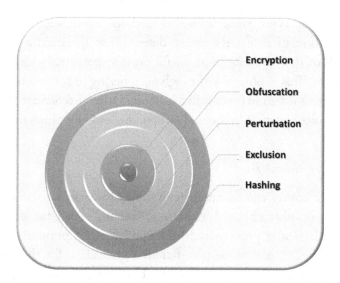

Encryption

Obfuscation

Perturbation

Exclusion

Hashing

Figure 5.6 Common techniques for masking.

Side Channel Attack Mitigation

A side channel attack is any attack that utilizes information gained from analysis of component or product behavior. Examples of this include such common approaches as timing analysis, power consumption analysis, and emanations, which are sometimes known as leaks. These all provide information that can be exploited. Because side channels do not directly involve the understanding of the internal structure of the component, they belong to black box types of attacks. In essence, these approaches all monitor electronic transmissions and other aspects of component performance and then apply statistically based estimation methods in order to draw conclusions about component operation or to obtain data by surreptitious means.

Side channel attacks rely on information that emanates from an unblocked or improperly shielded source. Therefore, the mitigation approaches tend to fall into two main categories. The first of these approaches is practical, simply plug the leak. This can be done through shielding, such as the TEMPEST regulations. It can also be done by a careful identification and analysis of all potential sources of leakage.

The second common method lies in an active attempt to break the linkage between a source of leaked information, such as a public operation that can be reverse engineered, and any protection of sensitive data.

Or in simple terms, since statistical methods are utilized to identify a protected relationship, the easiest defense is to specifically obfuscate any part of the operation that would provide potentially meaningful correlation. This is normally through enciphering or some form of statistical transformation process like hashing. Other defensive techniques include noise injection, frequent key updates, and randomization.

Anti-tamper Technologies

This topic covers the common techniques for making components resistant to physical and electronic assault. Anti-tamper technologies basically prevent modification of a component or product. Obvious countermeasures include obfuscation for the purpose of preventing reverse engineering. However, the most popular approach is the injection of some form of "poison pill" function into the component. That function will be activated if there is any attempt at modification. The iPhone password protection system is an example of this.

Tampering in the software domain is generally considered part of the malware universe. The most obvious example of this is the "backdoor." Because software is so dynamic, it is a bit of a contest between manufacturers and hackers to continue to come up with new attacks and countermeasures. Thus, anti-tamper protections can either be passive, in the form of code reviews, or component physical inspections. Also, with software it is possible to automate the review process using malware scanners and other forms of malicious code detection.

There are also more active approaches such as automata that are built into a product for the specific purpose of detecting common attempts at tampering and then reacting appropriately. This is also true for code in that software analyzers can be dedicated to detecting code elements that "don't fit" and either notifying or actually attempting to fix the problem. This response is built around heuristic detection of anomalies or variations from normal baseline configurations. That technology is capable of detecting and responding in such a way that the component is able to repair itself. Finally, the simplest form of anti-tamper response is the white list, which only allows permitted operations.

Knowledge Unit Two: Component Procurement

This knowledge unit describes the common techniques for ensuring the security of components throughout the procurement life cycle. Component procurement is normally associated with the security threats and risks that apply to products as they move through a formal organizational acquisition process. This process is often called, commercial off-the-shelf, or COTS purchasing. The aim of the security element is to establish a chain of trust from source to destination in any COTS process (Figure 5.7).

The assurance of a chain of trust in products obtained from a complex and remote set of suppliers involves a range of strategies including physical security assurance, as well as source control and traceability assurance. Much of this process is built around inspections and certifications of correctness. As a result, the discrete collection of practices that are aimed at ensuring trustworthy components is often associated with formal credentialing to a given set of criteria. Therefore, security control standards, like ISO 27000 and NIST 800-53, and their auditing are an important part of the execution of the process in this area.

Sourced products are developed through supply chains. The aim of a supply chain is to source a given product or service through coordinated work involving several organizations. The problem is that information and communication technology supply chains produce products that are either abstract, like software, or so infinitesimally complex that they cannot be overseen and controlled by conventional

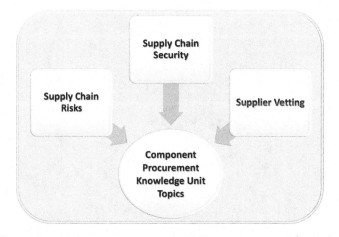

Figure 5.7 Component Procurement knowledge unit topics.

means. Those conditions imply the need for a different set of assurance activities. These are called supply chain risk management practices, and they were developed to address the unique assurance problems associated with the distributed supplier problem. Shown in Figure 5.8, supply chain risk management accomplishes this by providing a consistent, disciplined environment for the following:

- Developing a secure product
- Assessing what could go wrong in the process (i.e., assessing risks)
- Determining which risks to address (i.e., setting mitigation priorities)
- Implementing actions to bring high-priority risks within tolerance.

Typically, supply chains are hierarchical, with the primary contractor forming the root of a number of levels of parent–child relationships. From an assurance standpoint, what this implies is that every individual product of each individual node in that hierarchy has to be proven secure and then correctly integrated with all other components up and down the production ladder. Because the product development process is distributed across a supply chain, maintaining the integrity

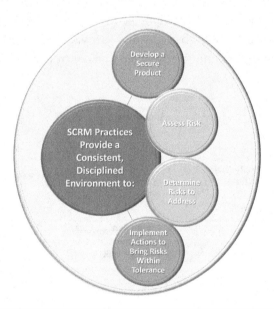

Figure 5.8 Supply chain risk management practice outcomes.

of the products that are moving within that process is the critical part of ensuring overall trust. The weak link analogy is obvious here.

Therefore, the activities within that product's supply chain have to be rationally sourced and precisely controlled in order to ensure against sabotage or unintentional harm. That requires a coordinated set of consistently executed activities to enforce visibility into the process. Thus, the aim of the activities in the CSEC2017 Procurement Knowledge Unit is to ensure the integrity of disparate objects as they move from lower level construction up to higher level integration.

Supply Chain Risks

The risks in information and communication technology supply chains generally fall into five categories, shown in Figure 5.9.

1. The installation of malicious logic on hardware or software. This is generally controlled by the acquisition of sufficient knowledge of supplier practices.
2. The installation of counterfeit hardware or software in the product. This is controlled by performing inspections for fraudulent items at appropriate places in the process.

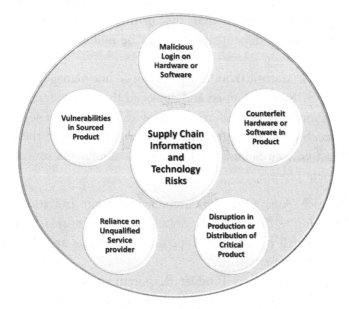

Figure 5.9 Supply chain information and technology risks.

3. The failure or disruption in the production or distribution of a critical product. This is generally addressed by knowing the supplier as well as the imposition of strategic business continuity management techniques.
4. Reliance on a malicious or unqualified service provider for the performance of a technical service. This requires the sourcing organization to always have detailed and intimate knowledge of every component supplier up and down the supply chain.
5. Finally, there is the age-old problem of the creation of unintentional vulnerabilities in one of the modules of the sourced product. This is addressed by consistent execution of a broad range of well-known, common software and hardware assurance practices.

The generic label for this kind of combined best practice is "supply chain risk management" or as it is more colloquially known SCRM.

Supply Chain Security

SCRM is ensured through comprehensive and systematic policies, which are designed to ensure optimum visibility and control. SCRM is deployed and operated as an organizational control function that should be no less rigorous than that of financial control. Thus, the process review and documentation must be maintained in auditable condition.

SCRM is a strategic requirement not an ad hoc managerial activity. Therefore, SCRM is planned and deployed through a strategic management process. It is built around a logical sequence of seven areas of practice. Shown in Figure 5.10, the relevant actions in these seven areas must be continuously performed throughout the sourcing and procurement process.

1. Practice Area One: Procurement Program Initiation and Planning – the customer organization prepares a business case, which defines the scope and boundaries and develops the procurement plan.
2. Practice Area Two: Product Requirements Communication and Bidding – the customer organization issues written requests for proposal to prospective suppliers. This request is

1. Procurement Initiation and Panning—Business case and procurement process is developed

2. Product Requirements Communication and Bidding—Written requests for proposals are issued

3. Source Selection and Contracting—Evaluation criteria for supplier selection is developed

4. Supplier Contract Execution—Process for artifact collection for contracted suppliers is executed

5. Customer Agreement Monitoring—A comprehensive process to monitor supplier is created and executed

6. Customer Acceptance—Customer executes the testing procedures for completed products

7. Project Closure—Product is installed in accordance with established contract requirements

Figure 5.10   Supplier sourcing and procurement process.

based on a formal specification of requirements. It specifies the SCRM terms and conditions and the official acceptance criteria. It might also specify an initial product architecture and assurance case.

3. Practice Area Three: Source Selection and Contracting – this stage develops and specifies the evaluation criteria for supplier selection. It also specifies the assurance criteria. Contract negotiations are performed here as well as the formal methods for product assurance reviews and audits. Along with this, the process for resolving issues is agreed on and the means for corrective action are defined.

4. Practice Area Four: Supplier Contract Execution – once a supplier or supply chain is contracted, the process for creating or delivering the artifact requires a plan to ensure the quality and security of the product. This normally involves a project management plan. That plan is implemented and executed in this phase, and the joint assurance process is executed.

5. Practice Area Five: Customer Agreement Monitoring – in conjunction with Practice Area Four, a comprehensive supplier monitoring process must be created and executed. This process ensures supplier activities up and down the supply

chain through the review and testing processes specified in the contract. The aim is to ensure that necessary information is available as needed.

6. Practice Area Six: Customer Acceptance – once the product is ready for delivery, the customer executes the testing procedures specified in the contract. Each deliverable is subject to acceptance reviews and acceptance testing and the product is accepted from the supplier once all of the specified conditions have been satisfied.

7. Practice Area Seven: Project Closure – the product is then installed in accordance with established contract requirements. Responsibility for the product or service is then transferred to the customer. Normally some form of customer assistance is also provided in support of the delivered product.

Supplier Vetting

Supplier vetting is actually one of the initial stages of every contracting process. Basically, the organization employs a tailored set of best practices, contractual tools, and acquisition methods in order to obtain a secure system component or service from a particular supplier organization. These strategies are oriented toward accumulating the maximum amount of knowledge about all potential supplier organizations.

This research must take place as early as possible in the procurement life cycle, because knowing the background of every potential supplier is an important aspect of supply chain assurance. The organization undertaking that study should make use of every available source of intelligence in order to develop a maximally effective acquisition strategy to guide the rest of the contracting process.

There are a number of different mechanisms that are available for ensuring the security of a supply chain. However, the one universal method is the contract. Contracts specify a concrete basis for the assurance of supply chain security. That includes strategic actions such as auditing or even credentialing suppliers as trusted sources. It also includes practical steps such as requiring a specific set of security measures as a condition of the contract.

Explicit documentation and reporting lines have to be specified for assuring transparency up and down the supply chain. Finally, specific methods for vetting of the processes and security practices of every node in the entire supply must be specified. This includes white–black lists of suppliers from parts of the world that have been known to be security risks. The aim is to ensure that all of the suppliers in the supply chain are fully aware of, and have implemented all of, the supplier's views on the actions that need to be taken to mitigate common methods of attack such as malicious code injection and counterfeiting. This is all embedded in the contract, and so, it is useful to have standard language already prepared that describes strict penalties for any supplier caught performing those actions. Finally, strategies like short delivery schedules and secure storage options can be used to tighten up the supply chain and thereby reduce the risk of exploitation of products in transit.

The organization should conduct a final audit or review of the potential supplier prior to entering into a contractual agreement with them. Considerations in these reviews include such things as the supplier's standard processes for the design, development, testing, implementation, verification, delivery, and support of the purchased product or service. It is also advisable to clarify the supplier's general capability and track record in developing and delivering similar types of products or components.

The reviews give the customer organization greater visibility into historical supplier performance, which serves to address the general problem of potential supply chain breakdowns and supplier malfeasance. Supplier reviews can also help to determine whether suppliers who are higher up the supply chain have sufficient security control over the processes and practices of their subcontractors.

The awareness of subcontractor practices needs to be complete for every element in the supply chain. This is an important consideration because products are integrated bottom up. So, a malicious item introduced at any one of a number of less visible companies at a low level in the supply chain can become a make-it-or-break-it security flaw in the final product.

Knowledge Unit Three: Component Testing

This knowledge unit introduces the specific testing techniques associated with unit design and assurance. It describes the tools and techniques that are employed to validate the security properties of a given component. It also makes the explicit provision for characterizing the approaches that will be used in order to ensure the comprehensive security testing of all of the artifact components or modules. That is the specific means of ensuring overall functional correctness in the design (Figure 5.11).

The unit testing process is what most people visualize when they think of testing. Unit testing is done for each individual component in the build to ensure its correctness prior to integration. The common practice of assuring a constrained set of components or units that comprise a target technology is the bedrock feature of testing any complex build. This is essentially the application of the scientific method. Essentially, the individual components or modules are evaluated using a well-defined set of testing cases. The purpose of the standardization is to get a homogenous assessment of a specific set of issues that are associated with a given product's usage or operation. A unit under test could comprise an entire component architecture, but unit testing is more commonly applied to an individual function or module within that larger structure.

In the end, unit testing is intended to aid in the identification of potential points of failure or exploitation of a given part. Often the constituent test cases, tools, and algorithms are combined into a suite of tests that can be applied in a number of instances for a given purpose. The goal is to determine whether a test unit is working as

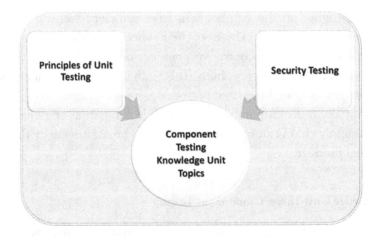

Figure 5.11 Component Testing knowledge unit topics.

intended and satisfies all stated qualification criteria. In essence, the aim is to prove that the component operates properly and will respond effectively to any inappropriate input.

Unit tests are an effective way to approach general assurance in that it makes the necessary understanding of the issues associated with a product clearer. That is because unit testing comes at the point in the build processes that focuses on the smaller, less complex aspects of the larger product. These smaller elements perform a single operation on a restricted set of data, rather than highly complex operations in a larger more monolithic architecture. Consequently, their performance is easier to evaluate in isolation.

The CSEC2017 makes the point that unit testing of components must be distinguished from system-level testing. Therefore, the component testing process is shaped by the characterization of areas of risk that apply only to the item being tested. That identification involves precise specification of the features that must be tested, the requisite test design, or test implementation strategies, as well as the existing sources of input, output, and state data. Finally, any relevant techniques for general data validation must be specified.

Principles of Unit Testing

The aim of unit testing is to isolate a unit in order to authenticate its correctness, independent of all other functions and inputs. Consequently, much of the general process of unit testing is focused on establishing the necessary isolation. Thus, the first step in the unit testing process is the identification and documentation of the specific components or architectural areas to be covered by the unit test set. This identification is a critical issue because unit testing has to be executed within a constrained test space. If that space is not well defined and controlled, the testing itself will be ineffective. The degree of rigor or coverage has to be specified for the same reason. In both instances, a badly defined testing space or inadequate resourcing will produce an outcome that does not ensure adequate confidence in the validity of the outcomes from that testing activity.

When testing is done at the unit level, every executable feature of the component must be covered by a test case. Therefore, every test case should be independent from any other test case that is executed.

Cases should specify the form of the test set, all relevant execution and follow-up activities, hardware or communications requirements, and testing tools and protocols.

Test cases are built around the critical or desired features of the component. These critical characteristics serve as the basis for testing all of the significant execution paths via all meaningful inputs. Finally, the parties responsible for unit testing and unit debugging must be explicitly identified based on the competencies required to ensure a proper outcome.

Rigorous testing discipline is mandatory in order to ensure consistent results. Every single component behavior must be actualized through a test case, except for those behaviors that actually originate in other modules and merely serve as input to the execution of the test subject.

The necessary specification is exhaustive. Specifically, all of the requirements for satisfying the completeness requirements must be made explicit. In addition, any conditions that would justify termination of a unit test process during its execution also must be specified. An example of that would be the detection of an unanticipated but serious anomaly, like a basic conceptual or logical error while the test is in process.

Security Testing

This CSEC2017 topic describes tools and techniques such as the classic stress and fuzz testing of Component Security properties. The aim of both of these is to evaluate functional correctness in a rational fashion, beyond established tolerances. The desired outcome is the identification of exceptions or corner cases – e.g., pathological events that might be created by events that happen just over the boundary between normal operation and the demands of the external environment of the component. Examples of that would be such contingencies as total component failure that might occur just at the boundary of normal operating parameters.

Security tests of this type, particularly of components, are a vital piece of the entire cybersecurity landscape because this type of testing is routinely done early on in the actual construction phase of the process. Consequently, it is the process that is most likely to identify those security problems that are hidden on or just beyond the periphery of normal component performance, at the appropriate time to make corrections.

Stress Testing

Stress testing is a standard element of system performance testing. But it can also be used for security testing. Stress testing puts a high degree of strain or stress on a component. Thus, security stress tests are typically done to map the subject's upper performance limits and to verify failure and recovery modes. Stress testing generally involves software-supported automated volume loading to evaluate performance. The automation is driven by programmed test scripts that execute a particular scenario of inputs for the purpose of producing meaningful information about the performance of the component under stress. Thus, security testing of this type is the most likely mechanism for identifying black swan-type events and other kinds of unwelcome surprises.

Fuzz Testing

Fuzz testing produces a similar set of results, but it is aimed at component reaction to unanticipated inputs, rather than performance issues like stress testing. Thus, fuzz testing normally utilizes automated means to provide a range of random, or unexpected, or invalid data inputs to a component for the purpose of identifying anomalous behaviors and/or performance exceptions such as memory leaks or denials of service.

Fuzz testing is an ideal way to evaluate the marginal correctness of the security performance of a module. As is the case with stress testing, this kind of security testing utilizes scenarios. The scenarios involve providing inputs within a "conceivably acceptable range of validity" that might be accepted as valid by the system but which are sufficiently incorrect to create an exception.

The aim is to identify the exact point where an input might cause a security failure or violate the boundary of secure space. An automated utility called a "fuzzer" is utilized to create a range of potentially valid inputs that could create a problem in special situations that might occur outside of normal operation of the component, such as the SYN flood and SQL injection attacks that seem to be the common stock of every hacker's inventory. Thus, fuzzing is a particularly effective method of security testing.

Penetration Tests

Penetration tests are perhaps the most common form of security testing. Penetration tests attempt to identify and exploit vulnerabilities in a component or a component architecture. A good penetration test will help the organization understand how attackers might infiltrate an existing protection scheme. Penetration tests are normally scenario based and methodology driven. The aim is to produce information that will lead to a solution to any identified security problem. These kinds of tests are frequently aided by automation. But creativity is the key to success in penetration testing. So, it is the individual penetration tester's understanding of component architectures that determines how effective the analysis will be.

All of these approaches are normally arrayed in the form of a test suite. The test suite is a formal organizational artifact that is created by plan and useful as a documentation of the security of a given component or component architecture. This documentation is particularly useful if the component is certified as acceptable by a third party. Thus, in general, security testing of components prior to acceptance and also in operational use is a major part of the overall business of computing.

Knowledge Unit Four: Component Reverse Engineering

This knowledge unit describes techniques for discovering the design and functionality of a component using incomplete information. Reverse engineering is essentially the same general process that a mechanic might follow in order to understand a new engine or scientists might use in order to draw up new theories. In the mechanics case, reverse engineering is the disassembly of the artifact in order to see and understand how it was put together in the first place. In the case of scientific inquiry, reverse engineering applies known principles and practices against an unknown object in order to draw a valid set of conclusions about how that something works (Figure 5.12).

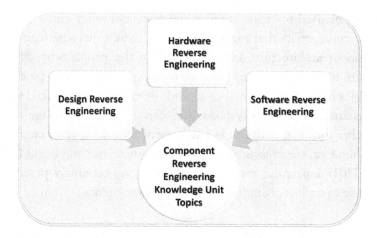

Figure 5.12   Component Reverse Engineering knowledge unit topics.

Reverse engineering is an important technology analysis technique in that it allows the reverse engineer to substantively understand the inner workings of an object that would otherwise be either unknown or a black box. The key condition is that the reverse engineer has little or no current knowledge of the components and/or architecture of the object under study, when they begin the process. So, it is necessary to analytically deconstruct the object in order to identify both its components, as well as their architectural interrelationships.

Reverse engineering is popularly considered to be a hacker activity. But that is not necessarily the case. One legitimate goal of reverse engineering is to simply understand old artifacts like legacy systems or existing hardware items for the purposes of properly documenting them. Another benign use of reverse engineering is to provide a means of identifying anomalous or malicious code in an existing product. This is a particularly important use in security because conventional inspection and validation processes are aimed at identifying and assuring "what is there," not "what shouldn't be there." A reverse engineering process will reveal the detailed operation of the object. Therefore, it is much more likely to identify undesirable or unwanted functions hidden in the artifact.

Obviously, there are nefarious uses for reverse engineering including understanding a competitor's product for adversarial purposes or even to ensure that the reverse engineer's products can seamlessly interface with the existing competitor product. Reverse engineering can also be used to create credible forgeries and other kinds of component counterfeits that can be embedded in an otherwise legitimate component architecture. Of course, all of the people who develop malware utilize reverse engineering techniques in order to plot their strategies for embedding malicious code in existing commercial applications and/or operating systems. The effectiveness of new-age virus's and other forms of malware is a testament to good reverse engineering. Therefore, the presence of a reverse engineering component in the CSEC2017 curricular recommendations is an extremely perceptive response to an increasingly troublesome phenomenon.

Design Reverse Engineering

This topic describes tools and techniques for discovering the design of a component at some level of abstraction. Given this definition, the distinction has to be made between the purpose and intent of design reverse engineering versus design reengineering. That is because much of the underlying methodology is the same.

Reverse engineering's basic goal is "understanding" versus "change." That distinction needs to be kept in mind when applying this process to component design. Design reverse engineering is done exclusively to discover the precise shape of the real-world components and architecture of a given artifact. The overall goal is to represent whatever is revealed through a zero-knowledge analysis using an acceptable form of abstraction. Nevertheless, the representation of a hitherto unknown object is as far as reverse engineering should legitimately go.

However, the aim of component reengineering is to do everything that reverse engineering did and then take the next step process by creating another entirely different form of the product. The latter is a development goal, and although a reverse engineering process may lead to the creation of something malicious or the development of an altered form of the product, those outcomes are derived from the knowledge that is gained via the reverse engineering process, not the aim of the reverse engineering process itself.

In its practical form, reverse engineering is composed of two general activities. These are redocumentation and recovery. Redocumentation amounts to the creation of new representation of the computer code so that it is easier to understand. Recovery is the application of the reverse engineer's contextual knowledge, plus any other external information, in service of the process of deduction. The aim is to secure an understanding of how the product operates. The purpose is to capture and portray the nitty-gritty elements of component structure and behavior. In essence, the goal of design reverse engineering is to understand the purpose and application of a given artifact, not just to characterize how it works. Given the inevitable structure of the computer, there are two logical aspects of design reverse engineering. These are hardware reverse engineering and software reverse engineering.

Hardware Reverse Engineering

This topic describes the tools and techniques that might be utilized in order to fully describe the component structure, and interconnections, as well as any other relevant properties of a component's hardware. This is by convention concentrated at the gate, circuit, and component level of the target artifact. Hardware reverse engineering is a popular pastime in the hacker community as well as with the cybersecurity professionals who do competitive research.

In general, hardware reverse engineering entails the normal reverse engineering processes. But these are aimed lower in the machine – e.g., at getting all of the necessary information about the essentials of internal representation and memory management, firmware programming, bus arrangement, and component interfaces of the target. Hardware reverse engineering can also involve lifting any stored, low-level password or cryptographic information. The information necessary to do proper hardware reverse engineering is usually obtained by any and all means necessary, including theft. However, conventional science-based inquiry is normally the path. This can be tool based and automated.

Popular enterprise platform security assessment frameworks like CHIPSEC support global the necessary functional process analysis questions like how system management is carried out, the shape and composition of the random access memory, all pertinent basic input/output system (BIOS) and buffer information, as well as BIOS access and interface integration. All of these analyses capture data that is vital to understanding the internal operation of the most atomic components of the machine. As shown in Figure 5.13, hardware reverse

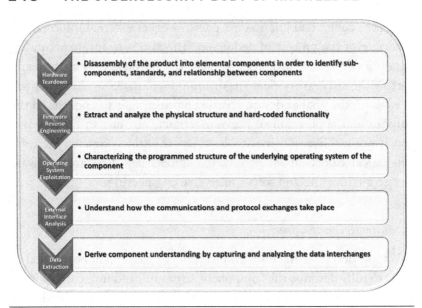

Figure 5.13   Hardware reverse engineering process.

engineering is normally accomplished by decomposing the object of analysis into its constituent elements and is normally done through the following five logical steps.

1. *Hardware Teardown* – the first step is the disassembly of the product into its elemental components. The aim is to identify every component at the subsystem level as well as any standard and/or unique aspect of the relationship between components.

2. *Firmware Reverse Engineering* – the next step is to extract and analyze the elements in terms of physical structure and the hard-coded functionality that operates it. This, of course, is built into every hardware entity, be it gate, circuit, or component physical representation.

3. *Operating System Exploitation* – the next step involves characterizing the precise programmed structure of the underlying operating system of the component. The aim is to capture and then document all of the interactions between the fundamental elements of the machine, such as registers and processing units, or even higher level component element interaction. This is done for the purpose of identifying points of access or exploitation.

4. *External Interface Analysis* – in the application universe, this is sometimes known as jailbreaking. The aim is to understand how the communications and protocol exchanges take place. This is done by capturing and decoding the electronic signals and other forms of interconnection and programmed interaction between components.

5. *Data Extraction* – this is the highest level of hardware analysis in that it derives component understanding based on capturing and analyzing the data interchanges that take place at all three levels of interaction – gate, circuit, and component.

Software Reverse Engineering

This topic encompasses tools and techniques such as static and dynamic analyses that are used to characterize the operation and properties of a given component's software functionality. Software reverse engineering is a popular exercise in the field. It can be used for constructive purposes like security testing and auditing and sustainment analysis for in-house patching or retrofits or even simple inquisitiveness. But it is most commonly used for nefarious purposes like subverting access controls or the removal of copy protection from proprietary files.

There are two main types of reverse engineering for software. The most common and simplest takes place if there is available source code. This activity is more common in the case of sustainment work where legacy code isn't adequately documented or the documentation isn't available. The second instance is the software reverse engineering approach that is more closely associated with security work. That takes place where there is no source code available. This approach is the one that depends on the analysis of the binary code.

Binary code reverse engineering is comprised of protocol analytic methods such as packet sniffers, which are used to understand the behavior of the software while accessing networks and busses. It also might utilize specialized tools like disassemblers, which translate the object code into assembly language statements. Finally, there are the decompilers. These take binary code in as input and then attempt to recreate it as source code. This in effect inverts the compiler function.

All of these methods are used for practical purposes in the field, not just cracking. Software reverse engineering is useful in understanding precisely how a software product will interface with another system and how both systems will interact in support of interoperability. It can also be used to do detailed competitive analysis of other people's products or to "repurpose" an obsolete application. But for the purposes of the CSEC2017, software reverse engineering is a useful tool to fully understand the security implications of the software inventory that is operated within the organization.

Forty Review Questions: Component Security

1. What is functional decomposition? How is it used to create views?
2. What is abstraction? Why is it critical to design?
3. Why is design considered to have management aspects?
4. Why are interdependencies an important part of secure design?
5. How does identification help with intellectual property theft?
6. What is the purpose of information hiding? Why is it important to security?
7. Why is embedding a malicious object a hostile act?
8. What specific problem do counterfeits cause in the design?
9. What is the specific design problem posed by leakages? How is this addressed?
10. What is tampering? How can it be addressed in the design?
11. What is COTS? How does it apply to Component Security?
12. What is a supply chain? What is it composed of?
13. What are the five types of supply chain risks?
14. What is the problem with supplier incapability? How does that affect security?
15. What is the problem with inadvertent defects in a product? Why is that a risk?
16. What is an area of practice? How many are these and how do they apply to security?
17. Why is supplier vetting important? What would happen if this wasn't done?
18. How do contracts control supply chains? What must a contract specifically ensure?
19. What is the purpose of reviews and audits? Where in the process does this apply?

20. Why is supplier certification a good idea for supply chain security?
21. What is a unit test?
22. What differentiates a unit test from other types of testing?
23. Why are unit tests the best place to ensure the security of the component?
24. Why is stress testing a useful security tool?
25. Why is fuzz testing a useful security tool?
26. What is the purpose of penetration testing? Why is it important to security?
27. What is the role of automation in testing? Why is this necessary?
28. What is a test case? How do test cases apply to security?
29. What is a test script? How are they used to ensure security?
30. Why is independence necessary in testing? What does it ensure?
31. What is the purpose of reverse engineering?
32. How does the concept of "zero knowledge" apply to reverse engineering?
33. How is reverse engineering used to steal intellectual property?
34. How is reverse engineering useful as a security mechanism?
35. What are the levels of focus of hardware reverse engineering?
36. What is software reverse engineering? Why is it potentially a problem?
37. Why is the availability of source code a help in reverse engineering?
38. What is binary? How does it apply in the reverse engineering process?
39. What is the role of teardowns in the reverse engineering process?
40. What is the difference between reverse engineering and reengineering?

You Might Also Like to Read

- Andriesse, Dennis, *Practical Binary Analysis: Build Your Own Linux Tools for Binary Instrumentation, Analysis, and Disassembly*, No Starch Press, San Francisco, CA, 2018.
- Britz, Marjie, *Computer Forensics and Cyber Crime: An Introduction*, 3rd Edition, Pearson, London, 2013.

- Clancy, Thomas K., *Cyber Crime and Digital Evidence: Materials and Cases*, 2nd Edition, Lexis-Nexis, New York, 2014.
- Erich, Gamma, Richard Helm, Ralph Johnson, John Vlissides, and Grady Booch, *Design Patterns: Elements of Reusable Object-Oriented Software*, 1st Edition, Addison-Wesley, Boston, MA, 1994.
- Fowler, Martin, *Patterns of Enterprise Application Architecture*, 1st Edition, Addison-Wesley, Boston, MA, 2002.
- Hugos, Michael H., *Essentials of Supply Chain Management*, Essentials Series, 4th Edition, Wiley, Hoboken, NJ, 2018.
- Martin, Robert C., *Clean Architecture: A Craftsman's Guide to Software Structure and Design*, 1st Edition, Prentice-Hall, Upper Saddle River, NJ, 2017.
- Monnappa, K.A., *Learning Malware Analysis: Explore the Concepts, Tools, and Techniques to Analyze and Investigate Windows Malware*, Packt Publishing, Birmingham, 2018.
- Sarkar, Suman, *The Supply Chain Revolution: Innovative Sourcing and Logistics for a Fiercely Competitive World*, AMACOM, New York, 2017.
- Schmalleger, Frank and Michael Pittaro, *Crimes of the Internet*, 1st Edition, Pearson, London, 2008.
- Sigler, Ken, Anne Kohnke, and Daniel Shoemaker, *Supply Chain Risk Management (Internal Audit and IT Audit)*, 1st Edition, Routledge, Abingdon, 2017.
- Wong, Reginald, *Mastering Reverse Engineering: Re-Engineer Your Ethical Hacking Skills*, Packt Publishing, Birmingham, 2018.

Chapter Summary

- The cybersecurity problem lies in the fact that the architecture of digital components is becoming increasingly complex and, as a result, much more vulnerable.
- The CSEC2017s Component Security knowledge area introduces the necessary process considerations, design concepts, and common development methodologies for a curriculum devoted to ensuring trust in digital components.

- Component Security is essentially a design issue. That is, good design practice is the one common factor that ensures the necessary trust in a component architecture.
- No two design activities are ever the same way. Therefore, each individual design process has to be considered to be different in its particulars. Thus, every organization must explicitly specify the process, concepts, methods, and tools that will be utilized in the creation of the desired component architecture.
- The basic premise of digital component design is that the elements of a given functional object have to be characterized to a level of detail that ensures that all constituent elements of that object are fully understood and are correctly interacting.
- The only general methodology that all design activities have in common is functional decomposition. This approach is a traditional conceptual modeling technique that achieves satisfactory understanding of the design space by means of a set of progressively refined views taken of the design object.
- Life cycle management ensures a stable base for the performance of commonly accepted best practices. These best practices dictate how the designers will think about the production of any given design and the necessary assurance concerns that are associated with that artifact.
- In order to create a proper digital component design, the designers draw up a tangible graphic model that conveys the complete picture of the tangible architecture of the entity.
- That model describes each of the various components that comprise the entity as well as their exact interrelationship.
- The real-world form of the design is the direct result of a complete specification of the discrete functional and qualitative requirements.
- Once a complete understanding is achieved of what's required, the designer conceptualizes and documents a complete and consistent top-level architecture.
- Along with a top-level description of the artifact, it is also important to specify how it will be tested and assured. The specification of the exact testing and qualification requirements for each component in the top-level design permits a

much greater level of assurance control over the quality and security of the product.

- Component design security applies sound scientific and engineering principles to the identification of vulnerabilities and the minimization or containment of the risks that might be associated with these vulnerabilities.

- The ability to individually mark and then indisputably associate a component to its source is a means of preventing intellectual property theft.

- The point of identification is to maintain explicit control over an inventory of things by uniquely identifying the components of a build, as well as differentiating its versions.

- Reverse engineering techniques center on the steps that are taken to obfuscate and/or mask a component design.

- Side channel attacks rely on information that emanates from an unblocked or improperly shielded source. Therefore, the mitigation approaches tend to fall into two main categories.

- The first of these approaches involve shielding, such as the TEMPEST regulations.

- The second common method lies in an active attempt to break the linkage between a source of leaked information, such as a public operation that can be reverse engineered and any sensitive protected data.

- Anti-tamper technologies basically prevent modification of a component or product.

- The most popular approach to tampering is the injection of a function that will be activated if there is any attempt at modification. The iPhone password protection system is an example of this.

- Tampering protections in the software domain can either be passive, in the form of code reviews and component physical inspections, or active through approaches like automata that are built into a product for the specific purpose of detecting common attempts at tampering and then reacting appropriately.

- Component procurement is normally associated with the security threats and risks that apply to products as they move through a formal organizational acquisition process.

- The assurance of a chain of trust in products obtained from a complex and remote set of suppliers involves a range of strategies including physical security assurance, as well as source control and traceability assurance.
- Much of this process is built around inspections and certifications of correctness.
- Sourced products are developed through supply chains. The aim of a supply chain is to source a given product or service through coordinated work involving several organizations.
- The problem is that information and communication technology supply chains produce products that are either abstract, like software, or so infinitesimally complex that they cannot be overseen and controlled by conventional means.
- Those conditions imply the need for a different set of assurance activities. These are called supply chain risk management practices, and they were developed to address the unique assurance problems associated with the distributed supplier problem.
- Supply chain risk management (SCRM) is ensured through comprehensive and systematic policies, which are designed to ensure optimum visibility and control.
- SCRM is a strategic requirement not an ad hoc managerial activity. Therefore, SCRM is planned and deployed through a strategic management process.
- Supplier vetting is one of the initial stages of every contracting process.
- The strategies are oriented toward accumulating the maximum amount of knowledge about all potential supplier organizations.
- There are a number of different mechanisms that are available for ensuring the security of a supply chain. However, the one universal method is the contract.
- The common practice of assuring a constrained set of components or units that comprise a target technology is the bedrock feature of testing any complex build.
- A unit under test could comprise an entire component architecture, but unit testing is more commonly applied to an individual function or module within that larger structure.
- In the end, unit testing is intended to aid in the identification of potential points of failure or exploitation of a given part.

- The aim of unit testing is to isolate a unit in order to authenticate its correctness, independent of all other functions and inputs. Consequently, much of the general process of unit testing is focused on establishing the necessary isolation.
- When testing is done at the unit level, every executable feature of the component must be covered by a test case.
- Test cases are built around the critical or desired features of the component. These critical characteristics serve as the basis for testing all of the significant execution paths via all meaningful inputs.
- The desired outcome of security testing is the identification of exceptions or corner cases – e.g., pathological events that might be created by events that happen just over the boundary between normal operation and the demands of the external environment of the component.
- Stress testing puts a high degree of strain or stress on a component. Thus, security stress tests are typically done to map the subject's upper performance limits and to verify failure and recovery modes.
- Fuzz testing normally utilizes automated means to provide a range of random, or unexpected, or invalid data inputs to a component for the purpose of identifying anomalous behaviors and/or performance exceptions such as memory leaks or denials of service.
- Penetration tests attempt to identify and exploit vulnerabilities in a component or a component architecture.
- All testing approaches are normally arrayed in the form of a test suite.
- Reverse engineering applies known principles and practices against an unknown object in order to draw a valid set of conclusions about how that something works.
- Reverse engineering is an important technology analysis technique in that it allows the reverse engineer to substantively understand the inner workings of an object that would otherwise be either unknown or a black box.
- One legitimate goal of reverse engineering is to simply understand old artifacts like legacy systems or existing hardware items for the purposes of properly documenting them.

- Another benign use of reverse engineering is to provide a means of identifying anomalous or malicious code in an existing product.
- Reverse engineering can also be used to create credible forgeries and other kinds of component counterfeits that can be embedded in an otherwise legitimate component architecture.
- Design reverse engineering is done exclusively to discover the precise shape of the real-world components and architecture of a given artifact. The overall goal is to represent whatever is revealed through a zero-knowledge analysis using an acceptable form of abstraction.
- In its practical form, reverse engineering is composed of two general activities. These are redocumentation and recovery.
- Redocumentation amounts to the creation of new representation of the computer code so that it is easier to understand.
- Recovery is the application of the reverse engineer's contextual knowledge, plus any other external information, in service of the process of deduction. The aim is to secure an understanding of how the product operates.
- Hardware reverse engineering involves the tools and techniques that might be utilized in order to fully describe the component structure, and interconnections, as well as any other relevant properties of a component's hardware.
- This is by convention concentrated at the gate, circuit, and component level of the target artifact.
- Software reverse engineering encompasses tools and techniques such as static and dynamic analyses that are used to characterize the operation and properties of a given component's software functionality.
- There are two main types of reverse engineering for software.
- The most common and simplest takes place if there is available source code. This activity is more common in the case of sustainment work where legacy code isn't adequately documented or the documentation isn't available.
- The second instance is the software reverse engineering approach that is more closely associated with security work. That takes place where there is no source code available. This approach is the one that depends on the analysis of the binary code.

Learning Objectives for the Component Security Knowledge Area

Mastery of the requisite learning outcomes for the Component Security knowledge area will be established through the student's ability to paraphrase and explicate the key contents of the knowledge units within this knowledge area (Bloom Levels Two and Three). In addition, the student will exhibit specific behaviors that demonstrate a capability to utilize the relevant concepts in common practical application. Specifically, the student will be able to paraphrase and explain the following 17 knowledge elements:

1. The common vulnerabilities in system components
2. Relevant ways in which discrete Component Security impacts the security of the system
3. The ways in which the concealment of a component's design might be compromised
4. Relevant ways to reverse engineer component design and implementation details
5. The common phases of a component's life cycle
6. The common design artifacts for a component, which might require protection
7. The pertinent principles for secure component design
8. The specific way in which each design principle serves to protect a given component
9. The relevant techniques for protecting the design elements of an integrated circuit
10. The common points of vulnerability in a component's supply chain
11. The common security risks in a component supply chain
12. Commonly accepted methods and principles to mitigate supply chain risks
13. The pertinent applicable differences between unit and system testing
14. Commonly accepted techniques for testing security properties of a component
15. The reasons why someone would reverse engineer a component
16. The difference between static and dynamic analysis in reverse engineering software

17. Relevant techniques for reverse engineering the functionality of an integrated circuit.

Keywords

Architecture – a complete entity or artifact that embodies a complete set of rational objects. These objects are commonly called "components."

Behavior – discrete actions performed that are observable by third parties.

Best Practice – commonly accepted means of carrying out a given task.

Component – an elemental unit or artifact that embodies a single function. These are assembled into structures called "architectures."

Controls – a discrete set of human, or electronic behaviors, set to produce a given outcome.

Critical Function – an action or object that is so central to an operation that it cannot be lost.

Cybersecurity – assurance of confidentiality, integrity, and availability of information.

Infrastructure – a collection of large components arrayed in a logical structure in order to accomplish a given purpose. Commonly used to describe the tangible elements of cyberspace.

Integrity – a critical quality of a component or component architecture.

Strategic Planning – the process of developing long-term directions aimed at furthering and enhancing organizational goals.

Reference

Joint Task Force (JTF) on Cybersecurity Education, "Cybersecurity Curricula 2017, Curriculum Guidelines for Post-Secondary Degree Programs in Cybersecurity, a Report in the Computing Curricula Series", ACM/IEEE-CS/AIS SIGSEC/IFIP WG 11.8, Version 1.0, 31 December 2019.

6

CONNECTION SECURITY

In this chapter, you will learn the following:

- The knowledge units of the Connection Security knowledge area
- The importance of Connection Security in the overall cyber-security process
- The knowledge elements of the Physical Media knowledge unit
- The knowledge elements of the Physical Interfaces and Connectors knowledge unit
- The knowledge elements of the Hardware Architecture knowledge unit
- The knowledge elements of the Distributed Systems Architecture knowledge unit
- The knowledge elements of the Network Architecture knowledge unit
- The knowledge elements of the Network Implementations knowledge unit
- The knowledge elements of the Network Services knowledge unit
- The knowledge elements of the Network Defense knowledge unit.

Introduction: The Challenge of Connecting the Enterprise

Connection Security underwrites trust in the organization's ability to ensure the confidential, correct, and reliable transmission of its information, from both internal and external threats. Thus, Connection Security comprises all of the technologies, processes, and practices that are deployed to protect the organization's networks, computers, programs, and constituent data from attack, damage, or unauthorized access. The unique issue with networks is the level of interconnectedness.

For example, according to SANS Institute, when you connect your private network to the Internet, you are physically connecting it to more than 50,000 unknown networks (Coffey, 2019). Therefore, networks have to be secured by specialized and robust technologies and practices.

Networks afford a host of benefits. But they also involve a boundless array of threats. Because of that fact, it's possible for everything from phishing attempts, to cyberterrorism, to be delivered to your doorstep along with your daily email messages. Consequently, the chief responsibility of Connection Security is to monitor and control the functioning of the organization's network systems. In doing that, Connection Security ensures the reliability of the organizations wide range of communication technologies.

The knowledge in the Connection Security area of the CSEC represents the current thinking about the appropriate response to electronic attack. The attack surface of a network is the sum of the different points where an unauthorized person can attempt to input or extract information. Simple examples of such attack surface vectors include user input fields, protocols, interfaces, and services. Because threats can show up at any time from any place in the world and be as diverse as the human mind can conceive, Connection Security might be the most difficult single aspect of the cybersecurity process. However, the security of connections might also be the most critical task of all, since our economy and our national defense both rely on the safe, stable, and accurate interchange of electronic information.

The specific mission of Connection Security is to protect electronic communications from unauthorized modification, destruction, or disclosure. As such, Connection Security has the unenviable task of guaranteeing that an exponentially growing number of anonymous virtual exploits will not impact a diverse and widely dispersed information infrastructure. It is the range, diversity, and scope and timing of those incidents, as well as the complexity of the medium itself, which makes network security such a compelling and difficult task.

Connection Security has a twofold mission. First, it must protect confidential information from unauthorized access. Second, it has to safeguard the transmissions themselves from malicious or accidental harm. In that task, the primary role of the Connection Security function is to ensure that the components of the network are operating correctly, as well as fulfilling their intended purpose. In addition,

Connection Security assures that the information transmitted through the network keeps its fundamental integrity. That latter responsibility involves all of the steps that are taken to ensure the robustness of the network equipment itself, as well as the media that record and retain information.

Accordingly, the Connection Security function involves carefully designed steps to protect all aspects of the transmission of electronic data. When people think of Connection Security, they normally think about the technological side of the operation. However, in fact, the body of knowledge in Connection Security actually encompasses a wide range of activities, many of which do not directly involve technical work. For instance, proper policy and effective procedures are always necessary to guide the Connection Security process, and even such indirect aspects as routine training and awareness are necessary adjuncts to ensuring the continuing capability of the network. Consequently, the Connection Security function cannot be seen as a strictly technical exercise. Instead, a Connection Security operation embodies a holistic mixture of mutually supporting topics. All of these will be discussed here.

Connection Security is enabled and enforced through a discrete set of countermeasures. Probably the best recognizable Connection Security countermeasure is a firewall. That piece of equipment limits the execution of files or the handling of data through the agency of specific hardware and installed programs. The most familiar hardware countermeasure might be the router. That can prevent the IP address of an individual computer from being directly visible on the Internet. Other countermeasures include encryption/decryption, antivirus, and spyware detection/removal programs.

The imperative is to be able to identify and evaluate risks and respond appropriately. The reality though is that we can't move as fast as the technology pushes us, so we're always forced to play catch-up. Consequently, business and governmental organization must constantly monitor the threat environment in order to identify potential sources of harm and devise the appropriate response as the threat changes. That's a continual process of identification, analysis, and design. Accordingly, there have to be a stable set of formal organizational mechanisms in place to ensure reliable oversight and response.

Fortunately, a large number of best practices have been developed over time, which are aimed at making the network more resistant to subversion. Security breaches occur when the organization does not adequately consider the ongoing changes to the security situation during life cycle network operation. The interfaces between the components of a network and between applications themselves alter as the organization evolves. These connection points are all potential points of vulnerability. Therefore, there is an attendant obligation to think about good Connection Security while undertaking normal business activities. In essence, the network operation always has guarantee that the business communication process and its many interactions, both internal and external, are satisfactorily assured. The term "robustness" is frequently used to describe that outcome.

The CSEC Connection Security Knowledge Areas

As shown in Figure 6.1, the following eight knowledge areas are considered to be elements of the rapidly growing field of Connection Security:

1. *Physical Media* – basic signaling and transmission concepts
2. *Physical Interfaces and Connectors* – connectors, their materials, and standards

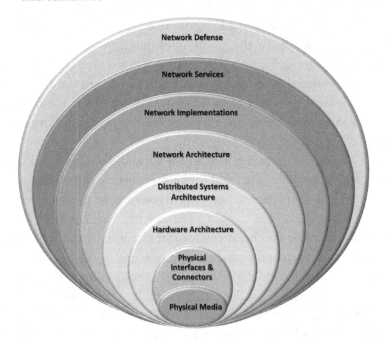

Figure 6.1 The Connection Security knowledge units.

3. *Hardware Architecture* – standard hardware architectures
4. *Distributed Systems Architecture* – the general concepts of distributed systems
5. *Network Architecture* – fundamental network connectivity concepts
6. *Network Implementations* – basic network architectural implementation concepts
7. *Network Services* – different models implementing practical connectivity
8. *Network Defense* – methods and models for effectively protecting networks.

Knowledge Unit One: Physical Media

This knowledge unit introduces the tangible signal transmission process (Figure 6.2). The physical layer of the Open Systems Interconnection (OSI) model (shown in Figure 6.3) is the foundation on which a network is built and its purpose is to transport bits from one computing device to another. Simply put, physical communication media enable the transportation of messages from one computing device to another. Physical communication media comprise the conduits that interconnect numerous devices in a way that allow them to interact in the most effective and efficient way possible.

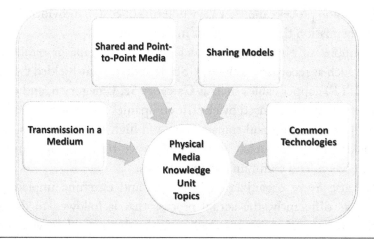

Figure 6.2 The Physical Media knowledge unit topics.

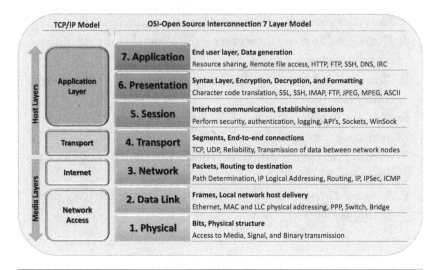

Figure 6.3 OSI model.

Contemporary physical communication media devices facilitate communication and data exchange among a range of entity types. Thus, physical communication media provide the foundation on which business transactions, personal Internet browsing, and countless other methods of interaction rest.

Networks transmit information from point to point in some rational fashion. They provide the physical and software infrastructures to allow many physical endpoints to interconnect and communicate with each other. A variety of physical media are employed in the actual transmission process and they vary in terms of cost, bandwidth capacity, transmission time, and ease of installation.

Examples of physical media include magnetic tape or removable media such as recordable DVDs; USB flash drives; unshielded twisted pair (UTP) copper cables such as Category 5e, Category 6, and coaxial cable; power lines used by electric companies for remote metering; fiber optics for long-haul transmission and high speed; wireless digital media; radio frequency waves, microwave transmission, infrared transmission, and communication satellites.

Because every organization is unique and everyone implements networks differently, the actual process that is followed to design, deploy, and sustain physical media will be distinct. However, there are a few basic areas that apply in every instance. As shown in

Figure 6.2, there are four sub-areas in the Physical Media knowledge area: (1) *Transmission in a medium* – signaling, (2) *Shared and point-to-point media* – communication characteristic of the media, (3) *Sharing models* – the various schemes for sharing media between multiple clients, and (4) *Common technologies* – this topic examines various implementations of the physical communication media topics that are listed above.

Transmission in a Medium

One of the oldest and still most utilized transmission media are twisted pair copper cables. There are two types of twisted pair cables: shielded twisted pair (STP) and UTP. By twisting a pair of two copper wires, Alexander Graham Bell discovered that it reduced electromagnetic radiation and crosstalk between neighboring pairs in telephone systems. STP incorporates a foil shielding around individual pairs of copper wire to provide an electrically conductive barrier to prevent electromagnetic interference. UTP is the most common cable used in computer networking and found in many Ethernet networks and telephone systems. For short- and medium-length connections, twisted pair cabling is often used due to its lower cost compared with fiber-optic or coaxial cable. Telephone cables are typically Category (Cat) 3 cables and is unsuitable for speeds over 16 Mbit/s. Most local area networks (LANs) use Cat 5 or Cat 5e cable.

Coaxial cable, or coax, is another common transmission medium and is used to carry high-frequency electrical signals with low losses. Compared to UTP cable, coax has better shielding and can span longer distances at higher speeds. It is widely used for cable television and metropolitan area networks (MANs), however, has been largely replaced by fiber optics for greater speed and distance. Due to the demands for high-speed Internet access, fiber-optic cabling has been installed in many communities. It is used for long-haul transmission in network backbones and fiber to the home (FttH) implementations. Fiber-optic cable is made of glass, which is made from the inexpensive raw material of sand. It transmits light as opposed to electronic signals and is not subject to electromagnetic interference like copper or coaxial cable types. Fiber-optic cable is also ideal for connecting buildings as it is not sensitive to moisture and lighting.

Wireless technology is increasingly in demand because people always want to be connected to the Internet, email, social media, GPS systems, etc. The most common wireless implementations use radio waves, which are electromagnetic waves of frequencies that travel at the speed of light. Compared to wired networks, wireless networks are frequently subject to electromagnetic interference, which can degrade the signal or cause the system to completely fail. Repeaters, amplifiers, and/or multiple wireless access points are often used to provide signal strength and higher throughput. Examples of wireless networks include satellite communication networks, cellular phone networks, wireless local area networks (WLANs), wireless personal area networks (WPANs), wireless sensor networks, and terrestrial microwave networks.

Shared and Point-to-Point Media

A point-to point connection on a LAN is a connection medium whereby a wire links exactly two endpoints or nodes. Switches provide point-to-point connections on the physical layer (of the OSI Model) and are designed using microsegmentation to allow each client to have a dedicated full-duplex connection to the network. Full duplex allows simultaneous communication in both directions using two channels as opposed to half-duplex where only one direction at a time may transmit. This differs from a hub or a walkie-talkie, in which all connected client nodes must share the same physical media. If more than one party transmits data at the same time, a collision occurs which will result in dropped messages.

A shared medium is where a channel for data transmission, such as a physical wire, wireless network, or radio channel, serves more than one user at the same time. This requires a channel access method as most channels only function properly when one user is transmitting at a time. A channel access method allows several data streams to share the same data transmission medium at the same time using multiplexing. Multiplexing is the interleaving of multiple data streams, which can be sent over a full- or half-duplex link.

To avoid collisions, a multiple access protocol and control mechanism are used, called a medium access control (MAC). Issues such as assigning channels to different users and addressing are handled by the MAC so that each available node on the network may communicate with other nodes on the network. A MAC address serves as a unique identifier for each piece of hardware and is also known as a physical address. To defer transmissions until no other stations are transmitting or regulate access to a shared Ethernet media, a common multiple access protocol is used such as CSMA-CD, carrier-sense multiple access with collision detection. When attaching to a local area or wireless network, a Transmission Control Protocol/Internet Protocol (TCP/IP) network will use both an IP and a MAC address. The MAC address remains fixed to the hardware device; however, the IP address may be dynamically assigned for each session.

Sharing Models

The IEEE, Institute of Electrical and Electronics Engineers, is a professional association formed in 1963, and due to the expansion of its scope into related fields, it is now the world's largest association of technical professionals. Over the years, the IEEE has developed numerous standards for engineering, telecommunications, computers, and allied disciplines. The standard that applies to the topic of sharing models for physical layer specification of technologies from Ethernet to WLANs and MANs is a family of standards referred to as IEEE 802. The IEEE 802 standards are restricted to networks carrying variable-sized data packets as opposed to fixed-sized cells that are transported in cell relay networks. Figure 6.4 shows a list of the active and most widely used standards.

Active IEEE 802 Family of Standards	
Standard Name	Description
IEEE 802.1	Higher Layer LAN Protocols (Bridging)
IEEE 802.3	Ethernet
IEEE 802.11	Wireless LAN, WLAN, & Mesh
IEEE 802.15	Wireless Personal Area Networks (PAN)
IEEE 802.15.1	Bluetooth certification
IEEE 802.15.4	Low-Rate wireless PAN (i.e., ZigBee, WirelessHART, MiWi)
IEEE 802.15.6	Wireless body area network (WBAN) or body sensor network (BSN) for wearable computing devices
IEEE 802.16	Broadband Wireless Access (WiMAX)
IEEE 802.20	Mobile Broadband Wireless Access
IEEE 802.23	Emergency Services Working Group
IEEE 802.24	Smart Grid Technical Advisory Group (TAG)

Figure 6.4 Active IEEE 802 family of standards.

Sharing media between multiple clients requires network access controls in order to identify user login credentials and the MAC addresses of machines on a network. A group of networking protocols for port-based network access controls, commonly referred to as IEEE 802.1X, provides an authentication mechanism for devices wishing to attach to a LAN or WAN. Several authentication protocols were developed for the 802.1X authentication process. The Point-to-Point Protocol (PPP), originally developed for dialup modems, now encapsulates the Ethernet frames and operates over Ethernet (PPPoE) and primarily used by telephone companies to provide digital subscriber line (DSL) connections. PPP includes the Password Authentication Protocol (Pap) and the Challenge Handshake Authentication Protocol (CHAP).

For cable modems and LANs, the extensible authentication protocol over LAN (EAPoL) was developed to provide a generic network sign-on for network resources and to support a wider range of authentication mechanisms to include certificates, public key authentication, and Kerberos, as well as hardware devices such as authentication dongles, USB tokens, and smart cards. The 802.1X authentication packetizes the EAP framework into Ethernet for transmission over a wired or wireless network. The 802.1X authentication process requires three parties: a supplicant which is a client/end user device such as a laptop, an authenticator such as an Ethernet switch or wireless access point, and an authentication server, which decides whether to accept the user's request for network access. The typical authentication process consists of: (1) Initiation – the end user's computer and authenticator device exchange a series of requests and responses before the user provides their user ID and password. The credentials are then encapsulated and forwarded to an authentication server. (2) Negotiation – the authentication server sends a reply to the authenticator device containing a request specifying the method it wishes the authenticator device to perform such as the EAP protocol. The authenticator device can either start using the requested method or respond with a negative acknowledgment and a different method in which it is willing to perform. (3) Authentication – if the authentication server and end user device agree on a method, requests and responses are sent until the authentication server responses with a success or failure message. If the authentication is successful, normal traffic is allowed.

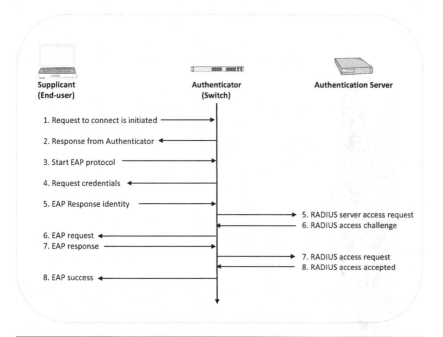

Figure 6.5   802.1X authentication process.

Figure 6.5 shows the 802.1X process to include the EAP protocol between the end user, switch, and authentication server.

Common Technologies

In addition to the standard for sharing media, the IEEE developed standards for the physical media and working characteristics of Ethernet, which is a LAN technology. The 802.3 standard started in 1980 and has evolved over the years to include faster speeds and a variety of cable media types. The increasing speeds have allowed for networks to handle transmissions of increasingly sizable files such as high-resolution photos/images, streaming video, MP3 and MP4 files, computer-aided design (CAD) drawings, and database files. The demand for faster speeds for Internet connectivity has allowed website designers to include all sorts of graphics, video clips, and features that were impossible at slower speeds.

Figure 6.6 outlines the evolution of advances in cable media types and communication standards that were developed under the IEEE 802.3 standard.

	Evolution of IEEE 802.3 Implementations	
IEEE Standard	Date	Description
Ethernet I	1980	10 Mbit/s (1.25 MB/s) over thick coax cable
IEEE 802.3	1983	10BASE5 10 Mbit/s (1.25 MB/s) over thick coax cable
IEEE 802.3a	1985	10BASE2 10 Mbit/s (1.25 MB/s) over thin Coax (a.k.a. thinnet or cheapernet)
IEEE 802.3i	1990	10BASE-T 10 Mbit/s (1.25 MB/s) over twisted pair
IEEE 802.3j	1993	10BASE-F 10 Mbit/s (1.25 MB/s) over Fiber-Optic
IEEE 802.3u	1995	100BASE-TX, 100BASE-T4, 100BASE-FX Fast Ethernet at 100 Mbit/s (12.5 MB/s) with autonegotiation
IEEE 802.3y	1998	100BASE-T2 100 Mbit/s (12.5 MB/s) over voice-grade twisted pair
IEEE 802.3ab	1999	1000BASE-T Gbit/s Ethernet over twisted pair at 1 Gbit/s (125 MB/s)
IEEE 802.3ae	2002	10 Gigabit Ethernet over fiber; 10GBASE-SR, 10GBASE-LR, 10GBASE-ER, 10GBASE-SW, 10GBASE-LW, 10GBASE-EW
IEEE 802.3af	2003	Power over Ethernet (15.4 W)
IEEE 802.3an	2006	10GBASE-T 10 Gbit/s (1,250 MB/s) Ethernet over unshielded twisted pair (UTP)
IEEE 802.3ba	2010	40 Gbit/s and 100 Gbit/s Ethernet
IEEE 802.3bm	2015	100G/40G Ethernet for optical fiber
IEEE 802.3bp	2016	1000BASE-T1 – Gigabit Ethernet over a single twisted pair, automotive & industrial environments
IEEE 802.3bs	2017	200GbE (200 Gbit/s) over single-mode fiber and 400GbE (400 Gbit/s) over optical physical media –Ethernet with speeds over 100 Gbit/s is Terabit Ethernet (TbE)

Figure 6.6 Evolution of IEEE 802.3 implementations.

As mentioned previously, the demand for and implementations of wireless technology have become ubiquitous. Wireless technology, also known as Wi-Fi, falls under the IEEE 802.11 standards and has evolved similarly to Ethernet in that speeds have improved significantly over the years. However, these improvements require hardware upgrades as the new protocols are introduced. For example, starting in 1997, wireless routers originally supported speeds of 1 Mbit/s (IEEE 802.11) and is now obsolete. In 1999, a dramatic increase in throughput led to the brisk adoption of the IEEE 802.11b standard and included additional devices such as cordless telephones and baby monitors. In June 2003, higher data rates of 54 Mbit/s and lower manufacturing costs were introduced in IEEE 802.11g; however, devices such as wireless keyboards experienced interference from other products operating in the 2.4 GHz frequency band. The standard, IEEE 802.11n, was introduced to improve upon the previous standards by adding multiple-input multiple-output (MIMO) antennas to operate at both the 2.4 and 5 GHz frequency bands with the data speeds increasing to 600 Mbit/s. In 2013, IEEE 802.11ac included wider channels (80 or 160 MHz versus 40 MHz) in the 5 GHz frequency band yielding speeds of 1,300 Mbit/s and added multiuser MIMO. Currently in development is the successor to 802.11ac that will increase the efficiency of WLAN with the goal of delivering four times the throughput of 802.11ac at the user layer of the OSI Model.

For consumers who live in rural areas with few options and have previously relied on dial-up connections for their Internet, fixed wireless broadband has been introduced in IEEE 802.16, a series of wireless broadband standards. Fixed wireless Internet uses stationary wireless access points and radio signals to connect directly to customer sites. There are no physical wires like fiber-optic or coax cables involved, and this technology is able to achieve speeds between 10 and 30 Mbit/s. The working group for this standard was established in 1999; however, it wasn't until the IEEE 802.16e-2005 amendment in which fixed wireless broadband was being deployed around the world. Fixed wireless Internet providers are much smaller than the large cable and DSL corporations and currently provide only 51% coverage nationwide although the demand is increasing (BroadbandNow.com, 2019). One significant limitation with this technology is the requirement to have a direct line of sight between a customer's antenna and

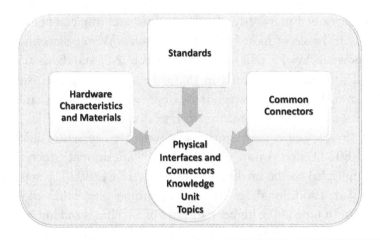

Figure 6.7   The Physical Interfaces and Connectors knowledge unit topics.

the ground station of the provider and severe rainstorms cause reductions in download and upload speeds.

Knowledge Unit Two: Physical Interfaces and Connectors

This knowledge unit describes the characteristics of connectors, their materials, and standards that define the characteristics of the connectors. Different materials have different characteristics and signal transmission capability. Even nontechnical security people need to understand that optical fiber is different than twisted pair and that each has different standards and specific standard connectors. As shown in Figure 6.7, there are three sub-areas in the Physical Interfaces and Connectors knowledge area: (1) *Hardware characteristics and materials* – linking characteristics of various media, (2) *Standards* – the various standards for connectors, and (3) *Common interconnectors* – this presents examples of connectors.

Hardware Characteristics and Materials

When architecting a network, the topology and size of the network will determine the type of cable chosen. So, it is important to understand the types of cable in regard to their connection characteristics, speed, and distance limitations. In networks using cable media, there are three choices: twisted pair, coaxial, and fiber-optic cables.

As mentioned previously, twisted pair cabling comes in two varieties: shielded and unshielded. One of the most popular selections and often the best option is UTP. The quality of UTP varies from telephone-grade wire to cables that have the ability to support very high-speed data transmissions.

A standard UTP cable has four pairs of wires, with each pair twisted together in varying number of twists. The higher number of twists per inch helps eliminate interference from surrounding electrical devices and also from the other pairs of wires next to it. Higher transmission rates are achieved when the wires are twisted together more tightly. This additional twisting also raises the cost per foot and can be a substantial cost of the overall network implementation. Established by the Telecommunications Industry Association (TIA) and the Electronic Industries Alliance (EIA), there are currently eight rated categories of UTP cables used for telephone and networking. Figure 6.8 outlines the category, application, speed, and distance limitations of networking cable.

STP is more expensive than UTP cabling; however, if the networking cable will be placed in environments with potential electrical frequency interference, STP may be a good solution. STP cable is available in three configurations: (1) Each pair of copper wires is individually shielded with foil, (2) a foil or braded shield

UTP Category	Application	Max Data Rate	Maximum Length
Level 1/Cat 1	Voice and modem cables	1 Mbit/s	
Level 2/Cat 2	Older legacy systems such as IBM 3270, LocalTalk & Telephone, deployed on Token Ring Networks	4 Mbit/s	
Cat 3	10BASE-T Ethernet and Token Ring Networks	10 Mbit/s	100 meters
Cat 4	Token Ring Networks, not commonly used.	16 Mbit/s	100 meters
Cat 5 (2 pair)	100BASE-TX Fast Ethernet	100 Mbit/s	100 meters
Cat 5 (4 pair)	1000BASE-T Gigabit Ethernet	1000 Mbit/s	100 meters
Cat 5e	1000BASE-T Gigabit Ethernet and 2.5GBASE-T, provides improved crosstalk specification, common for current LANs.	1000 Mbit/s	100 meters
Cat 6	5GBASE-T and 10GBASE-T Gigabit Ethernet, contains a physical separator between the four pairs to reduce electromagnetic interference. 10GBASE-T is supported for lengths up to 55 meters.	10,000 Mbit/s	100 meters
Cat 6a	5GBASE-T and 10GBASE-T Gigabit Ethernet, 10GBASE-T is supported for lengths up to 55 meters. Provides better immunization o crosstalk and electromagnetic interference.	10,000 Mbit/s	100 meters
Cat 7	5GBASE-T, 10GBASE-T, or POTS/Cat 5/1000BASE-T over a single cable. Is not currently recognized by the TIA.	10,000 Mbit/s	100 meters
Cat 8/8.1/8.2	25GBASE-T and 40GBASE-T, has designations by ANSI/TIA-568-C.2-1, ISO/IEC 11801-1:2017.	40,000 Mbit/s	30 meters

Figure 6.8 Categories of UTP cable.

inside the jacket wrapped around all pair of wires, and (3) a shield is placed around each individual pair as well as around the entire group of wires and is commonly referred to as double shield twisted pair.

Unlike UTP, coaxial cabling is highly resistant to signal interference and can support greater distances between network devices. Thin coaxial cable, referred to as thinnet, is a 10Base2 standard with the "2" referring to the approximate distance limitation of 200 m. Thick coaxial cable, referred to as thicknet, is a 10Base5 standard with the "5" referring to the approximate distance limitation of 500 m. Coaxial cabling has at its core a single copper conductor with a plastic layer providing insulation between the center copper conductor and the next layer of a braided metal shield. The metal shield's function is to block any outside interference such as fluorescent lights, which are often installed along with the coax cable in the ceiling.

The standard 10BaseF refers to fiber-optic cabling which costs comparable to copper cabling; however, it is more difficult to install and modify. The center of a fiber-optic cable is a glass core through which light propagates and is surrounded by a shield of either glass or plastic fibers to prevent breakage and keep all of the light in the core. The shield is then surrounded by an outer insulating jacket made of Teflon or PVD in order to protect the glass shield. Two types of fiber cables are single and multimode. Multimode fiber-optic cables are larger in diameter and have distance limitations shorter than sing mode; however, the single mode cable is more expensive.

Standards

The TIA/EIA developed wiring standards (both ends 568A or both ends 568B for straight-through cables or one end 568A and the other end 568B for a crossover cable) to specify the pin arrangements in RJ45 connectors on UTP and STP patch cables. The number 568 refers to the order of the wires (pin assignment) within a Cat 5/5e/6, etc. cable terminated in the plastic RJ45 modular connector. Although you can order varying lengths of patch cables with ends already connected, Cat 5/5e/6 cable also comes on a spool to make your own for greater lengths. Many network administrators

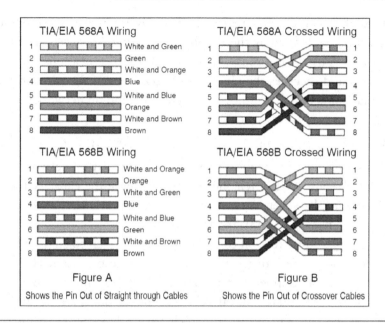

Figure 6.9   Pin assignments for the TIA/EIA 568A and 568B standards.

make their own patch cords by terminating the ends of the cable in a RJ45 connector by using a crimper and need to know the pin assignments. Figure 6.9 shows the pin number assignments for the 568A and 568B standards.

To interconnect similar devices such as hosts, switches, and routers, a crossover cable may be required. The difference between a straight-through cable and a crossover cable is that two of the wires are crossed when terminating into the plastic modular connector. Wires 1 and 3 and 2 and 6 are crossed for a crossover cable versus all wires running straight through. The hardware manufacturer generally notes in the specifications of the equipment when a crossover cable is required.

Common Connectors

In order to connect any of the abovementioned cable types to networking equipment, a variety of connectors are used. Connectors allow the transmission media to be physically connected into the different networking equipment used on a typical network. The standard connector for shielded and UTP cabling is an RJ45 plastic and modular connector that resembles a telephone connector (RJ11) only slightly larger. The registered jack (RJ) connection standard was originally defined by the telephone company; however, the RJ45 connector is used for a range of physical layer specifications such as Ethernet and specifies the pinout or the positions of the wires in the modular connector. The following is a list of common network media connectors:

- RJ45 – registered jack connectors are used with twisted pair cabling and are the most prevalently used today on networks.
- RJ11 – are used in telephone jacks and have the capacity for six pins; however, a standard telephone connection uses only two pins while a DSL model uses four.
- F-type – are screw-on connectors used to attach coaxial cable to cable modem or satellite Internet service providers' (ISP) equipment. Connector types are called RG-59 and RG-6.
- Fiber – there are several types of connectors for fiber and include the ST connector which uses a half-twist bayonet type of lock; the LC connector is similar to an RJ45 and uses snap lock, the SC connector uses a push–pull connector similar to common audio and video plugs and sockets, and the MTRJ connector is popular for two fibers and is half the size of an SC connector and slightly smaller than an RJ11 telephone connector. The compact design of the MTRJ is known as a small form factor (SSF) connector configuration for the demand for smaller components in network systems. There are at least three designs: LC by Lucent, VF-45 made by 3M, and the MTRJ by Tyco.
- USB – universal serial bus ports are now very common and come in types A and B, used for many peripheral devices.
- BNC – are associated with coaxial media and 10Base2 networks. These are legacy connectors for older network cards, hubs, and networks with using mainframe computers.
- RS-232 – recommended standard 232 is a TIA/EIA standard for serial transmission.
- IEEE 1394 interface – also known as FireWire, the 1394 connector is associated with the attachment of peripheral devices such as cameras or printers and comes in a four- or six-pin version.

Knowledge Unit Three: Hardware Architecture

This knowledge unit introduces the basic concepts and potential vulnerabilities of standard hardware architectures. Architecture is a tangible realization of a given intention by the designer. At its most basic, hardware architecture is chip design. At its broadest, hardware architecture involves huge multicomponent, global systems. Architecture as a generic term normally refers to the design constituents and interfaces of a system. It includes the discrete components themselves as well as the logic of their interrelationships. Architects conceptualize a rational array of "things" that achieve the basic purposes of a system. Those things are architected in such a way that they can be shown to most effectively achieve the intents of a given system. In creating that system, the developers simply integrate the concrete system elements into a tangible entity. In general, this is an umbrella process, in that the overall design process encompasses all of the activities that might be pertinent to the construction of a tangible system of components and interfaces.

Hardware architecture is not software architecture. That distinction needs to be kept in mind when considering this particular topic. Hardware architecture obeys the rules of the physical universe. The outcomes of a hardware architectural design are strictly linear and predictable, and they are derived based on modeling and design. The software architecture runs on the much more constrained hardware architecture, and it is the constraints of the hardware that dictate the shape of the software design. Also, software functionality can be embedded in hardware. Still, the two types of architecture are inextricably linked in the design process.

Hardware architectures have to get around the limitations imposed by the physical world. That makes it a design process at its base. A multifaceted arrangement of logic gates and other electronic components is required in order to fulfill the machine's particular purpose. That process is supported by mathematical proofs of desired performance as well as complex system modeling of the components and interfaces. In all respects, however, the actual rules for the execution of the process remain the same and they are all clearly constrained by the natural laws of physics. Thus, the steps that are involved in developing hardware architectures are rational in appearance and

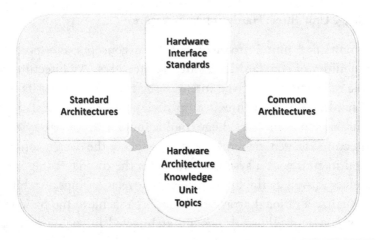

Figure 6.10   The Hardware Architecture knowledge unit topics.

they focus on building the proper arrangement of components and interfaces from bottom to top within a top-down structure of logical elements. The interfaces are the critical aspect of the process in that it is their interaction that provides the intended functionality. These range from the logic gates at the bottom of the hierarchy to the human–computer interface at the top. All of these things must be precisely aligned to achieve the purpose of the architecture. This is a very large consideration conceptually. As shown in Figure 6.10, there are three sub-areas in the Hardware Architecture knowledge area: (1) *Standard Architectures* – standard architectures and the advantages of standardization, (2) *Hardware interface standards* – the various hardware interface standards, and (3) *Common architectures* – this presents examples of current technologies (CPU chips, PC motherboard, Ethernet standards).

Standard Architectures

Standardization of network components over the years has dramatically improved compatibility, efficiency, and network support costs. An example of this is motherboard, also known as the system board or the main board of a computer and the backbone of a computer. A motherboard is a printed circuit board (PCB) within a typical desktop computer, laptop, or server and contains buses that interconnect electronic components such as central processing units

(CPUs), random access memory (RAM) modules, basic input/output system (BIOS) chips, and other chipsets. The form factor of a motherboard pertains to the dimensions, power supply type, location of mounting holes, and the physical layout of the various components and devices attached to the board. Although there have been many variations developed, there are three common motherboard form factors: (1) Advanced Technology eXtended (ATX) – this is the most common, (2) Micro-ATX – this is smaller than the ATX and has fewer expansion slots, however, but can use many of the same components, chipsets, and power connectors used in the full-sized ATX boards, and (3) ITX (Mini, Nano, Pico, Mobile) – designed for small devices with the Mini-ITX being the most popular. Mini-ATX motherboards were designed for thin clients and generate less heat.

The design and standards of motherboards have been influenced over the years as new generations of components were developed. For example, in 1981, IBM first developed the Industry Standard Architecture (ISA) 16-bit internal bus, designed to connect peripheral cards to the motherboard and was superseded in 1992 by Intel's PCI (peripheral component interconnect) 32-bit/64-bit Local Bus standard, which is currently used in most computers. Later revisions of PCI (PCI-Extended) added performance improvements such as higher bandwidth and new features. So, as components themselves have improved to add functionality, the standard size and layout (form factor), as well as the lists of required components on motherboards, have changed much more slowly.

Hardware Interface Standards

Because of the variety of devices and manufacturers, standards for the hardware interfaces have been critical in order to ensure reliability and compatibility. Hardware interfaces are designed to interconnect two devices together and are comprised of the cables, sockets, and electrical signals that pass through each line between the peripheral device and the CPU on the motherboard. The CPU handles all instructions from the hardware and software running on the computer. Examples of hardware interfaces include the CPU socket on the motherboard, which dictates what kind of CPU chips can be used; a USB port, in which a variety of devices can be plugged such as printers, external hard drives, cameras, flash drives, etc.; and an RJ45 Ethernet port in which a cable is plugged so that the computer can connect to the LAN.

At the heart of microprocessor chips and anything that uses radio waves are semiconductor chips created with silicon (hence, the expression "Silicon Valley"). Semiconductors require protection from the elements and physical damage, as well as a case (package) for mounting the electrical contacts connecting it to the motherboard. The package is called an integrated circuit or IC Package that contains the semiconductor device. IC Packaging elements that include a protective barrier, resins, encapsulants, substrates, and metal conductors have been developed and fine-tuned over time so that manufactures could determine which formulations best suited particular environments to ensure performance and reliability.

The chemical, electrical, and material of an IC Package determine the performance and reliability and require a standardized structure. So, organizations such as IEEE, NIST, and TIA/EIA developed standards for hardware interfaces. Figure 6.11 shows some of the standard bodies for hardware interfaces as well as other important elements of connectivity.

Common Architectures

The hardware architecture of computers refers to the system's physical components and their interconnectivity. Computing devices can be configured to be built with many different components, but there are certain components that are required for every device such as: motherboard and components directly attached to it, for instance: CPU – central processing unit, RAM – random access memory, Chipset, read-only memory, Busses, CMOS battery, video card, monitor, data storage and hard drive, graphics card, sound card, speakers, camera, and power supply. As motherboards are considered to be the backbone of the computer, the CPU is considered to be the brain and the most important element of a computer system. Modern CPU processor chips, called microprocessors, are contained on a single IC chip, have different form factors, and require a

The Organizations Responsible for Computer and Connectivity Standards	
Name of Standards Entity	Responsibilities
ANSI-American National Standards Institute	Oversees voluntary consensus standards for products, services, processes, systems, and personnel.
IEEE-SA-Institute of Electrical and Electronics Engineers Standards Association	Develops global standards for information technology, information assurance, telecommunication, and many others. IEEE 802 (LAN/MAN); IEEE 488.1 (Standard Digital Interface for Programmable Instrumentation); IEEE 1233 (System Requirements Specification); IEEE 1417 (System Architecture)
ETSI-European Telecommunications Standards Institute	Produces globally-applicable standards for Information and Communications Technologies (ICT), including fixed, mobile, radio, converged, broadcast and internet technologies.
NIST-National Institute of Standards and Technology	Develops U.S. standard reference materials that are certified as having specific characteristics or component content and used as calibration standards for measuring equipment and procedures, quality control benchmarks for industrial processes, and experimental control samples.
CCIA-Computer & Communications Industry Association	Dedicated to innovation and enhancing society's access to information and communications through open markets, open systems, open networks and full, fair and open competition in the computer, telecommunications and Internet industries.
TIA/EIA-Telecommunication Industry Association (TIA) and the Electronic Industries Alliance (EIA)	TIA's Standards division convenes communities of interest around nine engineering committees and is the administrator for a number of U.S. Technical Advisory Groups. These communities conduct the writing and maintenance of voluntary, industry-driven, consensus-based standards and specifications for the ICT industry. X.400 suite define standards for email.
IEC-International Electrotechnical Commission	Publishes consensus-based International Standards and manages conformity assessment systems for electric and electronic products, systems and services, collectively known as electrotechnology.
ISO-International Organization for Standardization	ISO is a membership organization that brings together experts to share knowledge and develop voluntary, consensus-based, market relevant International Standards that support innovation and provide solutions to global challenges.
ITU-International Telecommunication Union, ITU-T is the Telecommunication Standardization Sector	A specialized agency of the United Nations responsible for issues that concern information and communication technologies.
JEDEC Solid State Technology Association	semiconductor engineering trade organization and standardization body responsible for the standardization of part numbers, defining an electrostatic discharge (ESD) standard, and leadership in the lead-free manufacturing transition.
Japan Electronics and Information Technology Industries Association	Responsible for the research, development, and standards of electronics and IT industries.
PCMCIA-Personal Computer Memory Card International Association	Developed a standard for small, credit card-sized devices, called PC cards, that are often used in notebook computers.

Figure 6.11 Organizations responsible for computer and connectivity standards.

particular socket on the motherboard. There are two common architectures for CPU processors and sockets: (1) land grid array (LGA) – the pins to insert the chip to the motherboard are on the socket instead of the processor and (2) pin grid array (PGA) – the pins are on the underside of the processer, which are designed to be inserted into the motherboard CPU socket using zero insertion force (ZIF). As mentioned previously, the CPU handles the instructions between the hardware and software by use of an instruction set. There are two distinct types of instruction set architectures in which CPUs utilize, they are: (1) CISC – complex instruction set computer, uses a large set of complex specialized instructions to execute operations such as arithmetic calculations, a load from memory, and a memory store and (2) RISC – reduced instruction set computer, uses a smaller set of simpler instructions in a much quicker fashion than CISC instruction sets.

In advancing technology, manufactures have found ways to incorporate multiple CPU cores into a single IC chip which each read and execute program instructions. These CPUs are called multicore processors; however, any increase of performance depends on the software application's design use of multiple threads with the application and the operating system. Figure 6.12 shows the latest commercial multiprocessors developed from some leading vendors.

Knowledge Unit Four: Distributed Systems Architecture

The distributed systems topic introduces the general architectural principles that underlie the mechanism of connecting ourselves together. The aim of this topic is to help the student understand the concept of distributed systems and their interconnection methods. The idea of distributed systems really took off in the 1990s when client–server architecture first became popular. In essence, for the first time, a diverse array of computers could be interconnected using some type of centralized processor. The enabling software was typically termed "netware," or a "network operating system." The single, cohesive result was a comprehensive collection of components spread over a wide geographic area. That integration of processing power enabled an extensive range of capabilities, as well as allowed easier sharing. The

Examples of Commercial Multiprocessors	
Vendor	**Processor**
AMD	*Opteron* processor: single, dual, quad, 6, 8, 12, and 16-core server/workstation processors *Phenom* processor: dual, triple, and quad-core processors *Phenom II* processor: dual, triple, quad, and 6-core desktop processors *Sempron* processor: single, dual, and quad-core entry level processors *Turion* processor: single and dual-core laptop processors *Ryzen* processor: dual, quad, 6, 8, 12, 24, and 32-core desktop, mobile, and embedded platform processors *Epyc* processor: quad, 6, 8, 12, 24, 32, and 64-core server, and embedded processors
IBM	*POWER7* processor: a 4,6,8-core PowerPC processor, released in 2010 *POWER8* processor: a 12-core PowerPC processor, released in 2013 *POWER9* processor: *a 12 or 24-core PowerPC processor, released in 2017* *PowerPC 970MP* processor: a dual-core PowerPC processor, used in the Apple Power Mac G5 *Xenon* processor: a triple-core, SMT-capable, PowerPC microprocessor used in the Microsoft Xbox 360 game console *z10* processor: a quad-core z/Architecture processor, released in 2008 *z196* processor: a quad-core z/Architecture processor, released in 2010 *zEC12* processor: a six-core z/Architecture processor, released in 2012 *z13* processor: an eight-core z/Architecture processor, released in 2015 *z14* processor: a ten-core z/Architecture processor, released in 2017
Intel	*Core i3, Core i5, Core i7* and *Core i9* processors: a family of dual, quad, 6, 8, 10, 12, 14, 16, and 18-core processors, and the successor of the *Core 2 Duo* and the *Core 2 Quad* *Itanium* processor: single, dual-core, quad-core, and 8-core processors *Pentium* processor: single, dual-core, and quad-core processors for the entry-level market *Xeon* processor: dual, quad, 6, 8, 10, 12, 14, 15, 16, 18, 20, 22, 24, 26, 28, 32, 48, and 56-core processors *Xeon* Phi processor: 57, 60, 61, 64, 68, and 72-core processors
Nvidia	*GeForce* processor: 200 multi-core GPU (10 cores, 24 scalar stream processors per core) *Tesla* processor: multi-core GPGPU (10 cores, 24 scalar stream processors per core)
Sun Microsystems	*UltraSPARC T1* processor: an eight-core, 32-thread processor *UltraSPARC T2* processor: an eight-core, 64-concurrent-thread processor *UltraSPARC T3* processor: a sixteen-core, 128-concurrent-thread processor *SPARC T4* processor: an eight-core, 64-concurrent-thread processor *SPARC T5* processor: a sixteen-core, 128-concurrent-thread processor

Figure 6.12   Examples of commercial multiprocessors.

most common example of that concept now is the Internet. However, the student must still understand that the Internet is not the only network and TCP/IP is not the only protocol.

Architecture at its lowest level in the hierarchy is the interconnection of multiple CPUs in some form of LAN arrangement. At the highest level, a massive array of shared computing processes can be enabled in a wide area network (WAN) architecture that will produce the equivalent of a supercomputer. The wide area concept allows for everything from simple virtual private networks (VPNs) to the architecture of the World Wide Web. Normally, in the latter type of environment, all of the clients are stateless, and the sharing architecture can involve anything from simple client–server connections to peer-to peer arrangements. At the message transfer level, the interconnection of networks is normally enabled through various packet-based messaging protocols, such as TCP/IP, User Datagram Protocol (UDP), or Hypertext Transfer Protocol (HTTP). Each implementation has specific characteristics and different potential vulnerabilities. The focus of the learning should be on the similarities, and differences in these approaches, and why design choices are made.

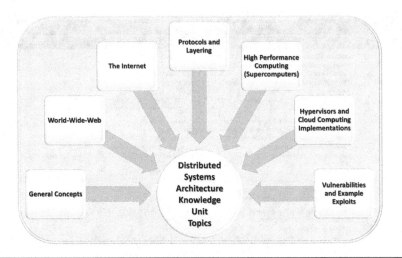

Figure 6.13   The Distributed Systems Architecture knowledge unit topics.

Network architectures are planned and designed. Therefore, knowledge of general principles, network constituents, and interconnection methods is a must. As shown in Figure 6.13, there are seven subtopic areas in the Distributed Systems Architecture knowledge area: (1) *Network Architectures, General Concepts*: designing and building an enterprise network; (2) *World Wide Web*: specific protocols that enable the worldwide web; (3) *The Internet*: evolution of the Internet; (4) *Protocols and Layering*: operational layers; (5) *High Performance Computing (Supercomputers)*: aggregating computer resources to accomplish a given task; (6) *Hypervisors and Cloud Computing Implementations*: infrastructure as a service (IaaS), software as a service (SaaS), and platform as a service (PaaS); and (7) *Vulnerabilities*: the attack surface of a network.

Network Architectures, General Concepts

Designing and building an enterprise network that is appropriate for its environment is no small undertaking. There are many options and decisions that must be made such as: How many users and locations are on the LAN? What about multiple locations and WAN needs? Whether to run wire to each desktop or just implement wireless; what firewalls, routers, switches, wireless access points should be installed? What speed is required such as gigabit Ethernet, gigabit Wi-Fi, or fiber optic? What IP addressing scheme should be used? What is the kind of intrusion detection systems (IDSs) (application, host, or network based)? Will there be remote users that require a VPN to securely access company resources? Will a storage area network (SAN) be required to retain high volumes of data? Will this be on premise or cloud based? What legacy systems need to be incorporated into the network design? What critical data needs to be backed up and how often? Should hardware- or software-based solutions be installed? What services and software applications are required and what are their bandwidth requirements?

The user must consider options such as *SaaS*, which is available via third parties over the Internet; *PaaS*, which are network components such as servers, storage, middleware, and tools managed by third parties; and *IaaS*, which comprises servers, storage, and network infrastructure managed by a third party. Or manage everything in house and on premise. These are just a few examples of things to take into consideration when architecting a network, and fortunately, there are best practices to follow.

Having a solid understanding of network basics and the OSI 7-Layer Model or the TCP/IP Stack Model allows the architect to determine the right mix of technologies that align with Layers 2–4 of the OSI Model. These are the layers most often concerned with designing a network. Layer 2 defines the type of topology. That is, the arrangement of the components that move the traffic around the network (i.e., Ethernet, token ring, Asynchronous Transfer Mode (ATM), DSL, etc.). Layer 3 defines the protocol that is used to route traffic and is typically IP. Layer 4 defines the protocol in which higher layer applications use to communicate across the network. Examples of protocols that work at the Layer 4 level are TCP and UDP. Examples of protocols that work at Layers 5–7 in the OSI Model are HTTP, HTTPS, Telnet, File Transfer Protocol (FTP), Simple Mail Transfer Protocol (SMTP), Dynamic Host Configuration Protocol (DHCP), Domain Name System (DNS), etc.

World Wide Web

This topic covers the specific protocol that enables the World Wide Web and it shows how that protocol is an example of a distributed processing standard. The World Wide Web is what makes the Internet valuable. It embodies the global collection of information resources, which are linked together through HTTP using URIs. It is a virtual resource that embodies the accumulated knowledge of our society. Hence, the World Wide Web. It is not the same as the Internet. The term "Internet," designates the global system of interconnected networks.

The foundation for data transfer on the World Wide Web is the HTTP. HTTP is a protocol and interconnection scheme that was developed by Tim Berners-Lee at CERN in 1989. It enables the seamless interchange of distributed hypermedia such as text, or images, video, sound, and embedded navigation features called hyperlinks. This interchange process is facilitated by a web browser which is a user application.

HTTP enables access control and authentication via a general framework which is based around a challenge-response concept. In this theory, the server will seek to authenticate a request from an external request for access. Thus, HTTP sessions establish a TCP connection to a server via a request to a designated access port. The server returns an acknowledgment and the session is conducted at the transport layer between the application and the IP. HTTP is a stateless protocol in that unlike TCP the server does not retain any information about the session. The security issues come from the use of various session management methods, such as cookies, which allows the server to record information about client requests, which in effect turns the HTTP session into a stateful protocol.

HTTP has evolved over the twenty years since it came into common use on the World Wide Web. Oversight for the HTTP medium falls under the purview of the Internet Engineering Task Force (IETF) which occasionally issues requests for comments (RFC) that specify evolutionary changes to the way internet connectivity will work. Given sufficient maturity, these will be translated into full Internet standards, as HTTP/2 was in 2015.

The Internet

This topic covers the evolution of the Internet as a distributed processing platform. In concept, the Internet is an information infrastructure. It's just that it reaches into the lives of anybody who owns a computing device and it is the medium through which the life's blood of our information society flows. In 1995, the Federal Networking Council (FNC) promulgated the following definition of the term "Internet." Internet refers to the global information system that is logically linked together by a globally unique address space based on the IP or its subsequent extensions/follow-ons and which is able to support communications using the TCP/IP suite or its subsequent extensions/follow-ons, and/or other IP-compatible protocols. Finally, it offers, uses, or makes accessible, high-level services which are layered on the lower level communications protocols and related infrastructure.

The modern Internet supports everything from e-commerce, through the control of remote devices, which is referred to as "the Internet of Things." The origin of the concept dates all the way back to 1962 when J.C.R. Licklider of MIT first outlined a "Galactic Network" theory for the Defense Advanced Research Projects Administration (DARPA). The initial realization of the concept came in 1969 when the first node of the ARPANET was established at UCLA. That idea was based on the concept of packet switching. In essence, the individual nodes in open architecture networks are separate and fit to their specific purpose while still internetworked with every other network underneath the common architecture of the Internet. That overarching architecture accommodates any type of network of any scope. This universal architecture was enabled by a new type of protocol called the Transmission Control Protocol/ Internet Protocol (TCP/IP).

Obviously, there was a need for some form of global addressing to enable flow control for the packets while the infrastructure itself had to be independent of any particular operating system. That is the role of TCP, which provides all the primary transport and forwarding services. IP then underwrites the addressing and forwarding of individual packets. An alternative called the UDP was added to the concept in order to provide direct access to the basic service of IP.

With the DNS, the Internet grew from the realm of research universities and the Department of Defense (DoD) into common usage. The DNS permitted a scalable distributed mechanism for resolving hierarchical host names into an Internet address. That final generic piece of the puzzle, plus Tim Berners-Lee's development of the HTTP is what brought us the structure that we today call the Internet.

Protocols and Layering

Protocol layering builds distinct information transmission protocols into a well-organized stratum of individual functions. The outcome of the layering process is a whole that is greater than the parts. In essence, layering breaks the networking function into distinct operational layers, each of which is managed by a protocol that is specifically designed to carry out each layer's task. Layered protocols allow high-level functions to provide a range of useful services while the lower level functions handle the actual connection process.

Protocol layering underwrites simplicity in the process of data transmission. Each individual protocol has a simple well-defined task. Therefore, it is easier to understand and control its operation. When these protocols are bundled, they accomplish a complex operation without sacrificing the reliability that comes with simplicity. This also allows the network architect the flexibility to tailor individual protocols into the bundle, for a particular application. For example, data delivery is one task and connection management is another. Those two processes are managed and operate at separate layers. In essence, one protocol does the data delivery, and another protocol does the connection management. The two protocols are oblivious of each other from an operational standpoint, which permits simplicity of design. It also creates a modular array, in that a similar specialized protocol can be used, where necessary, in place of the original; without disturbing the functioning of the rest of the protocols in the bundle.

The most important layered protocol designs are the OSI Seven-Layer Model and TCP/IP. OSI is the popular archetype of the idea of layering. That standard underlies and normalizes data transmission functions without regard to the underlying internal structure and technology. The concept of layering allows miscellaneous systems to communicate through a standard protocol at tiered levels of abstraction. Still, the concept of a layered protocol stacking was in use before the OSI Model was established. The TCP/IP model is not the OSI Model in that the two models use different assumptions and goals, particularly with respect to the relative importance of layering.

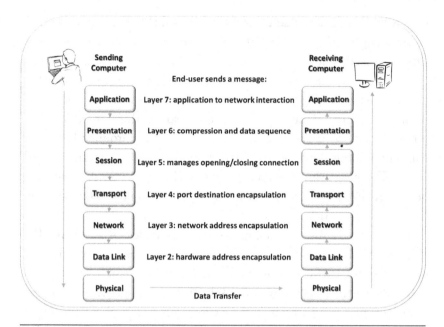

Figure 6.14 Network layer interaction.

TCP/IP embodies two architectural principles: encapsulation is the principle tool. It is used to provide abstraction of protocols and services. Encapsulation divides the protocol suite into layers of general functionality. The layers of the protocol suite near the top are logically closer to the user application, while those near the bottom are logically closer to the physical transmission of the data. As shown in Figure 6.14, an application, which is the highest level of the model, uses a set of protocols to send its data down the layers, which are further encapsulated at each level. The layering is a method of abstraction to isolate upper layer protocols from the details of transmitting bits over the communication medium.

High Performance Computing (Supercomputers)

High performance computing (HPC) is an illustration of the old saying about the sum being greater than the parts. The core concept of HPC involves aggregating computer resources to accomplish a given task. In simple terms, a large number of computer resources, which have conventional processing capabilities, are aggregated into a single processing entity that delivers much higher computing power than the individual devices that comprise it. Thus, HPC is useful in solving massive engineering or scientific challenges and for high performance situations in business.

The HPC concept is based on nodes that are harnessed together in such a way that they cooperate to address problems that you would normally require a Cray supercomputer to solve. This enhanced capability is possible because HPC computing is built around clusters of computers, each contributing their computing power to the overall effort. The networking element is involved because those nodes can be widely distributed, and they need to be able to talk to one another in order to cooperate.

The necessary internodal conversation is enabled by software. The software facilitates the cooperation between nodes. Linux currently dominates the process. However, it is perfectly possible to build an HPC cluster using Windows. The selection of the software and operating systems to utilize is based strictly on the application. Right now, factors such as business competition and product design drive the demand for HPC. But HPC is utilized in any field that requires intensive computer power such as weather forecasting. It is also used in such diverse areas as digital animation, graphics printing, quantum physics, and economic forecasting.

Hypervisors and Cloud Computing Implementations

This topic introduces such virtualized concepts as IaaS, SaaS, and PaaS. Hypervisors enable these services. A hypervisor is a software application that emulates a physical computer. The hypervisor sits at the lowest levels of the host processor and allows multiple virtual operating systems to execute on a single physical hardware platform. That includes a wide range of potential environments. Thus, the hypervisor concept is key mechanism to support any kind of virtual services.

One of the most popular and widespread applications of current hypervisor technology is cloud computing. That is, certain types of hypervisors run as a distinct software layer above both the hardware and the operating system of a given machine. That has enabled today's cloud computing industry. The flexibility of the cloud ensures a rich range of capabilities for any consumer. The cloud provides the option of being able to offload significant workloads into the cloud rather than on the host, which has generated the concept of IaaS. IaaS assumes that everything can be run in the cloud. IaaS solutions include such things as networking stacks and load balancing services.

The option to mix and match storage and workload solutions locally and in the cloud is a very persuasive argument for virtualized approaches. These solutions utilize a proprietary virtual platform that is virtual not actually on the premises. Instead, they are accessed via the Internet. Hence, the network security connection. Most of these are a proprietary managed service solutions. There are generally two types of clouds: public and private.

Public cloud architecture is categorized by its service model. Common service models include: SaaS, a third-party service provider is the host for a range of applications and services and makes them available in the cloud via the Internet and PaaS, in which a third-party provider actually provides discrete software and the accompanying hardware to its users as a service. This is normally for application development and it is on a fee basis. The advantage is that the customer does not have to invest in a permanent set of software and hardware tools. Finally, there is IaaS. As we saw earlier, here a third-party provider provides virtualized resources, applications, and storage, e.g., over the Internet or through dedicated connections. This is normally on a subscription basis. Along with public cloud services, there are also private cloud products. IBM, Microsoft, Hewlett Packard Enterprise (HPE), Oracle, and VMware are currently the most important private cloud providers. Private cloud services can range to any particular application or service that the customer requires.

Vulnerabilities

There are two broad categories of vulnerability in networks – malicious code and attacks. Malicious code is always a problem. However, there are commercial screening products that safeguard against the more common examples of malicious code. Attacks on the other hand are entirely different because they can be launched in so many different ways and from so many different places. The attack surface of a network or software environment is the sum of the different points – which are termed "attack vectors." These are the points where an unauthorized user can attempt to enter data or extract data from a computing environment.

Examples of attack vectors include user input fields, protocols, interfaces, and service. One approach to addressing vulnerabilities is to reduce the attack surface of a system or software. The basic strategies of vulnerability reduction here are to reduce the amount of code running, reduce entry points available to untrusted users, and eliminate services requested by relatively few users. By turning off unnecessary functionality, there are fewer security risks. By having less code available to unauthorized actors, there will tend to be fewer failures.

Although attack surface reduction helps prevent security failures, it does not mitigate the amount of damage an attacker could inflict once a vulnerability is found. This is done through a formal process to maintain a segmented architecture. The goal of that segmented architecture is to prevent intruders from exploiting other areas of the system, should one element be breached.

Knowledge Unit Five: Network Architecture

This knowledge unit introduces the concepts that are typically covered in a general computer networking course. It provides the foundation for the more specialized knowledge units in the Connection Security area. The network architecture topic provides a comprehensive picture of all of the many software applications, connectivity enablers, hardware devices, network protocols, and modes of transmission that are utilized by the network. Network architecture is typically layered. It serves as the detailed collation of all of the network layers. It is also based on the complete working definitions of the protocols. Consequently, network architecture also involves the practical planning and creation process. In that respect, network architecture is the embodiment of the entire framework for an organization's computerized communication function.

Network architectural elements include the hardware mechanisms, which are employed in the communication process, the cables and devices that facilitate the transfer, the network layout and topologies, and the physical and wireless connectors. In addition, the software functionality and protocols that populate the network architecture are also detailed in the architectural plan.

Network architecture is always overseen by a network manager. It is created and coordinated by the organization's network design and operation and function. The process is guided by the network architectural plan. The architectural plan is the blueprint for the complete network system. That blueprint provides a comprehensive picture of the tangible network elements with a listing of all of all of its inherent software and information resources. It allows people to understand the concrete network structure and the associated technology that underlies it. That understanding enables trustworthy and reliable design, construction, and management of a tangible network.

As shown in Figure 6.15, there are seven CSEC topics associated with this knowledge unit: (1) *General concepts*: topologies and the transmission characteristics, (2) *Common architectures*: this topic covers the IEEE 802 network architecture, (3) *Forwarding*: this topic covers packet forwarding, (4) *Routing*: this topic covers routing algorithms, (5) *Switching/Bridging*: this topic covers learning algorithms and IEEE 802.1, (6) *Emerging trends*: this topic covers emerging technologies and their impact as they emerge, and (7) *Virtualization and virtual hypervisor architecture*: e.g., native or host operating system virtualization.

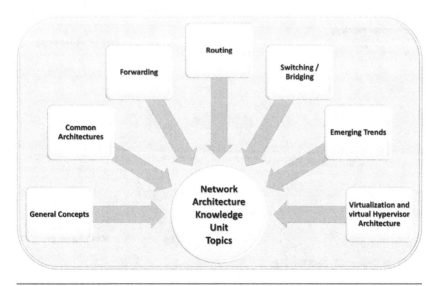

Figure 6.15   The Network Architecture knowledge unit topics.

General Concepts

This topic concentrates on the various topologies and the transmission characteristics of the topologies. As shown in Figure 6.16, there are four commonly accepted network topologies: (1) star networks, (2) bus or line networks, (3) loop or ring networks, and (4) mesh networks. These are generic patterns that can be laid out in different topologies. Those topologies include: local area networks (e.g., LAN), wide area networks (e.g., WAN), and metropolitan area networks (e.g., MAN).

As the name implies, a local area network (LAN) encompasses a limited geographic area such as a house, office building, or sometimes a small geographic area outside a single building. The resources of a LAN are linked together using wired Ethernet connectors (e.g., IEEE 802.3) which support efficient bit rates and distances. The other common connection technology is Wi-Fi, which is a radio frequency-based non-wired transmission technique. Because it is radio frequency based, Wi-Fi is potentially more vulnerable to attack than wired networks. Therefore, most Wi-Fi applications are secured

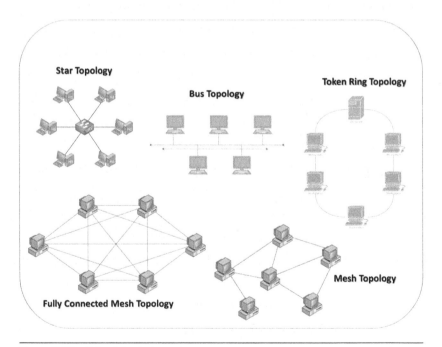

Figure 6.16 Network topologies.

by Wi-Fi Protected Access (WPA) which is a technology that protects information utilizing Wi-Fi.

By contrast, a WAN extends the communication net over a large geographical area. WANs are interconnected communication technologies that are employed to transmit data over long distances. By definition, WANs are able to intercommunicate with all other forms of communication topology including LANs and MANs. Thus, WANs are the go-to mechanism for any form of professional or commercial network application for business, government, or education. In essence, our entire internetworked world is built on wide area networking and in its most all-encompassing form, even the Internet might be considered to be a WAN. WANs normally communicate by packet switching methods. Thus, the most common transport and addressing protocol is TCP/IP. WANs can also be privatized using VPN technologies.

MANs are hybrid LANs. The concept was developed to describe a network that exceeds the communication capability of a LAN but which is nonetheless highly localized between such things as the office buildings of a business within a city. Thus, a MAN is a practical array of LANs that have been interconnected into a single larger network. MAN technology offers an order of magnitude greater level of efficiency between local nodes. MANs utilize the same backbone concepts as WANs. However, the interconnection might be point to point rather than ring based.

Common Architectures

This topic covers the IEEE 802 network architectures. As the name implies, the Institute of Electrical and Electronics Engineers (IEEE) is the professional society that serves the field of electronic and electrical engineering. It promulgates standards as part of that mandate. One of its areas of interest is the family of communication standards that standardizes the domain of LAN and MANs. These are the IEEE 802 series of standards; 802 provides a reference model for packet-based communications. The specifications of IEEE 802 apply to the OSI's data link and physical layers. In addition, the series divides the data link layer into two sublayers. The upper layer is the logical link control (LLC) which underwrites interoperability and the lower layer is the media access control (MAC) which is the packaging layer that allows for universal MAC use.

The standards set is maintained by a formally constituted IEEE LAN/MAN Standards Committee (LMSC). An individual working group serves as the focus for each area. There are twenty-four of these (e.g., 802.1–802.24). There are currently seven working groups active. These are: (1) *802.1 Higher Layer LAN Protocols* (Bridging) – LAN/MAN architecture and internetworking, (2) *802.3 Ethernet* – defines physical and data link layer MAC for wired networks, (3) *802.11 Wireless LAN and Mesh* – MAC and physical layer protocols for wireless local area networking, (4) *802.15 Wireless PAN* – specifications for WPAN implementations, (5) *802.15.1 Bluetooth Certification* – physical and MAC layer specifications for wireless connectivity in personal operating space, (6) *802.15.4 Low-Rate Wireless PAN* – physical and MAC layer specifications for low data rate long battery life devices with very low complexity, and (7) *802.15.6 Body Area Network* – low-power and short-range wireless standard for PAN devices used in or around the human body.

Forwarding

This topic covers packet forwarding in general. Forwarding and routing are the two most important network-layer functions. The difference between routing and forwarding is the difference between making travel plans versus stepping from the jetway onto the airplane. Routing does the planning. Forwarding takes the small steps to get there. Forwarding is the basic method for sharing information across systems on a network. The concept of forwarding simply implies the action of transferring a packet from interface to interface. With forwarding, packets are transferred between a source and a destination interface. It's like the post office. The system "forwards" packets with the destination IP address. Forwarding simply receives the packets from the local network and then outputs them using a forwarding table and the information in the packet. In that context, forwarding is the act of sending the packet to the next hop. Forwarding also has a more generic meaning of passing on something received from the network rather than accepting it on that host. If the destination is not on the local network, the packets are forwarded to the next adjacent network. The network layer decides on the path taken as the packets flow from a sender to a receiver. The algorithms that calculate that route are referred to as a routing algorithm.

Routing

This topic covers routing algorithms and explains how forwarding tables are built. Routing is the standard method for establishing a common basis for communication. Routing is the process by which systems decide where to send a packet. Routing protocols specify how routers communicate information that enables them to select routes between any two nodes on a computer network. Routing protocols on a system "discover" the other systems on the local network. The routing protocols learn the path to a destination interface and retain data about known routes in the system's routing table.

Routing algorithms determine the specific choice of route. Each router has a priori knowledge only of networks attached to it directly. The routing protocol shares this information first among immediate neighbors and then throughout the network. This way, routers gain knowledge of the topology of the network. The concept of routing is based around network address translation. An IP address is a numerical label assigned to each device participating in a computer network that uses the IP for communication. All packets on IP networks have a source and a destination IP address. The router tracks and stores basic data about each active connection (particularly the destination address and port) in an internal log. When a reply returns to the router, it uses the connection tracking data that it stored during the outbound phase to determine the private address on the internal network to forward the reply.

The router is typically connected to the Internet with a "public" address assigned by an ISP. The majority of network routing translators map multiple private hosts to one publicly exposed IP address. A router on that network knows a private address in that address space. As traffic passes from the local network to the Internet, the source address in each packet is translated on the fly from a private address to the public address.

The combination of IP address and port information on the returned packet can be unambiguously mapped to the corresponding private address and port information. This mechanism is implemented in any routing device that uses stateful translation tables to map the "hidden" private addresses into a single IP address and readdresses the outgoing IP packets on exit, so they appear to originate from the routing device. In the reverse communications path, responses are mapped back to the originating IP addresses using the rules ("state") stored in the translation tables.

The designers of the IP defined an IP address as a 32-bit number and this system, known as Internet Protocol Version 4 (IPv4), is still in use today. The simplest type of addressing protocol provides a one-to-one translation of IP addresses. Although there are many types of routing protocols, two major classes are in widespread use on IP networks. At the lowest level, an Interior Gateway Protocol (IGP) is a type of protocol used for exchanging routing information between gateways. By contrast, Exterior Gateway Protocols (EGPs) are used to exchange routing information between autonomous systems and rely on IGPs to resolve routes within an autonomous system. EGPs are the routing protocols that are used on the Internet for exchanging routing and reachability information between autonomous systems, such as Border Gateway Protocol (BGP). Some versions of the OSI networking model also distinguish routing protocols in a special sublayer of the Network Layer (Layer 3).

Switching/Bridging

Bridges connect physical network segments at the data link layer of the OSI model. Bridging communicates at the data link layer while isolating the physical layer. With bridging, only well-formed Ethernet packets are forwarded from one Ethernet segment to another; collisions and packet errors are isolated. Bridges are used to combine either smaller networks or network segments into a single entity. Bridge devices provide communication between them.

Bridging ties those elements together into an aggregate form rather than allow each discrete network to interact independently, which differentiates bridging from routing. In order to accomplish this, each network bridge keeps track of the MAC addresses associated with every one of its potential interfaces. Then it utilizes a simple store and forward method to do the forwarding. The bridge technology decides on a frame-by-frame basis whether or not to forward from one network to the other. The bridge uses the destination address to decide whether to forward or filter the frame. If the destination is on another segment, then it forwards it to the appropriate destination, and if it is local, it keeps it within that segment.

On the other hand, a switch is a type of multiplexing network bridge that uses packet switching to do the forwarding. The most common example is the Ethernet switch. Switches manage the flow of packets across a LAN by ensuring that a transmitted packet is directly sent to the device that it is addressed to. This is based on either the MAC or IP address. Switches use the addressing tables to make their forwarding decisions. They ensure the security and efficiency of the network that way because the packets are only sent to their proper destination. Because networks may be linked through multiple interconnected switches, it is necessary to implement algorithms that avoid redundant transmission loops. This problem was addressed by adding protocols (originally Spanning Tree Protocols), which have been enhanced by more robust protocols that essentially combine switching and routing into a single transmission process. Because these more enhanced protocols are essentially new additions, the development of switching architecture is still evolving. Thus, the CSEC recommends the presentation of both concepts.

Emerging Trends

This is essentially a placeholder in the CSEC model. It is necessitated because the evolution of network technology and thinking is so rapid. Thus, the CSEC suggests that there needs to be a consideration of emerging trends. The topic covers evolving aspects of the field and their potential impacts.

The CSEC identifies two potential topics: software-defined networks (SDNs) and the hybrid switching/routing capabilities discussed above. As the name implies, SDN is based in software rather than tiered hierarchies of switches arranged in a tree structure. Therefore, it is dynamic rather than static. There has been a demand for a new concept of networking architecture, because of the emergence of cloud-based services and mobile and IoT devices. SDN was developed to address that need.

SDN is gaining traction because it combines packet forwarding and data flow control into a single programmable network device or devices called SDN controllers. These are centralized functions that are intelligent and allow for a much more agile, directly manageable and dynamically configurable network solution. Of course, that is only one example of a potentially infinite number of topics in this area, but it does illustrate the importance of requiring consideration of future trends in the networking knowledge area.

Virtualization and Virtual Hypervisor Architecture

Virtualization was emphasized in the CSEC topic of Distributed Systems Architecture. However, it also has its place with hardware in that virtualization underlies the growing area of abstract machines. In essence, a virtualized machine represents an abstracted version of a hardware device which is instantiated and controlled through a software application called a hypervisor. Consequently, several instances of virtual operating systems can run independently on a common hardware resource. These are either type 1 or 2 hypervisors. Both abstract a guest operating system from the host operating system.

The type 1 hypervisor runs directly on the host machine's physical hardware. It overlays the characteristics of a foreign operating system on the physical host, thereby creating an abstract computing platform. Accordingly, it has direct access to the underlying hardware. The other type (type 2) runs as a process on the host. In essence, hypervisors allow a "guest" operating system to operate on the native operating system as if it were an independent entity. Both of these represent radical new opportunities for hardware architecture, and therefore, they are important components of the learning process in this area.

Knowledge Unit Six: Network Implementations

This knowledge unit explores specific technologies that implement the general concepts of networking. Network architecture can be understood through its specific implementation, but it should be understood that there are other ways to understand how a network

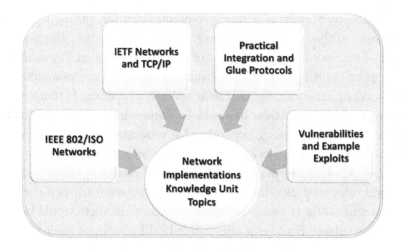

Figure 6.17   The Network Implementations knowledge unit topics.

operates. This very short subtopic area provides specific discussion of the history and basic ideas that underlie our current understanding of network design and implementation. Thus, this subtopic area serves as a summary device for the detailed CSEC content that has preceded it. As shown in Figure 6.17, there are four areas that stand out when considering the principles and practices of practical data transmission. These are the following: (1) *IEEE 802/ISO standards* – which are so central that they have been a topic in a number of other areas, (2) *IETF networking concepts and TCP/IP* – which enables the Internet, (3) *Practical integration and glue protocols* – which cover the practical network building concepts associated with ensuring the building blocks are properly and consistently fit together, and finally, (4) *Vulnerabilities and example exploits* – which look at generic points of exposure and attacks for the purpose of illustration.

IEEE 802/ISO Networks

This topic has already been extensively discussed. However, we have not talked about the reason for developing a family of standards for localized networks. Thus, we will concentrate on the rationalization for the 802 standards here. The IEEE 802 standards define standards and protocols for wireless and wired LANs at the physical and data link layers. Standards in general provide a guarantee of safety, predictability, and usability. Standards define a common point for linking together networks so that they can effectively talk to one another. Thus, some kind of commonly accepted point of reference is needed to guide the process of ensuring that the hardware and software components of a network, or networks, are able to seamlessly cooperate. If there were no networking standards, it would be almost impossible to reliably share information among networks that were made by different vendors. Also, computer networks are created by a diverse collection of entities for a range of purposes. The standard establishes a basic set of ground rules for packaging and sending data between any two entities across a network. If a standard did not exist, then there would be no common ruleset. Standards also enable healthy business competition. Since customers are not limited in their choices to a single vendor, they can buy hardware and software from any vendor who complies with the commonly accepted standard. This costs competitive.

As the area of local area networking grew in importance throughout the 1990s, the IEEE developed the 802 standards as a means of ensuring standardization of connection protocols for that area. That common basis has enabled the vast commercial word of wired technology. If there were no standards for the rules and protocols that connect us, we would not be able to communicate in the way we do today. Thus, an intimate knowledge of these standards is an essential part of any student's education.

IETF Networks and TCP/IP

In essence, the IETF standards regulate the Internet. This standard set is separate from the IEEE 802 series in that it is primarily focused on the IP suite (TCP/IP). Since 1993, the IETF has functioned as the standards development function for the Internet Society, which was chartered to provide a corporate structure to support the Internet standards development process. The Internet standards it oversees were originally developed by the DARPA and known as Transmission Control Protocol/Internet Protocol (TCP/IP). TCP/IP is the model for the underlying structure of the Internet. TCP/IP standardizes the process of data encapsulation into packets, addressed and transmitted, routed, and received through an end-to-end data communication system. TCP/IP implements four layers of abstraction: (1) *the link layer*, which defines the methods of transmission within a single network segment, (2) *the internet layer*, which enables communication between autonomous networks, (3) *the transport layer*, which handles host-to-host communication, and (4) *the application layer*, which underwrites process-to-process data exchange for applications. The IP suite predates the OSI Model, a more comprehensive reference framework for general networking systems. The range of difference should be noted since there is a common misperception that OSI is the only standard for networking systems. The diversity of the standard universe is something that the student needs to understand.

Practical Integration and Glue Protocols

We have extensively discussed the approaches to integrating data communication processes in both the network and the Hardware Architecture knowledge areas. This summary knowledge area focuses on the practical issues associated with the integration process. It goes without saying that networks are complex entities. They comprise a widely varied set of applications and protocols, end systems, switches, and various types of link-level media. As we saw, these are all brought together by the concept of layers. A layered architecture underwrites a modular approach. Each layer provides its services by performing certain actions within that layer and by using the services of the layer below. The fact that these layers exist means that application developers have to provide a means to integrate their functionality across various not necessarily compatible technologies.

For example, one of those approaches is to use some form of executable code to transparently adjust functionality that would otherwise be incompatible. This "glue code" supports interoperability. A construct called a "shim" is one example. It is a piece of program logic that allows a running program to operate in a different environment than it was developed for. Another option is the Address Resolution Protocol (ARP) that discovers such things as the MAC address associated with a given IP address. The various concepts and practical approaches to portaging between layers and among protocols are a necessary part of the student's basic understanding of the operation of networks.

Vulnerabilities and Example Exploits

It is important to understand the vulnerabilities of networks and the attacks that can be made against them. The whole point of the cyberdefense operation is to stay on top of the areas that represent the greatest danger. In practical terms, that means that vulnerabilities must be identified and either patched or fixed as part of the day-to-day operation of the system or network.

Vulnerabilities can typically be classified into one of the categories. First, there are backdoors in a computer system, a cryptosystem, or an algorithm. This is any secret method of bypassing normal authentication or security controls. They may exist for a number of reasons, including by original design or from poor configuration. Then there is spoofing, tampering, and privilege escalation. Spoofing of user identity describes a situation in which one person or program successfully masquerades as another by falsifying data. Tampering describes a malicious modification of products. So-called "Evil Maid" attacks and security services planting of surveillance capability into routers are examples. Privilege escalation describes a situation where an attacker with some level of restricted access is able to, without authorization, elevate their privileges or access level. Finally, there are phishing and social engineering attacks. Phishing is the attempt to acquire sensitive information such as usernames, passwords, and credit card details. It is typically carried out by email spoofing or instant messaging. It often directs users to enter details at a fake website whose look and feel are almost identical to the legitimate one. Social engineering aims to convince a user to disclose secrets such as passwords and card numbers by, e.g., impersonating a bank, a contractor, or a customer. These types of attacks can only be prevented by noncomputer means, which can be difficult to enforce, relative to the sensitivity of the information.

It is possible to reduce an attacker's chances by keeping systems up to date with security patches and updates, using a security scanner or/ and hiring competent people responsible for security. The effects of data loss/damage can be reduced by careful backing up and insurance. But the primary approach is to establish a segmented architecture. The design centers on controlling access through a number of perimeters, which have been termed a "defense-in-depth." The tangible components in a segmented network topology are the routers and firewalls that secure the perimeter of each layer. All of these potential vulnerabilities and the general countermeasure response are part of the student learning process.

Knowledge Unit Seven: Network Services

We have looked at the physical and data link levels of the OSI Model. Now, this knowledge area focuses at the applications and transport layers, where the functionality that provides the real visible usefulness of the system resides. Operations there can include all the functions associated with storing and retrieving of data for the purpose of manipulating, presenting, and intercommunicating data between hosts. There are a set of standard networking paradigms and methodologies that are associated with activity at these higher levels in the application universe. This includes the typical client–server or peer-to-peer architecture based on application layer principles. In all of these, the network service is provided by a centralized utility, which in its oldest form was a server that was accessed by a communication system made up of clients.

Network services are commonly built around an interface that allows numerous types of interactions for a range of services that utilize standard application layer communication across an IP network. The application layer protocols sit on top of the host-to-host communication services that the transport layer provides. Thus, the actual connection, flow control, and multiplexing process are handled at a lower level in the OSI-TCP/IP models. It should be noted that these models are not the same and they utilize different packet transmission techniques.

Communications that require accuracy and integrity are normally TCP based, and those where the actual transmission rate is paramount use UDP. The diversity of approaches is an important aspect of the network services area. As shown in Figure 6.18, there are six subtopics in the network services area, these are: (1) *Concept of a service*: a model for practical distributed computing, (2) *Service models (client–server, peer to peer)*: e.g., the classic models for network interchange, (3) *Service protocols and concepts (IPC, APIs, IDLs)*: which describes all of the ways components connect, (4) *Common service*

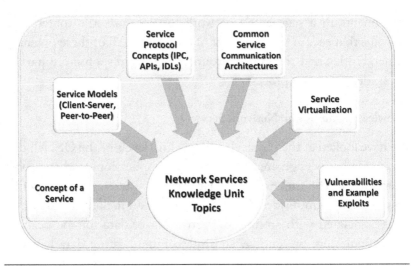

Figure 6.18 The Network Services knowledge unit topics.

communication architectures: which looks at specific services and how their protocols are implemented, (5) *Service virtualization*: communication service emulation, and (6) *Vulnerabilities and example exploits*: vulnerabilities of client–server, peer-to-peer, and virtualization services.

Concept of a Service

As the name implies, this is a fundamental descriptor for the network services topic. A service is a given set of discrete activities that are arrayed to satisfy the needs of a defined client. Services are normally a range of activities including repository, processing, delivery, or contextual functions, for this is by necessity distributed, with processes that are shared among service requestors and providers. It is worth calling out this subtopic at the beginning of the network service topic area because the basic concept of service is an essential differentiator between network services topic and the prior discussions of network architecture. In essence, we are looking at the methods and models for structuring and accessing, using, and transmitting the actual value that the data represents, rather than the methods and processes of transmitting and receiving date, which was the subject of the other CSEC topic areas.

Service Models (Client–Server, Peer to Peer)

The oldest and probably the best generic model for illustrating the concept of network service is the client–server network architecture. This concept is very simple from a network perspective, the client initiates a connection and a server responds. However, this service model encompasses everything from the distributed **browser, server, and the DNS** architecture of the Internet, all the way down to the client–server architecture of any humble local area or metropolitan network. In all of these instances, the concept is exactly the same. Client application and client devices on a network send messages, in the form of requests, to a server, or servers. The latter will respond to their clients by acting on each request and returning what has been requested. In this simple architecture, one server supports many clients, and multiple servers can be networked together to provide more computing power and enhanced capabilities.

Still, the client–server network service model is not the only approach to providing networked application capability. The most popular alternate approach is the peer-to-peer networking concept. As the name implies, all of the computers in a peer-to-peer architecture share equal responsibility for providing any necessary functionality and all of the devices have equivalent capability. With peer to peer, either side can initiate the request.

Comparatively, the client–server service model offers the advantage of being able to manage applications and data in one centralized location. Peer-to-peer networks are more scalable and the network itself has greater potential capacity. All of these factors are essential parts of the consideration that a student must be able to make.

Service Protocols and Concepts (IPC, APIs, IDLs)

This topic focuses specifically on interface protocols and methods. At its base, the activities and operating system mechanisms that are associated with inter-process communication (IPC) enable any running application process to manage shared data. That programmed sharing capability allows clients to request data and the server to respond at the basic operating system level of each device. The actual execution of the IPC process is dependent on external factors such as software functionality, design specifications, and performance and system requirements. Since distributed system architecture is built on specific sharing capability, IPC methods enable much of the network service function.

At the next level up, an application programming interface (API) supports the development of the software services and functionality that every client-side application requires in order to be useful. Accordingly, APIs might be considered to be the mechanisms that allow developers to build the interface mechanisms between the client and a server. APIs are protocol based. They utilize preprogrammed library implementations. The library enables a well-defined set of behaviors through a common interface that invokes them. The API is an abstraction. It specifies the requisite behavior while the library provides the actual running code that enables the functionality necessary to implement it. An API specification can take many forms but often includes specific subroutines or operating system or network-level calls.

APIs are programmed to ensure that any client request will always elicit a response in a specific format or in the form of a specific action. APIs provide an unambiguous functionality that carries out some commonly utilized processing operation, such as transferring data to a remote server, without requiring the application developer to understand the necessary underlying data transmission operations. As such, APIs are the driving force behind any form of client–server or web-based application development.

Interface Description Language (IDL) is an example of a specification language which can be used to describe the *requirements* versus the *manner* that a discrete program will interface with its environment. IDLs are both language and machine agnostic, software-based utilities that can be utilized to define system interfaces. IDLs allow components that are written in different languages to interface with each other and even execute on different machines through remote procedure calls. Given the diverse and distributed nature of network service, this is an essential capability.

Common Service Communication Architectures

By definition, a common service is a discrete unit of functionality that can be accessed remotely and acted upon and updated independently.

A service logically represents a real-world activity with a specified outcome. It is self-contained as a black box for the client. Still, it requires underlying services in order to operate. Thus, the common service communication model is any architecture that allows disparate services to connect and communicate across diverse platforms and languages. Obviously, this is an essential requirement for any distributed network environment. Service-oriented architecture entails and integrates distributed, separately maintained, and deployed software components. It is enabled by technologies and standards that facilitate components' communication and cooperation over a network, especially over an IP network. Different underlying network services are used in conjunction to provide the functionality of a distributed network. Consequently, network service communication architecture shares the principle of modularity with programming.

The architecture for a common service model is based on an approach to interconnecting network components so that they are interdependent to the least practicable extent. In essence, in a loosely coupled architecture, one element has little direct knowledge of another. While the concept of loose coupling is a fundamental part of software design, the term "loose coupling" in the case of network service architecture refers to the client's ability to be independent of the service that it is requesting. Thus, the service request is handled by discrete programmed components, which interface with the network's specific communication protocol. The basic principle of service-oriented architecture ensures independence from vendors, products, and technologies. Therefore, it is an essential part of network service architecture.

Service Virtualization

Service virtualization replicates specific interfaces, interactions, and behaviors that emulate situations where a communication system will interact with an application. Thus, service virtualization is useful in the development of cloud and service-oriented architecture applications or application program interfaces. Developers build a virtualized replica of the communication environment in order to test how well their specific product integrates. This provides a testbed that allows the developer to start testing the essential communication interfaces immediately rather than waiting until the dependent systems are fully developed in order to test integration.

The service virtualization process utilizes system logs to model the responses and behavior of a dependent system. This is often based on XML for web services and SQL for databases. Then developers test the new application in the virtualized service in order to confirm that a given application function elicits the same responses that the real one would be intended to have. The aim is to ensure that a new application, service, or feature will integrate with the existing infrastructure. The testing process can also examine extreme situations in the virtual environment, like high traffic volume, that would never be allowed in a real-world production system. Thus, service virtualization can work out bugs in the development phase rather than have to wait until the application has progressed all the way downstream to integration. This is an extreme benefit to the developers of sophisticated network solutions.

Vulnerabilities and Example Exploits

Since distributed systems represent the largest attack surface possible, the vulnerabilities and exploits that hit client–server, peer-to-peer, and virtualization network services are a critical final topic. There are two general categories that have specific application to network services: client–server and cloud-based services. Both of these have issues that are strongly associated with their assurance.

Client–server vulnerabilities are mostly a consequence of failures in the standard authentication and authorization services between client and server. That includes exploitation of network sockets to set up unauthorized connections or to drop malicious scripts on the server. Thus, student awareness of client-side vulnerabilities is a necessary element of network security.

Still, server-based vulnerabilities are a much more attractive target than the client, since the server is where the system resides. Thus, awareness of hardening measures that ensure against server vulnerabilities like SQL injection, cross site scripting and broken authentication, security misconfiguration, and sensitive data exposure vulnerabilities is an important aspect of the student learning process.

Also, cloud architecture has a different set of vulnerabilities associated with it. Things like insecure APIs, reliability and availability of service, insecure cryptography, session riding, and shared technology issues all have impacts that the student needs to be aware of. This is especially true in the case of SaaS and IaaS. These platforms are particularly vulnerable to such things. Thus, the CSEC requires that explicit attention be paid to the subtopic area of vulnerabilities.

Knowledge Unit Eight: Network Defense

This knowledge unit captures current concepts in network protection. Cybersecurity is implemented by conscious design, and the measures to defend it are embedded in the enterprise's systems. That activity lies within the general domain of network defense operations or network security architecture. The term network defense simply describes the tangible response to the threat environment for that particular setting. All required functions in a network defense must be substantively verifiable as embedded into a consistent and logical protection scheme.

As an activity, the term network defense describes a discrete, usually formal process that assures the development of a coherent and useful structure of operational countermeasures. Thus, the network defense is always established through a formal structural design. That process has to be explicit, because it serves two fundamental purposes. First, it supports the detailed thinking-through of the functions that will be required to ensure the necessary degree of security. Second, it describes the precise steps that will be taken to bake that solution directly into the programming of the network protection.

The network defense operations function is a requirement for effective cybersecurity. That is because it is the process that maintains continuous security functionality within the daily network operation. As such, network defense operations embodies the necessary practices to safeguard the organization against likely aspect of operational failure. The network defense operations function ensures that the appropriate set of security principles and best practice policies and practices are implemented and adhered to. Thus, the network defense operations function is the element that establishes and maintains the tangible activities that represent the assurance process to the rest of the organization. It monitors and evaluates daily electronic security practices to ensure that they are being performed in a disciplined and continuous manner. It assures the overall integrity of the network and application security operations by performing the necessary monitoring, testing, and housekeeping functions that are required to keep them functioning properly within the routine operational environment.

Because of its operational focus, the network defense function is less involved with strategy and more centered on issues of performance and execution. As shown in Figure 6.19, there are thirteen subtopics in the network defense topic area: (1) *Network hardening*: methods for ensuring against attack, (2) *Implementing firewalls and VPNs*: use of firewalls and VPNs, (3) *Defense in depth*: this topic introduces the idea that defenses must be layered, (4) *Honeypots and honeynets*: intentionally vulnerable networks for intelligence gathering, (5) *Network monitoring*: tools and techniques for monitoring network devices, (6) *Network traffic analysis*: tools and techniques for capturing and analyzing packet flows, (7) *Minimizing exposure (attack surface and vectors)*: tools and techniques for finding and mitigating vulnerabilities, (8) *Network access control (internal and external)*: tools and techniques for limiting packet flow based on content, (9) *Perimeter networks/proxy servers*: tools and techniques for implementing defense in depth, (10) *Network policy development and enforcement*: policies and requirements for network services along with enforcement, (11) *Network operational procedures*: procedures that are used to operate the network, (12) *Network attacks*: penetration testing methods, and (13) *Threat hunting and machine learning*: proactive threat hunting using machine learning to detect patterns of attack.

Network Hardening

This topic looks at the simple network configuration steps that you can take to make the security of your network's servers and routers more robust. Traffic into a network should be managed based on a set of access rules embodied in access control lists (ACLs). Hardening is also a function of disabling unnecessary services across the network as well

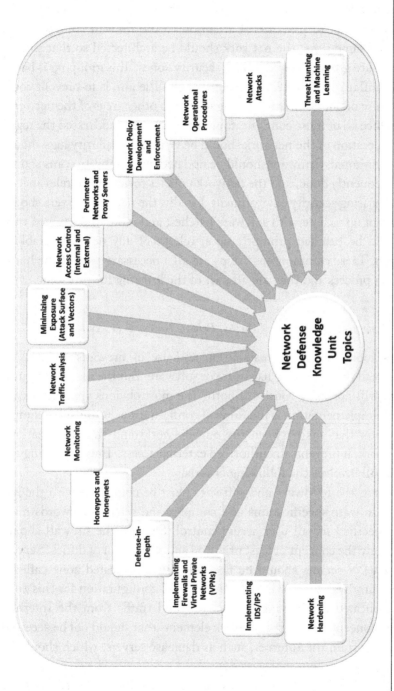

Figure 6.19 The Network Defense knowledge unit topics.

as configuring a logging function for the network. Firewalls are the first line of defense for any network with external links. Accordingly, it is essential to pay careful attention to the firewall configuration. At the same time, the network should be architected so that similar assets are grouped together into security zones. This grouping is based on similar sensitivity levels and function. The aim is to prevent compromise of one zone from propagating into other areas of the network.

Once all of these configuration items have been addressed the regular operation of the network should be tested, the security logs should be monitored, firmware should be updated, vulnerability scans should be frequently done, and the network policies reviewed for relevance to the existing security environment. Finally, the network servers should be kept up to date with software patches, and more importantly, they should be patched promptly upon release of any new vulnerability patch. These commonsense steps are all a necessary part of the hardening process and they are all part of the learning for this topic.

Implementing Firewalls and Virtual Private Networks (VPNs)

This topic covers the installation and use of firewalls and VPNs. Firewalls can be either hardware or software. But the ideal configuration will normally consist of both. The most obvious area of concern with implementation is the firewall configuration. A firewall is simply a router that sits between the outside world and the organization's network, it prevents unauthorized external access. Thus, installing the firewall involves the following criteria.

First, the hardware and software must be compliant with the latest firmware specifications and complex and secure passwords must be specified for all user access control. Second, the firewall should embody the concept of least privilege and separation of duties. Servers and VPN servers should be firewalled in a dedicated zone called a demilitarized zone or DMZ. The firewall configuration for this zone is dedicated to allowing limited inbound traffic from the Internet. That concept isolates the network elements that should not be accessed directly from the Internet, such as database servers, which should be firewalled into internal server zones.

A VPN server is a secure intermediary between a user and the Internet. It creates a connection to the Internet through a direct link to a third party. That connection firewalls your network by establishing a secure gateway connection to a remote server, which is run by the VPN provider. The VPN client authenticates itself to the VPN and a trusted key exchange takes place, which in essence creates a secure tunnel between your computer and the VPN service. Once authentication is established, all Internet communication through the VPN server is encrypted and, thus, secured. Thus, you are protected on public Wi-Fi, and your IP address is shielded from everybody else in all cases.

Defense in Depth

This topic has been discussed at length in other parts of this chapter. However, it is appropriate to revisit it here. Much of the current ideas about Connection Security involve the development of a network architecture that provides a multilayered defense. The purpose of a defense in depth is to prevent one compromised element from contaminating another part of the network. In practical terms, a defense in depth secures the network at every potential level of access to the organization's information assets. The essential element of a defense in depth is segmentation. The idea is to slow down potential attackers by forcing them to take the time to solve defenses at every level. That concept allows the designer to assure a high level of probability that a component or system will not fail or be breached within a given time within a specified environment. The strategy is based on the principle that it is more difficult to defeat a complex and multilayered defense system than to penetrate a single barrier.

The multilayered approach increases the security of a system by creating redundancies in the protection scheme. In essence, if a countermeasure fails, then one is waiting in the wings to take its place. Firewalls prevent access to and from unauthorized networks and will allow or block traffic based on a set of security rules. Intrusion protection systems often work in tandem with a firewall to identify potential security threats and respond to them quickly. Antivirus software protects against viruses and malware.

This concept addresses many different attack vectors, and it can significantly improve an organization's security status. The layered use of a series of different defenses, such as firewalls, anti-spyware programs, hierarchical passwords, data encryption intrusion detection, and biometric verification and integrity auditing solutions, addresses many of the electronic threats. In addition, physical protection measures combined with comprehensive behavioral measures for personnel are all part of good defense in depth.

Honeypots and Honeynets

Honeypot and honeynet operations are a sophisticated part of network defense. They mimic the behavior of a real system and appear as part of a network, shown in Figure 6.20. Honeypots look like a legitimate part of the site. But they are actually carefully shielded and monitored traps that are set to catch a thief. The honeypot lures intruders into accessing them. Then, the intruder's behavior is logged and analyzed as a means of improving security but is actually isolated and monitored, and that seems to contain information or a resource of value. This is similar to the kind of sting operations you see in TV police shows.

There are two kinds of honeypots in practice: (1) operational honeypots and (2) research honeypots. Operational honeypots are placed inside the business network to improve security. The honeypot detects, deflects, and counteracts unauthorized accesses that would normally hit operational systems. Research honeypots are used for intelligence gathering. They study the motives and tactics of the attackers who might target a given network. These honeypots look at how to better

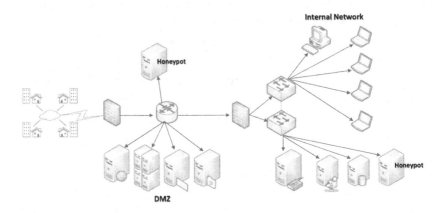

Figure 6.20 Network diagram showing honeypot servers.

protect the organization against the threats it might face. Two or more honeypots on a network form a honeynet. Typically, a honeynet is used for monitoring a larger and/or more diverse network in which one honeypot may not be sufficient. Honeynets and honeypots are usually implemented as parts of larger network IDSs.

Network Monitoring

This topic covers the tools and techniques for monitoring network devices and their associated logs. Network monitoring is a subset of network management. The term describes the systematic process of ensuring that the network hardware and software are performing within an acceptable range. This is normally automated in such a way that a failure in the network will be immediately detected by the network monitoring system and alerts will be broadcast.

Thus, the term really designates a dedicated set of management software tools that are set to ensure the reliable performance of computers and network services. For instance, network administrators frequently run speed tests or ping tests to verify connections and evaluate connection performance. Ping is one of the most basic-level network monitoring tools. The most common oversight mechanism is the network monitor. This is an automated entity that oversees the current status. To do that, it tracks and logs such things as data transmission rate, error rates, and response times.

Network monitoring is generally carried out through software applications and tools. The Simple Network Management Protocol (SNMP) is the most widely used network monitoring and management tool. It evaluates the performance of the hardware devices in the network as well as the software on those devices. An SNMP monitor gathers information on how much bandwidth is being used on the network, actively polls the network devices to ascertain status, notifying about device failure and collecting error reports, and does capacity management for storage devices.

Network Traffic Analysis

Network traffic analysis describes the simple process of capturing and analyzing network traffic. It obtains in-depth insight into what types of packets are flowing through a network. That continuous input is used to enhance network performance, evaluate its security, and improve the overall management of the network operation. Network traffic analysis is normally underwritten by manual and automated methods, all of which are aimed at understanding, in great detail, the traffic that flows through a network.

Typically, network traffic analysis is done through a network monitoring or network bandwidth monitoring software/applications. Network traffic analytics are employed to identify anomalies in the form of malicious or suspicious packets. This is a huge advantage in that other aspects of network defense, firewalls, and intrusion detection system (IDS)/intrusion prevention system (IPS) are focused on detection and prevention. However, traffic analysis is a proactive process. It tracks behaviors that are unique or which represent a small number of instances in comparison to the bulk of occurrences in an environment. By automating a rule-based detection capability, security professionals can then analyze sequences of events that represent suspicious behavior. The analysis of that behavior allows security professionals to implement custom responses.

Minimizing Exposure (Attack Surface and Vectors)

One common approach to improving security is to reduce the attack surface of a system or network. The attack surface of a network comprises sum of the different points or "attack vectors" where an unauthorized user can attempt to access the protected space. A vector in computing is the method that might be used to gain unauthorized access or damage the integrity of the system. Examples of attack vectors include user input fields, protocols, interfaces, and services.

Common methods of exploitation include buffer overflows and injection flaws, HTML and email weaknesses, or networking protocol flaws. The basic strategies of attack surface reduction are to reduce the amount of running code, reduce entry points available to untrusted entities, and eliminate services requested by relatively few users. By turning off unnecessary functionality, there are fewer security risks. By having less code available to unauthorized actors, there will tend to be fewer failures.

Network Access Control (Internal and External)

Much of establishing a secure network revolves around the proper configuration and operation of the functions that ensure authorized access. All cyberdefense activity is aimed at establishing and maintaining trust relationships by controlling access privileges for the files, directories, devices, and other data or code resident on the system. Once appropriate access is granted, the session is monitored and controlled by the operating system to ensure continuing compliance. The ability to do this is generally supported through the computer and network operating systems.

Access control is a persistent requirement as the network evolves and threats come and go. The function is based on the established policies and any other relevant condition that might be established for a given situation. Access control at the system and network level always requires the definition of types. The term "type" just denotes a label. Types are used to determine access rights. These labels can constitute a structure, a class, a module, a defined interface, or a user. They let the programmer assign privileges and other kinds of permission based on the attributes, roles, and relationships that each user presents to the system at the time access is requested.

Types are the basis for the decisions that the system will automatically make about the access mode that will be assigned to each request at the point where it is presented. Because this is preprogrammed, it must be possible to designate a decision for every type and mode of access. The architectural issues revolve around the establishment of the most effective and efficient processing structure for determining and enforcing types and permissions. Basically, access privileges have to be assigned, monitored, and revoked at the optimum level of permission for each type. Or in practical terms, it should be possible for the system to automatically determine what access to provide from a range of possible access permissions for a given user or system type. That decision is based on the relevant criteria that are preprogrammed into the system for it. These criteria can be temporal, transactional, or even defined. Access permissions that are granted can then be monitored and automatically enforced by the operating system based on those criteria.

This is normally overseen by a reference monitor. The control elements that launch and coordinate the granting of access usually lie within the operating system and the embedded firmware. That ensures a very high degree of organizational control at the automatic, or system level, because it guarantees that access rights will be directly managed by explicit policies embedded in the central software kernel of the system. In addition to the obvious assurance that this permits, the benefit of embedding security policy directly into the functioning of the system is that it makes system resource utilization much more efficient. That is because it is not necessary to invoke a separate program or application when security criteria are evaluated. The system administrator then configures the reference monitor to fit the requirements of the particular situation.

Perimeter Networks/Proxy Servers

This topic covers tools and techniques for implementing defense in depth using isolated networks and special servers. A perimeter network is the network that sits on the boundary. It is the last step out of your network and the first step in. Defense in depth is built around well-defined perimeters. Each perimeter represents a barrier that an attacker has to defeat in order to move to the next barrier. It is a layering concept that resembles the concentric walls of a castle. Thus, the key to defense in depth is establishing a solid boundary. With the Internet, that boundary marks the distinction between the private side of a network and the public side. The idea is that an organization's internal information assets are protected by a clearly defensible perimeter.

These perimeter networks are sometimes referred to as DMZs in that they are used to isolate and keep potential target systems separate, as well as to reduce and control access to those systems from outside of the organization. They are established and managed around the concept of proxy servers. A proxy server acts as an intermediary between two communicating parties. There is no direct communication between the client and the server. Instead, the client connects to the proxy server and the proxy server handles interactions with the external network or system. Most proxy servers are forward proxies. A forward proxy simply forwards request to the target server to establish a communication between the two.

Network Policy Development and Enforcement

This topic covers the creation of policies that provide guidance and requirements for the services provided by the network along with the measures to be used to see that the policies are followed. Because it is focused on maintaining the day-to-day reliability of the assurance, the network defense operation's function is built around a number of related security policies. These include policies that are not specifically technological such as architectural design and implementation concerns. It also includes such big picture requirements as ensuring that the most relevant security principles and practices are properly aligned with the organization's threat situation. It also entails monitoring the performance of the various security functions to ensure that they conform to proper procedure, as well as defining and executing standard operational testing strategies to validate that the security function continues to operate properly.

Nevertheless, the most important element of the network defense operations function may be its responsibility to ensure that there is always an effective response ready for every reported security incident. In that respect, the network defense operations policies represent both the corrective and the compensating element of a proper and systematic network operation. And accordingly, the effective implementation and management of those policies is a critical factor in the success of the overall network defense process. Obviously, besides policy making, it is important to define universal codes of best use and good conduct. That is also a role of the network policy process. It leads to the final element, which is policy enforcement. It is important to define a formal enforcement mechanism that will ensure every policy is uniformly and consistently enforced.

Network Operational Procedures

Policies are implemented by procedures. Thus, this topic is a logical follow on to the prior area. Network operational procedures entail the creation and enforcement of procedures that are used to ensure the complete and correct security of the network. Strictly within the domain of networks, the traditional role of operational procedures is to maintain management control over the organization's network and application systems and media. This is an essential contribution because network and application systems are both complex and for the most part incomprehensible to the better part of the organization. So, they are hard for line managers to keep track of and control with degree of certainty.

Consequently, a concrete set of procedures that underwrite the ongoing assurance of the effectiveness of the network operation across the entire organization is a very critical factor in meeting the overall goals of the business. Networks are relatively volatile. Thus, they always represent a primary security vulnerability. Therefore, it is the responsibility of the organization to develop, implement, and monitor the procedures that are needed to reliably ensure all of the various network elements.

These procedures establish consistent oversight over both managerial and technical assurance of the network. These procedures underwrite the integrity of the transmission of data both internally and externally in order to safeguard those transactions from such hazards as theft, fraud, repudiation, and dispute. Since electronic transactions are the lifeblood of modern business, that responsibility alone would justify a robust set of network defense procedures.

Network Attacks

The best way to counteract a network attack is to anticipate it and have the appropriate measures in place to either stop it or mitigate the harm. As shown in Figure 6.21, network attacks fall into eight generic categories: (1) password attacks, (2) social engineering, (3) sniffing, (4) IP spoofing, (5) denial of service, (6) man-in-the-middle attacks, (7) application layer attacks, and (8) insider attacks.

> *Password attacks*: A password attack is an attempt to access a computer by guessing its password. A successful password attack is a dangerous breach because once an attacker gains access, he or she has exactly the same rights as the authorized user. The best response to a password attack is a strong password that is regularly changed.

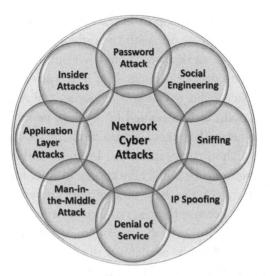

Figure 6.21   Network cyber attacks.

Social engineering attacks: These are very effective ways to penetrate a network. A social engineering attack depends on persuasion rather than technology. In it, the attacker uses claims of authority and other types of misrepresentations to fool users into allowing access. The countermeasure for social engineering exploits is education and awareness.

Sniffing/packet analysis: Sniffing is a technique that is software and sometimes even hardware based. Sniffing is a technological function. Sniffers are employed to read the information in packets being transmitted over a network. When sniffers are used for malicious purposes, the most common criterion used to identify an interesting packet is the presence of words like "login" or "password." Sniffers can also be used to compromise the integrity of the data stream by interjecting new information or changing the existing information in a packet. The proper countermeasure for a sniffer is encryption.

IP spoofing: It is a specific type of address attack. An IP spoofing attack occurs when an established session is intercepted and co-opted by the attacker. It is an exploit where the malicious agent attempts to impersonate another network party through its IP address. The intruder gains access to the target system by altering the sequence numbers of a packet's IP source address.

The aim is to make it appear as though the packet originated from a trusted site or one with the right type of access privileges. Normally, an IP spoofing attack is limited to such activities as adding data or commands to a data stream. However, if the attacker is able to change the routing tables in the target system to point to the spoofed IP address, he will be able to hijack the network packets addressed to the spoofed address. Methods such as the Secure Shell Protocol (SSH) use public key cryptography for both connection and authentication.

Denial of service (DoS): These attacks are different from most other attacks because they do not directly affect the information on the network. DoS attacks are a particular problem because they affect the availability of the transmission media itself. A DoS floods a network with traffic so that the network cannot respond normally and service is curtailed or denied. A DoS attack usually does not result in the loss of information. Instead, it is an information assurance compromise because DoS attacks degrade the availability of information.

Man-in-the-middle (MITM) attacks: These are often based on the use of network packet sniffers or by directly modifying routing and transport protocols. MITM attacks can be also launched through intermediate parties who function as proxies for the clients on either side, such as an ISP. If an agent is trustworthy, then there is little cause to worry. If they are not, then the clients on both sides of the communication link are in serious jeopardy.

Application layer attacks: These take advantage of weaknesses in popular applications and application services. These are usually Internet-based exploits that go after the web facing applications on an organization's server. They include such common attacks as buffer overflows, which exploit poorly written code that improperly validates input to an application. In most, but not all, cases, these attacks are exploitations of design flaws in a software application and center on the server. By taking advantage of these weaknesses, attackers can gain access at the same level of permission as the account running the application. Thus, many of these vulnerabilities can be addressed by proper application design and secure coding practice.

Insider attacks: It is well documented that the primary source of network breaches comes from insider action. Approximately three-quarters of all misuse incidents originate from the intentional or inadvertent actions of employees. Moreover, when that insider is disgruntled, considerable amounts of harm can ensure. The obvious first line of defense is good management. Thus, the essence of protecting from insider attacks lies in the monitoring function. Supervisors are the key security control points in cases of employee monitoring. In addition, software agents called policy managers or policy enforcement systems can be used to enforce security rules.

Threat Hunting and Machine Learning

Automated network security functions are proactive. The fundamental idea is to allow the network to make security decisions based on intelligence about end systems. This type of system is capable of making automated decisions about unauthorized access. As shown in Figure 6.22, there are five common approaches to network-based threat detection. These are: (1) pattern matching, (2) state matching, (3) analysis engine methods, (4) protocol anomaly, and (5) traffic anomaly. Two of these rely on patterns in the transmission data. The other three are oriented toward anomaly identification and statistical process control techniques.

The easiest approach by far is the simple pattern matching technology. Pattern matching offers a simple defense. It scans incoming

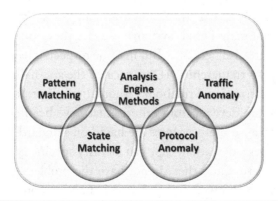

Figure 6.22   Five common approaches to network-based threat detection.

packets for specific byte sequences that are stored in a database of known attacks. In that respect, they operate like a standard virus checker does for viruses. They can identify and respond to commonplace attacks using that approach. But because they have to use known patterns to respond, attacks can be modified to avoid detection. Therefore, they require frequent updates.

A state matching approach is more reliable than pattern matching because it scans for attack signatures in the traffic stream itself rather than the presence of an individual packet sequence. Consequently, it can detect an incoming attack that is spread across multiple packets. Because it still relies on known patterns, it also requires frequent updates of attack signatures to be effective.

Analysis engine methods are state based. At their heart, they are anomaly detection systems in the sense that they use anomalous behaviors as the basis for their response such as multiple failed logons, users logging in at strange hours, unexplained system shutdowns, and restarts. Statistical anomaly-based threat detection systems are a common example of such methods. They get around the limitations of signature files because they are heuristic. Meaning they learn and develop baselines of normal traffic and then base their alerts on deviations from these baselines.

Because anomalous behavior serves as the basis for the established baselines, these systems can identify unknown attacks and such dynamic attacks as DoS floods. The problem with these systems is their complexity. Because they are so complex, they can be difficult to tune properly. And because they are reliant on their baselines to judge their responses, it always has to be ensured that the system understands what the "normal" traffic environment looks like.

Protocol anomaly-based systems are another form of analysis engine. They are also heuristic. But in some respects, they are also very close to the pattern matching IDSs, because the anomalies are defined based on an international rulebook. Anomalies in a protocol anomaly-based system are derived from criteria that have been established by the IETF. Because these systems are based on standard definitions of what constitutes a deviation, they can identify specific types of attacks without a signature and they do not have the problem of an analysis engine approach. However, the protocol analysis modules that drive these systems take a lot longer to deploy than a signature file.

Traffic anomaly-based systems are also analysis engines. These systems watch for unusual traffic activities, such as a flood of TCP packets or a new service suddenly appearing on the network. These threat hunters can identify unknown attacks and DoS floods, but they suffer from the same problem as the statistical anomaly-based approaches with ensuring that the "normal" traffic environment is properly understood.

Twenty Review Questions: Connection Security

1. Why is network security particularly difficult to achieve?
2. What is the basis for defining trust in networks and what does that imply in terms of the protection approach/requirements?
3. What is the difference between connection control and transmission control?
4. What are the physical components of a network and how are they secured?
5. What are the physical components of a network and how are they secured?
6. Why are network vulnerability assessments important? What differentiates network equipment from other kinds of computer equipment? What unique security issues does this difference raise?
7. How does connection control differ from transmission control? Why are both of these functions essential to secure transmissions?
8. Why is configuration an important aspect of both transmission control and connection control?
9. Why is sniffing a particularly dangerous vulnerability in a network? What are the specific properties of sniffing that make it that way?
10. What are the ways that a password can be compromised? What are some of the potential safeguards against that happening?
11. Why is employing a competent process an important consideration in application layer attacks? What does that prevent? What is gained by a proper approach to development?

12. How does access control policy relate to the network security plan? Why is it critical to the overall planning process?
13. What is the purpose of a risk analysis (besides to identify risks)? What particular feature of management does it support?
14. What does network defense in depth entail?
15. What is the generic function of a best usage policy?
16. Define a network security perimeter, what normally constitutes the dividing point?
17. Why are perimeters so important to the physical design of secure networks?
18. What is the role of DMZs in Internet security?
19. Why are human factors an important aspect of network security?
20. Why is IP spoofing always unethical, what are some examples from real life?

You Might Also Like to Read

- Bejtlich, Richard, *The Practice of Network Security Monitoring: Understanding Incident Detection and Response*, 1st Edition, No Starch Press, San Francisco, CA, 2013.
- Bhattacharjee, Sravani, *Practical Industrial Internet of Things Security: A practitioner's Guide to Securing Connected Industries*, Packt Publishing eBook, Birmingham, 2018.
- Brotherston, Lee, *Defensive Security Handbook: Best Practices for Securing Infrastructure*, 1st Edition, O'Reilly Media, Newton, MA, 2017.
- Brotherston, Lee and Amanda Berlin, *Defensive Security Handbook: Best Practices for Securing Infrastructure*, 1st Edition, O'Reilly Media, Newton, MA, 2017.
- Gilman, Evan and Doug Barth, *Zero Trust Networks: Building Secure Systems in Untrusted Networks*, 1st Edition, O'Reilly Media, Newton, MA, 2017.
- Kurose, James and Keith Ross, *Computer Networking: A Top-Down Approach*, 7th Edition, Pearson, London, 2016.
- Meyers, Mike, *CompTIA Network+ Certification All-in-One Exam Guide (Exam N10-007)*, 7th Edition, Mc-Graw-Hill, New York, 2018.

- Monnappa, K.A., *Learning Malware Analysis: Explore the Concepts, Tools, and Techniques to Analyze and Investigate Windows Malware*, Packt Publishing, Birmingham, 2018.
- Stallings, William, *Network Security Essentials: Applications and Standards*, 6th Edition, Pearson, London, 2016.
- Whitman, Michael E. and Herbert J. Mattord, *Management of Information Security*, 6th Edition, Cengage Learning, Boston, MA, 2018.

Chapter Summary

- Connection Security comprises all of the technologies, processes, and practices that are deployed to protect the organization's networks, computers, programs, and constituent data from attack, damage, or unauthorized access.
- The knowledge in the Connection Security area of the CSEC represents the current thinking about the appropriate response to electronic attack.
- Connection Security has a twofold mission. First, it must protect confidential information from unauthorized access. Second, it has to safeguard the transmissions themselves from malicious or accidental harm.
- At present, the following eight knowledge areas are considered to be elements of the rapidly growing field of Connection Security: *Physical Media* – basic signaling and transmission concepts, *Physical Interfaces and Connectors* – connectors, their materials, and standards, *Hardware Architecture* – standard hardware architectures, *Distributed Systems Architecture* – the general concepts of distributed systems, *Network Architecture* – fundamental network connectivity concepts, *Network Implementations* – basic network architectural implementation concepts, *Network Services* – different models implementing practical connectivity, and *Network Defense* – methods and models for effectively protecting networks.
- *Knowledge Unit One: Physical Media*: Networks provide the tangible infrastructure to allow many physical endpoints to interconnect and communicate with each other. There are four subtopics in the Physical Media knowledge area:

Transmission in a medium –, Shared and point-to-point media, Sharing models and Common technologies.

- *Knowledge Unit Two: Physical Interfaces and Connectors*: There are three subtopics in the Physical Interfaces and Connectors knowledge unit: Hardware characteristics and materials, Standards, and Common interconnectors.
- *Knowledge Unit Three: Hardware architecture*: There are three subtopics in the Hardware architecture topic: Standard architectures, Hardware interface standards, and Common architectures.
- *Knowledge Unit Four: Distributed Systems Architecture*: There are seven subtopics in the Distributed systems architecture topic: Network architectures, General concepts, World Wide Web, The Internet, Protocols and layering: HPC (supercomputers), Hypervisors and cloud computing implementations, Vulnerabilities.
- *Knowledge Unit Five: Network Architecture*: There are seven subtopics associated with this knowledge unit: General concepts, Common architectures, Forwarding, Routing, Switching/Bridging, Emerging trends, and Virtualization and virtual hypervisor architecture.
- *Knowledge Unit Six: Network Implementations*: There are four subtopics associated with this knowledge unit: IEEE 802/ISO standards, IETF networking concepts and TCP/IP, Practical integration and glue protocols, and Vulnerabilities and example exploits.
- *Knowledge Unit Seven: Network Services*: There are seven subtopics associated with this knowledge unit: Concept of a service, Service models (client–server, peer to peer), Service protocols and concepts (IPC, APIs, IDLs), Common service communication architectures, and Vulnerabilities and example exploits.
- *Knowledge Unit Eight: Network Defense*: There are thirteen subtopics in the network defense topic area: Network hardening, Implementing firewalls and VPNs, Defense in depth, Honeypots and honeynets, Network monitoring, Network traffic analysis, Minimizing exposure (attack surface and vectors), Network access control (internal and external),

Perimeter networks/proxy servers, Network policy development and enforcement, Network operational procedures, Network attacks, and Threat hunting and machine learning.

Learning Objectives for the Connection Security Knowledge Area

Mastery of the requisite learning outcomes for the Connection Security knowledge area will be established through the student's ability to paraphrase and explicate the key contents of the knowledge units within this knowledge area (Bloom Levels Two and Three). In addition, the student will exhibit specific behaviors that demonstrate a capability to utilize the relevant concepts in common practical application. Specifically, the student will be able to paraphrase and explain the following eighteen knowledge elements (CSEC, 2019):

1. Discuss the need for common models and architectures in order to describe systems.
2. Describe a model of systems that consists of components and interfaces for connections.
3. Explain why a component requires at least one interface.
4. List several standards that define models consisting of systems of components and interfaces.
5. Describe the components and interfaces of a networking standard provided. Physical component interfaces.
6. Explain why a hardware device is always modeled a physical component.
7. List several examples of physical component interfaces with their associated vulnerabilities.
8. Describe an exploit for a vulnerability of a physical interface provided.
9. Explain why every physical interface has a corresponding software component to provide a corresponding software interface.
10. Explain how software components are organized to represent logical layers in a standard model.
11. Discuss how the Internet five-layer model can be viewed as software components and interfaces that represent levels of services encapsulated by lower-level services.
12. Discuss how TCP/IP as a service is represented by different interfaces in different software systems.

13. Explain how connection attacks can be understood in terms of attacks on software component interfaces.
14. Describe how a specified standard interface could expose vulnerabilities in a software component that implements the interface.
15. Describe how an implementation could protect itself from a specified vulnerability in a specified standard interface.
16. Explain how transmission attacks are often implemented as attacks on components that provide the service of relaying information.
17. Describe an attack on a specified node in a TCP/IP network given the description of a vulnerability.
18. Explain why transmission attacks can often be viewed as connection attacks on network components (physical or software).

Keywords

Access Control – application of principles that define the level of authorization to data.

Architecture – a complete entity or artifact that embodies a complete set of rational objects. These objects are commonly called "components."

Behavior – discrete actions performed that are observable by third parties.

Best Practice – commonly accepted means of carrying out a given task.

Component – an elemental unit or artifact that embodies a single function. These are assembled into structures called "architectures."

Cryptography – assurance that data cannot be read by unauthorized parties.

Data Integrity and Authentication – practices that ensure that data is correct and verifying the identity of the people or systems accessing the data.

Forensics – the application of science to questions that are of interest to the legal profession.

Integrity – a critical quality of a component or component architecture.

Layering – a reference model for communication programs.

Protocol – a set of rules governing the exchange or transmission of data between devices.

Secure Communication Protocols – technical measures aimed toward secure transmission of data.

Strategic Planning – the process of developing long-term directions aimed at furthering and enhancing organizational goals.

Strategic Planning – the process of developing long-term directions aimed at furthering and enhancing organizational goals.

System – discrete components assembled into a synergistic whole to accomplish a purpose.

References

BroadbandNow.com., Terrestrial Fixed Wireless Internet in the United States. World-Wide-Web, 2019. Downloaded from https://broadband-now.com/Fixed-Wireless, August 2019.

Coffey, Charles, Informtion Warfare: It's Everybody's Battle. SANS Institute Reading Room, 2019. www.sans.org/reading-room/whitepapers/warfare/information-warfare-its-everybodys-battle-789.

Joint Task Force (JTF) on Cybersecurity Education, "Cybersecurity Curricula 2017, Curriculum Guidelines for Post-Secondary Degree Programs in Cybersecurity, a Report in the Computing Curricula Series", ACM/IEEE-CS/AIS SIGSEC/IFIP WG 11.8, Version 1.0, 31 December 2017.

7

SYSTEM SECURITY

In this chapter, you will learn the following:

- The concept and justification for a holistic approach to systems
- The role of security policy in the creation and maintenance of holistic systems
- The role of authentication in the assurance of System Security
- The role of access control in maintaining the integrity and confidentiality of systems
- The role of system monitoring in the assurance of overall secure operation
- The role of recovery planning and procedure in the assurance of trust in a system
- The role of testing in the assurance of secure system operation
- The role of documentation in the System Security life cycle process.

Assembling the Parts into a Useful Whole

In many respects, the System Security knowledge area (KA 5) is the glue that binds the knowledge areas associated with software (KA 2: Software Security), components (KA 3: Component Security), and connections (KA 4: Connection Security) into a single practical understanding. In essence, the System Security knowledge area is the one place in the CSEC2017 model where the "holistic view," which is integral to ensuring suitably complete and correct cybersecurity solutions, is fully represented and discussed as well as practically applied.

It should be clear at this point that cybersecurity is a complex field. Dealing with that kind of complexity requires concrete organizing principles that will ensure that a diverse collection of essential elements is properly integrated into a multifaceted and systematic appreciation of cybersecurity as a whole. The resulting understanding will then provide a unified way to provide the desired assurance outcomes.

In the case of cybersecurity, the ability to reliably counter any given real-world threat is inherently challenging. The problem stems from the fact that the constituent elements of the solution are diverse, often unique. And the requisite interactions, dependencies, or other types of relationships that exist between them are wide ranging and unpredictable. However, the principles that guide the creation of a rational cybersecurity response are no different than they would be for the construction of any other highly diverse and complex real-world system; whether it's the space program or Amazon's package distribution system. Therefore, the concept of system applies to all cybersecurity solutions.

Every system is a unified collection of interacting and interdependent objects. These objects are assembled by design into an intentional and well-defined structure of discrete components. The purpose of each element must be able to be specifically characterized. The "well-defined" criterion implies that a clearly recognizable structural and temporal boundary exists between every part in the system and that the elements can all be related to each other and that the system is specifically delineated from its environment.

The dynamic relationship implies that all systems are essentially living entities. Systems are composed of interdependent and interacting objects. Each object affects the system in the sense that a change to one will affect all other objects as well as the status of the system as a whole. However, in order to be systematic, the interaction of the parts must always act predictably, in a rational and rectilinear fashion.

Systems are almost by definition synergistic in the sense that ideally, the effect of the system should be greater than the impact of the sum of the individual parts. Systems are also emergent in the sense that they are in a continuous state of potential change as their purpose and the effects of the environment influence them. Finally, because they are dynamic, a system can be engineered in a substantively rational and deliberate fashion.

The Key Role of Design in Systems

Every security system is founded on a single, substantive, properly documented, logical design. That design specifies the major system objects and their protection goals and then proceeds to demonstrate how the associated assurance requirements will achieve those goals. The security requirements are underwritten by a set of concrete, mutually supporting security behaviors. In that respect then, the security design documents a complete set of actions that are deemed sufficient to ensure a satisfactory security solution.

The design provides an explicit itemization of system functions as well as their explicit interdependencies. In addition, a concrete set of organizational resources must be directly related to underwrite each of the actions specified. The design documents the systematic assurance activities that are required to ensure a specified level of security performance; as well as the people who will be accountable for their execution. The latter specification is necessary to ensure consistent day-to-day execution of the protection operation.

Every design process is conceptual in focus. The first step is for the designer to obtain a full and substantive understanding of the security problems associated with that particular system. Once sufficient overall knowledge of the security context is achieved, the designer will drill down to document the explicit security behaviors that enable the specific operational security goals of the system. These behaviors are the concrete control actions that must be developed and installed.

Following this step, each of the technical components and the practices that the designer has chosen to achieve each specified goal in that particular context must be fully and completely characterized. The description is done at a level of detail that ensures the systematic day-to-day performance of each requisite security duty. That requirement implies the need for a complete and effective documentation set, one that ensures the logical step-by-step execution of each behavioral and technical function. The aim is to guarantee consistent functioning of every system object within the context of the overall process.

Security is built on consistent and reliable performance of a proven set of specific best practices. These practices are embedded in repeatable processes. Repeatability ensures a stable and reliable security response. It also provides the basis for improving the security system over time by means of lessons learned. The process view explicitly states how the various intents and purposes of the system will be achieved. Process is a term that describes the consistent performance of a well-defined set of best practices. Accordingly, effective security systems are implemented as a real-world collection of intelligently designed and reliably repeatable processes. This representation is normally termed the "system engineering" approach. System engineering implies the application of best practice.

That development and instantiation of the appropriate set of security practices is essentially a matter of good system engineering. As we said in earlier parts of this text, the approach to creating the concrete system understanding entails such classic conceptual modeling techniques as top-down decomposition and analysis or object modeling. Just as was the case in the other areas of the CSEC2017, functional decomposition is the classic method for documenting abstract things. That approach relies on the development of a set of focused and progressively more detailed engineering views of the system space. In the end, a set of design objects are produced that represent the cybersecurity functions in the abstract.

The CSEC2017 System Security Knowledge Units

The requirement for system thinking is a key concept in overall cybersecurity theory and practice. In essence, some form of system thinking is imperative if you want the teaching and learning process to provide a full and coherent understanding of the problem space as a whole. The CSEC2017 specifies seven practical knowledge areas. As a complete set, these are intended to ensure that all approaches to cybersecurity are systematic. Thus, each of these knowledge units underwrites currently accepted system thinking.

The knowledge units that can be associated with these topics describe the full set of conceptual and practical activities related to the development of a complete, correct, fully synergistic, and effective real-world cybersecurity system. As a whole, the aim of each of these knowledge units is to specify a set of professional behaviors and capabilities that would be required to underwrite effective System Security design, development, and operational practice.

Hence, the areas that fall into the area of System Security mainly involve classic engineering and management concepts, which have traditionally been a part of the system development and sustainment process for information technology settings. These concepts are all intended to be embodied into a practical cybersecurity teaching and learning process.

That includes such standard approaches as development and abstract representation of real-world requirements, as well as a range of practical system management and system retirement concerns. These concepts all apply to conventional system thinking as a whole. There are a set of unique security factors that also have to be considered, such as classic access control principles and holistic thinking. In that respect then, the CSEC2017 knowledge units for System Security are as follows (Figure 7.1):

1. *System Thinking* – the process of intelligent design of holistic and synergistic systems
2. *System Management* – assurance of consistent and reliable oversight over a system
3. *System Access* – assurance of authorized entry for trusted entities seeking admission
4. *System Control* – assurance of reliable oversight and governance of the security solution
5. *System Retirement* – assurance of formal system extinction in a safe and secure manner

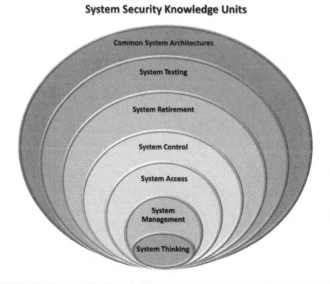

System Security Knowledge Units

Common System Architectures

System Testing

System Retirement

System Control

System Access

System Management

System Thinking

Figure 7.1 The Data Security knowledge units.

6. *System Testing* – processes for validating and verifying the correctness of the solution

7. *Common System Architectures* – classification of standard system models.

Knowledge Unit One: System Thinking

System thinking is colloquially called "The big picture." It is a mindset. It is the dynamic process that lets people comprehend the relationship between the parts of a thing and then adapt that understanding to the emergent elements of technological change. It is system thinking that applies the general principles of systems to any given real-world problem (Figure 7.2).

The system approach is essentially a structured way of understanding a complex thing. It is the way we learn how constituent parts interact with each other within the whole. In essence, the knowledge units that are contained in the System Thinking area underwrite the ability to view a particular artifact or entity as a single unified object and to deconstruct it into a collection of its logical components. It decomposes the security problem into its constituent elements and then addresses the overall concern by arraying a complete and correct

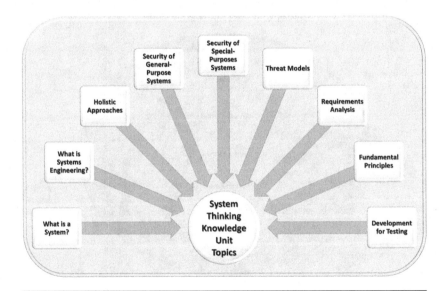

Figure 7.2 The Cryptography knowledge unit topics.

set of behaviors to respond to every aspect of the problem. System thinking is a holistic discipline in that it concentrates on understanding all of the ways that a given entity's parts interconnect and how the amalgamation of those parts into a whole will then proceed. Finally, system thinking views the environment of a particular system in terms of its contextual influences.

A system point of view sits in stark contrast to the classic areas of cybersecurity practice, such as networks or programming; in that it is fully inclusive of all types of security threats, comprehensive in scope, and top down from the environment in its analytic model. Thus, the system perspective embraces every conceivable aspect of threat and response, not just those considerations that are appropriate to a given discipline. This wide-ranging point of view ensures a balanced approach to the problem and it is characterized by three critical principles: factoring, equilibrium, and feedback.

Perhaps the most dominant principle is *factoring*. Factoring is commonly known as "functional decomposition." Factoring is the "go-to" strategy for understanding and organizing a complex thing, especially during the development process. It is based on breaking a problem into its logical parts in order to ensure a complete and accurate picture of the elements of a given entity, as well as the interrelationship of each of those elements in the overall structure. Typically, the goal of factoring is to categorize, document, and then build a model of the constituent elements and then to optimize the interaction between those things in order to ensure that they interact most efficiently.

The characteristic parameters that can be used to judge the effectiveness of a factoring process are "cohesiveness" and "coupling." Together, these concepts are normally called "modularity." The term cohesion describes the degree of relationship between the components of a given module. Cohesiveness is considered to be a measure of the logical correctness of the entity. That is because a module with a high degree of internal logic is generally considered to be more reliable, robust, and understandable. Therefore, modules that are highly cohesive are considered to be superior to modules that exhibit low cohesion. Loosely coupled elements underwrite the concept of modularity. Modules that are highly cohesive tend to be loosely coupled, in that the modules themselves are not dependent on each other. Thus, loose coupling is a primary indicator of the strength of the design architecture itself that is desirable practical quality in an architecture since the modules that comprise it can be interchanged in a plug-and-play fashion, while still providing the required functionality. A decoupled module also supports the concept of reliability, as well as information hiding; in that the failure of one module does not cascade to another. Finally, modular elements also support platform independence.

The *equilibrium* factor is a behavioral construct in that the behavior of a system can be judged by the stable interaction of its parts. The parts of a system have to interact in an intentionally harmonious fashion in order to satisfy its designed purposes. Systems are always dynamic, and therefore, a failure in any given part or interrelationship could potentially lead to overall system failure. The analogy is the human body. All of the organs in your body work together to ensure good health. If one of them fails, or interacts improperly, your body will suffer poor health or even death. Therefore, one of the essential qualities of a system is the maintenance of an optimum level of equilibrium between its components.

That leads to the concept of *feedback*. Feedback describes the need for the system to regularly obtain pertinent and suitable input from both the internal operation of the system, as well as from the environment as a whole. Thus, feedback is an essential consideration in all forms of system thinking. Using the body's example again, the information that is obtained from symptoms such as coughing, sneezing, or a runny nose will help the doctor diagnose and treat a common cold. In essence, the system feedback from the patient allows the medical staff to directly focus on and address the specific system problem. That diagnosis might be aided by the fact that the symptoms were presented during "cold season." Thus, the context is also a factor in effective decision-making and the specific provisions for obtaining feedback from the environment are critical operational elements of the system thinking process.

What Is a System?

In definitional terms, all systems are collections of logically interrelated parts, which are amalgamated into a fully integrated whole. The purpose of that amalgamation is always to achieve a given well-defined purpose. Consequently, by definition, a system is a functional architecture with clearly demarcated perimeters. The constituent elements within the perimeter of a system represent a well-defined and distinct environment. The system might be open or closed. If it is open, it interacts with the larger environment in intentional ways based on its purpose. If it is closed, all interactions take place within the system boundary of necessity then. The components of a system will share the same characteristics of structure and purpose with the overall system itself. As shown in Figure 7.3, the four primary qualities of a system are (1) boundary or scope, (2) architecture and complexity, (3) form of representation, and (4) behavior.

The first quality is *scope*. Because all systems exist within well-defined perimeters, they are characterized by the components that they circumscribe. Or in simple terms, you can differentiate a system through its constituent parts. The second quality is *complexity*. Systems are composed of a multifaceted array of components. There may be many or few and their interactions may be more or less intricate. Thus, system architectures are differentiated by the number of components and the intricacy of their array. That complexity is captured by a recognized form of *representation*. The common approach to representation is formal modeling. An accepted form of abstraction technique is employed to do formal modeling. Models explicitly depict the system components and the logic of their relationships. The aim of formal

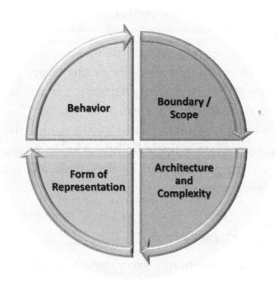

Figure 7.3 Four primary qualities of a system.

representation is to depict the intended *behavior* of the system. All systems have a purpose, which is achieved through a planned set of behaviors. Those behaviors can be evaluated through documented evidence of the consistent and reliable execution of the system functions. There can be both natural and man-made systems. However, for the purposes of cybersecurity, we are only considering the man-made variety.

What Is Systems Engineering?

Cybersecurity systems are complex and multifaceted by definition. So, the field of systems engineering is the academic area that is most closely identified with the design and management of complex cybersecurity systems. System engineering is by definition holistic and interdisciplinary. The general aim of the teaching of system engineering is to structure and present the concepts, methods, and techniques of system design and system management in a comprehensive and rational approach.

System engineering processes are primarily based on system thinking which the CSEC2017 quite appropriately presents as the topic just before this area in the System Thinking knowledge area. Systems Thinking principles and practices are utilized by the system engineer to deliver a rational, substantive, and fully engineered cybersecurity architecture. Done properly, this architecture embodies all of the requisite qualities of completeness, correctness, and synergy that a proper system should exhibit.

System engineering requires holistic understanding of the problem space. Thus, it is a multidisciplinary challenge. That also usually implies a team effort. System engineering is also more likely to be integrative than specifically creative in practice. That is because system engineering is oriented toward amalgamating the constituent parts of the system into a single holistic solution. Thus, the system engineering design process often involves trade-offs between every aspect of the eventual system.

Security of General-Purpose Systems

This topic really encompasses every aspect of what we typically call cybersecurity practice, in that general-purpose systems are the day-to-day things we call "computers." That includes every type of computer from mainframe to tablet as long as it runs a conventional operating system. The key concept here is "general purpose." Most computers do a wide variety of things. So, they require a single common operating system that can run a highly divergent set of software applications, thus the term "general purpose."

But the adaptability that a potentially unlimited array of software offers comes at a price. General-purpose systems are targets for attack because they are so ubiquitous. They are also more likely to have exploitable gaps. In that, they can only be as secure as the applications they are running. Since the application landscape for a general-purpose operating system like Microsoft Windows or Android constitutes a universe of things, it is hard to anticipate and counter all of the threats. That is the reason why the body of knowledge for security of general-purpose systems tends to be synonymous with that of cybersecurity as a whole and the teaching approach mirrors that state of affairs.

Security of Special-Purposes Systems

The point of the topic lies in the name, "special-purpose systems." These are systems that have been created to perform a single defined function such as control a production line device, or regulate electrical distribution, or even do banking like an ATM. Dedicated systems such as these are based on programmed logic. However, their single purpose makes them simpler and often much more efficient. That is due to the fact that the programmed logic can be hardwired without a need for an intervening operating system. Or, simple enough to be written in something like machine language.

One challenge is that the programming of most special-purpose devices does not incorporate security features that would normally be seen in a general-purpose application. The lack of attention to overall security would not be an issue in a completely closed system. But access to special-purpose systems, such as supervisory control and data acquisition (SCADA) controllers and even Internet of Things (IoT) special-purpose devices is often provided. When that happens, the constrained nature of the device's functionality, specifically the deliberate lack of security protection, makes special-purpose systems particularly vulnerable. Since special-purpose systems comprise most of our critical infrastructure, dedicated engineering practices to ensure their trustworthiness are a very high priority for the profession.

Threat Models

Threat modeling is a formal method that is employed to characterize attack vectors. The aim is to understand the threatscape in enough detail that all meaningful threats are identified and mitigated. Threat models are graphic portrayals of the system from the standpoint of entities, data flow lines, processing functions, and data stores. There is also an object modeling approach called "misuse cases." Specifically, threat models can be used to analyze and evaluate various types of attack. The aim is to describe what it would take to make a specific attack successful. That involves a number of "what if" type of suppositions and emulations. But the advantage of a good threat model is that impacts can be explicitly assessed and in detail.

All of these are aimed at understanding system functioning for the purposes of identifying potential points of weakness. In general, threat models form the link between real-world businesspeople and the security analyst. They provide the analyst with in-depth understanding of the system and its vulnerabilities. They also allow the analyst to explain the threat environment and associated attack vectors to the rest of the organization. In that respect, threat modeling is the language of cybersecurity systems work.

Requirements Analysis

Requirements analysis describes the difficult process of identifying, evaluating, and documenting those conditions and behaviors that will be "required" to satisfy a desired set of circumstances. Requirements analysis involves the painstaking process of elicitation, analysis, documentation, and assurance of a given set of system requirements along with their long-term sustainment. That includes fully describing all dependencies and interrelationships among the requirements set and making all of the potential design assumptions explicit.

Requirements are documented using the modeling methods discussed above. They are usually captured in the form of specific propositions such as use cases, data flow diagrams, and business cases. Requirements analysis underpins that process. The expectation is that the requirements analysis process will be sufficiently detailed to allow designers and stakeholders to agree on a final set of discrete system activities. These must assure that all identified threats are addressed by an acceptable array of countermeasures. The final product of the requirements analysis process underwrites the assurance that the requirements as specified are consistently correct, complete, and unambiguous, and that any identified conflicts have been fully and properly resolved.

Fundamental Principles

There are three fundamental qualities for judging security in systems. Those are the degree to which the system ensures the *confidentiality*, *integrity*, and *availability* of information. The basic principles for assuring these qualities were first published in 1974 (Saltzer and Schroeder, 1974). But they remain valid today and everyone involved with System Security needs to be aware of them. Most of these principles help in reducing the number of opportunities for an attacker to exploit a system. Since successful attacks can't always be prevented, several other principles are devoted to utilization of lessons learned. As shown in Figure 7.4, the principles are as follows:

1. *Least Privilege*: Each entity is granted the most restrictive set of privileges needed for the performance of authorized tasks. Application of this principle limits the damage that can result from accident, error, or unauthorized use of a system.
2. *Complete Mediation*: Every access to every (security-sensitive) object must be checked for proper authorization and access denied if it violates authorizations. This principle, when systematically applied, is the primary underpinning of the protection system.
3. *Fail-Safe Defaults*: Base access decisions on permission rather than exclusion. Thus, the default situation is lack of access, and the protection scheme identifies conditions under which access is permitted.

4. *Least Common Mechanism*: Minimize the security mechanisms common to more than one user or depended on multiple users or levels of sensitivity. These must be designed with great care to ensure against unintentionally compromising security.

5. *Separation of Privilege*: A protection mechanism that requires two keys to unlock is more robust and flexible. By requiring two keys, no single accident, deception, or breach of trust is sufficient to compromise the protected information.

6. *Psychological Acceptability and Work Factor*: The human interface is to be designed so that users apply the protection mechanisms correctly. Still, the cost of implementing a countermeasure should be commensurate with the cost of a loss.

7. *Economy of Mechanism and Analyzability*: Economy of mechanism simply states: *Keep the design as simple and small as possible*. This applies to any aspect of a system, but it deserves emphasis for protection mechanisms.

8. *Defense in Depth*: This principle ensures that an attacker must compromise more than one protection in a system. It integrates human, technological, and operational capabilities to establish protective barriers across multiple layers.

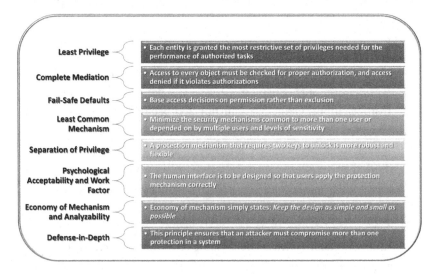

Figure 7.4 Basic principles to ensure security.

Development for Testing

The test strategy needs to embrace all of the phases of the system life cycle. A comprehensive view ensures common understanding across the entire process and it also assures the security and quality of the build. The aim of this unit is not "how to test." Instead it aims at conveying the simple belief that all planned tests have to satisfy basic conditions for economy and effectiveness.

A formal strategy for testing is important because economy and effectiveness tend to contradict each other. Effectiveness is achieved by targeting tests on the features that represent a concern for the security or operation of the system. That can be costly. Economy is achieved ensuring the least possible cost, effort, and time. That can cause you to miss things. Thus, development for testing optimizes the delicate balance between resource requirements and accuracy of findings. The depth and effectiveness of the planning and test documentation is what ensures the quality of the test outcomes. And the visibility of the process is what ensures the cost efficiency.

Knowledge Unit Two: System Management

This knowledge unit describes how a condition of cybersecurity is established and enforced throughout the operational life cycle of the system. System management typically embraces system operation and maintenance activities. These are the actions that are associated with the lengthy portion of the system life cycle that is termed "sustainment." Since the sustainment period will represent the greatest portion of time invested in the system, the operations and maintenance phase is an extremely influential participant in the overall goal of assuring the continuing security of any given system (Figure 7.5).

As the name implies, the purpose of the system management process is to supervise and administer the system operation in its intended environment. Essentially, this role implies a focus on the continuing assurance of proper system functioning as well as its effective security in day-to-day system use. Moreover, since system management involves attention to the hardware as well as the software within the practical operating environment, the process requires the

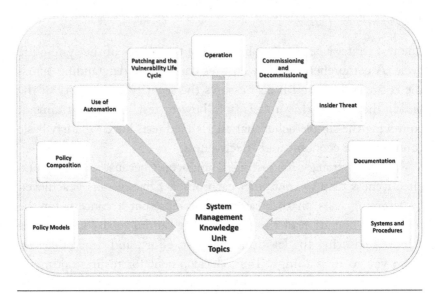

Figure 7.5 The System Management knowledge unit topics.

establishment of a comprehensive array of strategic policies to guide the everyday execution of the process.

The strategies center on establishing complete and consistent control over the security elements of the system operation within its intended environment. In addition to overall system management policies and strategic planning, there also has to be a reliable everyday means for ensuring continuing secure system operation and eventual retirement. Finally, there has to be an organization-wide approach for ensuring the internal integrity of the system from security challenges such as patching, automation, and insider attack.

The system management process involves a diverse set of tasks, which are performed across the entire organization. Therefore, an appropriate set of policy guidelines and task instructions need to be developed to guide the performance of the everyday work. The overall goal of system management is to define and maintain a stable set of routine activities to ensure the full and complete assurance of each system, system asset, or system service within the overall organizational structure of the company.

As a result, arrangements have to be made to integrate the policies and processes that have been developed for secure system management into the routine monitoring and control activities of the business operation as a whole. Consequently, much of system management takes place at the policy and procedure level. Appropriately then, the CSEC2017 System Management knowledge area begins with the development of policy approaches.

Policy Models

A policy is an applied statement of direction that is followed in a systematic fashion. Policies reflect the character and values of an organization. Policies are decisions that the origination makes about how it will operate in the long term. Accordingly, policies are comprehensively applied and semipermanent in approach. In the case of cybersecurity, policies specifically define how assets of value will be protected from identified threats in the organization's operational environment. Since much of this involves regulating access to the asset, one of the primary roles of policy is to govern and assure access control.

Policy models work exactly as the term implies. They are a well-defined protocol that is followed to ensure a comprehensive policy response. In general, policy makers make assumptions about elements of the environment that need to be addressed by concrete, long-term organizational behaviors – e.g., policies. In the case of cybersecurity policies, these assumptions can be a little more precise. That is because significant risks to target assets can be identified prior to the development of the specific policies to mitigate them. Thus, the cyber-risk analysis process is almost inseparable from cybersecurity policy development in most situations. The common element in policy is the continuous monitoring of the threat environment, which will then feed into the ongoing development of organizational cybersecurity policy responses.

Policy Composition

Security policies define how that assurance will be implemented in a given system. In most cases, the composition of those policies explicitly focuses on the risks and precisely how they will be mitigated for a particular situation. Cybersecurity policy is typically composed of procedures that are systematically carried out to preserve the integrity and confidentiality of target assets.

Since the general aim of cybersecurity is the assurance of the confidentiality, integrity, and availability of information assets, these specifications generally regulate how access to those assets will be controlled. Normally, these recommendations are a collection of statements about the restrictions that have been placed on access to system objects and mechanisms that will be implemented to ensure that enforcement.

Use of Automation

Automation is a real asset to security because it makes it easier for humans to manage the many growing intricacies of the threatscape. Artificial intelligence (AI) built into automated features can anticipate attacks and put measures in place to thwart them much quicker than human intervention. Artificially intelligent applications can predict and screen threats and undertake countermeasures when they occur. Firewalls and AI-based intrusion detection are two of the most common examples. Having numerous firewalls, each set up to protect its own segment, creates a defense in depth.

Still, the potential downside of automation is that it lacks the insight that human approaches provide. Both firewalls and intrusion detection systems (IDS) require policy parameters to make judgments. Thus, every formal system management policy statement has to specify the application and restrictions for automated features, both within and external to the system boundary.

Patching and the Vulnerability Life Cycle

This topic involves the security issues associated with patching, as well as how to handle vulnerability reports. Patching is a term that describes the technical and managerial actions that are taken to maintain the security and integrity of the system throughout its useful life cycle. Vulnerabilities that might threaten the security of a system will inevitably be discovered during its use.

Whatever the source of the discovery, every individually identified vulnerability requires a risk management decision about whether, or how, it will be patched or otherwise mitigated. There might be operational justification for not fixing or reporting a vulnerability or for not fixing it or reporting it as soon as possible. As shown in Figure 7.6,

Figure 7.6 Five stages of the system patching process.

the patching process entails the following five stages; (1) *Discovery* – a security vulnerability is identified, (2) *Notification* – finder notifies the effected parties, (3) *Investigation* – effected parties characterize the vulnerability, (4) *Resolution* – a patch is created to eliminate the vulnerability, and (5) *Release* – effected parties coordinate and release the requisite patch.

Organizationally persistent controls must be put in place to ensure that patching is done in a consistent and disciplined fashion. The patch management process ensures that all patches meet established criteria for good practice. Patches must be reintegrated into the operational system in a planned and rational manner. It is then necessary to conduct a technically rigorous process to assure that this reintegration has been done correctly. Thus, the reintegration is supported by a testing program. The testing certifies that the reintegration is satisfactory and that all interfaces are functioning properly.

Operation

Attacks on systems during their operational phase fall into the realm of System Security. Attacks and malicious behavior are undertaken by outsiders as well as insiders, including authorized users. Some of harm to the system might be the result of inadvertent misuse. So, consideration also has to be paid to the ease of operation during system design.

Each of the following common categories of attack may result in adverse operational outcomes. The severity of the consequence ranges from the annoying to critical. The specific techniques that are employed change as the technology evolves. As shown in Figure 7.7, attacks can be generalized into certain types:

1. *Spoofing*: gaining unauthorized access by impersonating an authorized user
2. *Snooping*: capturing data by multiple observations and deduction about the message
3. *Subversion*: actions resulting in modification, destruction, or undetected compromise
4. *Repudiation*: transferring information and subsequently denying having done so
5. *Covert Access and Abuse*: accessing information and performing harmful actions without permission
6. *Physical Abuse*: in certain situations, a physical attack
7. *Unintentional Abuse*: accidentally harming or transmitting sensitive information.

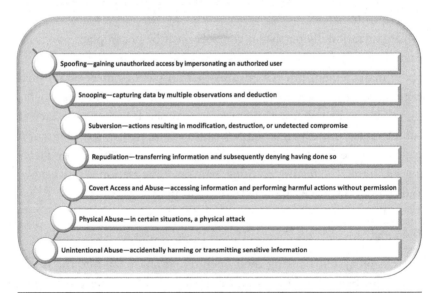

Spoofing—gaining unauthorized access by impersonating an authorized user

Snooping—capturing data by multiple observations and deduction

Subversion—actions resulting in modification, destruction, or undetected compromise

Repudiation—transferring information and subsequently denying having done so

Covert Access and Abuse—accessing information and performing harmful actions without permission

Physical Abuse—in certain situations, a physical attack

Unintentional Abuse—accidentally harming or transmitting sensitive information

Figure 7.7 General types of cyberattacks.

Commissioning and Decommissioning

Systems that have been decommissioned might still contain residual data in the software and firmware or backups. Alternatively, the attacker may be able to obtain archived software or data that has been replaced by later versions. Their aim would be to use knowledge gained from the archived entities to reverse engineer more effective attacks against the new version.

Insider Threat

Insiders are people who have been entrusted with authorized access as a result of the roles and duties that they fulfil in the organization. They abuse their status in order to cause harm. Insiders are dangerous because they are familiar with the organizations information assets as well as the methods that are in place to protect them. This makes it easier for them to circumvent any security controls. An insider may attempt to steal property or information for personal gain or to benefit another organization or country. The threat to the organization could also be through malicious code such as rootkits, backdoors, or other covert mechanisms.

An insider attack can also happen when someone close to an organization who has trusted access chooses to abuse that trust. This person does not necessarily need to be an employee. People with trusted access can include third-party vendors, contractors, and business partners. All of these categories of individuals can pose a threat. Insider threat falls into three generic categories: *malicious exploits*, *inadvertent negligence*, and *intrusion* – e.g., an attack by an external actor who has gained access to the system by legitimate credentials that have been obtained through social engineering.

Documentation

Documentation makes the system and its security functionality visible to the world at large. System Security documentation can be anything from the best-use policy to the specification of requirements for the System Security functions or the firewall operations manual. It can be simple end-user awareness, or something more technical, for the system administrator. Technical documentation can include code or architectural design documents. By convention, documentation is divided into process documentation and product documentation. Process documentation defines how the overall system and security process should be executed. It is normally expressed in end-user terms, and it is designed for a wide audience. Product, or system documentation, describes the system artifacts and how they are to be used.

System documentation is the heart of the active protection scheme. That includes security logs and other tracking and operational details. All of these must be systematic in terms of the records they generate and fully protected from loss or harm. That is because much of the items that they document are essential elements of proof of compliance with any outside security laws, regulations, or standards.

Systems and Procedures

All systems are managed by some type of planned or ad hoc procedure. These procedures specify the explicit activities and tasks appropriate to system use. The structure of these is top down from one process, to many activities for each process, to many tasks for each activity. Specifically, these instructions provide best practice advice on proper System Security management and use. They tend to concentrate on specification of the procedures for management of risk as represented by the National Institute for Standards and Technology Risk Management Framework (RMF).

Knowledge Unit Three: System Access

This knowledge unit introduces the critical issue of controlling access to the system. System access control is a management process that involves both documentation and record keeping as well as technical implementation. It requires the identification of authorized entities to an explicit level of granularity. Topics overlap with the Human Security knowledge area, but the focus here is on the system elements and not the human ones (Figure 7.8).

As it does in every other situation, access control at the system level requires the definition of types to support the authentication and authorization process. The term "type" just denotes a label. Types

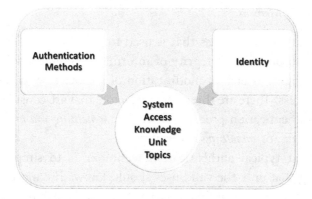

Figure 7.8 The System Access knowledge unit topics.

are necessary to establish identity, because they let the administrator assign privileges and other kinds of permission based on the attributes, roles, and relationships that each user presents to the system at the time access is requested. These labels can define a structure, a class, a module, an interface, or a user.

Types are the basis for the decisions that the system will automatically make about the access that will be assigned to each request at the point where it is presented. The architectural issues revolve around the establishment of the most effective and efficient processing mechanism for determining and enforcing types and permissions. Because this is preprogrammed, it must be possible for the system to make an explicit choice for every type and mode of access.

Access privileges are normally assigned, monitored, and revoked at the optimum level of permission for each type. That decision is based on the relevant criteria that are preprogrammed into the system for it. These criteria can be temporal, transactional, or even defined. Access permissions that are granted can then be monitored and automatically enforced by the system based on those criteria. Every attempt to access the system must be evaluated and acted on based on a specific security policy. The policy has to be set in advance by the administrator. The compliance criteria are embedded in the software of the access control system. Based on those policies, the session is either granted or denied. Access control embodies four basic functions: *Identification* – asserts the users identity, *Authentication* – verifies who the user is, *Authorization* – defines what the user is allowed to do, and *Accountability* – tracks what the user did and when it was done.

Authentication Methods

Authentication is a process that is used to confirm the identity of a person or to prove the integrity of information input. It verifies the identity, origin, or lack of modification of a subject or object that is seeking access. There are three generic factors that are considered during the authentication process. These are: *something you know, something you have,* or *something that you are.*

The most typical authentication technique is to simply ask for something that only the valid user should know. The most common example of that is the ordinary user ID (or username) and password. The problem is that this method of authentication is not particularly effective or secure. A second means of authentication is the use of something that only a valid user should have in their possession. Smart cards are the most common example of this type of authentication method. They work in collaboration with a "reader." The problem with this approach is that people lose their keys (or cards) all of the time which means that they themselves are prevented from accessing the system or even worse, if somebody else finds the card, then they will be able to access the system illegally.

The third method asks people to provide authentication using something that is unique about them, like handprint scans, this area is known as biometrics. In biometrics, the user must present a personal characteristic like their hand geometry or a fingerprint as the token for authentication. The system uses that token as the means for authenticating that the user is who they say they are. This is a particularly effective because individual characteristics, like a fingerprint, are very hard to duplicate and it is impossible to lose them. The most secure way to implement the authentication process is through multifactor authentication. Multifactor authentication increases the level of security, because more than one factor would have to be spoofed in order for an unauthorized individual to gain access.

Identity

Identity is based on the validation of unique properties, which are not shared by any other entity. The practical outcome of the identification process is accountability. Accurate identifications allow the system to track the activities of individuals and hold them responsible for their actions. Therefore, identifications are issued and maintained by means of a secure process. The most common of these is the password.

Knowledge Unit Four: System Control

This knowledge unit examines the models involved in defending against attacks. There are three types of control models that are currently in common usage in the industry. These are designed to specifically implement and enforce a desired level of confidentiality, or transactional integrity, for organizational data. These are classification-based models, such as Bell–LaPadula, integrity-based models, such as Biba, and transaction-based models, such as Clark–Wilson (Figure 7.9).

The most common classification-based security model is Bell–LaPadula. At its heart, the Bell–LaPadula model is specifically designed to limit the disclosure of information between security levels. The aim of Bell–LaPadula is to make it impossible for data to be disclosed to levels without the appropriate security clearances. The model employs both mandatory and discretionary access control mechanisms to implement its two basic security rules, which are: no read up and no write down. Authorization for access rights between

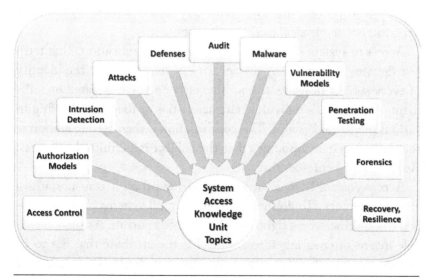

Figure 7.9 The System Control knowledge unit topics.

any subject and any given object is based on their individual security levels.

The Biba security model is a formal security approach that is centered on ensuring the integrity of subjects and objects in a system. Thus, integrity levels are utilized, instead of security classifications, to define access rights. Integrity levels indicate the level of "trust" that can be placed in information kept at different levels. The primary objective of Biba is to limit the modification of information, rather than its flow between levels.

Clark–Wilson uses transactions as the basis for its decision-making. It defines two levels of integrity. These are constrained and unconstrained data items. Access or change to constrained data items is subject to controls, while unconstrained data items are not controlled. Access is enabled through a trusted transformation process. This is a software function that ensures that the subject has the proper classification. Thus, access is granted to the control rather than the data itself.

Access Control

Access controls safeguard against threats and reduce vulnerabilities. They let management specify which users can access the system, what resources they can access, and what operations they can perform. By definition, access control is all of the security features that are employed to prevent unauthorized entry into a system, its attached network, or the physical facilities that house it.

Access to system objects requires proper authentication. That term just denotes the ability of the security system to verify the identity of every subject desiring access. The authentication is based on validating the subject's individual characteristics or their membership in various predefined groups. This confirmation is then used to authorize the data or system resources that the subject is permitted to access. Access control enforces this.

Access control is more of a required state than it is a substantive area of assurance. To do their jobs properly, all systems have to establish the specific access rights of authenticated parties. As such, a reliable means of ensuring access control is the attribute that has to be present in order for the system to operate securely. The concept of access just denotes the ability of a subject to interact with a given object. The definition of what constitutes a proper subject in the system sense can be very broad. In essence, the subject can be a person or a process. If it is the latter, it can either be a computer process or an organizational one. While the system object that is being accessed can be anything that might be legitimately accessed by that subject, that could be everything from the physical space the system resides in, to a file, to a hardware device.

Authorization Models

In practice, authorization involves the determination that a particular subject has the necessary level of permission to access a target resource. That is different from authentication which simply establishes the right of the subject to cross the system boundary. Authorization is built around the granting of "permission" or "privilege". Privileges are based on the concept of "trust."

Trusted identities are allowed access to specified services. Untrusted or unknown identities will not be granted access until they have been authenticated. In practice, authorization also describes the management function by which identities are granted access rights. In this process, each identity's specific rights of use are established. As shown in Figure 7.10, authorization is established by three generic methods: policy-based access control, mandatory access control (MAC), and role-based access control (RBAC).

> *Policy-based access control*: is by far the most common mechanism for controlling access. The most typical example of a policy-based access control method is the access control list (ACL). An ACL is just a list that specifies the authorized users of the system and their access rights. The list identifies not only the individual subject but the specific access that a subject has to each particular object. ACLs are typically attached to system objects. The list, which is automatically checked each time a service is requested, controls the subject's access to that system's objects and services.
>
> *Mandatory access control (MAC)*: is a means of restricting access to systems based on a fixed set of security attributes, which are attached to users and to files and other objects. The purpose of

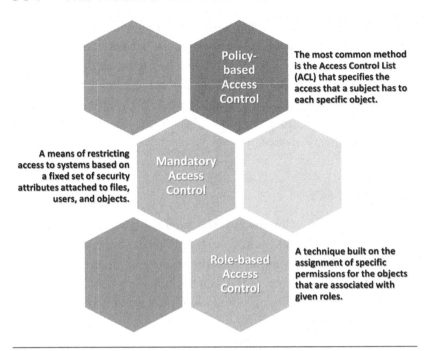

Figure 7.10 Three methods of establishing authorization.

MAC is to prevent users from sharing information arbitrarily. This technique uses a specific set of policies or security rules to define the sharing of data to the organization. These rules state the subjects and the access permissions that are allowed for each subject. In addition, the system actively controls what can be done with a given protected object.

Role-based access control (RBAC): is a technique that is built on the assignment of specific access permissions for the objects that are associated with given roles. Because of its simplicity and its flexibility characteristics, RBAC is a particularly effective means to secure access in large or complex systems. The main idea behind an RBAC controlled system is that access permissions are assigned based on the specific roles that the user fulfills. In practical application, the user is designated a set of roles that they may perform. Users and programs are granted permission to access the objects of the system based on the specific duties that they perform, not by their security classification. That makes the process of assigning the authorizations much more straightforward. In addition, it allows for greater flexibility in the day-to-day management and enforcement of the protection policies.

Intrusion Detection

IDS are the perimeter entries in any type of electronic access control system. They typically audit the operation of the system for intrusion attempts and report them in a timely fashion. Both intrusion detection and access control ensure integrity, and so, they are really effectively two sides of the same coin. Intrusion detection ensures that all attempts to gain unauthorized access are detected. Access control ensures that legitimate users are permitted into the system while unauthorized access is specifically blocked.

The precise function of an IDS is to attempt to identify and isolate attacks. It does that by monitoring traffic logs or assessing other types of audit data. This is a form of preventive control. There are two main types: network-based IDS (NIDS) – which detect attacks by capturing and analyzing packets and host-based IDS (HIDS) – which collect and analyze system information.

Attacks: In order to secure a system, it is important to understand the types of attacks that can be made against it. The typical attacks against computer systems can be classified into one of six generic categories. As shown in Figure 7.11, these are as follows:

Backdoors: are any secret method of bypassing normal authentication or security controls. They may exist for a number of reasons, including by original design or from poor configuration.

Spoofing: describes a situation in which one person or program successfully masquerades as another by falsifying data. Spoofing attacks are normally addressed by the use of intelligent firewall applications. These types of firewalls use various protocol measures to verify the IP identity of the sender or recipient of a message.

Tampering: deliberately destroys, obfuscates, or manipulates data. The process describes a malicious modification of products or data. Man-in-the-middle attacks are an example of tampering with data in motion. Malicious code is an example

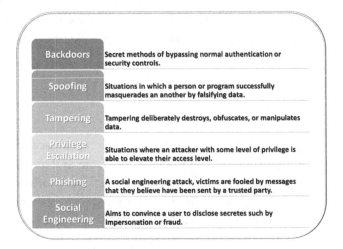

Backdoors	Secret methods of bypassing normal authentication or security controls.
Spoofing	Situations in which a person or program successfully masquerades an another by falsifying data.
Tampering	Tampering deliberately destroys, obfuscates, or manipulates data.
Privilege Escalation	Situations where an attacker with some level of privilege is able to elevate their access level.
Phishing	A social engineering attack, victims are fooled by messages that they believe have been sent by a trusted party.
Social Engineering	Aims to convince a user to disclose secretes such by impersonation or fraud.

Figure 7.11   Cyberattacks against computer systems.

of tampering with data at rest, in both instances, the intrusion is malicious.

Privilege escalation: describes a situation where an attacker with some level of privilege is able to elevate their access level. This is a management problem in both the Human and Organizational Security knowledge areas and is addressed more in depth there.

Phishing: is a type of social engineering. Victims are typically fooled by messages that they believe have been sent by a trusted party. Thus, phishing is typically done by email spoofing or instant messaging.

Social engineering: aims to convince a user to disclose secrets such as by impersonation or fraud. Social engineering can only be prevented by noncomputer means. Even in a highly disciplined environment, such as in military organizations, social engineering attacks can still be difficult to foresee and prevent.

Defenses

The system defense function ensures that the appropriate set of security principles and best practice policies and practices are implemented and adhered to in the system. These monitor and evaluate daily electronic transactions to ensure that they are being performed in a disciplined and continuous fashion. Defense concepts support the integrity of the overall network and application security operations by performing the necessary monitoring, testing, and housekeeping functions that are required to ensure proper functioning within the everyday operational environment.

Because it is focused on maintaining the day-to-day assurance process, the system defense function is built around a number of security practices that are not technological, such as architectural design and implementation. System defense also entails monitoring the performance of the various System Security functions to ensure that they conform to proper procedure. Finally, system defense includes defining and executing standard operational testing strategies to validate that the System Security operation continues to function as intended. Accordingly, defense concepts are a critical factor in the success of the overall process.

Audit

Audit-based System Security services reside on a host and detect intrusions. They do this by examining event logs, critical system files, and other auditable resources to identify any unauthorized change or suspicious patterns of behavior. Properly configured, an audit-based approach sends an alert when an unusual event is discovered.

Audit-based security approaches do their work by monitoring audit trails. An audit trail is just a record of system activities. The audit itself can be performed to capture data generated by the system, network, application, and user activities. Audit trails alert the human staff to suspicious activity, for potential further investigation. They also provide details concerning the extent of intruder activity and provide information for legal proceedings. The types of events that might be captured in an audit trail include such things as the network connection; system-, application-, and user-level event data; or even keystroke activity.

Malware

Malware is the common term for malicious code. Thus, malware always takes the form of executables. The term "malware" refers to any software that is intended to cause damage to a system. There seems to be an infinite variety of malware out there, but generally, it falls into six categories: virus, worm, Trojan horse, spyware, ransomware, and adware.

Malware is generally ubiquitous in cyberspace, and it is too large a topic to elaborate on in a section devoted to systems. However, it should be noted that the aim of all of the commercial malware products out there is to prevent harmful code from being induced onto a target computer. Therefore, most of the malicious code checkers concentrate on identifying malware and malicious activity and on recovering from successful attacks.

Vulnerability Models

Vulnerabilities are exploited by threats. A threat is any danger that might exploit a weakness to breach security and the related controls in a way that causes adverse impacts on an asset. A threat agent is an attack vector that exploits such a vulnerability. A threat can be either intentional – intelligent, e.g., an individual hacker or a criminal organization, or accidental. Accidents include the possibility of a computer malfunction or the possibility of a natural disaster or some other circumstance, capability, action, or event that causes harm.

A resource (both physical and logical) can have one or more vulnerabilities that can be exploited by a threat agent in a threat action. The result can potentially compromise the confidentiality, integrity, or availability properties of resources of the organization and other involved parties. The attack can be active when it attempts to alter system resources or affect their operation: so, it compromises integrity or availability. A "passive attack" attempts to learn or make use of information from the system but does not affect system resources, which compromises confidentiality.

Penetration Testing

The purpose of penetration testing is to directly evaluate System Security by attacking it. Penetration testing denotes the activities that are undertaken to identify and exploit security vulnerabilities. It is the act of simulating an attack on the system at the request of the owner. To be ethical, penetration testing must have clearly defined methodologies and goals. It is normally aimed at the security conditions that are the most common targets of intruders. To be effective, it must use the same methods or techniques as the adversary.

Penetration testing methods are based around four activities. The first of these is *discovery*, which is where the target is identified and documented. This is followed by *enumeration*, where the tester attempts to gain more knowledge about the target through intrusive methods.

Vulnerability Mapping

Vulnerability mapping takes place after that. This is where the tester maps the test environment profile to known vulnerabilities. Finally, testers attempt to gain user and privileged access using the knowledge they have gained. The final phase in the process is to *document* findings. The results of this report can help an organization to identify: existing vulnerabilities of the system, gaps in security measures, IDS and intrusion response capability, as well as potential countermeasures.

Forensics

The system forensics process centers on data collection and analysis of electronic threat and intrusion events. That includes evidence gathering, analysis, and documentation. This is a highly technical activity in that forensic evidence, in its raw electronic form, is very difficult to read or understand or even identify. The virtuality of cyberspace imposes unique complications of access and timing on the gathering and recording process. Therefore, proper management and planning is necessary to ensure that the digital forensics process is properly and effectively executed.

The primary focus of the digital forensics process is in the recovery, interpretation, and handling of evidence. The evidence itself is virtual, and so its trail is found in electronic sources such as computer log files, reference monitor files, and other hidden sources of information. The subsequent analysis supports decisions about the best means of identifying the source and reasons for an unauthorized access.

The forensics process is almost always associated with law enforcement. So, the most basic purpose of system forensics is to assist in gathering and preserving evidence that is used in the prosecution of computer crimes. Another important aspect is the potential use of forensic data to support the organization's own strategies for system defense. In doing this, the forensic examiner collects and analyzes any evidence that is generated by the actual cyberexploit. That might include such artifacts as source code, malware, and Trojans as well as attack methods and other forms of digital footprint.

Recovery Resilience

Resilience ensures the long-term viability of just those critical functions that the organization needs in order to continue to exist. Resilience centers on controlling access through a number of perimeters, which is termed a "defense in depth." That resilience is typically based on a segmented architecture. The goal of that architecture is to prevent intruders from exploiting other areas of the system, should one element be breached. The tangible components in a segmented architecture are the routers and firewalls that secure the perimeter of each layer. The short-term aim of resilience is to ensure effective system recovery.

The system recovery function ensures that the functions and data that are deemed essential are recoverable beyond a reasonable expectation of harm. In order to achieve this, the system recovery process ensures the timely preservation and recovery of critical assets under every likely scenario. That includes such concepts as recovery time, recovery point, backup strategies, hot sites, cold sites, and warm sites.

Knowledge Unit Five: System Retirement

The decision to retire a system does not take place in a vacuum. System retirement is founded on an explicit, analytic approach that is intended to draw a detailed roadmap of the elements and relationships of the system as a whole. The operational and technical criteria for retiring any given system or system element are formally documented in that plan. A detailed description of the system retirement impact is important because of interdependencies of elements in the system as a whole. Thus, any change to the system structure may affect the security of other systems or of the organization that used the system (Figure 7.12).

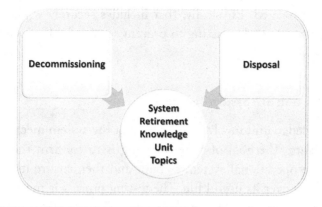

Figure 7.12 The System Retirement knowledge unit topics.

The plan will also ensure that the formal activity of changing the structure of the system as a whole is controlled and that the users of any other potentially involved system are notified of all related concerns, modifications, or new versions. Finally, the plan will describe how deletion of the element or system, from the system as a whole, will be performed.

Decommissioning

The purpose of decommissioning is to plan, establish, manage, control, and monitor an organization's retirement activities. It can probably be seen that system retirement is a strategic function. Therefore, the first step in the decommissioning process is the creation of an explicit system retirement plan. This plan is the organizationally approved process by which the system will be decommissioned. It considers all dependencies and defines the resources and procedures that comprise all of the system assets.

The first step in the actual decommissioning process is to evaluate all assets submitted for retirement in order to confirm conformance with the long-term system management strategy. Once an asset has been approved for decommissioning, it is archived using the provisions of the software configuration management process. The system manager is responsible for notifying all asset users and managers of any potential problems when the decommissioning takes place. Finally, the system manager is responsible for final notifications when the asset is deleted. Physically, that includes securely wiping media and other forms of degaussing to prevent sensitive information from being recovered.

Knowledge Unit Six: System Testing

This knowledge unit involves ensuring that the system meets security requirements. The goal of system testing is to confirm the correctness of the operational system as built and then ensure its continuing integrity over its useful life. The testing process is most typically viewed as being part of the development life cycle; requirement, design, and code validation, as well as system testing and acceptance. The rest of the activities in this knowledge area are considered part of the sustainment process. Sustainment normally takes place over a much longer period of time, during which time the product is operated and maintained and eventually disposed of in a safe and secure fashion (Figure 7.13).

Development-based testing is based on a specific set of testing and qualification requirements. These requirements are developed in advance for each element of the system. Once the mandatory review points are identified, a reasonable schedule for testing each system component should be specified. Ultimately, all system testing is done based on the criteria of traceability, external and internal consistency, appropriateness of the methodology and standards employed, and feasibility of both operation as well as the security features.

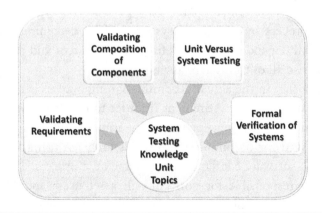

Figure 7.13 The System Testing knowledge unit topics.

Sustainment controls the operation of the completed system. Thus, the purpose of sustainment is to ensure that all software items, hardware items, and manual operations of the system operate as required, complete and correct. The system as a whole must be shown to satisfy the customers' continuing expectations as expressed in the contract. In order to ensure ongoing satisfaction, a sustainment strategy is devised that ensures the system according to contractual agreements involving the security and reliability of the system. In addition, criteria are employed to verify the continuing correctness of the interfaces between components. The effectiveness of the testing process itself is then verified and a regression testing strategy is developed for any component requiring retest.

Validating Requirements

The purpose of this topic is to demonstrate that requirements meet objectives. Consistency and traceability must be established between the system requirements and the components of the fully integrated system. The aim is to ensure that the operational form of the system is fully aligned with the system requirements and design.

Because the system validation activity involves testing, its items have to be compared to any formally specified requirements for them. Thus, there has to be validation outcomes to support acceptance of each requirement of the system. So, a set of tests, test cases and test procedures for conducting the system requirements validation have to be developed and documented and the developer has to ensure that the integrated system meets all contractual requirements.

A formal plan is created to do that. The plan must encompass all of the components coming out of the system development phase. It must ensure that those components have been integrated into a single seamless system that satisfies all contractual specifications. The plan aggregates all of the relevant testing strategies, procedures, data, technical responsibilities, and end schedules for each of the system functions into a single unified assurance process aimed at validating requirements as correct. The plan documents an explicit set of tests, test cases, inputs, outputs, and test criteria, as well as test procedures for conducting the requirements validation process and ensures that the system meets all security expectations.

Validating Composition of Components

The system has to be proven correct as built. So, each system component must be tested to ensure that it meets all of its qualification criteria as expressed in the design. This is a rigorous process, in the sense that the functioning of each of the system components must be fully tested and documented as correct.

The system developer, or manager, prepares and documents a set of tests, test cases, individual inputs, expected outputs, performance testing criteria, and test procedures to ensure the logical correctness of each component of the system. A set of criteria for judging compliance with system requirements is documented and the developer, or manager, will then test each component to ensure that it meets all stated qualification criteria, as well as the conformance with expected outcomes.

In doing the testing, the developer, or manager, is required to confirm the traceability, external and internal consistency, appropriateness of the testing methodology, and feasibility of the component as built. The system is tested using the defined criteria for evaluation. The test results are recorded, and any and all evidence is preserved.

Unit versus System Testing

Testing normally falls into two categories: unit testing and integration or system testing. Both of these types of testing are important. Unit testing is normally part of the coding phase. Integration testing is normally part of system integration. Both of these approaches typically address the formal requirements and are planned in advance.

The purpose of the *unit test* phase is to ensure the correctness of the components of a system. As a result, testing criteria must be defined for each system component. This is normally based on the formal specification of requirements. The components are evaluated for consistency and traceability to requirements. Test procedures and data for testing each component are developed and the developer, or system manager, then evaluates the functional performance of each unit under the specified testing criteria.

The purpose of *system integration* testing is to ensure the proper amalgamation of the components of the system product. Integration combines the system's components in a way that ensures their functional and nonfunctional correctness as a whole. As a result, an integration testing strategy is required. The developer or system manager evaluates the system integration plan, design, code, tests, test results, and user documentation considering the criteria of traceability to system requirements, external consistency, internal consistency, test coverage, appropriateness of testing methods, conformance to expected results, and feasibility of operation and maintenance.

The developer, or system manager, then documents a testing process to ensure proper integration. That includes specification of tests, test cases, inputs, outputs, test criteria, and test procedures. Evaluation criteria should include consistency and traceability between the software design and the components as an integrated whole. Proper integration is verified using the condition that each aggregated component must satisfy the requirements of the system as a whole and that each component is properly integrated into the operational entity.

Formal Verification of Systems

The organization calls on a formal verification process when it needs to determine whether a particular system is sufficiently consistent, complete, and correct to be trusted. Since this demands a good eye for detail, a growing body of literature talks about formal methods for verification. These are sophisticated approaches and require considerable knowledge and skill.

Basically, a verification process that embodies formal methods ensures that the system logic is provably proper in every case. A state machine concept is typically utilized to verify that the system elements are properly designed and consistently used. Formal methods can also be used during system design inspections. Because formal methods are highly constrained by the logic requirements, they are mainly used to evaluate embedded systems. In that universe, formal methods are used as proofs to verify that chip and advanced process control (APC) control functions are correctly implemented in their processors. However, unless the developer or manager is sufficiently well versed in these methods, they are only marginally useful.

Knowledge Unit Seven: Common System Architectures

Cybersecurity environments are complex, and the systems that comprise those environments are varied. The variability of systems both in terms of their application and structure makes their assurance a nightmare. That is the reason why common system architectures are such a useful means of categorization. These architectures provide a classification structure that allows the profession to approach security from the standpoint of commonalities among types.

The common characteristics of these models allow the trust element to be enforced by a standard approach (Figure 7.14).

The three factors that a standard model simplifies are *purpose, application*, and *risk*. Organizations have a particularly difficult time dealing with any of those three factors in the practical universe since it is likely that the operating context will contain a range of architectural types, all arrayed for a particular purpose. Each of these architectures has a standard real-world application and set of risks associated with it. Thus, an authoritative, mutually agreed-on means of categorizing and labeling is a first step toward understanding and controlling the system architectures that might exist in a given environment.

Still, "architecture" is a slippery term. It is perhaps easier to describe a common architecture in terms of its purpose and application. That enables a much more in-depth understanding of the risk factors associated with a given practical system application. Thus, a range of architectural applications have been much more commonly utilized as the classification

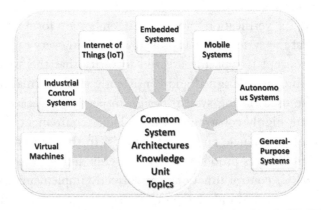

Figure 7.14 The Common System Architectures knowledge unit topics.

structure for potential System Security issues. The CSEC2017 includes consideration of seven common architectural types:

Virtual machines: are architectures that essentially don't exist. A virtual machine is a programmed entity that is created to mimic the behavior of a particular technology. Or in simple terms, virtual machines emulate the operations and functions of a given system. Virtual machines run through a hypervisor, which is essentially another programmed application that serves as an alternative operating system, running on an existing physical machine. In essence, the hypervisor creates the potential to run multiple virtual platforms, all segregated from one another, on a single host CPU. Given their flexibility, virtual machines are pervasive in the world of computing and they represent both an opportunity and a security challenge because of that ubiquity.

Industrial control systems: are items that are ubiquitous in the world of system applications. The term itself is associated with any system of program logic controllers (PLCs) that have been arrayed to perform some typically industrial task. These systems are like the insect world, they are everywhere, and they are mostly invisible because they do not involve human operators. Instead, they support everything from heating and air-conditioning to manufacturing. Industrial control systems process data from remote sensors. The controller utilizes a preprogrammed set of criteria to make a simple decision. If there is a need to correct the status of the object that the controller is monitoring, it activates a compensating device; think your home thermostat. Obviously, these systems are a simple and yet essential element of our entire existence as a society.

They have become an extreme security concern because of the increase in SCADA systems. The entire national infrastructure rests on a SCADA foundation. Thus, those systems must be protected. Many of them are Internet accessible which exacerbates the problem. The increase in the number of successful SCADA attacks indicates how vulnerable these systems are and the rising awareness of that importance is what dictates the inclusion of this system type in the list of CSEC2017 topics.

Internet of Things (IoT)

As system functionality becomes more powerful and available, the applications of that functionality have become more varied. Now connected devices in your home and everywhere else in your world have literally created an Internet of unimaginable things such as toasters, refrigerators, and even your TV set.

With all of that interconnectedness, it is difficult to even think about security in systematic terms, because not only do the operations of the various devices need to be ensured but also the network of potential connections. This is a serious concern from a security standpoint since the IoT has expanded the potential attack surface far beyond any point where it is possible to keep track of it, let alone secure it. The CSEC2017 really offers no solutions, because none exist right now. Still, awareness is the first step and that is precisely what is provided here.

Embedded Systems

This topic is exactly as advertised. It has been normal practice to embed specialized functionality, such as a programmed logic controller, into larger systems to perform some necessary function. In that respect, the prior two categories represent types of embedded systems. However, embedded System Security is a much older and more fundamental topic than SCADA or IoT System Security issues. The CSEC2017 raises embedded systems as a separate topic because they are specifically utilized in high-impact physical situations such as military applications or even the space program. Thus, the assurance of reliable and safe functioning of an embedded system is both an involved consideration as well as a very important consideration. Because embedded systems are omnipresent in modern life, there has been considerable study of best practice methods and models to ensure safety and resiliency. That body of knowledge is available for use in instructional situations.

Mobile Systems

Mobile systems are not the same as IoT in that mobile devices are data and communication oriented, rather than single function devices. Therefore, their security is a separate problem. That problem is a very involved concern in that mobile systems have expanded system assurance requirements into every nook and cranny of modern life. It used to be that everybody was connected to the mainframe. The advantage is that incredible amounts of data can be kept and processed at an individual's fingertips. The disadvantage is that data has to be secured.

The even greater problem is that the technology of mobile systems is evolving at light speed and it is almost impossible to develop and then implement an effective solution before the technology moves out from under it. The CSEC2017 raises the normal issues associated with mobile device security in reference to the other areas that are strongly affected: Organizational, Human, and Societal. However, it is clear that much work needs to be done in order to ensure that considerations of security are systematically included in the considerations of each of these knowledge areas.

Autonomous Systems

The security considerations associated with autonomous systems are similar to those of the other topics in this knowledge area. However, the dimension of independent movement is added to the equation. This category embraces a wide range of leading-edge development topics but perhaps the most important are the robotics and autonomous vehicle areas.

There is a kinetic factor in both of these areas that makes the security of the products particularly important. It would be one thing to have your data stolen from your mobile device. It is something else entirely to be run over by a self-driving car because of a minor system glitch. Therefore, the topics of safety and reliability take on a much greater importance in the teaching in this area. That implies the kind of rigorous attention to detail that not just gets the programming right. It also involves issues of decision-making and choice that are simply not part of the PLC universe of considerations. Thus, the autonomous topic area is perhaps the one place where the study of computing is truly blended with the more human and behavioural-oriented content of the social sciences.

General-Purpose Systems

It isn't possible to ignore general-purpose systems when introducing the area of common architectures. That is because general-purpose computing is essentially what we think about when we contemplate the topic of System Security. The common architectural principles of the general-purpose computer were really laid down by Von Neuman and have not changed much in the ensuing years. What has changed is the number and variety of general-purpose devices.

It would seem like general-purpose computing architectures constitute 99% of the devices out there. But we have seen that the controller universe is vastly larger. However, general-purpose computing powers government, business, and academia; and therefore, the universal laptop and desktop is the thing we are most familiar with. Therefore, in order to complete the set, the CSEC2017 has introduced the obvious need to master the concepts of the general-purpose universe. In many ways that is a fitting way to close this knowledge area.

Seventy Review Questions: System Security

1. What is the general outcome of system thinking?
2. What is a holistic view?
3. Why is a holistic view important to System Security?
4. What is the role of design in system engineering?
5. What is the role of modeling in System Security design?
6. What is the role of requirements analysis in secure system development?
7. How do fundamental principles add to the definition of a secure system?
8. Why is a formal testing strategy important in system development?
9. Why do tests have to embrace the entire life cycle to ensure security?
10. What is the difference between a testing strategy and the actual testing process?
11. What is the role and purpose of system management?
12. What is the role of policy in system management?

13. Why is automation useful in system management?
14. What is the role of inadvertent misuse in system management? Is it important?
15. Why are patches required in system operation?
16. Why is patching part of system management?
17. Why must retired systems be decommissioned?
18. What is the role of documentation in system management?
19. What the role of procedure in managing systems? Why is procedure important?
20. What is the role of the security log in ensuring proper procedure?
21. Why is access control a critical security feature?
22. What is the role of "type" in system access control?
23. How are access privileges assigned?
24. What are the general criteria for granting access?
25. What are three common authentication methods?
26. What is the difference between authentication and authorization?
27. What is the principle of least privilege and how does it apply to authorization?
28. Why is identity a factor in access control?
29. What is identity based on?
30. What is the role of accountability in identity?
31. What are the three types of generic models for defending against attack?
32. What is the role of "levels" in Bell–LaPadula?
33. How does Biba differ from Bell–LaPadula?
34. What is a privilege? Why is it needed? How is it granted?
35. What are authorization models? Why are they different?
36. What is the difference between authentication and authorization?
37. What is the role of audit in system defense?
38. Why is penetration testing necessary? What does it provide?
39. What is the problem with forensic evidence in cyberspace?
40. What is the role of resilience in recovery?
41. Why is it necessary to retire systems?
42. What is the purpose of planning in decommissioning?

43. Why is it necessary for stakeholders to approve the plan in advance?
44. Why is it necessary to evaluate assets prior to decommissioning?
45. What are the consequences of unwiped media?
46. Why is it a good idea to archive decommissioned systems?
47. What is the role of software configuration management in archiving?
48. What is the reason to notify all affected parties prior to decommissioning?
49. What is the role of the system manager in retirement?
50. What is the purpose of degaussing? How does it relate to decommissioning?
51. How does system testing relate to qualification?
52. What is the reason to test against requirements?
53. What is the role of testing during sustainment?
54. What is the difference between unit test and integration test?
55. What is a test case?
56. What is the role of traceability in system testing?
57. What are the criteria for evaluation? Why are they necessary in system testing?
58. How does testing support integration?
59. Why is component correctness a factor in system testing?
60. What is a formal method? When is it appropriate to use?
61. What is the purpose of a common architecture?
62. What three factors does a common model clarify?
63. What is the role of a classification structure in architecture?
64. What is the relationship between IoT and the attack surface?
65. What is the purpose of a virtual machine? Why is it useful?
66. How does a hypervisor operate?
67. What is the primary vulnerability of a SCADA system?
68. What the difference between and embedded system and SCADA?
69. Why are autonomous systems suddenly areas of interest for security?
70. What is the primary reason why general-purpose systems are important?

You Might Also Like to Read

- Conklin, William Arthur and Daniel Shoemaker, *CSSLP Certification All-in-One Exam Guide*, 2nd Edition, McGraw-Hill Education, New York, 2019.
- Danielle, Lacamera, *Embedded Systems Architecture: Explore Architectural Concepts, Pragmatic Design Patterns, and Best Practices to Produce Robust Systems*, Packt Publishing, Birmingham, 2018.
- Diogenes, Yuri and Erdal Ozkaya, *Cybersecurity: Attack and Defense Strategies*, Packt Publishing, Birmingham, 2018.
- Du, Wenliang, *Computer Security: A Hands-on Approach*, 1st Edition, CreateSpace Independent Publishing Platform, Scotts Valley, CA, 2017.
- Engel, Avner, *Verification, Validation, and Testing of Engineered Systems*, 1st Edition, Wiley, Hoboken, NJ, 2010.
- Gregg, Brendan, *Systems Performance: Enterprise and the Cloud*, 1st Edition, Prentice Hall, Upper Saddle River, NJ, 2013.
- Gregory, Peter H., *CISM Certified Information Security Manager All-in-One Exam Guide*, 1st Edition, McGraw-Hill Education, New York, 2018.
- Harris, Shon and Fernando Maymi, *CISSP All-in-One Exam Guide*, 8th Edition, McGraw-Hill Education, New York, 2018.
- INCOSE, *INCOSE Systems Engineering Handbook: A Guide for System Life Cycle Processes and Activities*, 4th Edition, Wiley, Hoboken, NJ, 2015.
- Ingeno, Joseph, *Software Architect's Handbook: Become a Successful Software Architect by Implementing Effective Architecture Concepts*, Packt Publishing, Birmingham, 2018.
- Kim, David and Michael G. Solomon, *Fundamentals of Information Systems Security*, 3rd Edition, Jones & Bartlett Learning, Burlington, MA, 2016.
- Maras, Marie-Helen, *Computer Forensics: Cybercriminals, Laws, and Evidence*, 2nd Edition, Jones & Bartlett Learning, Burlington, MA, 2014.

- Martin, Robert C., *Clean Architecture: A Craftsman's Guide to Software Structure and Design*, 1st Edition, Prentice Hall, Upper Saddle River, NJ, 2017.
- Mike, Chapple, Bill Ballad, and Tricia Ballad, *Access Control, Authentication, and Public Key Infrastructure*, 2nd Edition, Jones & Bartlett Learning Information Systems Security, Burlington, MA, 2013.
- Mittal, Saurabh, Saikou Diallo, and Andreas Tolk, *Emergent Behavior in Complex Systems Engineering: A Modeling and Simulation Approach*, Stevens Institute Series on Complex Systems and Enterprises, 1st Edition, Wiley, Hoboken, NJ, 2018.
- National Institute of Standards and Technology, *Attribute Considerations for Access Control Systems*, NIST Special Publication 800-205, NIST, Gaithersburg, MD, 2019.
- Rutherford, Albert, *The Elements of Thinking in Systems: Use Systems Archetypes to Understand, Manage, and Fix Complex Problems and Make Smarter Decisions*, Amazon, Seattle, WA, 2019.
- Shiu-Kai, Chin and Susan Beth Older, *Access Control, Security, and Trust: A Logical Approach*, Cryptography and Network Security Series, 1st Edition, Chapman & Hall/CRC, Boca Raton, FL, 2010.
- Shoemaker, Daniel and Ken Sigler, *Cybersecurity: Engineering a Secure Information Technology Organization*, 1st Edition, Cengage, Boston, MA, 2014.
- Whitman, Michael E. and Herbert J. Mattord, *Management of Information Security*, 6th Edition, Course Technology, Boston, MA, 2018.

Chapter Summary

- The System Security knowledge area is the one place where the "holistic view" is fully discussed.
- Every system is a unified collection of interacting and interdependent objects.
- Objects are assembled by design into an intentional and well-defined structure.

- Systems are composed of interdependent and interacting objects.
- Systems are almost by definition synergistic.
- Systems are in a continuous state of potential change.
- Systems can be engineered in a substantively rational and deliberate fashion.
- Every security system is founded on a single, substantive, properly documented, and logical design.
- System engineering implies the application of best practice.
- The requirement for system thinking is a key concept in overall cybersecurity theory.
- The CSEC2017 specifies seven knowledge units.
- The aim of each of these knowledge units is to specify System Security practice.
- The system approach is essentially a structured way of understanding a complex thing.
- It decomposes the security problem into its constituent elements.
- All systems are collections of logically interrelated parts, which are amalgamated into a whole.
- The purpose of a system is to achieve a given well-defined purpose.
- System engineering principles and practices are utilized by the system engineer.
- System engineering requires holistic understanding of the problem space.
- Threat modeling is a formal method that is employed to characterize the threatscape.
- Modeling is aimed at identifying potential points of attack.
- Requirements analysis is elicitation, analysis, documentation, and assurance of requirements.
- Requirements are documented using modeling.
- Fundamental principles reduce opportunities for attack.
- Development for testing optimizes the balance between resource requirements and accuracy.
- Planning and test documentation ensures the quality of the test outcomes.
- System management administers system operation in its intended environment.

- The process requires a comprehensive array of strategic policies.
- System management entails a diverse set of policies.
- A policy is an applied statement of direction that is followed in a systematic fashion.
- Policy models are a deliberate protocol that is followed to ensure a comprehensive response.
- Security policies define how that assurance will be implemented in a given system.
- Policy is typically composed of procedures that are systematically executed.
- Automation makes it easier for humans to manage the intricacies of the threatscape.
- Patching is a term that maintains the security and integrity of the system.
- Patch management ensures that all patches meet established criteria for good practice.
- Attacks on systems occur during the operational phase.
- These fall into the realm of System Security.
- The severity of the consequence ranges from the annoying to critical.
- The specific techniques that change as the technology evolves.
- Systems that have been decommissioned are still a risk.
- They might contain residual data in the software and firmware or backups.
- Insiders abuse their trusted status in order to cause harm.
- Documentation makes the system and its security functionality visible.
- By convention, documentation is divided into process and product types.
- All systems are managed by some form of written or ad hoc procedure.
- Procedures specify the explicit activities and tasks appropriate to system use.
- The structure is top down one to many.
- System access control involves documentation as well as technical implementation.
- Types are necessary to establish identity.

- They assign privilege based on the attributes, roles, and relationships.
- Types are the basis for the decisions that the system will automatically make about the access.
- Access permissions are monitored and automatically enforced by the system.
- There are three types of level-based control models that are in common usage in the industry.
- The most common classification-based security model is Bell–LaPadula.
- The Biba security model is centered on ensuring the integrity of subjects and objects.
- Clark–Wilson uses transactions as the basis for its decision-making.
- Access controls let management specify which users can access the system.
- Access to system objects requires proper authentication.
- Authorization determines that a particular subject has the necessary level of permission.
- Trusted identities are allowed access to specified services.
- IDS are the perimeter sentries in any type of access control.
- The precise function of an IDS is to attempt to identify and isolate attacks.
- System defense ensures the appropriate set of security practices.
- System defense entails monitoring the performance to ensure proper procedure.
- System defense executes operational testing strategies.
- Audit-based System Security services reside on a host and detect intrusions.
- Audit-based security approaches do their work by monitoring audit trails.
- Malware always takes the form of executable code.
- Vulnerabilities are exploited by threats.
- A threat is any danger that might exploit a weakness to breach security.
- A resource (both physical and logical) can have one or more vulnerabilities.

- The purpose of penetration testing is to directly evaluate System Security by attacking it.
- The system forensics process centers on data collection and analysis of electronic threat.
- Digital forensics focuses on recovery, interpretation, and handling of evidence.
- The purpose of system forensics is to assist in gathering and preserving evidence.
- Resilience ensures the long-term viability of critical functions.
- Resilience centers on "defense in depth."
- System recovery ensures that functions and data deemed essential are recoverable.
- System retirement uses a detailed roadmap to ensure change control.
- System retirement is a strategic function; thus, it is plan based.
- The plan is the organizationally approved process for decommissioning the system.
- The goal of system testing is to confirm the correctness of the operational system as built.
- Development-based testing is based on a specific set of testing and qualification requirements.
- Criteria are employed to verify the continuing correctness of the components.
- A formal plan is needed to do that.
- The system has to be proven correct as built.
- This involves tests, test cases, individual inputs, expected outputs, criteria, and test procedures.
- Testing normally falls into two categories: unit testing and integration or system testing.
- The unit test phase ensures the correctness of the components of a system.
- System integration testing ensures the proper amalgamation of the components.
- That involve tests, test cases, inputs, outputs, test criteria, and test procedures.
- A formal verification process determines whether a system is consistent, complete, and correct.

- A state machine concept is typically utilized to verify that the system elements are proper. Common system architectures are such a useful means of understanding systems.
- Architectures provide a classification structure that enables understanding among types.
- These models allow the trust element to be enforced by a standard approach.
- A virtual machine is an entity that is created to mimic a particular technology.
- The hypervisor creates the potential to run multiple virtual platforms.
- Industrial control systems are associated with any system of PLCs.
- These systems are everywhere, and they are mostly invisible.
- They have become a security concern because the infrastructure rests on a SCADA foundation.
- Interconnected devices in your home have created an IoT.
- This expands the potential attack surface beyond any point where it is possible to secure it.
- The assurance of reliable and safe functioning of an embedded system is important.
- Embedded systems are omnipresent in modern life.
- Mobile systems are data and communication oriented, rather than single function devices.
- The expanding system assurance requirements are seeping into every nook and cranny of modern life.
- Autonomous systems involve leading-edge issues like robotics and autonomous vehicles.
- General-purpose computing powers government, business, and academia.
- Thus, the obvious need to master the concepts of the general-purpose universe is important.

Learning Objectives for the Component Security Knowledge Area

Mastery of the requisite learning outcomes for the System Security knowledge area will be established through the student's ability to paraphrase and explicate the key contents of the knowledge units within this knowledge area (Bloom Levels Two and Three). In addition, the student will exhibit specific behaviors that demonstrate a capability to utilize the relevant concepts in common practical application. Specifically, the student will be able to paraphrase and explain the following twenty-five knowledge elements (CSEC, 2019):

1. What a system is, and system thinking.
2. Explain the concepts of trust and trustworthiness.
3. Explain what is meant by confidentiality, integrity, and availability.
4. Explain what a security policy is and its role in protecting data and resources.
5. Discuss the importance of a security policy.
6. Explain why different sites have different security policies.
7. Explain the difference between configuration and procedures to maintain security.
8. Explain three properties commonly used for authentication.
9. Explain the importance of multifactor authentication.
10. Explain the advantages of pass phrases over passwords.
11. Describe an ACL.
12. Describe, compare, and contrast physical and logical access control.
13. Distinguish between authorization and authentication.
14. Discuss how IDS contribute to security.
15. Describe the limits of anti-malware software such as antivirus programs.
16. Discuss the uses of system monitoring.
17. Explain what resilience is and identify an environment in which it is important.
18. Discuss the basics of a disaster recovery plan.
19. Explain why backups pose a potential security risk.
20. Describe what a penetration test is and why it is valuable.
21. Discuss how to document a test that reveals a vulnerability.
22. Discuss the importance of validating requirements.
23. Discuss the importance of documenting proper system installation and configuration.
24. Be able to write host and network intrusions documentation.

25. Be able to explain the security implications of unclear or incomplete documentation.

Keywords

Architecture – an artifact that embodies a complete set of rational objects called "components"

Behavior – discrete actions performed that are observable by third parties

Best Practice – commonly accepted means of carrying out a given task

Component – an elemental unit that embodies a single function assembled into "architectures"

Controls – a discrete set of human or electronic behaviors set to produce a given outcome

Critical Function – an action or object that is so central to an operation that it cannot be lost

Cybersecurity – assurance of confidentiality, integrity, and availability of information

Infrastructure – a collection of large components arrayed in a logical structure in order to accomplish a given purpose. Commonly used to describe the tangible elements of cyberspace.

Integrity – a critical quality of a component or component architecture

Strategic Planning – the process of developing long-term directions aimed at furthering and enhancing organizational goals

System – discrete components assembled into a synergistic whole to accomplish a purpose

References

Joint Task Force (JTF) on Cybersecurity Education, "Cybersecurity Curricula 2017, Curriculum Guidelines for Post-Secondary Degree Programs in Cybersecurity, a Report in the Computing Curricula Series", ACM/IEEE-CS/AIS SIGSEC/IFIP WG 11.8, Version 1.0, 31 December 2019.

Saltzer, Jerome H. and Michael D. Schroeder, The protection of information in computer systems, *Communications of the ACM*, 17, 7, 1974.

8
HUMAN SECURITY

In this chapter, you will learn the following:

- The knowledge units of the Human Security knowledge area
- The importance of Human Security in the overall cybersecurity process
- The challenges that human behavior represents in formulating a cybersecurity process
- The knowledge elements of the Access Control knowledge unit
- The knowledge elements of the Social Engineering knowledge unit
- The knowledge elements of the Awareness knowledge unit
- The knowledge elements of the Compliance knowledge unit
- The knowledge elements of the Privacy knowledge units.

Human-Centered Threats

Every organization is accountable for ensuring the confidentiality, integrity, and availability of all of its information assets of value. This responsibility implies the creation of substantive measures to protect the organization from every credible threat, including any non-virtual ones. The last part of that statement is particularly important because longitudinal surveys, conducted over the past decade, have consistently pointed the finger at human-based exploits as the main source of record loss (PRC, 2015). Specifically, a large percentage of the record losses that have occurred over the past ten years are attributable to non-virtual attacks such as insider theft, social engineering, or human error (Kelly, 2017; Laberis, 2016).

The root of the issue is that information is complex and highly dynamic, and it can exist in many states, and thus, it can be stolen in many ways, not just electronic. The fact that data can be lost through the simple act of a stolen laptop, or tablet, or even a smartphone makes the entire information protection problem multidimensional. Therefore, it is incumbent on the organization to research and implement secure processes and procedures that will ensure against every credible threat and weakness, including the weakest link, the human element.

Secure personnel procedures describe a set of recommended best practices for the way in which people should carry out their assigned duties. However, there are all sorts of human factors that can influence how closely a given person will adhere to any particular practice. For instance, most businesses use robust firewalls to protect their information from external threats. However, they rarely dictate explicit instructions about how an authorized individual should secure proprietary information that is kept on their own personal devices (Kelly, 2017). As a result, critical or classified information is stolen, lost, or even given away through a sheer lack of proper care by a user. Therefore, the duty to ensure that the people in the organization have sufficient knowledge of, and follow specific organizational procedures for, securing their work and personal space is a key aspect of the cybersecurity process.

Ensuring Disciplined Practice

The requirement for the consistent performance of good security practice implies the need for a substantive and well-documented means to ensure proper Human Security discipline. The discipline must guarantee that the required organizational security practices are consistently and reliably performed. Thus, cybersecurity in the human realm is built around the systematic execution of pre-designated tasks that are chosen to mitigate a given threat. Therefore, the consistent execution of those tasks is essential to ensure continuous protection. Given the requirement for consistency, the designated cybersecurity procedure must be performed in a coordinated fashion by every member of the organization, at all times. Accordingly, one of the first conditions for establishing a systematic Human Security process is to precisely define the practices that are intended for each of the organizational roles that either access information, or who manage the process.

It is generally assumed that, disciplined practice will guarantee the desired level of security. But the problem is that security tasks also impose additional work requirements on the people who make up the organization and it is axiomatic that the workforce does not like additional work requirements. Therefore, some of the people in that organization will probably not carry out the practices that they need to execute in order to assure the requisite state of security. The lackadaisical execution of the security process is obviously not an acceptable condition. So, the organization has to install substantive mechanisms to ensure that all workers perform all requisite tasks in a coordinated way. Since that necessary oversight has to more-or-less reliably ensure proper Human Security behavior, it will add another dimension of complexity to the overall design and execution of the cybersecurity operation.

The Challenging Case of Human Behavior

Classic technological attacks can be objectively analyzed and controls can be planned and deployed to achieve a reliable outcome. Moreover, if the resultant countermeasures are properly maintained it can be assumed that they will consistently achieve their preprogrammed purpose. Human beings, on the other hand, are an entirely different challenge. The problem with human beings is that their behavior is difficult to predict and even harder to control. Nonetheless, the cybersecurity function must be able to ensure, with certainty, that the people who are legitimately authorized to access and manage organizational information are doing so in a secure and disciplined way.

The challenge that cybersecurity professionals face is that humans do not behave rationally or predictably. That is due to human variability. Technology is generally reliable and if it is properly installed and operated correctly, it will consistently do what it was designed to do. So, it is possible to model and predict its outcomes. But that isn't even close to the case with human beings. The current field of cybersecurity is essentially computer-oriented, and thus the foibles of basic human behavior are more-or-less a mystery to a profession that focuses almost entirely on devising discrete technological processes. But it's a given that every credible threat has to be countered. So, substantive measures have to be designed and added to the overall cybersecurity function, which can be proven to be capable of ensuring proper human behavior.

One issue is that humans are unique and their behavior is personal. Human threats can come from so numerous directions and they can be "sophisticated" incidents, like insider-thefts, spear-phishing, or social engineering scams. However, threats can also originate from such "low-tech" places as simple misuse, or human error. So, it is almost impossible to deploy a single effective solution that will ensure against every way a human can threaten an organization.

Worse, cybersecurity defenses are primarily oriented toward detecting and preventing attacks that originate from outside the security perimeter, not the hostile actions of a trusted insider. Still, it only takes one disgruntled worker with top-secret access to information, or a system manager with, for instance, a financial or a personal problem, to topple the entire security infrastructure of a business.

Threats that originate from human users and operators can be classified in two categories, outsider and insider, shown in Figure 8.1. Threats posed by outside attackers are the more commonly understood. People such as hackers, or cyber-criminals are the best examples of outsider threats. However, malicious actions by the trusted personnel within an organization are far too easy to execute and very hard to prevent. These actions include such things as fraud, misuse, theft and human error. Because they are often random acts and their motivation is much less well understood, these types of threat pose a much more serious hazard then the potential actions of any outsider. In fact, studies have

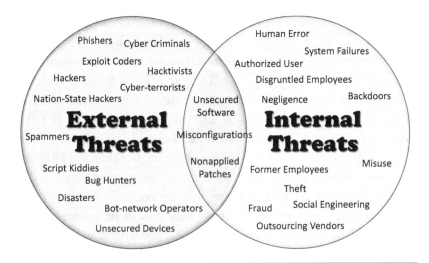

Figure 8.1   External versus internal threats.

found that human behavior-based threats such as these described here might constitute up to 90% of the total record loss (Kelly, 2017). As such, it is an absolute requirement that the organization take substantive steps to ensure consistently secure behavior by the human element.

The CSEC2017 Human Security Knowledge Units

Since securing the human element is a serious challenge, the developers of the CSEC2017 felt that a separate category, which was strictly oriented toward shaping human behavior, was justified. Accordingly, the knowledge units and topics in this category were designed to make the assurance against human-based exploits more understandable and applicable. Consequently, the commonly accepted practices in the CSEC2017 Human Security knowledge area offer a wide-ranging discussion of the actions that the organization ought to take in dealing with its Human Security issues. The CSEC2017 also recommends essential capabilities that employees should master in order to protect the organization against misconduct and unintentional error.

Logically, the first step in the process is to develop and implement a tangible set of practical controls on human behavior. These controls must be arranged to ensure consistent suitable performance of each individual worker's security duties. These measures are embodied in the following seven knowledge units that comprise the Human Security knowledge area (Figure 8.2):

1. *Identity Management* – identification and authentication of people and devices
2. *Social Engineering* – psychological manipulation the human attack surface
3. *Personal Compliance with Cybersecurity Rules/Policy/Ethical Norms* – enforcement of security decisions and norms
4. *Awareness and Understanding* – education, awareness, and training
5. *Social and Behavioral Privacy* – human behavioral factors
6. *Personal Data Privacy and Security* – privacy of personal information
7. *Usable Security and Privacy* – personal privacy enablement and enforcement.

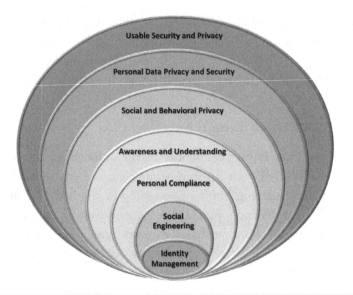

Figure 8.2 Human Security knowledge units.

Knowledge Unit One: Identity Management

The Identity Management topic describes the knowledge elements that can be associated with the assignment and authentication of trust. The ability to establish personal identity and subsequently authenticate that individual for every instance are important concepts in the study of cybersecurity because, in the real world, a diverse set of actors ranging from trusted key employees to unknown potential customers will seek to gain access across the security perimeter. And in this respect, the organization must be able to ensure that every individual person who crosses the system boundary is verified trustworthy, every time that person seeks to gain access (Figure 8.3).

The request for access can come from a human or even a running process. The type of access that is requested might be virtual or even physical. But in all cases, the entity's access rights must be correctly and accurately verified in order to ensure that only the appropriate entry privileges are granted. Thus, this generic assurance process falls into the category of "access control." And the knowledge units describe the access control practices that are recommended as the proper approach to ensuring the trustworthiness of the people and processes who access controlled space.

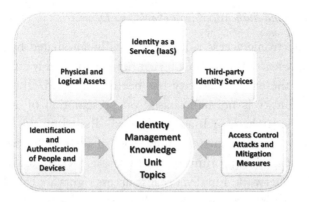

Figure 8.3 The Identity Management knowledge unit topics.

However, there is one caveat here. Identification and authentication are far too important as concepts to be limited to a single knowledge area. Consequently, the ideas in the Human Security area are cross-cutting throughout the entire CSEC2017. Nonetheless, identity and authentication DO play a particularly important role in the Human Security area, in that the maintenance of suitable identifications and subsequent authorizations is cybersecurity's responsibility.

The authentication of access rights is a principle requirement of any security function. People approach a system anonymously. They might be known and trusted. They might be known and untrusted, or they might be unknown altogether. Consequently, there always has to be a designated point on the perimeter of secure space, where the organization takes the opportunity to evaluate the level of trustworthiness of the person or process requesting access before allowing entry. Once that identity is established, the authentication decision can be made.

The information technology arm of the organization is normally responsible for the grunt work of assigning and maintaining identities. The cybersecurity function is primarily responsible for documenting access privileges and assigning suitable individual access to the assets within the virtual perimeter of the system. Because access must be continuously available, the authentication function is typically based on an automated set of rules, and these rules are not innate. They have to be programmed and continuously maintained so that they are current and accurate. Therefore, the specification of the rules for identity management and the assignment of privileges are important supporting elements of the identification and authentication process.

Identification and Authentication of People and Devices

Because electronic access rules are typically automated by software, the access control system must be configured to reliably enforce those rules once the entity's identity has been established. The establishment of identity is normally based on presentation of an assigned authentication token, such as a password. Therefore, the knowledge elements in this topic area encompass all of the recommended practices for authenticating running processes, as well as access through the external network. Finally, because access rights are based on identity, this category also includes the knowledge elements for assigning and managing identities for enforcing generic human access control.

In conjunction with that topic, the authentication area also includes methods for multifactor identification and authentication based on the assignment of roles. The assignment of a role is a pure business function that is enabled within the cybersecurity operation. Nevertheless, the assigned system identity, which is related to that role is assigned by management and must be appropriate to the level of function as well as the level of sensitivity. Identities must permit individual access privileges to be assigned based on a desired level of trust. That level of trust is determined by management prior to any attempt to cross the system boundary.

Physical Asset Control

Notwithstanding electronic access, a physical authentication perimeter might be even more important to the overall security of the organization. The access control mechanisms are the only difference in the case of physical security. Since access control in the physical universe is typically based on human surveillance and barrier mechanisms such as gates, guards, and credentials, the control of access to physical assets normally constitutes the space that can be adequately surveilled and ensured by means of a fixed set of checkpoints and physical resources such as fences, monitoring devices, and checkpoints.

Thus, CSEC2017 topics in this area focus on the various methods for scoping secure space in a way that ensures sufficient access control over physical assets within that defined area. The methods themselves involve various forms of inventory identification and asset tracking schemes for tangible hardware and network property.

Identity as a Service (IDaaS)

This topic is in response to the identity management issues raised by such recent technological innovations as the cloud and software as a service (SaaS). IDaaS is usually a cloud-based "as-a-service" platform operation that performs turnkey identity and access management functions for each customer. All normal identification and access control services are performed by a third party rather than the organization's own local staff.

IDaaS typically include the classic single sign-on and multifactor authentication services that are characteristic of advanced automated access control capabilities, both local and cloud based. The primary issues raised by this topic are the implications of the loss of local control over the processing and storage of the organization's data. However, since the basic access control over cloud and SaaS functionality is offloaded to a remote provider, the alternative means of assurance, which is presented in this area, are logging and auditing processes aimed at ensuring acquiescence to basic corporate security rules and enforcing compliance if those rules are violated.

The topics in this area represent leading-edge inquiry. So, the CSEC2017 only raises the issue of third-party identification requirements without being too specific about how to control the process. Still, this item is an excellent example of the CSEC2017 mission which is to itemize the elements of a comprehensive body of knowledge, with the expectation that as more extensive knowledge is developed, it will be plugged in under this category.

Third-Party Identity Services

This is the logical extension of the identification-as-a-service item outlined above. Third-party identity services introduce the topics related to the general authentication infrastructure. That discussion is oriented toward how various service modalities such as cloud or commercial identity services can provide third-party identity management, password management, endpoint access privilege management, and cloud directory services for user data and credentialing control.

Access Control Attacks and Mitigation Measures

This topic provides an overview of various types of access control attacks and the explicit control measures that can be utilized to combat them. This is an extensive area and so the list is potentially long and evolving. General topics include access aggregation attacks such as password, dictionary, brute force, and spoofing. This area also discusses mitigation measures including such classic assurance mechanisms as policies for strong password and encryption, practices that underwrite multifactor authentication, and the methods for maintaining protected password files.

Knowledge Unit Two: Social Engineering

Social engineering is the practice of manipulating people in a way that causes them to give up confidential information. The statistics make social engineering's destructive potential clear. Humans account for 90% of security incidents, 92% of malware is delivered by email, 56% of IT decision makers say targeted phishing attacks are their top security threat and the average ransomware attack costs a company $5 million (Fruhlinger, 2018).

Social engineering exploits are a pure type of human-based attack, rather than an electronic one. Consequently, it is the most difficult form of threat to defend against. That is because automated means alone cannot be used to detect or mitigate social engineering attacks. That might be the reason why social engineering attacks are perhaps the fastest growing area of concern in the current cybersecurity universe (Figure 8.4).

Social engineering is used either as a means in itself, for instance to convince the target to give up their password or financial information, or to allow the attacker to secretly install a malicious object. Social engineering is what old-time con artists would call a, "confidence game." But it differs from a traditional "con" in that a social engineering exploit is often just the first step in a larger and more complex attack. In fact, social engineering tactics and techniques are components of many, if not most, cyberattacks and the primary channel through which attacks are initiated (Palagonia, 2016).

The reason why social engineering exploits are so prevalent is that it is a lot easier to manipulate human weakness than it is to spend

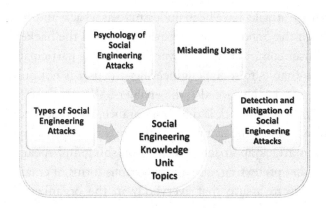

Figure 8.4 The Social Engineering knowledge unit topics.

time and effort on busting through a firewall or password cracking. Practically speaking, why go to all of the trouble of brute forcing a user's access credentials, when a simple phone call will get the same information. Therefore, the root of social engineering lies in deception. The attacker uses psychological manipulation methods to mask their true identity and motives.

The aim of the social engineer is to convince the target that he is an individual who can be trusted. In that respect then, many social engineering exploits simply rely on people's desire to be helpful and their willingness to trust people they know. For example, the attacker might pretend to be a co-worker who has some kind of urgent need for a sensitive piece of information. As such, the organization needs to take substantive steps to ensure that its employees are sufficiently well versed in the methods and approaches of social engineering attackers. And this implies that measures to identify and mitigate social engineering attacks need to be developed and promulgated out to the organization's workforce. These measures are embodied in the topics that comprise the four Social Engineering knowledge units of the CSEC2017.

Types of Social Engineering Attacks

This topic provides an overview of the different ways that various adversaries exploit our weaknesses. The main aim of the cybercriminal is to develop and utilize psychologically valid approaches to evade detection and hide their malicious activity. Up to the present, cybersecurity attacks have been understood as a back-and-forth struggle between the organization's security team and the hacker community. The user community has never been seen as participants in that fight. Now thanks to social engineering, the user is not only the target of the attack, they are also the enablers. Whether user participation in a successful attack is due to ignorance, bad practice, or simple absent mindedness, the fact remains that users need to be made aware of common attack approaches such as phishing and spear phishing, deception and pretexting, and all the various forms of email scams.

Being able to assure that everybody in the organization understands what these are and how they work is the single most critical requirement in protecting the organization against social engineering attacks. That is because, no matter how robust and extensive the security scheme might be, there is almost no chance that the organization will be able to secure itself if its people do not properly understand the various ways to protect themselves from human-oriented exploits. So, the topics in this area concentrate on making the user community explicitly aware of the categories and types of social engineering attacks as well as their impact on the corporation at large.

Psychology of Social Engineering Attacks

This topic provides an overview of the psychological and behavioral factors related to why individuals fall for social engineering attacks. People think that social engineering is a new phenomenon because it's new to cyberspace. The truth is, as long as people have been around, there have always been people trying to con them.

Social engineering scams are successful because they take advantage of the ordinary weaknesses built into human nature. Since it relies on manipulating the way the human mind works, social engineering exploits continue to be effective. However, if the individual targets are aware of the psychology and understand the psychological triggers, it is possible to mitigate the increasing impact of social engineering attacks.

It is those underpinnings that the CSEC2017 topics seek to explore. In general, there are seven generic triggers that have been associated with successful social engineering exploits. These are strong effect, overloading, reciprocation, deceptive relationships, diffusion of responsibility and moral duty, authority, integrity, and consistency. The CSEC2017 topics in this knowledge unit allow organizations to better understand adversarial thinking, how emotional responses impact decision-making, cognitive biases of risks and rewards, and trust building.

Misleading Users

Social engineering is all about deception. In fact, the most famous social engineer of all, Kevin Mitnick, titled his book on the topic *The Art of Deception*. Most of this is based around exploiting user trust and ignorance. Misleading users is not a simple matter of pretexting. It can involve strictly electronic means such as Transmission Control Protocol/Internet Protocol (TCP/IP) header and email address spoofing. But primarily, deception is based around the fact that people are not aware of the ways they can be attacked via social engineering and are careless about protecting themselves when they are.

Thus, the CSEC2017 provides an overview of the technology that underlies information systems communication processes as well as the human psychological issues that are utilized to mislead potential targets. Proposed topics include the mechanics of the technological and psychological factors that might enable exploitation.

Detection and Mitigation of Social Engineering Attacks

There is no "generic" approach to identifying social engineering attacks, since they are as varied as the human imagination. That is one of the primary reasons why social engineering succeeds. Since the individual user is the target, mitigations are strictly limited to increasing the awareness of the user community. Users have to learn to question and withhold information when things don't add up. For instance, any attempt to rush a target user into divulging information or the refusal of a caller to verify their identity when requested, even things like misspellings in an email or embedded hyperlinks can all be treated as warning signs.

The user has to always remember that just because they think they know who's calling or who sent the message, it doesn't actually mean that person actually sent it. So, the best approach to identifying and mitigating a social engineering attack is an informed user. That is why it is important to try to get the caller to identify things that only a legitimate person would know and to always assume that a request needs to be checked out. Thus, the CSEC2017 topics emphasize scenario-based, hands-on activities via simulation or virtual tools. The aim of these exercises is to create an environment that simulates the emotional impact of various social engineering attacks. There is also the suggestion that the student should be familiar with technological mitigations such as email filtering, security blacklists, and intrusion detection systems.

Knowledge Unit Three: Personal Compliance

Personal compliance is an important topic because, like every other profession, cybersecurity practitioners need to know and exhibit authorized behaviors. Guidance is particularly important in the case of cyberspace, because the entity itself is virtual. If the rules for working in virtual space were as clear as they are for jobs in traditional physical areas, the issue of proper behavior might not be such a big concern. That is because, the elements of professional practice in long-standing fields, like medicine, or even the law, are well established and have not changed much over time. That is not the case with a field as new and rapidly evolving as cybersecurity. Moreover, because of continuous, and in some respects outrageous, advances in the technology, the actual rules themselves keep changing (Figure 8.5).

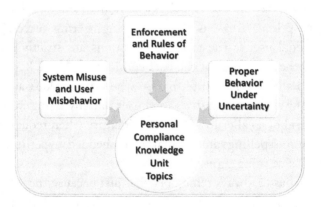

Figure 8.5 The Personal Compliance knowledge unit topics.

Technology creates serious problems when it comes to deciding how to behave. The problem is that technological advances often come without ethical instructions. That is because the abilities that the new technology provides advance human capability into some new realm. Thus, the technology itself has consistently exceeded society's ability to define how to use it appropriately. As a result, people who might have a desire to do the right thing have no guidance about how to draw the line between correct and incorrect. So, given the intangibility of the product and the relentless evolution of the technology, there are an ever-increasing number of ethical gray areas. Absent a clear understanding of the implications of a particular capacity, it is hard to draw conclusions about its use.

Consequently, the list of gray areas associated with technological advances seem endless. These gray areas range from minor issues like misuse of information, all the way up to institutionalized data mining. The practical outcome of that lack of understanding is that none of the stakeholders in cyberspace have a frame of reference. In all organizations, the formal documentation of proper behavior is called a code of conduct. Codes of conduct define the values and beliefs of a profession. They delineate the specific duties and obligations that the members of the profession owe each other and their clients. Professional codes of conduct describe the proper way for members of a practitioner group to relate to each other. Finally, and most importantly, they define how the overall profession proposes to interrelate with society as a whole.

It must be recognized though that, because codes of conduct define group norms and all groups are different, there is probably no such thing as a universally valid set of rules. For instance, the code of conduct for the hacker community is different from the code of conduct of the Business Software Alliance. Although the legitimacy of the former group's ethics may be questionable, nonetheless, their code represents their accepted group behavior. Accordingly, the underlying basis and intent of the supporting ethical system has to be fully understood when judging what any code of conduct means.

A code of conduct is the organization's standard of behavior. It defines the accepted values and principles of the people within a given domain. Codes of conduct dictate the duties and obligations of individual workers in reference to group norms. Codes of conduct also provide the concrete basis to manage the ethical behavior of any given group of individuals. The rules captured within a code of conduct are either normative, that is, they establish an understanding of general right and wrong or descriptive. Descriptive norms define what the group believes and how the members of the group should act in reference to that belief.

Professional codes of conduct communicate the formal ethical models that embody the norms a specific group has chosen to adopt. Those models are based on each individual organization's understanding of correct professional behavior. In the case of the assurance process, the professional code must explicitly describe the organization's position with respect to safeguarding the confidentiality, integrity, and availability of data assets, as well as the policies for appropriate use. As such, it is important for both individuals and corporations to develop and utilize a frame of reference to ensure that proper behavior in cyberspace. That is the role of compliance in cybersecurity.

Since those group norms are the measuring stick for judging individual behavior, the interrelationship between individual ethical decision-making and the associated requirement for a common point of reference must be kept in mind when attempting to understand ethical systems. It is the code of conduct, not personal ethics, that dictate how individual workers act within an organization. For example, individuals working at a credit-reporting agency may have a different ethical perspective than the actual code of conduct that is required for its members. If that is the case, the behavior of the individual employee should comply with the code of conduct established by the organization. Moreover, if the individual employee is not able to accept the required code of conduct, then the only option is to leave.

The formally documented code of conduct is a concrete point of reference. As such, it is important to ensure that each individual understands the organization's code of conduct as part of the screening and hiring process. More importantly, from a personnel security standpoint, a defined ethical code also helps an organization decide when an individual is not behaving correctly.

Correct behavior can be defined as the individual's capacity to make consistently proper decisions in the light of the normative values of the organization. A properly designed ethical system will always provide a concrete reference for that decision-making as well as a precise explanation of the consequences of deviation from group norms. Accordingly, in the practical use of codes of conduct, an explicit enforcement mechanism is an absolute necessity.

System Misuse and User Misbehavior

This topic provides an overview of the issues associated with intentional and unintentional misbehavior in cyberspace. Individuals who use the computer to do illegal, or unethical things are often shielded from thinking about the appropriateness of their actions by the intangibility of the commodity and the anonymity that computing provides. Information is the only resource that can be stolen without anybody knowing that it is missing. As such, the ethical question is… "If you could commit a crime that nobody knew about, would you?" The right answer to that depends on the individual's ability to recognize that what you are doing is incorrect.

There are nine functional areas, shown in Figure 8.6, where specific guidance about ethical behavior should be provided. These

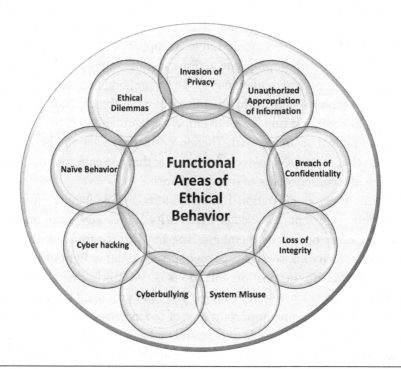

Figure 8.6 Functional areas of ethical behavior.

are invasion of privacy, unauthorized appropriation of information, breach of confidentiality, loss of integrity, system misuse, cyberbullying, cyber hacking, naive behavior, and ethical dilemmas related to system security decisions.

Enforcement and Rules of Behavior

This knowledge unit deals with the human issue of personal compliance. The motivation to comply with a security rule or practice is an important factor in the cybersecurity process. Motivation initiates, directs, and sustains all forms of cybersecurity behavior. Motivation is the factor that ensures a person's willingness to consistently execute a given task or achieve a specific goal, even if the performance of the task itself is personally inconvenient. It also dictates the level and persistence of a person's commitment to the overall concept of security. Therefore, motivation underwrites secure performance.

Motivation is typically geared to accountability. This accountability comes from the enforcement of appropriate-use policies. Appropriate-use policies are developed and documented by the organization to guide everything from the use of computers, to the use of expense accounts. They are then monitored for compliance. The accountability system will reward appropriate actions and discourage inappropriate ones, with respect to defined policy. Therefore, organizational control is in effect implemented through enforcement of these behavioral policies. However, it is impossible to enforce accountability if the policies are not known or understood. Therefore, the organization also has to ensure that all of its employees know what they are expected to do, as well as the consequences of noncompliance.

Thus, every organization has to undertake a deliberate effort to maintain sufficient knowledge of security duties and accountabilities for every one of its members. The need to ensure a continuous level of security knowledge is particularly essential in light of the fact that membership in most organizations is constantly changing, with trained workers leaving or changing jobs and untrained people being added. Therefore, one important aim of the cybersecurity function is to make certain that people understand and adhere to the policies that have been laid down for secure and proper behavior. That includes making certain that every individual is assigned the accountability and knows the consequences of a failure to comply as well as document individual performance when it comes to compliance.

So, it is every organization's responsibility to ensure that its membership is sufficiently knowledgeable about the expected rules of behavior for each individual, as well as how that person is supposed to perform. The mechanism that organizations typically employ to fulfil that obligation is called an awareness, training, and education in the proper rules/policy/ethical norms as well as the consequences of noncompliance.

Proper Behavior under Uncertainty

Unlike the other three units, this knowledge unit is oriented toward reasoning, rather than compliance to rules. It ensures an intelligent response to a heretofore undefined situation. It establishes the ability to reason based on the principles of good cybersecurity as well as the critical thinking abilities that will be needed to react appropriately in a continually changing and uncertain virtual landscape. The individual must be able to analyze, evaluate, and then select the optimum security response from all alternatives. Thus, people are encouraged to critically examine and evaluate the present problem and to respond appropriately by tailoring fundamental principles into a solution that precisely fits the situation.

This capability is normally based on a formal and in-depth education program. Education can be distinguished from training by its scope, as well as the intent of the learning process. In a training environment, the employee acquires skills as part of a defined set of job criteria. In an educational context, the employee is taught to think more critically about the implications of what he or she is doing. The practical aim of education is to ensure the individual learner's ability to integrate new knowledge and skills into day-to-day security practice. The specific outcome of an institutionalized education process of this type is the ability of the people in the organization to adapt to new situations as they arise. Given what has been said throughout this text about the constantly changing nature of threats and vulnerabilities in cyberspace, this is an essential survival skill for the workers in any organization. CSEC2017 topics include an emphasis on intellectual adaptability, critical thinking, understanding the right versus wrong choices, how to make those choices under uncertainty, rational versus irrational thinking, ethical thinking decision-making, and learning how to react when there is no clear process available to follow.

Knowledge Unit Four: Awareness and Understanding

Awareness is the building block on which all other levels of learned security behavior rest. At its fundamental basis, awareness learning is very broad in scope but the knowledge requirements themselves are limited in depth. Thus, effective awareness programs ensure that all employees at every level in the organization understand, appreciate the need for, and are capable of executing disciplined security practices in an organized manner. So, in this respect then, awareness meets basic security aims. However, the requirement for awareness varies across the organization. Awareness at the highest levels of the corporation sets the "tone at the top." Consequently, awareness programs at the executive level should be focused on ensuring strategic awareness of the cybersecurity issues facing the organization, as well as the costs, benefits, and overall implications of security (Figure 8.7).

At all of the other levels, it is necessary to maintain a relatively high degree of awareness of relevant threats and the associated cybersecurity assurance practices. Thus, there has to be a formal effort to ensure that everybody in the organization is aware of the specific security requirements that apply to their role. In addition, the people in the organization have to be motivated to practice security in a disciplined

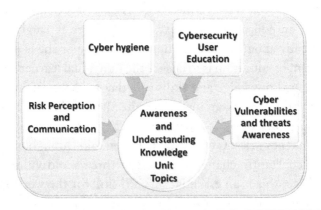

Figure 8.7 The Awareness and Understanding knowledge unit topics.

fashion. In essence, a good awareness program will strengthen motivation, the program must motivate all users to practice security; ensure effective focus, the program must concentrate on relevant and appropriate topics; maintain participant interest, the program must ensure that individual participants will continue to be interested in security; underwrite capable performance, the program must ensure effective actions with respect to security; and integrate the cybersecurity content, the program must ensure the full integration of the proper set of practices into the organization.

However, awareness alone does not assure a capable state of cybersecurity. As such, it is also necessary to ensure that individuals responsible for executing specific security functions are knowledgeable in the precise requirements of their role. Therefore, it is essential to ensure that every security function is performed correctly. That implies the requirement for a greater degree of awareness with respect to how to perceive and understand risk. Thus, awareness trains individual learners how to properly perceive, judge, and respond to cybersecurity risks.

Since the response will revolve around effective communication, cybersecurity awareness programs must also provide a standard means of communicating information about security risks in a systematic way. Finally, awareness programs need to help the user formulate a personal vision of how their individual actions impact their own and the organization's level of cybersecurity and privacy.

Cyber Hygiene

The organization is essentially defenseless until a fundamental state of good cyber hygiene practice is established. That is because no form of cybersecurity is being practiced by the organization's stakeholders. Thus, the topic of "cyber hygiene" provides a discussion and the essential activities that are focused on the most fundamental level of good cybersecurity practice. Here, the outcome is simply group recognition that cybersecurity is a valid and necessary concern. This is normally implemented in the form of a basic awareness program.

Once adequate awareness and understanding is established however, individual members will begin to understand that security is a concern. Thus, members of the organization will be more conscious of security in their day-to-day work. Every worker will follow rudimentary procedures in response to that appreciation. Workers may not necessarily act in any large-scale or organizational fashion, but they will persistently apply basic cybersecurity practice.

The awareness program that underlies the topic of cyber hygiene focuses only on those few security issues that have been expressly identified as the greatest concerns. It will also present general practices to address these concerns. The practices are not sufficiently specific, and their performance is not overseen enough to ensure that security is embedded in the standard operational model. However, the individual accountability for cyberthreat mitigation is understood and topics like secure password creation, password storage, and cyberthreat mitigation tools, as well as simple good practice on the Internet are presented.

Cybersecurity User Education

This topic involves a consciously planned and formally deployed cybersecurity effort. Here, the organization accepts and acts on a commonly acknowledged understanding of the need for some form of formal cybersecurity education process. The response is recognizable in that security procedures are planned and documented, and the organization implements a formal cybersecurity education program to convey them. The education is typically aimed at enforcing understanding of the requisite security practices, which are associated with each worker's individual role. For instance, there might be targeted programs for executives, a different one for managers, and another for workers. The worker programs might be subdivided by operation.

The aim of these educational programs is to foster understanding of the security procedures that are considered appropriate to that role or function. They are generally not oriented toward imparting specific skills beyond the understanding of the security practices that are required to carry out the basic work as well as the impact of the training program on users' subsequent knowledge and behaviors. The topic touches on methods for educating end users on generic cybersecurity threats and behaviors and is supported by standard pedagogy for delivering cybersecurity education to diverse populations.

Cyber Vulnerabilities and Threats Awareness

This topic provides an overview of end-user-facing threats. The aim is to increase the user's level of understanding with respect to the cybersecurity threat universe. The security of an organization largely depends on the capability of its users, specifically with respect to their data privacy and security awareness. For instance, many studies have shown that providing employees with proper data privacy and security training significantly reduces social engineering attacks (Trend-Micro, 2015). The outcome of the training is evidence that the user community is aware of and follows proper security procedures.

The aim of the whole effort is to ensure a minimum level of good security practice. This topic does not go beyond ensuring that employees take simple precautions. That is leveraged by ensuring that users can associate common security threats with the best practices that are designed to prevent or avoid them. For example, people will recognize that worms exist and that they are often forwarded in email, so they will consistently avoid clicking on links that they do not recognize. Once that recognition is created, users will be more likely to think twice when they are offered the opportunity to… "Take a look at this!"

This level of knowledge also applies to other basic security practices related to virus and malware checking and workstation security. This knowledge is publicized by means of formal awareness programs that emphasize typical vulnerabilities and threats, such as identity theft; business email compromise; open Wi-Fi networks; and malware, spyware, and ransomware awareness.

Knowledge Unit Five: Social and Behavioral Privacy

Privacy is a very important and desirable quality in any society. That is because privacy underwrites personal freedom. On the other hand, a society's need to know something about each of its citizens requires that records be kept and information gathered. The specific concern with respect to cybersecurity is finding the proper balance between knowing enough about a person but not too much (Figure 8.8).

Issues of privacy were less important seventy years ago. That was because it was not possible to collect and efficiently retrieve information about every individual citizen. Moreover, people in a highly

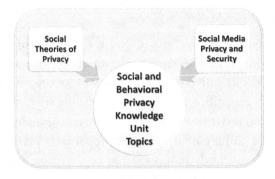

Figure 8.8 The Social and Behavioral Privacy knowledge unit topics.

mobile society were difficult to track. However, times have changed. Large organizations now have an insatiable appetite for information about each individual citizen living in this country. In fact, throughout the 21st century, every business in the Fortune 100 has dedicated enormous economic and staff resources to developing a better understanding of all of us. That thirst for data has created a massive data-mining industry that is capable of providing complete, aggregated, in-depth, and up-to-date information about every person in the United States, which means that any concept of personal privacy is now relegated to the realm of fiction.

The shredding of personal privacy by institutional means raises serious ethical concerns around the subject of an individual's rights, and at a minimum, it violates the principle of confidentiality. Yet at this particular moment, there is very little awareness and almost no regulation when it comes to virtual invasions of privacy. That is the case because there is no suitable ethical point of reference to judge the appropriateness of information gathering actions. Moreover, because the technology continues to evolve faster than society can develop the necessary personal and social awareness and understanding, many more gray areas of this type are likely to develop in the future. Therefore, it is particularly essential for the cybersecurity professionals to understand the basic social and personal requirements that underlie the concept of privacy.

The goal of that social and behavioral understanding is to know how to better balance what is good for the individual against the greater good of society. The balancing act is dynamic; there are no correct answers. Consequently, good ethical behavior centers on the understanding of a commonly accepted set of principles that can serve as a practical rule of thumb for determining appropriate actions.

These principles comprise a value system for the profession and must be formally defined as well as commonly accepted and understood by the profession at large. The interpretation of how these principles should be applied is up to the individual. However, that interpretation requires an overall understanding of the personal and social implications of each situation.

Social Theories of Privacy

This topic provides an overview of the various ideas that have emerged from social psychology and social science regarding privacy and privacy rights. There are many instances where what might be considered an invasion of privacy takes place in virtual space. For instance, credit-monitoring services are a growing industry. These agencies collect more than credit history. They know the legal, marital, employment, and medical histories and even what magazines an individual reads. The question is, what does this do to individual rights?

What this means in terms of the overall societal understanding of the field of cybersecurity is still up in the air. But the behavioral sciences have long-standing theories about the impact of relationships and social behavior on something like privacy. All of these have contributed to our understanding of where cybersecurity fits in the overall picture of privacy rights and privacy protection. The aim of this topic then is to provide a deeper and richer understanding of the sociological thinking with respect to where the cybersecurity fits in the big picture of human life. Therefore, this topic looks at various formal personal and group social interaction theories and the risks and trade-offs they represent as well as such larger topics as personal monitoring, regulatory protections, and concerns on maintaining social privacy.

Social Media Privacy and Security

Social media has drastically changed people's everyday lives. There are some estimates that the average person spends up to a quarter of their daily lives on social networks. Now, it is possible to communicate the basics of your personal reality on a basis that was formerly unheard-of, with every friend and stranger in the world. But that immediacy poses serious privacy risks. Because of its scale, social media is also one of the major threats to personal and organizational security in decades. Therefore, it's critical that people know and understand the risks they face when they put themselves out there on social media.

The Internet is like the Wild West. That's because every online move you make leaves cyber footprints that are making yourself fodder for third-party research about you, without you ever realizing it. Bad guys stalk the social media networks looking for victims. Their intent is to fool people into visiting harmful sites or to inject spyware that gives them information about things you possess like passwords. Because social media sites have information that's required, like birthday and email address, identity thieves like to do all kinds of mischief. The same is true with location-based services, which reveal the user's location to every potential malicious actor out there. That invites every kind of weirdo and burglar to your front doorstep.

So, this topic provides an overview of privacy concerns when using social media. Proposed topics include users' online disclosure decisions and behaviors, personas and identity management, determining audience and social access controls, interface and coping mechanisms for managing privacy on various social media sites, challenges of managing time boundaries, as well as personal and workplace boundaries of social media.

Knowledge Unit Six: Personal Data Privacy and Security

This knowledge unit assumes that individuals have the fundamental right to control the way in which their own personal data is collected and used. That simple assumption implies the basic obligation for organizations to be more accountable for data protection. Personal data is any information that is related to an identified or an identifiable natural person (GDPR, 2018). In other words, any information that is clearly about a particular individual and in certain circumstances, this information could include everything from someone's name to their physical appearance. This topic is so critical that it has been subject to international and national regulation (Figure 8.9).

The obligation for protecting sensitive personal data (SPD) has been formally codified on the European Union's General Data

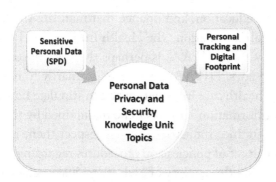

Figure 8.9 The Personal Data Privacy and Security knowledge unit topics.

Protection Regulation (GDPR, 2018). The GDPR mandates auditable proof of an organization's continuing commitment to the protection of the personal information that it collects. That means that the organization must provide documented evidence that it has installed processes and practices that will ensure all of its information processing practices will effectively handle any emerging privacy and security risks. In many respects, proof of this is a business advantage in that the ability to demonstrate evidence that the complex and challenging requirements of the GDPR have been met will improve both the organization's cybersecurity function, as well as build customer trust and accordingly improve competitive position.

The protection of personal data is built around the principles of accountability and governance; the organization needs to create a substantive governance structure devoted to data protection. The governance structure ensures that the information processing function is transparent and legal, that the information itself is collected only for legitimate purposes, and that the collection process is adequate, relevant, and limited to what is necessary, accurate, and securely stored (GDPR, 2018). Finally, it ensures that the privacy rights of individuals are protected, and that valid consent has been given for its use (GDPR, 2018). Finally, if all else fails, the GDPR lays down formal rules for data breach reporting. It mandates that it will report all breaches of personal data within seventy-two hours of the discovery. This particularly applies if there is a risk to the personal rights and freedoms of the subjects of the data (GDPR, 2018).

The United States does not have such a sweeping data protection regulation. However, it does have laws in several sensitive areas such as health care, education, and finance that mandate the legal protection of personal information. The Health Information Portability and Accountability Act (HIPAA) is perhaps the best illustration of such sector specific laws. HIPAA was created primarily to modernize the processing of health care information and to stipulate how "Personally Identifiable Information" (PII) is to be maintained by the health care and health insurance industries. In that respect then, HIPAA mandates an explicit set of policies and procedures regarding the assurance of the privacy and the security of each individual's personally identifiable health information.

HIPAA ensures organizational accountability by describing a formal set of offenses with respect to the handling of health information, and it establishes legal consequences for violations. HIPAA compliance is built around its "Privacy Rule," which stipulates the right of an individual to request that any organization holding their health information corrects any inaccurate protected health information. Also, it requires health organizations to take realistic steps to assure the confidentiality of all health-related communication. Organizations must also track any disclosures of an individual's personal information and document its privacy policies and procedures for ensuring that (HIPAA, 1996).

Perhaps the most significant feature of this act is the requirement that every organization designate a privacy official who is responsible for overall compliance as well as a formal contact person accountable for receiving customer complaints. Because of the importance of this knowledge unit, the CSEC2017 has captured the essence of these advancements in two generic topic areas: SPD and the personal tracking.

Sensitive Personal Data

Personal data can be a varied collection of things. In that respect then, this topic area gives the learner a formal description of the categories of data that fall under the heading of sensitive personal information. The data is designated that way because it might be especially vulnerable to misuse for the purpose of significantly harming an individual in an occupational, fiscal, or societal way. This topic provides specific examples of the types of SPD that might fall into the "special categories." These are the types that must be treated with extra security. Those categories are racial or ethnic origin, political opinions, religious or philosophical beliefs, union membership, genetic data, and biometric data which can be used to uniquely identify someone (GDPR, 2018). However, there are also such obvious items as social security number and bank account number and credit card numbers.

Personal Tracking and Digital Footprint

Personal tracking enabled the ability of people and organizations to keep track of individual actions in virtual space. Personal tracking is such a ubiquitous exercise that anybody who is active on a computer in virtual space is being tracked. Automated trackers keep tabs on everybody's daily activity. They know your name and interests and share information back and forth. Moreover, unknown organizations may have recorded more about you than you might recall about yourself, using that capability.

Most of this tracking is based around the electronic transactions that are an unavoidable part of daily life. That includes everything from the stuff that you buy with your credit or loyalty card all the way to the websites you visit. That power to surveil you is enhanced by the use of third-party cookies that the website sets on your computer. These little features are embedded in websites in order to report back to the website provider whenever you've viewed a page. These cookies also gather statistics on your browsing history. This isn't limited to websites. All of the social networking services do the same thing.

The important point to note is that this all happens without your knowing it. It happens entirely behind the curtain and without your knowledge or approval. That is the reason why the personal tracking and digital footprint topic is such an important area in the CSEC2017. Areas of suggested coverage include (CSEC 2017) location tracking, web traffic tracking, network tracking, personal device tracking, and digital assistants such as Siri or Alexa recordings. Topics include user behaviors and concerns with regard to each of these kinds of tracking, as well as current methods for limiting tracking and protecting privacy.

Knowledge Unit Seven: Usable Security and Privacy

Let's face it, security can be a pain in the neck, and unfortunately, security measures are the features that users are most frequently subverted. Whether it's complex passwords or long, extensive authorization security takes extra time and imposes onerous tasks on users. Saltzer and Schroeder (1974) were the first people to describe this phenomenon. They called it the "Usability Principle." Even now, the greater security that an organization demands, the more likely it is that the user community will develop ingenious ways of getting around it. So, the issue of usability in the design of security systems is a major concern and that is the reason why the CSEC2017 introduces this knowledge unit and its topics (Figure 8.10).

Usability and User Experience

The challenge is that a well-designed security system has to be used properly in order to be effective, and human beings are not cut out to do that regularly and consistently. That's a psychological problem as much as it is anything else. Experience has taught people that it is likely that the more security they have, the less usable the system will be. Therefore, an important part of the design process is ensuring that the system's security features are easy to configure and painless to use.

This topic falls under the umbrella term "usability." The political term "think global and act local" applies in the case of usable security. Most people know that cybersecurity is a worldwide problem. But at

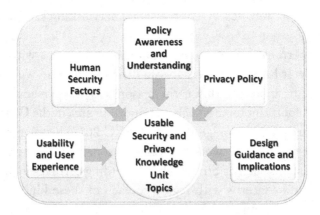

Figure 8.10 Usable Security and Privacy knowledge unit topics.

the same time, they tend to resist the security features that are put in place for their own safety, like frequent password changes. That is because those are the things that affect them directly. Thus, user security has to be very easy to configure and operate. That's a design problem.

Security needs to be a given state for any system. So, cybersecurity professionals have to provide security for the users without making them work for it. Specifically, the product has to have its security built in because the user community cannot be expected to configure it later. In that respect then, user education and engagement is crucial where security cannot be built in. Therefore, this knowledge unit concentrates on defining usability as it relates to the user experience. Topics include (CSEC, 2017) examples of usability problems in traditional security systems such as authentication or encryption, usability and security trade-offs in systems, and methods for evaluating the usability of security and privacy systems.

Human Security Factors

Security is an amalgam of technological architectures blended with human motivations and capabilities. That is a tough interface to bridge but it is essential if the organization is ever going to achieve an acceptable level of cybersecurity. So, this topic area concentrates on the human–technological interface. Students are expected to be able to integrate knowledge about the computer, human psychology, and classic assurance processes into a single understanding of what constitutes a holistic solution. Thus, topics in this knowledge unit include the psychological aspects of adversarial thinking as well as the standard business issues of security policy, economics, and legal and regulatory issues as they relate to the assurance of a secure organization.

Policy Awareness and Understanding

Policy is perhaps the lynchpin of Human Security since it sets the strategic course for all the individuals in the organization. An organization's security policy lays down the strategic directions, processes, and procedures for information asset security. Ideally, the policy should fit the organization's culture as well as reflect the perspectives of the people in the organization. It should also lay out exactly what risks will be addressed and how much tolerance each will have. The overall policy reflects how stakeholders will use as well as value their information.

As the CSEC2017 views it, much of policy is driven by the requirement for proper legal and regularity accountability. In general, that security policy document is a living thing in that it must be continually updated to adapt with the evolving business environment. The content in this area is highly crosscutting, so the topics include the regulatory items covered in the Personal Privacy knowledge unit as well as in the Privacy Policy topic area below. It also includes the educational and awareness topics covered in several areas. For this topic in particular, the focus is aimed at ensuring that all policy requirements are satisfied.

Privacy Policy

This topic area provides an overview of privacy policies as they are applied in specific settings. Essentially, this looks at privacy from a local jurisdictional point of view. As we said in the abovementioned section, the organization's specific security policy lays down the strategic directions. Ideally, the policy should fit the organization's culture as well as reflect the perspectives of the people in the organization. So, as the CSEC2017 views it, much of the policy is driven by the requirement for proper legal and regularity compliance.

Still, in general, the security policy document is a living thing in that it must be continually updated to adapt with the evolving business environment. Thus, this topic explores the relationships between larger scale privacy policies from the individual and organizational perspective. CSEC2017 suggested topics include the impact of privacy policy on new tools/software and identifying a need for tools and techniques. There is an emphasis on best use privacy policy.

Design Guidance and Implications

This final area provides advice on the factors that go into ensuring proper security usability design decisions. This is a more applied set of formal best practice recommendations about how to ensure and sustain practical and usable features in a security system. The CSEC2017 topics in this area include hands-on methods and techniques for reducing user burden and making security decisions easier and more rational; it also looks at the Saltzer and Schroeder principle of security by default. Finally, this topic area addresses the various methods for reducing unintentional security and privacy errors. Since up to 90% of the actual harm falls into the category of inadvertent error, this is an important topic. The CSEC2017 suggests that this reduction is done by simplifying the process and making threats along with their risks concrete to the user. It also entails reducing technical language and jargon.

Seventy Review Questions: Human Security

1. What is the generic purpose of the identification and authentication process?
2. Besides humans, what is the other category of things that might seek access to a system?
3. Why are identification and authentication topics crosscutting?
4. Why is assignment of trust a key issue with identification?
5. What is the method that is used to authenticate to an automated system?
6. Besides electronic, what is the other area that requires authentication?
7. Why is identity as a service (IDaaS) necessary?
8. What is access auditing and why is it an important protection measure for IDaaS?
9. What do third-party identity services provide?
10. What is an access aggregation attack and how is one executed?
11. What is the aim of social engineering?
12. Are social engineering attacks electronic? If not, what is the method of attack?
13. Why are social engineering attacks so prevalent?
14. Why is awareness of social engineering an important countermeasure?
15. What are the triggers that social engineering attacks exploit?
16. What are social engineering attacks "all about?"
17. What is spoofing?

18. What is an example of an electronic spoof?

19. What are some of the signs of a social engineering attack?

20. Why are scenario-based cases useful in teaching about social engineering?

21. Why is the issue of defining correct professional behavior so important?

22. How do codes of conduct and group norms equate?

23. Why is a code of conduct an essential element in ensuring secure behavior?

24. Why is it important to specify the conduct with respect to confidentiality of data?

25. What is the primary influence behind personal willingness to comply?

26. How is compliance enforced?

27. What organizational function dictates the rules of conduct for a given situation?

28. How does organizational turnover justify detailed rules of behavior?

29. What is the one ability that a person must possess in an uncertain situation?

30. How is that ability formally developed for all of the workers in an organization?

31. What is the chief problem with putting security features in a system?

32. What does awareness underwrite in terms of subsequent worker development efforts?

33. What generic human behavior does a good awareness program strengthen?

34. Why is it vital to ensure that people are aware of the precise requirements of their role?

35. Why is a personal vision of the way an individual's actions impact security important?

36. What is the role of cyber-hygiene awareness in creating the overall security function?

37. What is the role of prioritization of concerns in establishing a cyber-hygiene program?

38. Why must procedures be planned and documented to start a cyber education program?

39. Why is targeting of the educational effort to specific roles necessary?
40. What is the positive impact of education on end user behavior?
41. How is end user threat understanding publicized?
42. What freedom does privacy underwrite?
43. What is the chief concern regarding balance and privacy?
44. Why are common principles an important element in ensuring privacy?
45. Why is data mining a threat to societal privacy?
46. What is do the behavioral sciences contribute to privacy enforcement?
47. Why are social group interaction theories particularly relevant to cybersecurity?
48. Why is personal monitoring an issue when it comes to workplace privacy?
49. What is social media a threat to privacy, specifically what concerns does it raise?
50. What does social media posting threaten in terms of individual identities?
51. How do disclosure decisions impact individual security?
52. What is the definition of personal data?
53. Why do individuals need to control their personal data?
54. Why does the GDPR require auditable proof of compliance?
55. Why is consent an issue when it comes to personal data?
56. What is the HIPAA Privacy Rule?
57. Why is a privacy official a key individual in HIPAA compliance?
58. Why is it necessary to define the things that can be considered SPD?
59. What feature is personal tracking built around?
60. What do cookies do?
61. What is a digital footprint?
62. What does configuration have to do with ensuring security functionality?
63. What are the large components of a security system and how do they interrelate?
64. Why are human factor interfaces a point of concentration?

65. Why is policy an important element in ensuring Human Security?
66. What is a security policy document and what does it ensure?
67. The difference between local and global jurisdiction in security policy guidance?
68. Why is risk enumeration an important part of security policy documentation?
69. What is the role of perspective in security policy formulation?
70. What aspects of security does a usability design decision impact?

You Might Also Like to Read

- Achutha, Raman, *Build a Better Privacy Policy: EU GDPR Compliance for Privacy Managers*, Kindle Edition, Amazon, Seattle, WA, 2018.
- Bertino, Elisa and Kenji Takahashi, *Identity Management: Concepts, Technologies, and Systems*, Artech House Information Security and Privacy, Artech, Norwood, MA, 2010.
- Hadnagy, Christopher, Paul F. Kelly, and Paul Ekman, *Unmasking the Social Engineer: The Human Element of Security*, 1st Edition, Wiley, Hoboken, NJ, 2014.
- Hadnagy, Christopher and Paul Wilson, *Social Engineering: The Art of Human Hacking*, 1st Edition, Wiley, Hoboken, NJ, 2010.
- Hallas, Bruce, *Re-Thinking the Human Factor: A Philosophical Approach to Information Security Awareness Behaviour and Culture*, Kindle Edition, Hallas Institute, Nottingham, UK, 2018.
- Kennedy, Gwen E. and L.S.P. Prabhu, *Data Privacy Law: A Practical Guide*, Interstice, 2017.
- Leichter, William and David Berman, *Global Guide to Data Protection Laws: Understanding Privacy and Compliance Requirements in More than 80 Countries*, Amazon, Seattle, WA, 2017.
- McNamee, Roger, *Zucked: Waking Up to the Facebook Catastrophe*, Penguin, Tamil Nadu, 2019.

- Microsoft Corporation and Michael McLoughlin, *Digital Transformation in the Cloud: What Enterprise Leaders and their Legal and Compliance Advisors Need to Know*, Kindle Edition, Amazon, Seattle, WA, 2018.
- Mitnick, Kevin D., William L. Simon, and Steve Wozniak, *The Art of Deception: Controlling the Human Element of Security*, Wiley, Hoboken, NJ, 2003.
- Orondo, Omondi, *Identity and Access Management: A Systems Engineering Approach*, Amazon, Seattle, WA, 2014.
- Pfleeger, Charles and Shari Lawrence Pfleeger, *Analyzing Computer Security: A Threat/Vulnerability/Countermeasure Approach*, 1st Edition, Prentice-Hall, Upper Saddle River, NJ, 2011.
- Saydjari, O. Sami, *Engineering Trustworthy Systems: Get Cybersecurity Design Right the First Time*, 1st Edition, McGraw-Hill, New York, 2018.
- Singer, Peter W. and Allan Friedman, *Cybersecurity and Cyberwar: What Everyone Needs to Know*, Oxford University Press, Oxford, 2014.
- Steinberg, Joseph, *Official (ISC)2® Guide to the CISSP®-ISSMP® CBK® ((ISC)2 Press)*, 2nd Edition, Auerbach, Boca Raton, FL, 2015.
- Vasileiou, Ismini and Steven Furnell (Editor), *Cybersecurity Education for Awareness and Compliance*, Advances in Information Security, Privacy, and Ethics, Information Science Reference, IGI Global, Hershey, PA, 2019.
- Webb, Amy, *The Big Nine: How the Tech Titans and their Thinking Machines Could Warp Humanity*, Kindle Edition, PublicAffairs Publishing, New York, 2019.
- Williamson, Graham, David Yip, Ilan Sharoni, and Kent Spaulding, *Identity Management: A Primer*, 1st Edition, MC Press, Boise, ID, 2009.
- Worstell, Karen, *Your Amazing Itty Bitty® Personal Data Protection Book: 15 Keys to Minimize Your Exposure to Cybercrime Using These Essential Steps*, Kindle Edition, Amazon, Seattle, WA, 2017.
- Zinatullin, Leron, *The Psychology of Information Security*, IT Governance Publishing, Cambridgeshire, 2016.

- Zuboff, Shoshana, *The Age of Surveillance Capitalism: The Fight for a Human Future at the New Frontier of Power*, Kindle Edition, PublicAffairs Publishing, New York, 2019.

Chapter Summary

- The requirement for the assurance of the confidentiality, integrity, and availability of all information assets of value implies the need for substantive measures to protect the organization's information assets from non-virtual threats.
- It is incumbent on the organization to research and implement secure processes and procedures that will specifically control the human element.
- Cybersecurity in the human realm is built around the systematic execution of pre-designated tasks, which are chosen to mitigate a given threat.
- Human threats can come from many varied directions. So, it is almost impossible to deploy a single effective solution.
- The organization has to install substantive mechanisms to ensure that all workers perform all requisite tasks in a coordinated way.
- A key aspect of the cybersecurity process is the requirement to ensure that all of the people in the organization have sufficient knowledge of and follow specific organizational procedures for securing their personal work and personal space.
- Malicious actions by the trusted personnel within an organization are far too easy to execute and very hard to prevent.
- The commonly accepted practices in the CSEC2017 Human Security knowledge area offer a wide-ranging discussion of the actions that the organization ought to take in dealing with the Human Security issue.
- The CSEC2017's measures are embodied in the seven knowledge units that comprise the Human Security knowledge.
- In general, the first area **Identity Management** describes the knowledge elements that can be associated with the assignment and authentication of trust.
- Knowledge Unit Two, **Social Engineering,** is the practice of manipulating people in a way that causes them to give up

confidential information. Consequently, it is the most difficult form of threat to defend against.

- Knowledge Unit Three, **Personal Compliance** is an important topic because like every other profession, cybersecurity practitioners have to know and be able to exhibit a proper set of authorized behaviors. A code of conduct defines the accepted values and principles of the people within a given domain.

- Knowledge Unit Four, **Awareness and Understanding** contains the building blocks on which all other levels of learned security behavior rest. Effective awareness programs ensure that all employees at every level in the organization understand, appreciate the need for, and are capable of executing, disciplined security practice, in an organized fashion.

- Knowledge Unit Five, **Privacy** underwrites personal freedom. The specific concern with respect to cybersecurity is finding the proper balance between knowing enough about a person but not too much.

- Knowledge Unit Six, **Personal Data Privacy and Security** assumes that individuals have the fundamental right to control the way in which their own personal data is gathered and used. That simple assumption implies the basic obligation for organizations to be more accountable for data protection.

- It's axiomatic that the greater security that an organization demands, the more likely it is that the user community will develop ingenious ways of getting around it. So, Knowledge Unit Seven, **Usable Security and Privacy** is the CSEC2017 area that deals with the issue of usability in the design of security systems.

Learning Objectives for the Human Security Knowledge Area

Mastery of the requisite learning outcomes for the Human Security knowledge area will be established through the student's ability to paraphrase and explicate the key contents of the knowledge units within this knowledge area (Bloom Levels Two and Three). In addition, the student will exhibit specific behaviors that demonstrate a capability to utilize these relevant concepts in common practical application. Specifically, the student will be able to paraphrase and explain the following twenty-eight knowledge elements (CSEC 2017):

1. The difference between identification, authentication, and access authorization
2. The importance of audit trails and logging in identification and authentication.
3. How to implement the concept of least privilege and segregation of duties.
4. The nature and behavior of access control attacks and mitigation measures.
5. The common types of social engineering attacks.
6. The psychology of social engineering attacks.
7. Common techniques employed to mislead users.
8. How to identify types of social engineering attacks.
9. How to detect and mitigate social engineering attacks.
10. The importance of cyber hygiene.
11. The importance of cybersecurity user education.
12. The importance of cyber vulnerabilities and threat awareness.
13. The major topics within Security Education, Training, and Awareness (SETA).
14. The importance of SETA as a general countermeasure.
15. The importance of risk perception in the context of cybersecurity and privacy.
16. The importance of communication in the context of cybersecurity and privacy.
17. The various theories of privacy from social psychology and social science.
18. The concepts of privacy trade-offs and risks in the social context.
19. The concepts of personal control and awareness of data consent.
20. The concepts of personal information monitoring.
21. The importance of regulatory protections and concerns in maintaining social privacy.
22. The importance of social media privacy and security.

23. The importance of personal data privacy and security.
24. The importance of protection of SPD.
25. The importance of PII.
26. The importance of regulations governing collection, use, and distribution of SPD.
27. The possibilities for inference of SPD.
28. The ethics of personal tracking and digital footprinting in the context of privacy.

Keywords

Awareness – a sense that an idea or concept exists and has meaning to the individual

Behavior – individual personal actions performed that are observable by third parties

Code of Conduct – documented rules outlining expected behaviors for an organization

Compliance – authenticated actions that indicate that a requirement, rule, or law is followed

Controls – a discrete set of human or electronic behaviors set to produce a given outcome

Critical Asset – a function or object that is so central to an operation that it cannot be lost

Cybersecurity – assurance of confidentiality, integrity, and availability of information

Human Security – assurance of consistently correct behavior by individuals in the organization

Infrastructure – a collection of large components arrayed in a logical structure in order to accomplish a given purpose

Privacy – assurance that personally identifiable data is safeguarded from unauthorized access

Reliability – proven capability to perform a designated purpose over time

Strategic Planning – the process of developing long-term plans of action aimed at furthering and enhancing organizational goals

Third Party – additional participant in a process involving a user and a service.

References

Fruhlinger, Josh, "Top Cybersecurity Facts, Figures and Statistics for 2018", *CSO Magazine*, 10 October 2018. www.csoonline.com/article/3153707/security/top-cybersecurity-facts-figures-and-statistics.html, accessed February 2019.

General Data Protection Regulation (GDPR), On the Protection of Natural Persons with Regard to the Processing of Personal Data, EU2016/679, 27 April 2016, Effective date 25 May 2018.

Joint Task Force (JTF) on Cybersecurity Education, "Cybersecurity Curricula 2017, Curriculum Guidelines for Post-Secondary Degree Programs in Cybersecurity, a Report in the Computing Curricula Series", ACM/IEEE-CS/AIS SIGSEC/IFIP WG 11.8, Version 1.0, 31 December 2017.

Kelly, Ross, "Almost 90% of Cyber Attacks are Caused by Human Error or Behavior", Chief Executive, 3 March 2017. https://chiefexecutive.net/almost-90-cyber-attacks-caused-human-error-behavior/, accessed February 2019.

Laberis, Bill, "20 Eye-Opening Cybercrime Statistics", Security Intelligence, IBM, 2016. https://securityintelligence.com/20-eye-opening-cybercrime-statistics/, accessed 18 December.

Palagonia, Gamelah, "Social Engineering Is Bigger than Hacking: But Countermeasures Work", Willis Towers Watson Wire, 21 January 2016. https://blog.willis.com/2016/01/social-engineering-is-bigger-than-hacking-but-countermeasures-work/, accessed February 2019.

Privacy Rights Clearinghouse, *A Chronology of Data Breaches*, PRC, San Diego, CA, 2015.

Saltzer, Jerome H. and Michael D. Schroeder, The protection of information in computer systems, *Communications of the ACM*, 17, 7, 1974.

The Health Insurance Portability and Accountability Act (HIPAA), Pub.L. 104–191, 110 Stat. 1936), 104th Congress, 1996, Enacted 21 August 1996.

Trend-Micro, Report on Cybersecurity and Critical Infrastructure in the Americas, Organization of American States, Trend Micro Incorporated, 2015.

9

ORGANIZATIONAL SECURITY

In this chapter, you will learn the following:

- The challenges organizational threats represent in the overall cybersecurity ecosystem
- The integrative function of the Organizational Security knowledge area
- The importance of risk in the overall cybersecurity process
- The importance of security governance and policy in formulating a response
- The application of analytical tools to cybersecurity operation
- The critical importance of effective systems administration
- The methods and practices of cybersecurity planning
- The application of continuity, recovery, and incident management practice
- The relevance and practices of Security Program Management
- The critical importance and practical implementation of personnel security
- The large-scale issues associated with security operations.

Introduction Securing the Entire Enterprise

The Organizational Security knowledge area is arguably the highest level of concept among the CSEC2017 cybersecurity functional areas, and it is the one that is most broadly relevant. It is also probably the oldest of the CSEC2017 areas in the sense that its best practices derive from old-fashioned organizational management principles, rather than the new world of digital technology. Essentially, Organizational Security ensures that the actual performance of the cybersecurity function is both reliable and consistent. That typically involves the use of a set of policies and standard operating procedures, which explicitly dictate how each of the other seven CSEC2017 knowledge areas interacts, as well as the best practices associated with each subset unit.

In general terms, the Organizational Security knowledge area represents the governance aspect of any cybersecurity operation. An everyday Organizational Security governance framework is extremely important in the conduct of the cybersecurity function. That is because it embodies the planning and control aspects of conventional organizational management. These traditional business aspects are important because the cybersecurity process does not operate in a vacuum. The big-picture understanding of organizational threat and the development of strategies to respond to those threats is the valuable contribution that Organizational Security brings to the party.

The Organizational Security knowledge area centers on the creation of an organizational assurance system. This system originates in the strategic policy domain. Essentially, the business creates a complete and coherent framework that embodies all of the necessary management roles, organizational behavior, and strategic policies necessary to underwrite organization-wide assurance. The complete array of these countermeasures is capable of addressing any potential threat, tangible or intangible, that the business might face. The Organizational Security knowledge area integrates all of those across-the-board countermeasures for each of the other areas of the CSEC2017.

Typically, the process of policy development starts with the creation of a top-level framework. The organization's specific cybersecurity strategy is referenced directly to, and communicated by means of, a set of defined policies, which are developed through the organization's overall strategic planning process. Subsequently, this "strategic" point of reference provides the consistent roadmap necessary to tailor a particular cybersecurity solution down to the most concrete level of implementation.

Integrating the Elements of Cybersecurity into an Applied Solution

The manner in which the areas of protection are planned, deployed, and overseen within the day-to-day operation will govern the effectiveness of the response. All of the other CSEC2017 areas constitute an aspect of the solution. It is the Organizational Security knowledge area that integrates those disparate components into a single unified approach.

Therefore, the knowledge elements of Organizational Security might be considered to lie at the fundamental basis of cybersecurity.

Logically, there are two straightforward conditions that must be met in order for the cybersecurity process to be effective. First, the cybersecurity solution has to be complete, in the sense that everything that must be protected is assured by a provably effective mechanism. Second, the cybersecurity solution has to be institutionalized, in the sense that there must be an organizationally persistent and consistently performed, well-defined process that ensures concrete cybersecurity governance.

The latter stipulation is particularly important because organizations do not become secure by chance. Organizations have to embark on a deliberate and disciplined set of steps to establish and maintain an acceptable condition of cybersecurity, and the state must operate as a stable twenty-four hour a day corporate function. That kind of operation is normally resource intensive. Therefore, executive decision makers have to understand that the Organizational Security function is a formal entity and that it is a long-term commitment that cannot be sidetracked by short-term budget concerns.

From an implementation standpoint, the requirement for a fully holistic organization-wide security process implies the need to adopt a systematic security management strategy that continuously aligns the security response to conditions as they appear in the threat environment. The second condition implies that the organization must be both willing and able to define and enforce a substantive set of management controls that ensure that all of the explicit security requirements, as specified in the organizational assurance strategy, create and enforce an organization-wide cybersecurity culture.

As we said earlier, all of these requirements consume time and resources. Nonetheless, there are very real and practical consequences if the cybersecurity solution is not complete or consistently practiced. For instance, a highly secure network without equally robust assurance that the personnel who operate it have been properly vetted is wide open to social engineering attacks no matter how sophisticated the technology is. In fact, according to Verizon, up to 58% of the theft of personal health information is attributable to insiders (Team ObserveIT, 2018).

One illustration of how this exact scenario played out is an incident, where the information for 18,000 Medicare patients was stolen by an insider. That information included Medicare ID numbers, social security numbers, health plan ID numbers, names of members, and dates of enrollment (Team ObserveIT, 2018). That particular insider's tendency toward bad behavior was well known to human resources (HR). But nobody thought to pass the information along to the people who operated the system. This is a perfect illustration of the reason why the cybersecurity function must be fully coordinated across all organizational areas.

Accordingly, the Organizational Security knowledge area provides mutually supporting and interlocking recommendations for understanding best practice in organizational development. These are basically governance concepts. But they are derived from, and apply directly to, the oversight and optimization of the performance of all of the technical knowledge areas in the CSEC2017 model. In terms of their application, the most narrowly focused topics of the Organizational Security build the organization's security response capability by means of specifically focused areas of practice such as analytics and system management. These two areas directly impact the day-to-day operation of the technology and embody all of the best practices associated with the assurance of system and network security. In that respect, these two Organizational Security knowledge units represent the essential, high-level governance concepts that are needed to tie the elements of the technology operation together. Those concepts apply in the first five areas of the CSEC2017: Data, Software, Component, Connection, and System Security.

However, they do not specifically address the more abstract concerns of risk, or the essential contextual issues of holistic security. Those large-scale concerns include everything from planning, to program and operational management, to incident response and recovery, to methods that can be used to assure the integrity of the people who operate and maintain the system. Those Organizational Security knowledge units encompass the actions that incorporate specific best practice for governance and control into a single coherent organizational approach to strategic and operational management. They ensure that a single well-defined and commonly understood process is sufficiently capable of ensuring the overall reliability and integrity of the everyday cybersecurity functioning of the business. These units embody a real-world cybersecurity operation through the explicit organizational controls that they deploy as well as the planned inter-actions that take place between them.

The integration of the entire set of Organizational Security knowledge units into a single substantive planned response ensures that every aspect of the threat is addressed in a holistic fashion. The embodiment of the holistic solution that the Organizational Security knowledge area enables does not simply ensure that the system implements access control. It ensures that those accesses are logged, analyzed, and evaluated for the purpose of long-term system planning and development. It also ensures that any requirements for continuity and compliance are fully addressed in the access con-trol solution as well as recommending managerial corrective action where they are not.

The CSEC2017 Organizational Security Knowledge Units

The Organizational Security knowledge area is composed of nine dis-tinct areas of operation. We will discuss and illustrate their applica-tion in each of the succeeding sections (Figure 9.1). The nine areas are as follows:

1. *Risk Management* – identification, assessment, and mitigation of risk
2. *Security Governance and Policy* – strategic policy and management
3. *Analytical Tools* – analytic support elements of the planning and management process
4. *Systems Administration* – practices for assuring optimum System Security performance
5. *Cybersecurity Planning* – strategic and operational planning
6. *Business Continuity, Disaster Recovery, and Incident Management* – concept and method
7. *Security Program Management* – security governance opera-tional practices
8. *Personnel Security* – behavioral control policy and application of practices
9. *Security Operations* – operational security management practice.

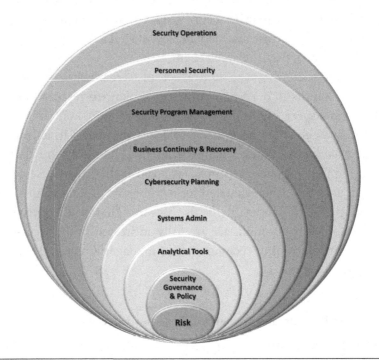

Figure 9.1   The Organizational Security knowledge units.

Knowledge Area One: Risk Management

Risk management entails finding and controlling risks to organizational assets. It is a formal process that is set up to protect an organization's information and information processing equipment from harm due to inadvertent, or deliberate, acts. Risk is a fundamental aspect of human life in the sense that risk is always a factor in any situation where the outcome is not precisely known. And the necessary calculations that we make about the probability of some form of harm resulting from an action that we take, are normally a given in our decision-making processes. Whether the risk assessment involves the decisions about a major corporate initiative, or just making the decision to walk down the street, we are always identifying, and evaluating, the potential of harm from the risks involved. So, in that respect, we can be said to be constantly managing risk in everything we do.

Risk management is a holistic process in that it rationally deploys the complete set of controls necessary to prevent unauthorized use, loss, damage, disclosure, or modification of information assets. The reason why risk management is a particularly important aspect of the cybersecurity body of knowledge is that information and communication technology assets are more difficult to account for and control than the most conventional physical ones. This is because information and communication technology always involves the production and management of virtual, highly dynamic products, which makes it difficult to identify WHAT to secure let alone how to do it.

The intangibility puts effective risk understanding center stage in the consideration of how to establish and maintain a holistically secure information and communication technology environment. In practical terms, the risk management process evaluates whether a given threat behavior will adversely impact something of value to any given organization. That includes such threat factors as people, physical events, or electronic actions. Once those risks are known, the risk management process deploys all necessary countermeasures to ensure against any form of consequent harm.

Certain types of organizations manage risk in a highly quantified and data-driven way. For example, corporations require high levels of integrity in their products, as well as the segments of the critical infrastructure where the potential failure of a crucial system could result in highly undesirable consequences. Other organizations spend less on managing risk. It all depends on the nature of the threat environment and the value and sensitivity of the assets that are being protected. Because the need to accurately characterize and understand the threat environment plays such an important part in risk management, the assessment of threats and their impacts constitutes the essential focus of the process.

Thus, risk management is operationalized by means of a continuous assessment of the organizational environment, which is aimed at identifying, understanding, and controlling all of the potential threats and the negative impacts that might impact the business. Once these threats have all been identified and characterized, the specific steps are devised and implemented to mitigate any adverse outcomes. Given its reliance on substantive decision making concerning threat, an important underlying factor in risk evaluation is the uncertainty principle. Uncertainty is a key element in assessing threats because risk entails future consequences. In essence, the outcomes of any given threat have to be fully understood in order for an intelligent decision to be made about the long-term costs of addressing it. However, a number of unknown, and therefore unevaluated, factors are always involved. Thus, the institution of a standardized and persistent set of practices to identify, understand, and respond effectively becomes the essential element of the risk management process.

In the real world, organizations develop, implement, and follow some form of systematic process to establish a persistent state of operational risk management. That design and management process is a strategic activity, in that it involves long-range considerations. Thus, planning for strategic risk management is necessary in order to ensure continuous risk assurance. And a formal strategic planning process is necessary to implement an organization-wide risk management control. Risk management itself must incorporate all of the elements of the business within its scope, and the process should reach the boundaries of the organization.

The outcome of a risk management process is a concrete, organization-wide risk management scheme. That scheme will balance the aims of long-term risk control policy with real-world conditions and constraints. The atomic-level components of the risk management process are a set of substantive controls that ensure the requisite level of assurance against loss. These controls should be traceable directly to the policies that defined their need. This is a closed-loop process in that the ongoing alignment of risk controls to policies fine tunes the evolution of the substantive risk management process and ensures its effectiveness in all operational settings.

Nevertheless, because every organization is unique and everyone implements security differently, the actual process to identify, evaluate, and ensure the meaningful risks involves the same general steps. As shown in Figure 9.2, there are five subtopics of the Risk Management knowledge unit: (1) *Risk identification* – cataloging risk, (2) *Risk assessment and analysis* – understanding risk, (3) *Insider threat* – dealing with risk from trusted individuals, (4) *Risk measurement and evaluation models and methodologies* – empirical analysis tools, and (5) *Risk control* – control measures to mitigate identified risk.

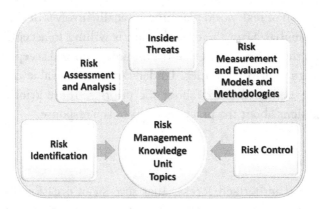

Figure 9.2   The Risk Management knowledge unit topics.

Risk Identification

Risk identification involves the cataloging of the information assets for the express purpose of evaluating and controlling risk to them. The aim is to evaluate potential harm should those assets be compromised or lost. Risk identification might be the most important subtopic in the risk management area because the control assignment process is based on it.

The risk identification process formulates a detailed and comprehensive picture of the entire organizational asset base, as well as a clear understanding of the acceptable levels of risk for each asset, within any applicable constraints.

Risk Assessment and Analysis

In order to maintain the necessary understanding of the threat environment, the organization has to undertake a specialized empirical risk analysis process. That function should be able to achieve acceptable qualitative and quantitative understanding of any new, or emerging, threat and its associated risks. The ideal outcome of this process would be a continuous assurance that all of the relevant risks are properly understood and that any emerging risks will be identified and accurately described.

Because cost is a factor, a precise specification of the maximum degree of acceptable risk is a prerequisite to doing practical risk identification. The specification of the maximum level of risk is necessary because much of real-world planning typically involves deciding what level of potential harm the organization is willing to accept. A decision about the degree of risk that the organization will accept will lead to an assignment of priorities. Understanding the value of an item enables an explicit decision about the priority. Those priorities then drive decisions about the practical form of the response.

Insider Threats

Insiders have authorized access. That access can occasionally lead to knowing, or unknowing, damage to the organization. An insider threat is a security threat that originates from employees, former employees, contractors, or business associates. All of the categories may have legitimate credentials to access the organization's resources, including its proprietary information and technology. An insider threat action is any malicious act that is perpetrated from within the organization by any of those groups.

The primary concern is that insider threats cannot be mitigated by traditional security measures. The type of electronic means that defend against such activities as conventional hacking, or that prevent unauthorized access across the organizational perimeter, won't raise the same security flags as a former employee who is using an authorized login in an outside attempt to gain access to a company's network.

Risk Measurement and Evaluation Models and Methodologies

In practice, organizations always implement and follow some form of the systematic assessment process in order to establish a persistent operational risk management process. That evaluation is a strategic activity, in that it involves organization-wide considerations. Thus, an explicit standard model for strategic risk evaluation is utilized in order to ensure uniform ongoing risk measurement.

Threat modeling is normally used to support risk measurement. Threat modeling allows risk data to be modeled and subsequently communicated among team members. The major steps of threat modeling begin with a determination of the scope of protected space that the model corresponds to. Then, threats that might impact the components of that space are enumerated, and specific details as to the potential likelihood and impact of the threat are collected.

The concerns are categorized into a single common understanding of the threat environment and the concomitant risks. This assessment will likely require the organization to develop lead indicators that will allow senior management to determine whether the risk control process is meeting its overall assurance goals. This amounts to the definition of a set of critical success factors, which can be used to evaluate the performance of the most important elements of risk management in the specific threat environment.

There are a number of industry-accepted methodologies that are designed to support the evaluation and communication of the resultant threat picture. They entail both quantitative and qualitative risk assessment approaches. As shown in Figure 9.3, the risk models include the National Institute of Standards and Technology's Cyber Resilience Review self-assessment; ISO 31000:2009, Risk Management/ISO. IEC 31010:2009 – Risk Management – Risk assessment techniques; COSO's Enterprise Risk Integrated Framework; and the HI-Trust Common Security Framework (CSF). There are also different specific risk requirements that are dictated by various business or regulatory circumstances: HIPAA for healthcare, or Sarbanes Oxley for corporations, for instance.

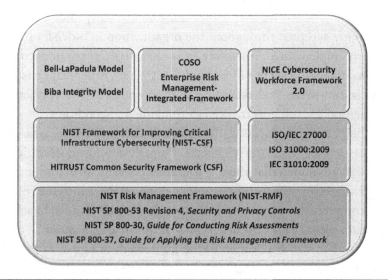

Figure 9.3 Risk models.

Risk Control

Risk control is not one-size-fits-all. It has to be designed to fit the particular environment and overall operating circumstances of the organization. Once the threat environment is understood, the scope or area of coverage, of the actual controls, has to be explicitly defined. The controls themselves are based on general priority. Priority is directly related to the sensitivity of each item of information within the system. That is because the sensitivity of the information determines the levels of confidentiality, integrity, and availability required. Each organizational asset is classified based on the severity of potential negative impacts on the organization and the degree to which the ability of the organization to perform its mission would be affected, should the information be compromised. A checklist of items for analysis is useful in facilitating this process. It provides the necessary structure for the analysis. A checklist will also ensure that the right data is captured for each category as well as ensuring that the eventual analysis is appropriate.

Knowledge Area Two: Security Governance and Policy

Security governance establishes a fully integrated and documented policy framework that ensures the confidentiality, integrity, and availability of the organization's information assets. In practice, the organization's cybersecurity stance must be explicitly understood and commonly accepted throughout the organization in order for it to be properly implemented. Therefore, it is always necessary to document and make public a set of tailored policies that are suitable for ensuring organization-wide understanding and acceptance. The relationship between policy and governance is a fundamental condition.

Policies must be expressed in sufficient detail to ensure a tangible state of security across the workplace. Properly developed strategic policies will guarantee that there is a uniform control structure in place that reaches from the top of the organization all the way to the bottom. That comprehensive framework of controls must be planned to achieve optimum security effectiveness across the entire organization.

The day-to-day application of the framework brings us to the concept of a security governance process. Governance simply denotes the tangible mechanism that is implemented to ensure best practice in normal operation. Security governance processes are always concrete and are not created by accident. Governance processes are normally implemented as part of the conventional strategic planning process. They require both an acceptable reference model for guidance and a well-defined method of ensuring the overall administration and oversight of the process.

The Security Governance and Policy knowledge unit focuses on the elements of the security policy development life cycle, from initial research to implementation and maintenance to practical use. As shown in Figure 9.4, there are six subtopics in the Security Governance knowledge area: (1) *Organizational context* – factors effecting how security is implemented, (2) *Privacy* – cultural and organizational attitudes toward individual rights to confidentiality, (3) *Laws, ethics, and compliance* – legal and regulatory factors effecting cybersecurity, (4) *Security governance* – methods for managing the cybersecurity operation, (5) *Executive- and board-level communication* – methods for ensuring top-down accountability, and (6) *managerial policy* – principles of explicit command and control in an organization.

Organizational Context

In simple terms, organizational context is the array of factors that influence, or impact, a given corporate situation. Organizational context is composed of the company's beliefs, values, and approaches. The corporate leadership team is always explicitly responsible for establishing

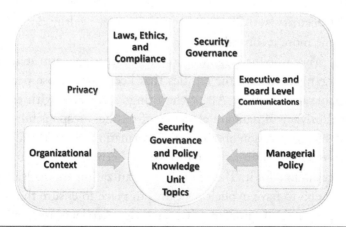

Figure 9.4 The Security Governance and Policy knowledge unit topics.

the organizational context. However, context is also an outcome of the organization's business purpose, and concept of marketing and operation. Those factors control the internal policies and practices, as well as the work environment. Context also entails the clientele of the business, including contractors, customers, and suppliers.

In the case of security, the context clarifies security policies and the governance process as well as the way that a given set of controls is deployed. Context is obviously situational within the organization. But it also embodies the external legal and regulatory climate that surrounds a given organization. Finally, context is also cultural, in terms of both the local and country-specific issues; things such as the type of business and the industry/sector should also be evaluated. There is a significant difference in the approach to cybersecurity among organizations in various business, vertical industry segments. Thus, context is an important matter in considering the shape of the response.

Privacy

The classic definition of privacy is a state or condition of freedom from observation or disturbance by other people. As people utilize cyberspace, they give up their right to privacy. Their browsing, on-line shopping, and social media habits expose large quantities of personally identifiable information to faceless organizations. Personal information that is in the custody of those organizations might subsequently be stolen or misused, which can lead to identity theft. Therefore, privacy is a major topic of concern throughout the CSEC2017; both the Societal Security and Human Security have a healthy dose of it as well as the more technical areas.

Still, privacy is an Organizational Security concern at its root. Since organizations are the entities that keep and expose personally identifiable information. All of the things associated with ensuring personal privacy of data are elements of business responsibility. That is, once an organization obtains your information, either through your direct consent or indirectly, that business becomes legally and ethically accountable for it. Therefore, the organization and its leadership are obligated to have explicit measures in place to ensure the protection of personal information. That fact is an excellent justification for the inclusion of privacy in any discussion of Organizational Security.

Laws, Ethics, and Compliance

In a discussion about something as abstract as laws ethics and compliance, it is important to provide a definition of terms. The term "ethical" is frequently used interchangeably with the term "legal." However, that is not strictly speaking correct. Ethics are logical assumptions about how moral principles should be applied in practice. Ethical systems become legal systems when the morality they capture is formalized into law. Laws are different from ethics in that they are explicitly stated and have specific enforcement mechanisms and sanctions built into their structure. Legal frameworks are prescriptive and oriented toward the enforcement of defined standards of behavior. Legal frameworks are important in the world of cybersecurity because the policies that shape the assurance process must be formulated in light of existing regulations and laws.

Most of the laws that have been passed so far have to do with protecting privacy or regulating commercial transactions using computers. They all have something of a governmental and bureaucratic focus. As shown in Figure 9.5, they can be classified into four generic

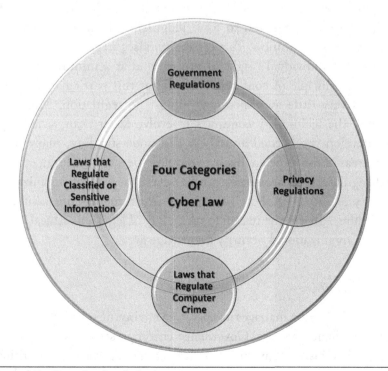

Figure 9.5 Four categories of cyber law.

categories: (1) governmental regulations, (2) privacy regulations, (3) laws that regulate computer crime, and (4) laws that regulate classified or sensitive information. Because each of these entails different compliance requirements, there is a need to think about each of these categories separately.

Technology creates serious problems when it comes to ethics. That is because technology has consistently advanced at a rate that exceeds society's ability to decide about its suitability. As a result, there is no formal guidance about where to draw the line between ethical and unethical. For example, many third-party cookies are spyware. They are placed on a system via surreptitious means, to gather data without the owner's consent. There would probably be plenty of outrage if the average person understood that the purpose of third-party cookies is to track Internet usage. However, that permission is normally buried in the end user license agreement, so it is not against the law.

Thus, the general problem with the laws ethics and compliance category is that most people do not understand, or even know about, the specific implications of any of these factors. In an increasing number of important instances, such as job interviews and credit, this body of information is utilized to form judgments about an individual's personal trustworthiness. That capability raises serious legal concerns around the individual's right to privacy and at a minimum; it violates the principle of confidentiality. Yet at this particular moment, there is very little awareness and almost no regulation. Moreover, because the technology continues to evolve faster than society and can develop the needed awareness and understanding, many more gray areas of this type are likely to develop. Because the legal, ethical, and regulatory consequences can be severe, a prudent organization will try to anticipate those concerns by instituting routine assurance procedures. That is the reason for the study of legal and ethical topics in the Organizational Security knowledge area.

Security Governance

Each organization manages its operating environment through a security governance process. Governance encompasses every identifiable activity and task that an entity carries out in the process of governing. That applies to any defined thing, be it corporate, governmental, or even something like an informal society. Governance comprises a set of standard principles that are applicable in every instance of coordinated control. Essentially what this implies is that the organization needs to establish a formal structure of rational, coherent, and systematic policies for cybersecurity assurance. In effect, this structure has to ensure the protection of, as well as management control over, the organization's information technology (IT) assets. In practice, this formal control array is implemented through a strategic planning process that is designed to accurately reflect the long-term protection needs of the organization and its resource base. The specific mission and responsibility of security governance is to ensure the full and ongoing protection of all information assets. Thus, it has to be continuously audited and enforced by an established business process.

Governance is normally implemented through a well-defined and commonly accepted set of policies and practices that are designed to accomplish the organizational purpose. The formality of the process by which these procedures are enacted depends on the organizational culture and the nature of the external actors. For instance, a military organization will have a different governance climate and structure than a day-care center. Consequently, the actual governance process may be executed differently in different settings and may be subject to different types of motivations and stimuli.

Executive- and Board-Level Communication

The responsibility for proper security is normally vested at the top of the organization. Corporate leaders are the only people who are capable of influencing employee behavior across the board. Therefore, the security of the organization as a whole is particularly reliant on the top leadership. This is necessary to ensure accountability for compliance among the rest of the organizational actors. Thus, cybersecurity is the responsibility of the senior management of an organization. Corporate leaders define the formal planning, risk management, and regulatory compliance capabilities for the organization, which are usually achieved through the development of comprehensive plans, programs, and operational planning controls that are designed to ensure that corporate executives and external decision makers are properly informed as to the present state of the cybersecurity process.

Consequently, this CSEC2017 topic primarily revolves around the development of effective communication processes up and down the organization. That includes both systematic and human-centered reporting systems. Because of the importance of coordinated action at all levels of the organization, this particular topic is a critical part of the curriculum for Organizational Security.

Managerial Policy

This CSEC2017 topic area provides exposure to real-world security policy and practices. Policies define acceptable behavior. Consequently, policies are in effect a set of formal rules of behavior for a particular application, system, employee, or corporate entity. They are communicated as a prescribed means of controlling the cybersecurity behavior of employees and the organization as a whole. That specification normally includes all of the policy elements and factors that are relevant to a given situation. They dictate the specific activities and tasks that must be executed to achieve a given policy goal.

Managerial policies are a compendium of best practice advice or externally imposed directions that specifically enable the management of the cybersecurity function within a particular organization. NIST 800-12 differentiates those policy decisions into three basic types: program policy, issue-specific policy, and system-specific policy (Nieles et al., 2017). Managers need that direction in order to make the day-to-day decisions essential to managing, protecting, and distributing information. It isn't easy to manage scare resources with so many difficult threats. Without concrete guidance, those actions can fluctuate among levels. Therefore, it is important to have a concrete set of policies in place to guide managerial decisions about the technical and behavioral response that needs to be deployed in a given situation.

Knowledge Area Three: Analytical Tools

This knowledge unit entails a set of techniques using data analytics to recognize, block, divert, and respond to cyberattacks. Analytical tools at both the host and network layer in a system are important. Automated analytics can inspect the configuration of endpoints to determine whether they may be susceptible to attack. It can also analyze activity across a network and compare it to known attacks or attack patterns (this is called network-based intrusion detection system (IDS)). A well-tuned analytic system can identify malware inside an infrastructure before it can cause damage. For example, let's say an attacker managed to slip a Trojan into your network. With the right analytical tools in place, an organization can identify the activity and react.

The most common of these is network analytics. Network analytics monitors the perimeter in any type of system. It typically audits the operation of the system looking for attempts to violate the perimeter. When such an effort is detected, the monitor reports it in a timely fashion. Both network monitoring and analytics and access control systems ensure integrity, and so they are effectively two sides of the same coin. The network monitor ensures that all attempts to gain unauthorized access are detected. Access control ensures that legitimate users are permitted into the system while unauthorized access is specifically blocked. The precise function of analytics is to attempt to identify and isolate attacks. It does that through real-time analysis or by assessing audit data. This is a form of preventive control. Monitoring real-time network activities enables agile decision making, detection of suspected malicious activities, utilization of real-time visualization dashboard, and employment of a set of hardware and software to manage such detected suspicious activities. As shown in Figure 9.6, there are three subtopics of Analytical Tools knowledge area: (1) *performance measurements* (*metrics*) – objective ways to judge

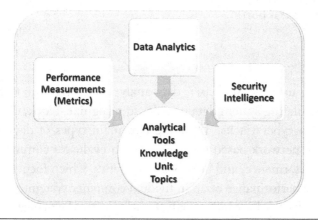

Figure 9.6 The Analytical Tools knowledge unit topics.

the security program, (2) *data analytics* – automated means of management control based on data analysis, and (3) *security intelligence* – threat reporting and data mining to support the security response.

Performance Measurements (Metrics)

Performance measurement is based on general criteria that define an entity's required level of functioning. These are agreed on as part of the management control/governance process. According to the CSEC2017, their aim is to understand the process of design, implementation, and management of specific measures to characterize the effectiveness of the overall security program. That process is built on metrics, which is a term that might describe any detailed statistical analysis technique. But it is now commonly synonymous with performance measurement. The aim is to identify a discrete set of measurable behaviors that can be used to judge the success, or failure, of the function they are associated with. Performance measurement is done to capture data about system, network, application, or user activities. The types of events that might be captured include such things as the network performance, system performance, individual application performance, user behavior, or even isolated actions by specified users. The most important success factor is the establishment of a clear and unambiguous understanding of performance. That includes such routine activities as access control system and physical measurement, intrusion detection and response, internal monitoring of authorized and unauthorized activity, and security performance measurement recording and reporting.

Data Analytics

According to the CSEC2017, data analytics involves the techniques for manipulating system data in order to recognize, block, divert, and respond to cyberattacks. There are two main types of data analytic processes: network-based analytics, which evaluates communication system performance, and host-based analytics, which focuses on analyzing the performance of an individual computer system.

Network-based analytics analyze real-time performance and other relevant transmission information and can send alerts, or terminate, an offending connection, if a problem is detected. Host-based analytics examine and characterize intrusions. They do this by scrutinizing event data, critical system data, and other auditable resources to identify any suspicious patterns of behavior. Properly configured, a host-based analysis will alert management to the situation and any required responses.

Security Intelligence

This topic area focuses on the collection, analysis, and dissemination of security information, including but not limited to threats and adversary capabilities. In many respects, this is the classic role of intelligence, and in that respect, its appearance in a framework that is focused on the cybersecurity body of knowledge reflects the growing role of intelligence in the global effort to keep our systems secure. This topic area describes the knowledge necessary to gather intelligence information about any foreign or domestic adversary.

It is the emphasis on the gathering of any pertinent information in any form that primarily differentiates this topic from the other ones in the Analytic Tools knowledge area. Essentially, this topic does cover the information gathering and preparatory work that allows an organization to connect the dots in order to understand another entity's plans. The general aim is to ensure that the organization takes the necessary steps to make itself safe from an anticipated attack.

Dissemination of that intelligence typically includes information sharing and analysis centers as well as public service organizations like InfraGard.

Knowledge Unit Four: Systems Administration

System administration is an important function in an information and communication technology organization because it curtails the natural tendency toward chaos in complex organizational settings. The knowledge in the systems administration area is focused on maintaining the secure performance of the information and communication technology system during its operational life cycle. Thus, the system administration process always takes place within a given technological environment. The organization or functional area responsible for system administration defines a strategy and criteria for ensuring that the system achieves its organizational purposes. The system administration function will periodically evaluate performance in order to ensure that the systems under its care are operating correctly and that the requisite level of operation is fully sustained within the target environment. The system administration function will also offer specialized assistance and consultation for end users and customers in accordance with the business's operational plan.

Because of its everyday focus, system administration is probably the most overlooked and underestimated process in the entire information and communication technology assurance process. Yet, because it underwrites the functions necessary to ensure the effective operation of the software and provide operational support to users, the system administration function is perhaps the most pivotal process in the organization's defense against cybersecurity threats and vulnerabilities.

The system administration process begins with a plan, but it also includes a requirement to select an appropriate set of explicit standards to guide the work. The overall goal of this portion of the process is to establish a stable set of guidelines from which a given system, hardware, or software operation, or software service, can be effectively ensured and maintained. The system administration function does not imply construction; thus, the actual products or services it assures originate with external sources.

From the point where the system is placed into use, the activities in the System Administration knowledge area are characterized by the ongoing performance of the system's normal operational functions, which could include a range of routine user support activities, database administration, system and network administration tasks, and change management and problem resolution. The system administration process also does provide organizational support for the product, such as training or operating a help desk.

The system administration process uses routine testing and evaluation procedures to demonstrate that system requirements are being met. In addition, system administration is responsible for installing product upgrades and the modifications of all existing systems. System administration normally comes into play when a product requires modifications to supporting technology, code, or associated documentation.

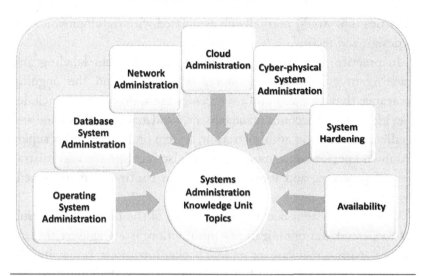

Figure 9.7   The Systems Administration knowledge unit topics.

Such changes are usually a consequence of a reported problem or a request for a change or refinement. As shown in Figure 9.7, there are seven subtopics in the System Administration knowledge area: (1) *Operating system administration* – activities related to operating system assurance, (2) *Database system administration* – activities related to database system assurance, (3) *Network administration* – activities related to network system assurance, (4) *Cloud administration* – activities related to cloud system assurance, (5) *Cyber-physical system administration* – activities related to supervisory control and data acquisition (SCADA) assurance, (6) *System hardening* – concepts related to system reliability, and (7) *availability* – concepts related to system access.

Operating System Administration

This topic covers the upkeep, reliable operation, configuration, and troubleshooting of technical systems, especially multiuser systems and servers. In general, operating system administration is composed of planning, control, assurance, and communication activities. The goal of operating system administration is to maintain and control changes to an organization's systems or products in a way that preserves their integrity, while providing a basis for ensuring their security and availability. In conjunction with the routine practices of upkeep, the system administrator may also be required to perform activities that would normally be associated with development, such as design and testing.

In practice, the process focuses on the consistent labeling and tracking of components, products or services, and the ongoing assurance that user and process accesses are appropriate. It includes user identity and account management, local and remote storage and media assurance and administration, system process, and task supervision and performance monitoring. It also includes the administration of processes and tools for long-term continuity management assurance.

Operating System Security oversees all of the preventive controls set to defend the organization's information assets against threats, viruses, worms, malware, or remote hacker intrusions. It may involve any, or all, of the following functions: operating system updating and patching; automated operating system defense automation, including antivirus software, firewall configuration, and administration on the system side of the communication process; and user account management and privilege assignment.

Database System Administration

Database system administration ensures that operational database assurance is performed in the most effective and efficient manner. It ensures that the functioning of the operational assurance process for databases is continuously monitored. The aim is for management to identify and report any operational problems that are encountered in the operation of the databases. As such, it is a requisite of good database administrative practice to (1) assess and audit the policies, procedures, tools, and standards used for operational database assurance; (2) document the outcomes of assessments and audits and make recommendations for remediation, or improvement to the system; and (3) specify and maintain proper database and application software configurations and settings, including resource-based security configurations, and facilitate any patches that might have a significant impact.

Automated tools might also be used to examine the internal configuration of the database for possible exploitable vulnerabilities. Finally, database security administration might perform a static analysis of specifications and designs for potential logical vulnerabilities that might be exploited. Coverage should include the data storage technologies in wide use as well as emerging data management technologies.

Network Administration

In an era where electronic commerce is the norm, administrative control of networks is a critical function. Networks are particularly hard to assure, which is mainly due to the fact that they are so diverse and dispersed. Plus, networks are volatile and way too public, which always represents a primary security vulnerability. So, although physical security and access control provide the procedures for assuring connections, somebody has to be responsible for ensuring data in transit. That task normally falls to the network security administration function. It is the responsibility of that function to develop, implement, and monitor the practices needed to protect the various forms of network media either physical or electronic. The network security administration function guards against potential threats by procedural and technical assurance. This is not to be confused with the role of network security, which is to ensure the integrity of the communication process itself. The role of the network security administration function is to underwrite the integrity of the transmission functions in order to safeguard electronic transactions from such hazards as theft, fraud, repudiation, and dispute.

Monitoring the performance of a network link is also known as network analysis. Network analysis is an important area of network measurement, which deals with monitoring the health of various links in a network using end-to-end probes sent by agents located at vantage points in the network/Internet. Route analytics is another important area of network measurement. It includes the methods, systems, algorithms, and tools to monitor the routing posture of networks. Incorrect routing or routing issues cause undesirable performance degradation or downtime. Automated monitoring services can check HTTP pages, HTTPS, FTP, SMTP, POP3, IMAP, DNS, SSH, SSL, TCP, UDP, Media Streaming, and a range of other ports with a variety of check intervals ranging from every 4 hours to every 1 minute.

Cloud Administration

Cloud administration manages network links that serve the storage space that users access remotely. In many respects, this is a network administration task. However, the cloud administrator's network is open and accessible to a large number of unaffiliated people, who do not have an explicit connection to the servers that they manage beyond the role of the customer.

The term "cloud security" refers to specific policies, technologies, applications, and controls that are used to secure virtualized intellectual property, data, applications, services, and the associated infrastructure of the cloud computing establishment. The notion of the "cloud" is a concept that arose out of the early 21st-century idea of distributed systems. Before the cloud, companies networked their resources through local servers that ran programs in a centralized environment. However, as Internet connectivity developed over time, it was possible to create remotely accessible servers that could be accessed by a wide range of people. That served the notion of software as a service. Now software developers allow purchasers to remotely access their proprietary software, giving the user their own secure work environment and storage space, which is virtually located on the service provider's servers. Cloud administration manages that environment.

Cloud administrators work directly within the computer operating system to ensure a stable server environment. Because the servers that enable cloud functionality have to operate around the clock, cloud administration is responsible for load balancing and maintaining peak efficiency. Cloud administration sustains the proprietary software and processing capabilities as well as the security protocols. Thus, at its core, cloud administration is a server administration task. The cloud administrator ensures that the provider's infrastructure is secure and that the customer's data and applications are protected, while the user is responsible for ensuring proper access control and authentication on their side of the transaction.

Cyber-Physical System Administration

The term "cyber-physical system" just designates a computerized device that controls something in the physical universe. Because almost everything from the electrical grid to your pop-up toaster is run by program logic, the cyber-physical universe can be compared to the insect world, in that it is everywhere. The term that has been adopted to describe the cyber-physical system universe is the "Internet of Things," or IoT. However, the realm of SCADA lies within that infinitely wide domain, and it is a major national security concern. SCADA systems perform the functions that underwrite our daily life. Complex cyber-physical system control networks are central to the operation of every sector in the critical infrastructure.

Cyber-physical systems administration is built around ensuring safety, capability, adaptability, scalability, resiliency, security, and usability, as shown in Figure 9.8. Essentially, the body of knowledge of cyber-physical system assurance comprises all the formal steps, "To prepare for and adapt to changing conditions and withstand and recover rapidly from disruptions." The aim is to ensure the survival of critical systems in light of every conceivable risk. Consequently, resiliency must be baked into a cyber-physical system architecture by design, which implies the requirement to ensure that strategic design is a factor in any educational process focused on cyber-physical System Security.

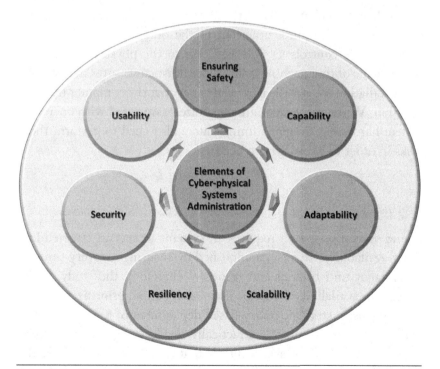

Figure 9.8 Elements of cyber-physical systems administration.

System Hardening

In simple terms, system hardening aims to "strengthen" the attack surface of a computer by reducing the running software and services accessible to an unauthorized user down to the bare minimum required. The purpose of system hardening is to eliminate as many security risks as possible. This is typically done by removing all non-essential software programs and utilities from the computer. Keeping the attack surface as small as possible is a basic security measure. The aim is to reduce the potential attack vectors by which data can either be entered or be extracted from the system.

Hardening is done through suitable tools (firewall, antivirus, IDS, honeypot). Still, hardening is as much a process as it is a technical act. This topic covers securing a system by finding and remediating risks. This may include hardening or securing configuration, system software, firmware, and application. The administrator needs to think security from the very beginning of the hardening effort. It begins with the decisions made about how to properly configure the security features of the system.

Hardening includes disabling unnecessary accounts, ports, and services. It also requires attention to the detailed configuration of system access controls as well as access to the physical and logical components of the machine itself. More drastic measures may involve the installation of only the bare necessities that the computer needs to function. While these steps are most often associated with operating system hardening, system administrators also need to perform these tasks in order to boost System Security.

Availability

Sound system operation requires all systems to sustain targeted levels of availability. This is accomplished by ensuring recovery through redundancy and backup and recovery. Therefore, the study of the concept of availability is founded on classification, prioritization, and comprehensive strategic policy-based deployment of a rigorous set of real-world security controls. Practically speaking, the best argument for a focused study of availability is that it concentrates on just the essentials of security protection.

Organizations establish an "availability strategy and architecture" that gives them the ability to withstand and recover rapidly from disruptive events. Availability requires methods that react to breaches by locking down the asset that they are designed to protect. These protection processes are both electronic and behavioral in focus, and they are designed to protect key assets, as well as to ensure optimum recovery of the overall system in the event of a successful attack.

Availability recognizes that there are too many cutting-edge hacking tools to prevent sophisticated attackers from finding the cracks in even the most robust cybersecurity perimeter. Thus, availability requires a well-defined, explicit set of controls to ensure the survival of just those critical elements that cannot be subject to compromise. The topic includes but is not limited to identifying key assets and administering controls to ensure reliable system backup and recovery. The controls must assure provable protection of the designated functionality and the interdependencies among the elements in the enterprise's ecosystem.

Knowledge Area Five: Cybersecurity Planning

The generic role of cybersecurity planning is to develop the organization's strategic goals and tactical objectives and then lay out the specific steps necessary to achieve them. Thus, planning has both a vision and a practical resource allocation component to it. Strategic planning is long term, and thus, it is normally the responsibility of the organization's upper management. Tactical plans implement the overall strategic direction, and so they are more limited in scope. They are typically drawn up by unit managers.

Cybersecurity planning is both strategic and tactical. Upper-level managers decide on the larger questions regarding scope, priority, and resource commitments. The unit managers create the explicit response. Planning is an iterative process in the sense that plans are tied to the organizational context and that context changes constantly because of the rapid pace of technology. Because they are meant to set the long-term course, strategic planning windows are normally in the 3- to 5-year timeframe. Tactical plans can be revised as the contextual environment changes. But at a minimum, these plans are revisited once a year.

Planning is generally scenario based. That is a logical and likely range of scenarios is developed and plans are developed for the ones with the highest likelihood and impact. Thus, one of the unique features of the planning process is the need for creativity and vision. Preparation of the necessary steps to assure the effective response for each of the target eventualities requires precise and detail-oriented assignment of tasks and alignment of the necessary resources. The creation of a timeline is an essential part of this process in that it allows planners to monitor and understand the ongoing success, or failure, of their plans to a given point. As well as how far they still need to go to achieve their planning objectives. As shown in Figure 9.9, the CSEC2017 calls out the two logical components of planning: (1) *Strategic planning* – the setting of long-term goals and directions, and (2) *Operational and tactical management* – the actions taken to achieve a set of planning goals.

Strategic Planning

Strategic planning defines the cybersecurity strategy. In conjunction with that process, it determines the direction and resources that will be allocated to achieve those goals. Thus, the strategic planning process links the technology, processes, resources, and information assets of the business to the overall aims of cybersecurity for that particular organization. Therefore, top-level decision makers define a coherent security strategy to explicitly perform information asset protection within the particular environmental context of the organization.

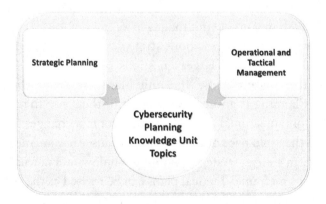

Figure 9.9 The Cybersecurity Planning knowledge unit topics.

There are seven universally desirable characteristics, called success factors, which a strategic planning process must embody. The first is effectiveness – in that the protection scheme should be planned in such a way that all information that is relevant and pertinent to a given business process is available in a timely, correct, consistent and usable manner. The second is efficiency – in that the information must be provided through optimum, competent, and economical practices. The third is confidentiality – in that sensitive information must be guaranteed protected from unauthorized disclosure, or access as well as tampering. The fourth is integrity – in that the accuracy and completeness of information as well as its validity must be assured. The fifth is availability – in that information must be available when required by the business process. The sixth is compliance – in that all information and information processing must comply with existing laws, regulations, and contractual. And finally, there is reliability – in that the information will support decision making sufficient for management to fulfill its fiscal and business responsibilities.

These qualities are operationalized through the formal strategic plan for the business. The plan explicitly documents and maintains a level of control sufficient to secure the organization. The outcome is a concrete cybersecurity plan, which is capable of maintaining a desired state of assurance for the organization. The required organizational structure, control policies, practices, and procedures must be specified in the strategic plan. These specific practices are developed to meet the desired level of effectiveness, efficiency, confidentially, integrity, availability, compliance, and reliability for the organization.

Operational and Tactical Management

Operational management plans link the cybersecurity strategy to the business purpose in the day-to-day setting. In that respect, operational management can be considered to be short-term and highly focused statements about what the cybersecurity function must do to further business goals at a given point in time. Operational management plans specify a concrete tactical behavior for every single strategic intention. In that respect, operational management planning specifies an explicit set of tactics for control of threats in the cybersecurity ecosystem. Each of the planned control behaviors must be tied to an identified requirement for cybersecurity protection for a given area of need. In addition, each of these control objectives must be directly traceable to the information asset it protects.

Finally, there must be some form of tangible specification of the approach that will be employed to implement each tactical objective, and each control objective must be tangibly evaluated. Therefore, the tactical behaviors must be expressed in precise measurement-driven terms. And they must be focused by priority on the protection targets that are most critical to the business process. Accordingly, measurement and prioritization become the means for determining if, or when, a process has been successfully completed.

Knowledge Unit Six: Business Continuity, Disaster Recovery, and Incident Management

Continuity and recovery embody the methods and techniques to ensure continuity. These are a logical extension of the general goals and assumptions that underlie the overall cybersecurity scheme. So, in many respects, continuity is just cybersecurity in depth. Where the body of knowledge for continuity differs from regular cybersecurity thinking is in its orientation. All other cybersecurity topics are focused on prevention and response. Continuity is oriented toward preserving business value after the fact. Nevertheless, continuity can be both proactive and reactive. Continuity seeks to ensure that, no matter what the cause is, the extent and effect of a shutdown are minimized. Thus, the continuity process has two primary goals: The first is to avoid the complete disruption of critical information services in the event of a disaster, and the second is to get information functions back in operation as quickly and efficiently as possible should one occur. As a consequence, most business continuity programs embody a range of concrete measures to either prevent or minimize damage from events that could be anticipated and restore operation in the shortest feasible time. To do this, continuity management targets the three basic components of any operation: systems, personnel, and facilities.

The continuity process entails the creation and use of various types of incident response, business continuity, disaster recovery plans, as well as the processes and situations where revisiting a plan is justified. The plans are all explicitly threat based. Therefore, the continuity planning process employs a continuous risk assessment to identify all of the credible threats to the operation. It then undertakes a formal prioritization and planning activity to decide which ones have to be addressed by a preparedness response and in what order of priority.

Since an active response is resource intensive, it is important to limit them only to events that are likely to occur and that will cause a great deal of harm. The likelihood estimate is almost always a matter of "best guess" since it involves too many factors to ensure an absolutely reliable estimate. However, if the planner focuses on developing a standard response to categories, or types of harmful events, it is possible to ensure an appropriate and effective response for a range of eventualities that might fall within a given group, some of which could seem quite unlikely. As shown in Figure 9.10, there are three subtopics in the Business Continuity, Disaster Recovery, and Incident Management knowledge area: (1) *Incident response* – planned process for responding to potentially harmful events, (2) *Disaster recovery* – planned process to restore operation following a harmful event, and (3) *Business continuity* – activities related to ensuring survival of the business operation.

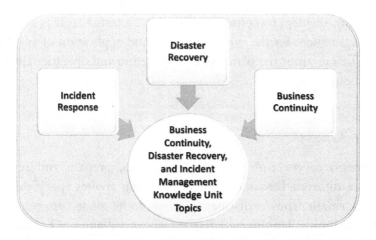

Figure 9.10 The Business Continuity, Disaster Recovery, and Incident Management Knowledge unit topics.

Incident Response

Incident response embodies actions taken to anticipate, detect, and mitigate the effects of an incident. Incident response planning is both a long-term and short-term perspective. In the long term, an effective incident response plan centers on anticipating incidents and ensuring the proper solution has already been developed. However, in order to do that properly, all potential risks and their likelihood have to be identified and categorized. Since anything could be possible, the actual feasibility of the risk is the key concept. So, there is a requirement to establish and maintain a balanced and realistic understanding of the threat. The assumptions that underlie this process are almost always based on selecting and adopting the most likely incident scenarios and then doing a regularly scheduled update of their feasibility.

Planners have to specify the precise steps that will be taken if a particular incident occurs. The events in that anticipated scenario have to be clearly understood, laid out, and cross-referenced to the recommended procedures. This is always based on an explicit plan, and it is implemented through clear and unambiguous instructions that are referenced to each individual circumstance. This normally involves assigning the staff responsible and the itemization of the roles and responsibilities of all of the participants. Incident management also encompasses the motivation and education of the executive managers and other stakeholders who will be specifically accountable for ensuring that the plan is updated and maintained.

Finally, incident response plans have to be tested. This is an absolute requirement for the implementation and application of any such plan. This requires the planners to both refine and operationally test their assumptions.

Disaster Recovery

Disaster recovery embodies the actions to, prepare and recover from, a disaster. Disaster recovery planning applies specifically to the aftermath. Thus, a distinction needs to be made between business continuity planning and disaster recovery planning. Essentially, disaster planners are focused on a narrower aspect of the continuity mission. They are specifically seeking to recover the information asset after an event has occurred rather than to prevent that occurrence in the first place. Their aim is to identify every feasible harmful contingency and then prepare specific mechanisms to respond effectively. The tangible representation of this thinking is captured in a disaster recovery plan.

As the term is used in the industry, the disaster recovery plan is usually oriented toward restoring the technical side of the operation. It typically aims to bring a specifically identified set of critical systems back up to a desired level of operation. This is normally based on the practical task of migrating damaged systems, or applications, to an alternate site after the disaster. Accordingly, the disaster recovery plan only comes into effect when a catastrophic event such as a major fire, or a natural disaster, denies access to normal processing facilities.

The goal of a disaster plan is to minimize loss of information and the interruption of work should a disaster occur. The types of disasters that must be planned for will vary based on the specific requirements of the situation and even things like geographic location. Therefore, one of the initial practical requirements is that all of the things that might happen should be listed. Then, this list has to be prioritized. A disaster recovery plan is necessary for all credible threats. Although the range of potential disasters might vary, as shown in Figure 9.11,

Figure 9.11   Elements of a disaster recovery plan.

the plans that address them always have the same three generic elements: (1) disaster impact description and classification, (2) response deployment and communication processes, and (3) escalation and reassessment procedures.

Disaster impact classification entails the understanding and description of the implications of the threat. Once the precise threats have all been identified and described and their likelihood of occurrence assessed, the preplanned response can then be described. Responses are always prepared in advance. These responses are generally based on assigned roles rather than fixed procedures. Finally, because all disasters involve the unknown, there have to be a defined set of escalation and reevaluation procedures. These are helpful if the situation turns out to be worse than anticipated or was not properly understood in the first place.

Business Continuity

Business continuity is based around an involved planning process. That process encompasses all of the strategies and operational measures to ensure that the organization will continue to survive in the event of a disaster. In essence, the continuity process entails the steps to be taken to react to a given disaster. It details a set of prescribed actions that must be taken through a preparedness plan. This plan itemizes the specific policies and procedures to prevent or minimize damage, as well as to secure, or recover. Likewise, it also details the precise mechanisms necessary to assure the continuous off-site transmittal and storage of information. Finally, it provides explicit processes for assigning and notifying key personnel who might be needed to immediately reestablish the operation.

Because of the importance of the business's information assets, that plan is always developed through a formal strategic planning process. In particular, it itemizes replacement or restoration procedures that will ensure the continuing integrity of the organization's information base. In its most basic form, the continuity plan lays out the steps that the organization will take to ensure that its critical functions are preserved. The information that is used to develop an effective continuity plan is obtained through the same threat identification and risk assessment process that establishes the overall assurance scheme.

That similarity of approach has to be kept in mind when the organization establishes cybersecurity processes.

Continuity plans embody two things: The first is a set of assumptions about the circumstances and the events that could affect them, and the second is a coherent strategy for maintaining continuity. Assumptions are based strictly on an understanding of the threats to the organization. This is a dynamic situation in the sense that the threat scenario is constantly changing and so the assumptions have to be periodically updated. As new risks emerge, assumptions have to be made about their impact on critical business functions. This could include the timing and extent of the threat as well as the areas of potential harm. In addition to the approach, the plan also specifies when, where, and how it applies and when it will terminate.

Knowledge Unit Seven: Security Program Management

The term "Security Program Management" describes the organizational function that underwrites due diligence in the assurance of the organization's information resources. Security Program Management consciously builds and sustains a rational structure of interorganizational behaviors that control and ensure the company's information assets. The business defines a coherent framework of explicit controls that embody all of the necessary behaviors to ensure reliable assurance.

The Security Program Management process includes large activities such as project integration, project scope management, project time and cost management, quality management, HR considerations, communications, risk management, and procurement management. Thus, it goes without saying that all of these actions must be fully coordinated. Coordination of complex work requires a common point of reference to benchmark performance against. That common point of reference is a formal set of security management best practices embodied in a formal, well-defined Security Program Management function.

As with any complex deployment, this can only be ensured through rational and explicit project planning. Strategic planning for the security program aims specifically at optimizing the effectiveness of the security function. Accordingly, the most straightforward approach to initiating the program management process is to do it from the top, as a comprehensively planned effort. The strategy will effectively describe how the security management program is instituted. Thus, the four large elements embodied in the CSEC2017 characterize a wide range of strategic functions, which are not stand-alone. Taken as a whole, they constitute the aggregate body of knowledge for security management. As shown in Figure 9.12, the four basic knowledge areas are as follows: (1) *Project management* – the principles and practices of managing security projects, (2) *Resource management* – the ability to effectively achieve a given objective, (3) *Security metrics* – the ability to monitor and make visible security performance, and (4) *Quality assurance and quality control* – the ability to assure adherence to best practice.

Project Management

Project management is the application of knowledge, skills, and techniques to shape project activities to meet security project requirements. There are five practical principles that underwrite the achievement of these goals. The organization can manage security-oriented projects by implementing the activities embodied in these five elements. The end result of this process is a coherent and fully integrated security response.

The first of these is scope. Scope establishes the boundaries of the solution. In day-to-day practice, this means that it must be possible

Figure 9.12   The Security Program Management knowledge unit topics.

to make an intelligent decision about the level of risk that can be accepted for the resources available.

The second principle is the assessment. This principle just signifies that the organization fully understands its security requirements. The end product of an assessment always describes all relevant threats and impacts.

The next principle is planning. The outcome of the planning process is a design that concretely addresses each issue identified in the risk assessment and that fulfills all known constraints.

The largest principle in terms of the actual time spent is integration. Its product is the actual, substantive security system.

The final concept is measurement. That function provides consistent monitoring to confirm that appropriate controls are in place and functioning properly. It ensures that confidence in a given security solution can be ensured through data.

Resource Management

Resource managers must know how to classify and make decisions about the level of criticality of each particular information asset and then be able to assign a level of resource commitment to be able to dependably assure it. Resource management planning is a necessary part of the overall security project because there are never enough resources to reliably secure every organizational asset. Therefore, it is essential for every organization to devise a process to systematically evaluate and prioritize the assets that it wishes to place in the protection scheme. This is the first step in developing the targeted protection plan for the organization as a whole. The CSEC2017 discusses ways to manage virtual assets. Most of these are standard economic analysis techniques, which employ performance metrics to customize the resource allocation.

The chief benefit of a resource management strategy is that it dictates the practical sequence for securing assets. As data are collected and refined, the organization will be able to improve its resource management effectiveness. This effectiveness sharpens its control over the security of the asset base. The eventual outcome of the resource management process is precise operational control over the day-to-day security of all of the major items in the information protection scheme.

Security Metrics

This topic includes the elements of security metrics, and how to design, develop, validate, and organize them. Metrics are used to characterize and communicate security program performance. Security management programs are based on the use of quantitative measures to characterize security system performance. This is an important aspect of ongoing security management, in that the ability to base management decisions on explicit data lets the organization evaluate the performance of its overall security operation as well as rationally assign accountability for the success of that operation as a whole.

Properly established and maintained, the security metrics program will allow managers to empirically assess the performance of the security function and bring deviations from expectations to the appropriate person's attention. This is ensured by regularized tests and reviews of each discrete operational element, at preplanned and mutually agreed on times. An effective security metrics program should exhibit three fundamental attributes. As shown in Figure 9.13, the three fundamental attributes are as follows: (1) factual, in that the values are directly observable versus inferred; (2) adaptable, in that the measures appropriately fit the circumstance; and (3) meaningful, in that the outcomes are fully understandable to all stakeholders. The rule for this is straightforward, whatever definition and measures that

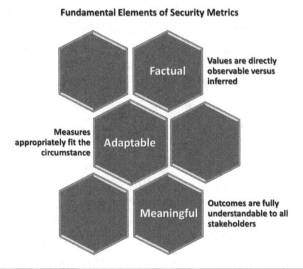

Figure 9.13   The fundamental attributes of security metrics.

are selected must be well defined and commonly accepted. If measurement data is properly classified and documented, it is possible to monitor and evaluate the overall security management process.

Quality Assurance and Quality Control

Realistically, it isn't possible to assure every artifact in the organization's security process. That is because many of the information assets and their protection controls are virtual. So, most of the quality control processes depend on a regularized assessment of a defined set of variables in the Organizational Security environment. This takes place at preplanned and mutually agreed-on points in the operational process. The unit that is responsible for fulfilling that role is normally termed "quality assurance."

The CSEC2017 quality assurance and quality control topic entails the approaches that are used to ensure organizational functioning. These are important topics in the CSEC2017 because a great degree of oversight is required in order to ensure a state of consistent and reliable security. The formal quality assurance process provides such a means. These practices are specifically derived from standard methods that are developed and implemented to increase the quality of any form of system performance. Thus, quality assurance and quality control are particularly important aspects of security management.

The purpose of quality assurance is to monitor the ongoing operation of the organization's security control functions for the purpose of assuring their ongoing correctness. This must be a formal part of organizational management. Therefore, quality assurance is always based on a strategy and a plan. That plan ensures that evidence of successful control performance is produced and maintained; problems and/or nonconformances are identified and recorded for remediation; and the adherence of products, processes, and activities to the specifications of any applicable best practices, procedures, and requirements is verified.

There are several organizational givens built into the quality assurance operation. The assurance mission entails monitoring and reporting on the performance of the operational process. In that respect, quality assurance inspects all of the qualitative and security plans for completeness. It also participates in design and operational inspections, reviews all test plans and test results, and audits the established security controls to insure compliance with all criteria. It is also responsible for registering nonconcurrence where a deviation is identified. Because of that responsibility, it also must embody an effective enforcement mechanism. A number of commonly accepted models for how to do this properly exist, e.g., ISO 27000 and FIPS 200. Those models become the organization's blueprint for maintaining a fundamental level of quality in the security operation.

Knowledge Unit Eight: Personnel Security

Personnel security entails formally established policies and procedures to assure the actions of the people within the organization. These policies and procedures define each individual's explicit responsibility for security, as well as their resulting accountabilities. Both responsibility and associated accountability have to be clearly stipulated to ensure that every individual knows their duties and obligations in the process. The overall success of the cybersecurity operation depends on the organization's ability to guarantee a minimum level of competency and commitment to those specified rules of behavior.

Consequently, the first step in the process of establishing control over the actions of employees is the development of personnel security policies based on known threats. In essence, to properly secure itself, every organization needs to make a conscious decision about the threats involving people and then prepare an appropriate strategy. This strategy has to take into consideration, as well as to prioritize, the control requirements for the personnel in the organization. In large corporations, this might amount to a major HR initiative. With smaller businesses, this might require nothing more than getting the necessary information to decide specific threats. In every case however, the role of personnel security is to put in place the concrete controls for every threat that has been identified.

Personnel security controls include such things as the steps to ensure that each business unit follows the required security procedures. However, they can also include such complex tasks as strategic planning to secure information assets. More importantly, personnel security also includes awareness and training processes to ensure that all employees in the organization are fully and completely cognizant of their specific duties and accountabilities. As shown in Figure 9.14,

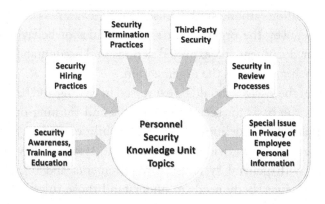

Figure 9.14 The Personnel Security knowledge unit topics.

the six common-sense topics in the personnel security area are as follows: (1) *Security awareness, training, and education* – ensuring the individual knowledge of duties and responsibilities, (2) *Security hiring practices* – ensuring trustworthiness of individuals brought into the organization, (3) *Security termination practices* – ensuring secure separation from the organization, (4) *Third-party security* – ensuring the reliability of outsiders while within the Organizational Security perimeter, (5) *Security in review processes* – ensuring the confidentiality of feedback to employees, and (6) *Special issue in privacy of employee personal information* – ensuring confidentiality of HR data.

Security Awareness, Training, and Education

The formal organizational awareness and training function is geared toward assuring that the employee is informed and competent. Once an individual has been hired, it is essential to provide sufficient security training to ensure that the employee complies with the stated policies, practices, and rules of behavior that apply to their position. For that reason, the training requirements themselves are frequently embedded in the position description. This is important from the standpoint of control because accountability depends on having a clear knowledge of the consequences of inappropriate behavior.

In addition to ensuring the capable performance of security tasks, the awareness, training, and education function also underwrites enforcement. This is no trivial matter, because the lack of adequate knowledge of policy and procedure is one of the primary causes of security violations among staff. Consequently, awareness and training programs convey the organization's formal rules of behavior. Rules of behavior document the expected actions and accountabilities that apply to each member of the organization.

The rules themselves should be expressed in writing and be available to serve as the basis for security awareness and training operations. They should clearly delineate the responsibilities and expectations for each and every individual who uses the system. They must be consistent with general system-use requirements and overall security policies. Everybody needs to understand those rules before they are allowed to access the organization's information assets. Potential awareness and training topics include physical security, desktop security, password security, wireless networks, security phishing, file sharing and copyright, browsing, encryption, insider threat, international travel, social networking, and social engineering.

Security Hiring Practices

Since HR is the unit that is responsible for the overall job assignment process, it would be logical for it to be responsible for the creation, implementation, and oversight of the security hiring function. That assignment makes sense, because the HR function documents and manages the rest of the company's numerous job categories, as well as general hiring and orienting new employees.

The assignment of access privileges is a joint activity involving both HR and IT. Logically, the entry point into the process of assigning security privileges to individuals is the job definition function. Job definitions are typically documented for all of the positions in the company. Therefore, the common-sense place to embed security requirements into the organization is at the point where all of the other relevant aspects of the job are defined. The security criteria adopted by the organization are the driving force behind the screening process. Background screening helps the organization confirm that the prospective employee fits the security requirements for a given position.

With sensitive positions, background checks could include an examination of the prospective employee's legal history, their financial and/or credit history, their medical history, their immigration and/or internal revenue service (IRS) records, and anecdotal observations about their overall business behavior. This level of examination is necessary because, besides the obvious reflection on their personal character, employees who have a personal vulnerability from their past are easy to compromise. So, it is important to ensure that people who hold sensitive positions are not susceptible to blackmail.

Security Termination Practices

Security termination practices ensure that privileges associated with any person who has left the company, for any reason, are revoked in as timely a fashion as possible. In that respect, there are two entirely different scenarios for that termination, namely, friendly termination and unfriendly termination. Because the situation is different in these two cases, the security response is also different. No matter what the cause is however, a carefully planned response is essential to assure the security of all company information in the case of termination of employment.

With a friendly termination, the employee is normally leaving the company under mutually acceptable terms. As employees follow their individual career paths, these types of terminations are common. Nonetheless, a disciplined process has to be followed to ensure that the employee transitions out of the company in a secure fashion. That is the case no matter how mutually satisfactory the conditions of separation might be. That disciplined process is built around a set of routine operational procedures that ensure the secure separation of outgoing or transferring employees. These procedures are usually established and supervised by the HR function.

In the case of a friendly termination, the purpose of the secure separation procedure is to ensure that user account privileges are removed from the system. This must be done in a timely manner. Any physical property that might contain company data must be secured. If the person separating from the company has had access to sensitive data, it might be necessary to obtain formal nondisclosure agreements as well as to secure all cryptographic material.

A different set of procedures apply when an employee leaves the organization under unfriendly circumstances. Unfriendly terminations are usually for some specific cause and involve a unilateral decision on the part of one of the parties. Since it might be ill-feeling, there is a much greater potential for mischief. Consequently, the company has to pay a lot more attention to the security implications. The procedures associated with unfriendly terminations are generally no different from those associated with friendly ones. However, with an unfriendly termination, each step has to be more judiciously executed. So, if the company has decided to fire an employee, access privileges should be removed at the time of the decision and the employee should not be allowed to access the system under any circumstances.

Third-Party Security

Organizations must establish an explicit set of rules to ensure the security behavior of contractors and outsourced work. These policies and procedures should ensure that contractors are following the same required security procedures as everybody else in the organization. In addition, they should guarantee the protection of assets accessed by contractors, either on the site or off the site. In most cases, contract employees have to have the same access to information as the regular employees who are doing the same type of work. However, contractors present a special problem in that they are not regular employees of the organization and may not have gone through the same screening and orientation processes. Consequently, access rights have to be narrowly and explicitly assigned in the case of contractors and then strictly overseen. That oversight includes formal and informal reviews and other explicit forms of control, such as policy management software, to ensure proper use and accountability.

Security in Review Processes

The overall success of the security function depends on the organization's ability to determine whether its people and processes are operating at the required level of effectiveness. Consequently, the regular review of the performance of all individuals is an essential part of good security practice. In particular, regular reviews to ensure the performance of the individuals responsible for the security process are especially necessary. Accordingly, a formal personnel review is the accepted mechanism for evaluating and controlling the performance of individuals in the organization. In a practical sense, these reviews require a clear set of observable criteria. The only feasible way to assess the actions of the individuals in the process is through the use of expert judgment.

The outcomes of the personnel security process are personally sensitive. Therefore, the findings for each person are treated as classified information. The criteria and process for assigning and ensuring confidentiality should be periodically reviewed for each category. The aim is to confirm that the individual's personal review findings are kept strictly confidential.

Special Issue in Privacy of Employee Personal Information

The organization holds personal data of others. The CSEC2017 raises this as a matter of principle. However, it also has legal and ethical implications. The organization is legally obligated to prevent unauthorized or harmful viewing or use of the data it holds. The security issue lies in whether it took reasonable care in protecting that information. If it is found that an organization did not practice due care, then the custodian of the data is legally liable for whatever damage ensues.

Still, legal is not the same as ethical. The ethical test is simpler. The failure to protect private information is always an infringement of ethical rights no matter what the finding of a court may be. People who work for or deal with a particular organization have the right to assume that the information that they provide will be kept confidential. Therefore, a breach of confidentiality violates this reasonable presumption.

Thus, the protection of the confidentiality of information, which is one of the prime directives within the field of cybersecurity in general, has both a security and an ethics character to it. And no matter what ambiguous concerns there may be with respect to the invasion of privacy represented by an unauthorized appropriation of information, the ethical obligation to ensure confidentiality is clear-cut and indisputable.

Knowledge Unit Nine: Security Operations

The origin and traceability of sourced system components is hard to establish, let alone assure. This is particularly difficult where complex technology, or development, and integration projects are involved. That is mainly due to the layers of complexity built into our global sourcing operations. This is especially the case given the fact that most products are integrated through a multilevel collection of suppliers who are often based offshore. Consequently, the importance of a formal, comprehensive, understanding of the activities and tasks that the communities of practice undertake is an essential part of cybersecurity knowledge.

Attacks can originate from any number of global sources. Most products, either developed or acquired, are managed through multi-layered, multi-vendor, and even multicultural team approaches. All the activity at every level in the process must be fully coordinated and controlled up and down the process to ensure trust in the eventual product. Coordination of multifaceted elements of work requires a commonly recognized and coherent model of control processes and activities. The aim of these processes is to fully encapsulate and relate the activities that a given set of, typically globally based, managers will utilize to understand the precise security status of any given product from initial design to final product integration, testing, and assurance.

The ever-increasing reliance on globally sourced hardware and software components leverages the importance of the assurance of trust. Still, the accelerating trend toward multinational approaches makes it almost impossible to utilize a given supplier's reputation, or even overall corporate ownership, as a basis for obtaining that assurance. That is the case because the construction of complex things involves a product tree that integrates parts from a diverse range of small suppliers to products of ever-increasing size and scope.

This tendency will obviously reduce any given organization's ability to understand and track the various components that make up a final product. Therefore, the specific purpose of this topic in the CSEC2017 is to call out the need for a working understanding of the factors that must be considered when developing a defense-in-breadth-and-depth solution. As shown in Figure 9.15, this includes two large areas of thought: (1) *Security convergence* – the growing tendency for holistic approaches to global cybersecurity work, and (2) *Global security operations centers* (GSOCs) – the formal combination of a range of security disciplines into a single organized response.

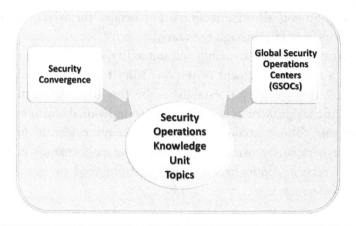

Figure 9.15   The Security Operations knowledge unit topics.

Security Convergence

Security convergence is a term that refers to a phenomenon that is long overdue. That is the merging of relevant personnel and physical security functions into the cybersecurity operation. In the past, physical security and information security were traditionally two separate operations. That is not a logical approach since information assets are embedded in tangible things and those things have to be protected from loss, theft, and damage.

We have already looked at the importance of personnel security. Still, physical security protects all of the physical assets that fall within the protected space in the cybersecurity scheme. In essence, the items in protected space represent the complete inventory of all of the assets that the organization needs to secure. The size of the protected space is typically dictated by the security resources that are available and the required level of protection. In that respect, it is essential to maintain a continuous understanding of the relationship between the physical items and the information they process, or store.

In essence, the value and importance of items of physical property is directly related to the information they contain or can access, and therefore, the contents of a physical device and its interconnections have to be known and continuously evaluated. This principle is holistic. It is implemented top-down throughout the organization and is applicable among all organizational partners. Otherwise, protected information can fall through the cracks.

Because of the need to assign accountability, it is also important to provide a specific statement of responsibility for all protected property. That responsibility is established by the organization through the specific assignment of security tasks to individuals, who are then accountable. Those accountabilities are always explicitly assigned in the cybersecurity plan. Subsequently, the performance of those assigned security duties is monitored and enforced to ensure their proper performance.

Global Security Operations Centers (GSOCs)

The concept of GSOCs is not new; however, they are becoming more and more common as the necessity to merge physical and virtual security operations becomes more in demand. GSOCs give a global organization the ability to have local situational awareness in far-off places, as well as do risk mitigation and real-time monitoring of events worldwide. A GSOC is able to determine the type, profile point of origin of a specific attack vector, and then disseminate that information to the other security operation centers. This makes the organization much capable of responding to local security situations as they occur.

GSOCs tend to be mergers of existing capabilities into a converged form. Factors such as the mission and global reach of the organization, as well as resource considerations, all apply to this process. If the GSOC is a new concept, it will generally have to be built from scratch in terms of the equipment and staff, and it all depends on the funding priorities of the organization. GSOCs not only monitor large things like strategic or geopolitical events, but also monitor such things as social media, looking for any approaching hazard. Consequently, when it comes to threat identification and mitigation, a GSCO gives the organization proactive capability, which implies that a properly organized GSOC could become a potential epicenter for all relevant security information. It will also underwrite ongoing improvement in the overall Organizational Security capability.

Forty Review Questions: Organizational Security

1. What is governance? How does it apply to Organizational Security?
2. Why is a holistic approach necessary? What happens if the solution isn't complete?
3. What is the role of strategy in Organizational Security? Why is it system oriented?
4. What is the best practice? How does it relate to creating sufficient management control?
5. What is the role of uncertainty in risk assessment?
6. Why is risk management considered to be a holistic process?
7. Why are assets cataloged prior to the risk assessment? Why is this essential?
8. What are the two factors in a risk assessment? Why is it essential to estimate them?
9. Why are insiders particularly risky? What specific threat do insiders represent?
10. Why is modeling an essential tool for risk measurement and evaluation?
11. What is the role of priority in risk control? Why is it necessary to prioritize risk?
12. What is the role of policy in security? Why are policy frameworks necessary?
13. Why must governance frameworks be tangible? What are they composed of?
14. How does context effect security? What are the relevant contextual factors?
15. How does privacy relate to organizational responsibility? What are the legal concerns?
16. Distinguish legal from ethical? Why is there a difference? How does it apply to security?
17. Why is executive-level communication a concern? How does it relate to security?
18. Relate managerial policy to best practice? How does one implement the other?
19. What is the role of data analytics in ensuring a substantively secure operation?

20. How does intelligence gathering play a part in ensuring Organizational Security?
21. What is the value of unified system administration? What does it curtail?
22. Distinguish network administration from cloud administration? What is the difference?
23. Why is the area of securing cyber-physical systems increasingly important?
24. What is an attack surface? How do you harden one?
25. How do you characterize availability? Why is it a factor in system administration?
26. Distinguish continuity from disaster planning? Why is there a difference?
27. Continuity is scenario based. Why are scenarios used? What do they capture?
28. Disaster planning is oriented toward the organization's systems. Why?
29. Distinguish strategic planning from tactical planning? Why is there a difference?
30. How are tactical plans linked to the business purpose? Why should that happen?
31. How are metrics used for resource monitoring and allocation? Provide an example?
32. Is quality assurance a process? If so, how is it structured and run?
33. Why is personnel security often overlooked? What is the role of HR?
34. Why is security awareness and training a critical factor in ensuring security?
35. What is the role of IT in security hiring? How does that relate to the HR function?
36. Distinguish friendly from unfriendly termination? Does that imply different approaches?
37. What is the role of review in personnel security? Why is review information sensitive?
38. Why is employee information sensitive? What is the consequence of losing it?

39. Distinguish cybersecurity from regular security? Why is cybersecurity so difficult?
40. What is the justification for convergence? Why are GSOCs useful tools to support this?

You Might Also Like to Read

- Baase, Sarah and Timothy M. Henry, *A Gift of Fire: Social, Legal, and Ethical Issues for Computing Technology*, 5th Edition, Pearson, London, 2017.
- Craig, Brian, *Cyberlaw: The Law of the Internet and Information Technology*, 1st Edition, Pearson, London, 2012.
- Fennelly, Lawrence J., *Effective Physical Security*, 5th Edition, Butterworth-Heinemann, Oxford, 2016.
- Halbozek, Edward and Gerald L. Kovacich, *The Manager's Handbook for Corporate Security: Establishing and Managing a Successful Assets Protection Program*, 2nd Edition, Butterworth-Heinemann, Oxford, 2017.
- Johnson, Brian and Patrick J. Ortmeier, *Introduction to Security: Operations and Management*, 5th Edition, Pearson, London, 2017.
- Kamata, Keisuke, *Introduction to Cybersecurity Management*, Amazon Digital Services, Seattle, WA, 2019.
- McCrie, Robert, *Security Operations Management*, 3rd Edition, Butterworth-Heinemann; Oxford, 2015.
- Spinello, Richard, *Cyberethics: Morality and Law in Cyberspace*, Jones & Bartlett Learning, Burlington, MA, 2016.
- Tyson, Dave, *Security Convergence: Managing Enterprise Security Risk*, 1st Edition Butterworth-Heinemann, Oxford, 2007.
- Watson, Scott, *The Art of War for Security Managers: Ten Steps to Enhancing Organizational Effectiveness*, 1st Edition, Butterworth-Heinemann, Oxford, 2007.

Additional Web Resources

- (GISS) exploring the most important cybersecurity issues facing organizations today.

www.ey.com/Publication/vwLUAssets/ey-global-information-security-survey-2018-19/$FILE/ey-global-information-security-survey-2018-19.pdf

- Privacy by Design Centre of Excellence Papers
- CERT's Podcast Series: Security for Business Leaders
  www.sei.cmu.edu/publications/podcasts/index.cfm
- Twenty Critical Controls for Effective Cyber Defense: Consensus Audit Guidelines
  https://www.sans.org/critical-security-controls
- Resource Center: Cyber-Risk Oversight
  www.nacdonline.org/insights/resource_center.cfm? ItemNumber=20789
- How Much Security Is Enough?
  https://resources.sei.cmu.edu/library/asset-view.cfm? assetid=295902
- 20 questions directors should ask about IT
  www.cpacanada.ca/en/business-and-accounting-resources/ other-general-business-topics/information-management-and-technology/publications/20-questions-on-information-technology
- Center for Cyber Security & Intelligence Studies
  http://liberalarts.udmercy.edu/academics/cis/center-for-cyber-intel-studies
- IWS – The Information Warfare Site
  www.iwar.org.uk/cip/
- The Psychology Behind Security
  The Psychology of Security – Schneier on Security

Chapter Summary

- Organizational Security involves the use of a set of policies and standard operating procedures that explicitly dictate how each of the other seven CSEC2017 knowledge areas interacts.
- Organizational Security represents the governance aspect of any cybersecurity operation.
- The big-picture understanding of the organizational threat and the development of strategies to respond to those threats is the valuable contribution of Organizational Security.

- The Organizational Security knowledge area embodies all of the necessary management roles, organizational behavior, and strategic policies necessary to underwrite organization-wide assurance.
- The requirement for a fully holistic organization-wide security process implies the need to adopt a systematic security management strategy that continuously aligns the security response to conditions as they appear in the threat environment.
- The organization must be both willing and able to define and enforce a substantive set of management controls that ensure all of the explicit security requirements.
- The integration of the entire set of Organizational Security knowledge units into a single substantive planned response ensures that every aspect of the threat is addressed in a holistic fashion.
- The Organizational Security knowledge area is composed of nine distinct areas of operation: (1) *Risk management* – identification, assessment, and mitigation of risk; (2) *Security governance and policy* – strategic policy and management; (3) *Analytical tools* – analytic support elements of the planning and management process; (4) *Systems administration* – practices for assuring optimum System Security performance; (5) *Cybersecurity planning* – strategic and operational planning; (6) *Business continuity, disaster recovery, and incident management* – concept and method; (7) *Security Program Management* – security governance operational practices; (8) *Personnel security* – behavioral control policy and application of practices; and (9) *Security operations* – operational security management practice.
- Risk management entails finding and controlling risks to organizational information assets. It is a formal process that is set up to protect an organization's assets from inadvertent, or deliberate, acts.
- Risk management is a holistic process in that it rationally deploys the complete set of controls necessary to prevent unauthorized use, loss, damage, disclosure, or modification of information assets.

- The outcome of a risk management process is a concrete, organization-wide risk management scheme.
- There are five subtopics of the Risk Management knowledge area: (1) *Risk identification* – cataloging risk, (2) *Risk assessment and analysis* – understanding risk, (3) *Insider threat* – dealing with risk from trusted individuals, (4) *Risk measurement and evaluation models and methodologies* – empirical analysis tools, and (5) *Risk control* – control measures to mitigate identified risk.
- Security governance and policy establishes a fully integrated and documented policy framework that ensures the confidentiality, integrity, and availability of the organization's information assets.
- Policies must be expressed in sufficient detail to ensure a tangible state of security across the workplace.
- Properly developed strategic policies will guarantee that there is a uniform control structure in place that reaches from the top of the organization all the way to the bottom.
- The Security Governance and Policy knowledge unit focuses on the elements of the security policy development life cycle, from initial research to implementation and maintenance to practical use.
- There are six subtopics in the Security Governance knowledge area: (1) *Organizational context* – factors effecting how security is implemented, (2) *Privacy* – cultural and organizational attitudes toward individual rights to confidentiality, (3) *Laws, ethics, and compliance* – legal and regulatory factors effecting cybersecurity, (4) *Security governance* – methods for managing the cybersecurity operation, (5) *Executive- and board-level communication* – methods for ensuring top-down accountability, and (6) *Managerial policy* – principles of explicit command and control in an organization.
- The Analytical Tools knowledge unit uses data analytics to recognize, block, divert, and respond to cyberattacks.
- There are three subtopics in the Analytical Tools knowledge area: (1) *Performance measurements (metrics)* – objective ways to judge the security program, (2) *Data analytics* – automated means of management control based on data analysis, and

(3) *Security intelligence* – threat reporting and data mining to support the security response.

- The Systems Administration knowledge area is focused on maintaining the secure performance of the information and communication technology system during its operational life cycle.
- The system administration process begins with a plan, but it also includes a requirement to select an appropriate set of explicit standards to guide the work.
- The system administration function does not imply construction; thus, the actual products or services it assures originate with external sources.
- The system administration process uses routine testing and evaluation procedures to demonstrate that system requirements are being met.
- There are seven subtopics in the System Administration knowledge area: (1) *Operating system administration* – activities related to operating system assurance, (2) *Database system administration* – activities related to database system assurance, (3) *Network administration* – activities related to network system assurance, (4) *Cloud administration* – activities related to cloud system assurance, (5) *Cyber-physical system administration* – activities related to SCADA assurance, (6) *System hardening* – concepts related to system reliability, and (7) *Availability* – concepts related to system access.
- Cybersecurity planning articulates the organization's strategic goals and tactical objectives and then lays out the specific steps necessary to achieve them.
- Strategic planning is long term, and thus, it is normally the responsibility of the organization's upper management.
- Tactical plans implement the overall strategic direction, and so they are more limited in scope. They are typically drawn up by unit managers.
- Because they are meant to set the long-term course, strategic planning windows are normally in the 3- to 5-year timeframe. Tactical plans can be revised as the contextual environment changes. But at a minimum, these plans are revisited once a year.

- Planning is generally scenario based. That is a logical and likely range of scenarios is developed and plans are developed for the ones with the highest likelihood and impact. Thus, one of the unique features of the planning process is the need for creativity and vision.
- The CSEC2017 calls out the two logical components of planning: (1) *Strategic planning* – the setting of long-term goals and directions, and (2) *Operational and tactical management* – the actions taken to achieve a set of planning goals.
- Business continuity, disaster recovery, and incident management entail the methods and techniques to ensure continuity.
- Continuity seeks to ensure that, no matter what the cause is, the extent and effect of a shutdown are minimized.
- The continuity process entails the creation and use of various types of incident response, business continuity, and disaster recovery plans. The plans are all explicitly threat based.
- There are three subtopics in the Business Continuity, Disaster Recovery, and Incident Management knowledge area: (1) *Incident response* – planned process for responding to potentially harmful events, (2) *Disaster recovery* – planned process to restore operation following a harmful event, and (3) *Business continuity* – activities related to ensuring survival of the business operation.
- Security Program Management consciously builds and sustains a rational structure of interorganizational behaviors that control and ensure the company's information assets.
- Strategic planning for the security program aims specifically at optimizing the effectiveness of the security function.
- Taken as a whole, they constitute the aggregate body of knowledge for security management. These four basic knowledge areas are as follows: (1) *Project management* – the principles and practices of managing security projects, (2) *Resource management* – the ability to effectively achieve a given objective, (3) *Security metrics* – the ability to monitor and make visible security performance, and (4) *Quality assurance and quality control* – the ability to assure adherence to best practice.

- Personnel security entails formally established policies and procedures to assure the actions of the people within the organization. These policies and procedures define each individual's explicit responsibility for security, as well as their resulting accountabilities.
- Both responsibility and associated accountability have to be clearly stipulated to ensure that every individual knows their duties and obligations in the process.
- The six common-sense topics in the Personnel Security area are as follows: (1) *Security awareness, training, and education* – ensuring the individual knowledge of duties and responsibilities, (2) *Security hiring practices* – ensuring trustworthiness of individuals brought into the organization, (3) *Security termination practices* – ensuring secure separation from the organization, (4) *Third-party security* – ensuring the reliability of outsiders while within the Organizational Security perimeter, (5) *Security in review processes* – ensuring the confidentiality of feedback to employees, and (6) *Special issue in privacy of employee personal information* – ensuring confidentiality of HR data.
- The ever-increasing reliance on globally sourced hardware and software components leverages the importance of the assurance of trust.
- Therefore, the specific purpose of this topic is to call out the need for a working understanding of the factors that must be considered when developing a defense-in-breadth-and-depth solution.
- That includes two large areas of thought: (1) *Security convergence* – the growing tendency for holistic approaches to global cybersecurity work, and (2) GSOC*s* – the formal combination of a range of security disciplines into a single organized response.

Learning Objectives for the Organizational Security Knowledge Area

Mastery of the requisite learning outcomes for the Organizational Security knowledge area will be established through the student's ability to paraphrase and explicate the key contents of the knowledge units within this knowledge area (Bloom Levels Two and Three). In addition, the student will exhibit specific behaviors that demonstrate the capability to utilize these relevant concepts in common practical application. Specifically, the student will be able to paraphrase and explain the following fifteen knowledge elements (CSEC, 2019):

1. Describe risk management and its role in the organization.
2. Describe risk management techniques to identify and prioritize risk factors for information assets and how risk is assessed.
3. Discuss the strategy options used to treat risk and be prepared to select from them when given background information.
4. Describe popular methodologies used in the industry to manage risk.
5. Discuss the importance, benefits, and desired outcomes of cybersecurity governance and how such a program would be implemented.
6. Describe information security policy and its role in a successful information security program.
7. Describe the major types of information security policy and the major components of each.
8. Explain what is necessary to develop, implement, and maintain the effective policy and what consequences the organization may face if it does not do so.
9. Differentiate between law and ethics.
10. Describe why ethical codes of conduct are important to cybersecurity professionals and their organizations.
11. Identify significant national and international laws that relate to cybersecurity.
12. Explain how organizations achieve compliance with national and international laws and regulations, and specific industry standards.
13. Explain strategic organizational planning for cybersecurity and its relationship to organization-wide and IT strategic planning.
14. Identify the key organizational stakeholders and their roles.
15. Describe the principal components of cybersecurity system implementation planning.

Keywords

Awareness – a sense that an idea or concept exists and has meaning to the individual

Behavior – individual personal actions performed that are observable by third parties

Code of Conduct – documented rules outlining expected behaviors for an organization

Compliance – authenticated actions that indicate that a requirement, rule, or law is followed

Controls – a discrete set of human, or electronic behaviors, set to produce a given outcome

Critical Asset – a function, or object, that is so central to an operation that it cannot be lost

Cybersecurity – assurance of confidentiality, integrity, and availability of information

Infrastructure – a collection of large components arrayed in a logical structure in order to accomplish a given purpose

Organizational Security – assurance of consistently correct security practice

Privacy – assurance that personally identifiable data is safeguarded from unauthorized access

Reliability – proven capability to perform a designated purpose over time

Strategic Planning – the process of developing long-term plans of action aimed at furthering and enhancing organizational goals

Tactical Planning – explicit actions aimed at achieving a particular objective

Third Party – additional participant in a process involving a user and a service

References

Joint Task Force (JTF) on Cybersecurity Education, "Cybersecurity Curricula 2017, Curriculum Guidelines for Post-Secondary Degree Programs in Cybersecurity, a Report in the Computing Curricula Series", ACM/IEEE-CS/AIS SIGSEC/IFIP WG 11.8, Version 1.0, 31 December 2019.

Nieles, Michael, Kelley Dempsey, and Victoria Yan Pillitteri, *An Introduction to Information Security*, NIST Special Publication 800-12 Revision 1, National Institute of Standards and Technology, Gaithersburg, MD, 2017.

Team ObserveIT, "Five Examples of Insider Threat-Caused Breaches that Illustrate the Scope of the Problem", 22 March 2018. www.observeit.com/blog/5-examples-of-insider-threat-caused-breaches/, accessed July 2019.

10
SOCIETAL SECURITY

In this chapter, you will learn the following:

- The relevance of Societal Security in the worldwide digital milieu
- The behavioral challenges that worldwide interconnectedness poses to our society
- The knowledge units of the Societal Security knowledge area
- The knowledge elements of the Cybercrime knowledge area
- The knowledge elements of the Cyber-legal knowledge area
- The knowledge elements of the Cyber-society knowledge area
- The knowledge elements of the Cyber Policy knowledge area
- The knowledge elements of the Societal Privacy knowledge area.

Security and Worldwide Connectivity

The anonymity of cyberspace makes it difficult to judge the correctness of human actions, and due to its virtuality, there is no clear basis for making that judgment. Thus, a stable and tangible point of reference must be available if society is ever going to understand and enforce acceptable individual and/or group behavior. This is the role of CSEC2017 Knowledge Area Seven, Societal Security.

Societal Security is the domain that explicitly characterizes and explores the overall implications of acceptable social behavior in the virtual world. In essence, this knowledge area focuses on the applicable concepts and relevant behavioral constructs that define and govern legal and ethical behavior in cyberspace. Such guidance is necessary in order to ensure productive citizen behavior in a virtual society.

Accordingly, the CSEC2017 Societal Security knowledge area focuses on various relevant societal factors as they influence the overall conduct of the residents of cyberspace. Societal issues are not topics that are usually called out within a cybersecurity curriculum. Therefore, the inclusion of this knowledge area is something of a departure from previous models of the field. Still, ensuring proper behavior of the citizenry of an interconnected universe is a critical factor in the assurance of reliable societal interaction. Therefore, societal issues are a fundamental consideration in the overall understanding of how cybersecurity impacts people's lives.

Virtual Behavior and Diversity

The inclusion of Societal Security in a curriculum is justified in that cyberspace is an impossibly diverse place where acceptable behavior is pretty much in the eye of the beholder. Consequently, knowledge of what constitutes correct legal and ethical behavior is a prerequisite in the development of a proper understanding of cyberspace, since issues are almost always ill-defined and highly relative. Accordingly, it is almost impossible to ensure a consistent understanding of the proper actions that individuals, or organizations, should take in a virtual and anonymous environment.

Practically speaking, cybersecurity students and practitioners must be able to both characterize and evaluate the common conventions, concepts, and concerns of human interactions in a virtual society. That requirement is particularly relevant in guiding our understanding of how virtual rules apply to the assurance of proper personal and professional conduct in people's day-to-day lives. In this respect, the true value of the Societal Security knowledge area is that it formally documents a complete set of overarching concepts, or ethical principles, that must be considered in deciding on the appropriate response to the inevitable legal and ethical challenges that pop up daily in virtual space.

The presence of a statement of formal principles allows individuals and corporations to formulate an ethical approach to virtual space, as well as to better control their subsequent behavior and interactions. In any conversation about something as abstract as ethics and law, it is important to have mutually agreed-on and well-defined principles at your disposal. These constitute a formal point of reference for judging correct behavior.

A point of reference is particularly necessary where decisions must be made about the appropriateness of individual and corporate conduct in society at large. That is because the understanding of what constitutes "social responsibility" is a very hazy notion in a milieu where the actual interactions are cybernetic and might include every single individual on the Internet. Thus, the common-sense requirement for responsibly managing all of the "squishiness" is something that every responsible individual and corporate entity might want to formally document. The process for formalization of those ethical principles and commitments implies the need for a logical set of implicit legal, ethical, and moral guidelines that are appropriate to real-world practice. That is the topic for discussion in the Societal Security section of the CSEC2017.

Three Large-Scale Security Concerns: Why We Need Societal Security

As we have alluded to many times, the contents of the CSEC2017 Societal Security knowledge area are a fundamental departure from how we normally educate cybersecurity professionals. Given the technological basis of the field, we tend to focus on the narrow electronic concerns. Of course, these are critical issues. But it is also a fact that, when it comes to cyberspace, the societal framework that we have employed to define whether the behavior is ethical or legally correct, is quaintly out of date. That's because cyberspace extends individual and institutional reach far beyond any physical horizon that was ever conceived of by traditional moralists and philosophers, not to mention any of the judgments captured in the precedents and principles of our legal system.

Since everything in computing happens in the anonymous virtual universe, people who use the computer can do unethical things insulated to some degree from any perception of responsibility for the consequences. In fact, in all but a pitiful few cases, nobody even knows anything has happened. Consequently, a thorough knowledge of the inner workings of the Internet will give a malicious user a more-or-less ironclad guarantee of invulnerability.

Thus, there are three major societal concerns where specific guidance about appropriate behavior is likely to be required: (1) legal and ethical considerations of property rights and personal privacy, (2) legal or regulatory considerations including what constitutes a crime, and (3)

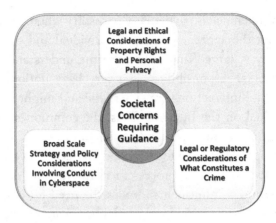

Figure 10.1 Societal concerns requiring guidance.

broad-scale strategy and policy considerations involving conduct in cyberspace (Figure 10.1). These concerns represent the foundation of the study of proper societal behavior, and the CSEC2017 presents and discusses them in a logical order.

The critical need for a concrete point of reference has to be kept in mind when attempting to understand the CSEC2017 Societal Security knowledge area. Cyberspace is dynamically changing and full of unique, often undiscovered challenges. Therefore, an explicit statement of acceptable societal conduct is put there to serve as an unambiguous landmark to ensure suitable formal decision making and adequate management control. For instance, an individual working at a credit reporting agency might arrive with a different perspective about something important, like how sensitive information ought to be handled. Reasonably then, the behavior of the employee must be realigned with organizational ethical norms in order to ensure the integrity and confidentiality of the credit information as the organization views it, which also implies that the organization has already defined an explicit enforcement mechanism, which can be utilized to ensure sufficient realignment is effectively accomplished. If that has been done, a process can be followed to either ensure the reconciliation of that difference or terminate the employee. If no point of reference is available, there is no basis for control.

Finally, it must be remembered that an organization's societal culture embodies its common norms and all groups are different. Therefore, there is no such thing as a universally valid set of behaviors. That is the reason why the underlying group norms for every organization need to be fully and completely documented. That clear statement of norms is necessary in order to understand the behavior that a particular group believes is correct. For instance, it is very likely that the acceptable use policy for the hacker community will be considerably different from the acceptable use policy for the Business Software Alliance. Although the legitimacy of the former group's behavior might be questionable, that behavior is nonetheless the accepted norm for that group. Therefore, it is important to understand what that group considers to be correct in order to understand and judge its behavior.

The CSEC2017 and the Profession

Perhaps the first and most important purpose of the elements of the CSEC2017 Societal Security knowledge area is to formally codify what should be expected in a capable cybersecurity curriculum. In essence, the individual units in the CSEC2017 specify the knowledge and requisite behavior required to comprehensively educate students about the societal duties and obligations of a cybersecurity professional. That formal specification of a minimum level of knowledge serves to create a basic statement of professional performance that can be used to develop targeted courses and teaching material. The Societal Security knowledge area describes a floor level of ethical decision making that a reasonable person should expect from a cybersecurity professional under a specified set of circumstances. Therefore, the knowledge units in this area apply to the role requirements of the profession as well as the circumstances in which those competencies apply.

The role that the CSEC2017 plays in the formalization of professional expectations has been a theme throughout this text. The point with all of that discussion has been that the requirement for a reliable frame of reference has been recognized with the CSEC2017 and the problem has been responded to in the form of asset of structured curriculum topics. The specification of societal competencies within such a curricular framework is a particularly novel and important aspect of this process. The contents of this chapter lay down the minimum expectations about how professionals should behave in light of radical changes to our conventional social structure.

This specification goes directly to the establishment of cybersecurity as a true profession, in that it formalizes the criteria for social responsibility when performing cybersecurity work.

The CSEC2017 Societal Security knowledge area establishes the minimum commonly agreed-on areas of societal concern. These areas are generally associated with the legal and ethical performance of cybersecurity work, especially as regards privacy. Knowing those areas and their associated performance criteria are is an important next step in creating an educated professional workforce because up until now, people working in the field have not been subject to any definitive form of requirement for understanding the big picture.

A vague set of general expectations for managerial vision and leadership has always been part of the mythology of the profession, and there have always been commercial certifications that attest to a particular set of acquired skills in the traditional areas of the field. But up till now, there has been no formal mechanism for evaluating the large-scale strategic policy knowledge and abilities of professional workers in the cybersecurity domain. Consequently, there has never been any assurance that the education process will ever be able to see past the machine in order to help students understand the long-term impact of their actions on the society that they serve.

This might be the single most important implication of the Societal Security knowledge area. This area builds a formal basis for trust in the actions of the profession. It's a fact that, even though the belief exists among members of the public that cybersecurity practitioners bring an elevated level of knowledge, skill, and ability to any problem involving information protection, there is no actual assurance that cybersecurity workers understand anything more than the problems associated with their particular area of expertise. For example, it would be nice to think that network security managers understand the basics of privacy law and regulation and where they apply. But there is no formal assurance that these individuals know anything more about those issues than the average person in the street. Thus, there is no formal attestation that your network manager knows, or even cares about, the preservation of the privacy of your personal information. And in that respect, the ordinary stakeholder has no guarantee that their trust in the fundamental professional capabilities of that manager has not been misplaced.

As the Internet continues to grow and more and more human interaction becomes computerized, the problems discussed here will increase in importance. Consequently, a universal education process that is aimed at ensuring proper and correct societal conduct is the right and proper thing to do to advance the profession.

The CSEC2017 Societal Security Knowledge Units

As the name implies, the Societal Security domain encompasses five large-scale constructs that incorporate ideas that broadly impact society as a whole. The aim of the knowledge elements in the Societal Security domain is to document and clarify the interrelationship of each of the relevant facets of ordinary human social interaction as they apply to the assurance of proper virtual citizenship. Thus, the areas that fall under the purview of Societal Security comprise the usual list of suspects That list includes such obviously relevant societal functions as crime, law and the legal space, applicable ethical considerations, and the elements of social policy as they apply to the assurance of security and privacy. As shown in Figure 10.2, the areas are as follows:

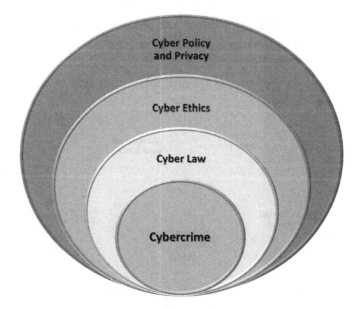

Figure 10.2 The Societal Security knowledge units.

1. *Cybercrime* – all forms of criminal behavior in cyberspace
2. *Cyber law* – the current and emerging framework of laws and regulations governing cyberspace
3. *Cyber ethics* – fundamental principles that underlie and motivate communal good behavior
4. *Cyber policy* – strategic decision making with respect to socially acceptable corporate directions
5. *Privacy* – assurance of a fundamental right to personal privacy in virtual space.

Knowledge Unit One: Cybercrime

This knowledge unit provides students with an understanding of the scope, cost, and legal issues relating to cyber-based criminal activity. Cybercrime has grown in importance as the computer has become central to commerce, entertainment, and government. As we learned in the first chapter, the current cost of cybercrime approaches $3 trillion worldwide and that is expected to double, or triple, in the next 3 years (Microsoft, 2018). So needless to say, cybercrime is a critical issue (Figure 10.3).

In broad terms, cybercrime simply involves the use of a computer to perpetrate an illegal act. The most common examples of this are Internet fraud, personal property and identity theft, child pornography, or statutory privacy violations. But it can also embrace such complex criminal activity as corporate tax evasion and stock manipulation. At one end of the continuum are crimes that involve a basic

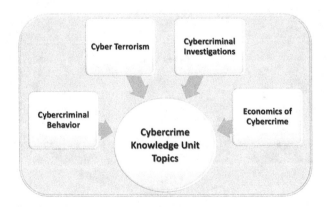

Figure 10.3 The Cybercrime knowledge unit topics.

violation of personal or corporate privacy, which includes such acts as simple theft of information, forms of blackmail, such as ransomware, or real acts of sabotage.

The most ubiquitous example of this kind of crime is the rapidly growing problem of digital identity theft. These are more conventional crimes in that they impact specific victims.

Then, there are the transaction-based crimes such as cyber-fraud and deception, digital piracy, money laundering, and the various types of digital counterfeiting. These are organizational, or corporate, in nature in that they are typically perpetrated for financial gain. Finally, there are those crimes that involve actual attempts at wides-cale, or strategic, disruption. These range from targeted hacking and denial-of-service attacks to intentional acts of cyberterrorism either by state or by nonstate actors.

Cybercrime usually doesn't affect physical things per se. Instead, it impacts a virtual aspect of a person or an organization, which usually amounts to stealing or compromising an electronic asset that belongs to that person, or institution. Because cyberspace is not limited to national boundaries, the potential for criminal activity inevitably encompasses all of the residents of the Internet. Hence, cybercriminals are not jurisdictionally restricted.

The most common type of cybercriminal is the hacker. In fact, the term "hacker" has become a catchall phrase for any person who violates the security of a computer, or its information. A hacker is an outsider who seeks to intrude on protected space in order to perform some illegal act. Hackers seek unauthorized access to computer systems through various electronic and physical subterfuges. Although the common perception is that all hacking attempts are electronic in nature, the actual loss of data indicates that modern cybercriminal attacks tend to also be physical and human-centered exploits. The crimes associated with hackers can range in severity from simple trespass through serious acts that corrupt or destroy data.

Cybercriminal Behavior

This knowledge unit examines the behavioral impetuses of the individuals, or groups, who perpetrate a cybercrime. There are five generic "incentives" that might lead a criminal to attack your system:

(1) curiosity or recreational attacks, (2) business or financial attacks, (3) grudge attacks, (4) intelligence attacks, and (5) military or terrorist attacks. These reasons obviously span the gamut of cybercriminal behavior. However, the general motivation factors are commonly classified into eight behavioral signatures, or methods of operation (MOs), which are as follows (Figure 10.4):

1. *Ego*: behavior motivated by an inflated sense of pride, or individual superiority to others
2. *Exposure*: behavior meant to reveal information that the owner does not want to be revealed
3. *Deviance*: abnormal behavior, not fitting society's norms and therefore unacceptable
4. *Monetary gain*: behavior designed to obtain money, which motivates targeted crimes
5. *Extortion*: behavior intended to force the victim to unwillingly do something

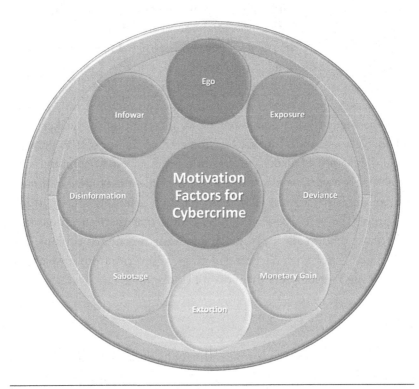

Figure 10.4 Motivation factors for cybercrime.

6. *Sabotage*: behavior intended to damage or destroy the credibility of a resource

7. *Disinformation*: behavior intended to achieve a dishonest purpose by spreading lies

8. *Infowar*: behaviors conducted to achieve a national or organizational purpose.

The motivations and general goals can be aggregated into criminal profiles. Thus, it is possible to describe at least 12 distinct behavioral profiles in the cybercriminal population.

1. *Script Kiddies*: Kiddies use programmed scripts. Their intent is trespass, and their motivation is ego. Because they do not know what they are doing, they can be very destructive.

2. *Cyber-Punks*: Cyber-punks are the counterculture and are ego-driven. The motive is exposure. Cyber-punks target establishment organizations, companies, and products.

3. *Old-Timers*: Old-timers are perhaps the most technologically proficient members of the hacker community. They are ego-driven and relatively harmless.

4. *Code Warriors*: Code warriors are the first of the more aggressive profiles. Their crimes are built around code exploits. They are driven by ego or revenge or monetary gain.

5. *Cyber Thief*: Their motive is always monetary. This profile uses tools. They are also adept at social engineering. This is the first profile that could be part of an organization.

6. *Cyber Huckster*: Cyber hucksters are the general purveyors of malware. Their motive is commercialization. They are adept at social engineering. They also use spoofing.

7. *Unhappy Insider*: The unhappy insider is dangerous because they are authorized to access the organization's information. Their distinctive characteristic is unhappiness with the organization.

8. *Ex-Insiders*: Ex-insiders are unfriendly terminations. Their motive is extortion, revenge, sabotage, or disinformation. They are focused on harming organizations that fired them.

9. *Cyber-Stalkers*: Cyber-stalkers are motivated by deviance. This profile is different from the other ego-driven profiles by the fact that they are driven by a psychological craving.

10. *Conman*: This category is motivated by simple monetary gain. They are adept at social engineering. This group runs traditional cons, as well as newer exploits like phishing.

11. *The Soldier*: This is organized crime's entry into the field of cybercrime. It is differentiated from all of the other categories by its high level of determination and skill.

12. *Warfighter*: This is not a criminal type when it is fighting on your side. However, when the warfighters are on the other side, their actions would be viewed as destructive.

Cyberterrorism

This knowledge unit is significant due to society's growing dependency on digital technology. Because much of our infrastructure is powered by computers, cyberspace can be utilized in such a way that it is possible to bring about mass panic, or fear, in a population. Thus, any use of the computer to cause significant harm for personal ideological reasons, such as political motivations, could also be considered cyberterrorism.

The term "cyberterrorism" is somewhat slippery since, in the broadest sense, any act of widespread sabotage, for instance, a denial of service, might be interpreted as "terrorism." That would include any act that falls under the general rubric of "cybercrime." So conventionally, in order for an incident to be considered "terrorist," the purpose of the attack must only be to create a perception of fear, intimidation, or disruption.

The Internet allows groups driven by political or ideological motives to conduct asymmetric attacks on large chunks of a target population, and these attacks carry the potential for large-scale destruction, or loss of life. Therefore, such a cyber-based attack allows any country or nonstate group to anonymously, and comparatively inexpensively, enforce their personal agenda. The aim of these attacks is to achieve a particular purpose through widespread threat and intimidation. And in the Clausewitzian sense, this is the definition of war.

Virtual terrorist attacks are appealing to every second-rate power and small group actor because they do not require huge investments in military hardware in order to create havoc. Thus, they, in effect, "even the playing field." , because of the potential for massive amounts of harm and the concept of cyberterrorism is on the top of the priority list for state and federal agencies in this country. Moreover, the importance of cyberterrorism is expected to increase as the Internet becomes more diversified into areas like the Internet of Things (IoT). Accordingly, cyberterrorism is a particularly important conversation to have in any cybersecurity curriculum.

Cybercriminal Investigation

This area encompasses all of the standard methods for investigating cyberattacks, which includes investigations of individuals, organizations, overseas actors, nation-state adversaries, and terrorists. At its core, the actual practice of cybercriminal investigation is an individualistic exercise that is no different than the deductive exploits of Sherlock Holmes. From a curricular standpoint, cybercriminal investigation requires a mix of skills which, on the surface, might not intuitively relate to each other. For instance, intimate knowledge of how electronic data is represented and manipulated is required. However, it is also essential to have a lawyer's command of legal procedure and the investigative skills of a trained police detective.

Moreover, strict deterministic rules do not apply to the collection of legal evidence, because that evidence resides in a diverse and highly dynamic virtual environment. So, in most cases, the abilities of the practitioner and the appropriate use of tools typically determine the success of an investigative exercise. However, there are some basic principles that must be included in every curriculum. These principles define the elements and sequence of a cybercriminal investigation process. In order to perform a proper cybercriminal investigation, three generic, sequential activities have to be performed: (1) evidence collection, (2) evidence retrieval and analysis, and (3) forensic reporting.

The practices in a cybersecurity investigation curriculum have to support critical forensic functions such as data collection after criminal acts, data collection in support of civil proceedings, and data collection in response to internal investigations. It is very important that the forensic staff is trained to execute these properly. The requirement for intensive detail in the forensic work must be part of the design of a curriculum in cybercriminal investigation.

Finally, scientific analysis cannot always determine what was accessed, taken, or harmed. This investigative element is a particularly unique condition of virtual information, which is because virtual information is one of the few things that can be taken or tampered with without any physical sign that anything has happened. For instance, things would clearly be missing after a robbery in the physical world. However, information can be stolen without any obvious sign that it has ever been accessed. Since it is hard to even tell what items have been affected, the exact focus of the investigation has to be specified in advance in order to narrow down the items that have to be considered.

Economics of Cybercrime

As we said in Chapter 1, cybercrime is profitable. In fact, it is the most profitable form of crime; they are far exceeding the profits of the drug trade and other more conventional ways of making money illegally. This is mainly due to two things: First, information is virtual. Therefore, it can be easily stolen, transported, and sold without any of the conventional problems associated with physical theft. Second, law enforcement always runs into jurisdictional issues in a worldwide milieu like the Internet.

The average cost of a cyberattack now exceeds $1 million (Radware, 2019). The top economic impact of cyberattacks is operational/productivity loss (54%), followed by negative customer experience (43%). What's more, almost half of the respondents (45%) reported service disruption. Another third (35%) said the goal was data theft (Radware, 2019). Most organizations have experienced some type of attack within the course of a year, with only 7% of respondents claiming not to have experienced an attack at all. Twenty-one percent reported daily attacks, representing a significant rise from 13% last year (Radware, 2019). However, 78% of respondents hit by a cyberattack experienced service degradation or a complete outage, compared to 68% last year (Radware, 2019). So, the economic implications of cybercrime are an important motivating issue for the study of cybersecurity.

Nowhere is that more evident than in the rise of an entirely virtual culture, where lawlessness and criminality have a place to hide. That is the Dark Web. The Dark Web should not be confused with the Deep Web. The latter is simply the 96% of the Internet that has not been indexed by the spiders of the various search engines. The presence of all of that unexplored territory is intimidating in-and-of-itself. But the Dark net on the Dark Web enables fully anonymous transactions that are not visible to anybody outside that particular peer-to-peer connection. This guaranteed anonymity creates fertile ground for crime.

The criminal behavior is enabled by the availability of cryptocurrencies such as bitcoin. These cryptocurrencies underwrite the purchase of any illicit thing from child pornography, to a professional hitman. That economy has encouraged the establishment of commercial Dark net markets, which function primarily as sellers, or brokers, of every illegal commodity from drugs, to guns, to stolen credit cards and forged documents. So, in essence, the Internet has its "bad side of town."

The economics of this phenomenon has actually been studied in a way similar to the research examinations of the legitimate stock market. Since the place is by definition surreptitious, very little is known about the details of the Dark Web and its contents. But cybersecurity professionals need to be educated in their nuances in order to be considered fully capable. Therefore, CSEC2017's inclusion of content on the topic of cybercrime economics indicates how forward thinking it is.

Knowledge Unit Two: Cyber Law

The Cyber Law knowledge unit is intended to help students understand the basic elements of law in cyberspace. In a discussion about something as abstract as the law and legal systems, it is important to provide a definition of what that the term "law" implies. Laws are explicitly stated and have specific enforcement mechanisms and sanctions built into their structure. Because there is not a lot of precedent in cyber-based legal cases, the specific understanding of what constitutes a violation is not well defined by U.S. law. This particularly applies to the relevant international implications (Figure 10.5).

The comprehensive understanding of law in cyberspace is important because the policies that shape the substantive cybersecurity process of any organization must be developed in light of existing regulations

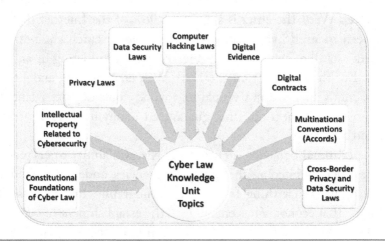

Figure 10.5   The Cyber Law knowledge unit topics.

and laws. Legal systems are prescriptive and oriented toward the enforcement of defined standards of behavior. Most of the laws that have been passed so far as they apply to cyberspace have to do with protecting privacy or regulating commercial transactions using computers. They all have something of a governmental and bureaucratic focus. They can be classified into five generic categories.

1. Governmental regulations
2. Privacy regulations
3. Laws that regulate intellectual property rights
4. Contract and tort law
5. Laws that regulate computer crime.

Because each of these entails different compliance requirements, the CSEC2017 deals with each of these separately (Figure 10.6).

Constitutional Foundations of Cyber Law

Legally, individuals have the right to control some, but not all, of their information. This is based on precedents that have evolved over the past 50 years. However, these are all derived from the first and most concrete directive that was provided to support the confidentiality of individual information. That is the Bill of Rights to the U.S. Constitution (1791). The Fourth Amendment explicitly guarantees individual protection against unreasonable search and seizure. It is a

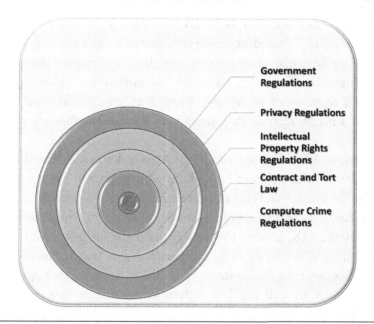

Government
Regulations

Privacy Regulations

Intellectual
Property Rights
Regulations

Contract and Tort
Law

Computer Crime
Regulations

Figure 10.6 Five categories of cyber law.

common myth that this Amendment offers an explicit guarantee of a right to privacy. Still, there are several privacy laws that are relevant to cyber law that derive directly from that Amendment.

The first of these is the Freedom of Information Act (FOIA). The FOIA (5 U.S.C. 552 Public Law 890554) enacted in 1966 actually provides the first electronic age protections. Prior to the passage of this Act, the burden of proof was placed on the individual if they wanted to see records that the government might have about them. Under FOIA, the burden of proof shifted to the government and the "need to know" standard was replaced with a "right to know." Specifically, the FOIA guarantees access to the documents that are held by agencies in the Executive Branch including all cabinet departments.

FOIA requires that federal agencies must provide the fullest possible disclosure of information to the public. It sets standards for determining which records should be made available for public inspection and which records can be withheld from disclosure. It provides administrative and judicial remedies for those denied access to records. The records that can be requested under the FOIA include all records of a federal agency.

In 1986, amendments to FOIA gave agencies some authority to deny access to a record or refuse to confirm its existence. There are three specific instances where this applies: First, there are the records that might interfere with an active law enforcement investigation. Second, records can be denied if they are from confidential informants. Finally, records that pertain to foreign intelligence can be withheld.

Then, in 1974, Public Law 93-579 better known as the "Privacy Act" defined the rights of individuals with respect to the computerized information that is kept about them. This Act is the first instance of the omnibus regulation of electronic information. The Privacy Act requires the U.S. government to safeguard the integrity, confidentiality, and availability of all of the personal data that is processed by federal agency computer systems. In addition, agencies are required to provide ways for individuals to determine what information is being recorded about them, and it mandates that there must be a way to correct inaccuracies.

The purpose of the Privacy Act was to safeguard individuals from invasions of privacy by the federal government. It did this by regulating to some extent the way the government collects, maintains, uses, and disseminates personal information. This Act essentially ensures that the collection, maintenance, use, or dissemination of information is for a necessary and lawful purpose. It gives individual citizens the right to see what computerized records are kept about them as well as to modify that information if it is not correct. It prevents personal records from being used for purposes other than those that were intended or where the owner did not provide express consent.

All federal agencies and, by implication, any agency engaged in interstate commerce, such as an Internet Service Provider (ISP), are subject to legal damages from willful or intentional acts that violate an individual's rights under this Act. The Act was further expanded by the Right of Financial Privacy Act (1978). It establishes that a depositor's bank accounts are private and can only be accessed by court order and due and proper notification. The Electronic Funds Transfer Act (1979) that followed it then specifically safeguarded the privacy of transmissions related to funds using electronic funds transfer (EFT).

The Electronic Communications Privacy Act of 1986 (Public Law 99-508, 18 U.S.C. 2510) supplemented this and offers a single clear statement of the rights of individuals with respect to electronic information. It expressly prohibits the unauthorized interception of communications regardless of how the transmission took place. This was extended to include the transmission that was made through a wide range of common media.

This Act was passed because the actions of law enforcement agencies had wandered too far afield in the electronic surveillance of various organized crime figures. It makes it illegal for governmental agency to intercept telecommunications, such as EFTs and electronic mail, without prior authorization. This Act specifically defines which transmissions are protected and which ones are not. It mandates that public electronic communication providers, such as ISPs, may not give the contents of the messages that they transmit to anyone but the sender and the addressee.

The Privacy Act was further amended by U.S. Code 552a (1988), which is entitled the Computer Matching and Privacy Protection Act. The Act requires that federal agencies must follow certain specified procedures in the way that they transmit information between agencies. If an individual can prove that a federal agency intentionally or willfully violated the provisions of this regulation, they can recover monetary damages, and if it can be demonstrated that that disclosure was deliberate, the fine can be substantial.

This Act is significant because its passage served to raise the overall awareness of the potential for government misuse of the growing body of personal information collected on computers. When it passed the Act, Congress was particularly concerned about the increasing use of computers and sophisticated information technology to acquire and analyze information. This law places explicit limits on how federal agencies can develop supplemental information on citizens through matching computer data from various separate databases.

Intellectual Property Related to Cybersecurity

The CSEC2017 Cyber Law knowledge area specifically states that it is important to help students understand the scope, cost, and legal environment associated with cyber-based intellectual property theft. Thus, there is a strong emphasis on intellectual property rights both legal and ethical in the CSEC2017 model. The theft of intellectual property can involve everything from plagiarism to outright pilfering of other people's products or ideas. Still, because intellectual property is transmitted and stored in the unconstrained world of the Internet, it is almost impossible to protect.

The legal issue with respect to litigating intellectual property theft revolves around the concept of intangible property. Real property has substance and obvious worth. It can be seen and counted. Therefore, it is possible to assign a clear value in a court of law. Intellectual property is abstract, so its value is strictly in the eye of the beholder. Thus, because it is hard to value the contents of intellectual property, the legal process is complicated. So, the best hope for preventing intellectual property violations is an established law or legal precedent to enforce penalties for infringements. In that respect, the most important step in addressing the theft of intellectual property might be increasing the awareness in the minds of lawmakers and the legal system that intangible products have tangible value.

Three general conditions are necessary to leverage general awareness: First, there has to be an understanding within the legal community that item of intellectual property represents an investment by the individual of their time, which has monetary worth. More importantly, because it is intangible, there has to be some means, particularly when it comes to the Internet, of designating ownership. Finally, there has to be a mechanism to guarantee and enforce the right of possession. The latter is obviously the key to implementing effective control of the intellectual property. But it has yet to be put into practice. The only instance where there has been a well-organized effort is in the case of software piracy, which is because piracy represents a monumental drain on the profits of the software industry.

Intellectual property protection in cyberspace specifically applies to software piracy. The deliberate act of stealing software is called piracy. Legally, computer programs are copyrighted works. They do not have to be registered with the U.S. Copyright Office for that to be enforceable. So, when you "buy" software, you don't buy the copyright. What you buy is a license to use it. Accordingly, you must be able to produce valid proof, which in the form of that license, to demonstrate that all of the copyrighted software that you are running has been legally acquired.

Piracy is a worldwide problem because computer programs are so easy to copy. According to the Business Software Alliance, about 23% of the software used in the United States is pirated (BSA, 2018). The problem is much more serious overseas. For instance, the estimated piracy rate in China was 66% and in Russia was 62%, with a business value of $1.3 billion (BSA, 2018). The rate in Eastern Europe was around 55%, while the rates in the rest of the world followed the same general trend. As a result, the software industry estimates that it loses upward of $10 billion per year to piracy (BSA, 2018).

Privacy Laws

Because the legal consequences can be severe, a prudent organization will try to anticipate the litigation that possession and handling of private and personal information represents. This is typically done by instituting routine assurance procedures. However, in addition to the general risk, there are also a number of actual laws that affect privacy. Compliance with these has to be factored into the equation. Many of them have to do with defining the rights of individuals to the assurance of confidentiality. Violations of these can lead to specific penalties, so their dictates have to be understood.

Technology creates serious problems when it comes to privacy. That is because technology has consistently advanced at a rate that exceeds society's ability to decide about its suitability. As a result, there is no formal guidance about where to draw the line between legal and illegal. For example, many third-party cookies are spyware. They are placed on a system via surreptitious means, to gather data without the owner's consent.

There would probably be plenty of outrage if the average person understood that the purpose of third-party cookies is to track Internet usage without individual consent. However, that is not against the law. Thus, the general problem with cyber law is that most people do not understand, or even know about, the specific implications of such violations. Moreover, because the technology continues to evolve faster than society and can develop the needed awareness and understanding, many more gray areas of this type are likely to develop.

Data Security Law

In general, the legal framework for data protection in the United States is ad hoc; highly regulated industries like healthcare and finance have rather robust laws that protect the data they hold. For instance, Title II of The Health Insurance Portability and Accountability Act (HIPAA) establishes policies and procedures for maintaining the privacy and security of personally identifiable health information (PII), HIPAA gives individuals the right to request a covered entity to correct any inaccurate PII, and it requires the holders of that data to take reasonable steps its confidentiality. In that respect, it establishes civil and criminal penalties for violations.

The financial sector is regulated by Gramm-Leach-Bliley (G-L-B) (1999). That law governs the collection, disclosure, and protection of consumers' nonpublic personal information or PII held by financial institutions. G-L-B compliance is mandatory whether a financial institution discloses nonpublic information or not; there must be a policy in place to protect the information from foreseeable threats in security and data integrity. However, general data protection in the United States is currently regulated on a state-by-state basis. The California Consumer Privacy Act of 2018 is perhaps the strictest of these state-level laws. Beginning in 2020, citizens will have comprehensive control over their personal data. For instance, companies like Facebook and Google must state what they are collecting about each individual, why they are collecting it, and who they are sharing it with. Consumers will have the option of barring data mimes like those from selling their data, and children under 16 must opt into allowing them to even collect their information at all.

There are other national laws to ensure data privacy, specifically the United Kingdom's Data Protection Act, which ensures that personal data is accessible to those whom it concerns and provides redress to individuals if there are inaccuracies. The Data Protection Act states that only individuals and companies with legitimate and lawful reasons can process personal information and cannot be shared. Finally, the General Data Protection Regulation (GDPR) of the European Union (EU) became law on May 25, 2018. Under this law, organizations face significant penalties if they do not comply with the regulation. It is anticipated that the GDPR will force organizations to comprehensively address their data privacy risks and take the appropriate measures to reduce the risk of unauthorized disclosure of consumers' private.

Examples of industry-specific data protection rules include the Payment Card Industry Data Security Standard (PCI DSS) for the credit card companies and the Family Educational Rights and Privacy Act (FERPA) for education institutions. These are industry specific and do not rise to the level of enforceable rules outside that particular area.

Computer Hacking Laws

The first real law that addressed crimes committed using a computer was Public Law 99-474, the Computer Fraud and Abuse Act (1986). This Act establishes through a federal mandate that a person is in criminal violation of the law who (Figure 10.7)

- Knowingly accesses a computer without proper authorization
- Exceeds their permitted access
- Uses that access to cause a loss > $1,000
- Performs an act, such as launching a denial-of-service attack that prevents other authorized users from using their computers.

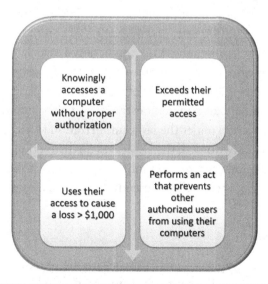

Figure 10.7 A person is in criminal violation of the law who.

The Fraud and Abuse Act further prohibits unauthorized or fraudulent access to government computers. It specifically prohibits access with intent to defraud, and it prohibits intentional trespassing, which is the legal term for "hacking." The Act is restricted to "federal interest computers," which are not as narrow as it might seem. It applies not only to computers that are owned by the government or used by the government but also to computers that access federal data or computers that are located in two or more states, e.g., the Internet.

Notwithstanding the provisions of the Tenth Amendment, separation of state and federal rights, that provision extends federal jurisdiction into every nook and cranny of the private sector.

In the years before the advent of the Internet, the Fraud and Abuse Act was intended to apply strictly to computers containing national defense, banking, or financial information. It established a range for criminal acts that took place, i.e., from a fine of $5,000 or twice the value of thing obtained by the illegal activity up to 5 years in jail for "criminal" offenses. However, Robert T. Morris was convicted and sentenced in 1990 under this federal law for the first true cybercrime.

Morris's case serves as a very good illustration of the problem of trying to assign penalties for crimes involving things of abstract value. Even though his act was considered a "six" under sentencing guidelines, meaning he was found guilty of fraud and deceit, the sentencing judge departed from the stipulations of the law and gave him 3 years of probation, a $10,000 fine, and 400 hours of community service.

The Supreme Court upheld his conviction a year later by deciding not to hear his case. It was their opinion that the wording of PL 99-474 was sufficient to define the facts of unauthorized access. Their view was that the defendant had demonstrated sufficient intent to injure to justify his conviction under the laws authorization to access provisions. However, currently worded, the law leaves no distinction between people who use computers for recreational hacking versus those who use it for the crime. So, there will be amendments as the precedents evolve.

Digital Evidence

Digital evidence typically entails the gathering of a correct and accurate copy of digital information. This material then becomes the target for forensic analysis. Since the evidence usually resides in a number of virtual places, the collection process always involves the identification and indexing of all of the locations where instances of relevant data exist. This is basically a tool-supported inventory process. Nonetheless, it is critically important to adopt a well-defined and formal protocol to ensure that the collecting agent has looked in all of the places that they need to look.

Because that evidence is typically electronic, the forensic collection process must be guaranteed to be technically sound. That assurance is necessary to ensure beyond a shadow of doubt that all of the evidence that is collected will be a true and accurate reflection of the facts of the case, at a given point in time. Most importantly, the organization has to have mechanisms in place to guarantee the integrity of the chain of custody. In its simplest form, the chain of custody requires the documentation of each step of the process as it occurred. Consequently, a formal protocol to ensure integrity has to be spelled out in any plan to establish a cybersecurity criminal investigation process, and all of these steps must be included in any comprehensive study.

Electronic evidence is basically intangible. Therefore, in the case of any form of prosecution, or litigation that relies on electronic evidence, it is critical that the investigating organization is able to certify that the evidence that was collected was obtained in a legal manner and not tampered with. The risk of having an ironclad case thrown out of court because of an illegal search, or a broken chain of custody, is the reason why the absolute assurance of the authenticity of virtual information is such an important aspect in the overall cybercriminal investigation process.

Digital Contracts

The most common application of law in cyberspace is the simple assurance of compliance with a contract. A contract is any legally recognized agreement. Contracts might be explicit between a customer and a supplier, or a primary contractor and a subcontractor. Contracts might also be implicit, for instance, between a supplier and an in-house customer. In every case, however, if a legally binding agreement exists, then the terms of agreement must be followed.

Contracts are based on "offer and acceptance." In simple terms, the contract involves an offer to another party, who accepts the offer. For example, in the fine print of most software sales, there is a window that says, "Do you accept these terms and conditions?" The buyer's clicking on the "I accept" button is a necessary part of creating a binding contract for the sale. In order to be valid, the parties to a contract must exchange something of value. In the case of the sale of a software product, the buyer receives something of value in the form of the functionality in the product, and the seller receives money.

There must be an express or implied agreement in order to form a contract. The essential requirement is that there be evidence that the parties had each engaged in conduct manifesting their assent and a contract was to be formed. A contract is made when the parties are demonstrated to have met such a requirement. All contracts based on offer and acceptance terms must be enforceable. The terms themselves must make it clear that the parties gave affirmative assent.

Because a contract can be made for any product or service, there is no single way to define how compliance should be legally ensured. However, the governing principles for how to go about are contained in the body of law that defines the rights and obligations of parties who enter into agreements. This is called contract law. Contract law serves as the basis for standardizing all commercial agreements.

All valid contracts must have terms. A term is a representation of fact made to induce another person to enter into a contract. Terms are a set of clauses defining the exact set of promises agreed to. The terms and conditions of a contract comprise its actual content. Only if a term is explicitly stated can a party sue for breach. The other part of the contract is the consideration. Consideration must be legally sufficient. There must be "consideration" given by all contractual parties, meaning that every party is shown to confer a benefit on the other party, or himself.

Contract stipulations must spell out the obligations of each party. Those stipulations constitute the elements of the contract. Typically, in order to be enforceable, a contract must involve an offer that another accepts. There must be evidence that the parties had each engaged in conduct manifesting their assent, and a contract was formed when the parties met such a requirement.

The action stipulated by the contract must be completed. In a typical "breach of contract" action, the party alleging the breach will attest that the party performed all of its duties under the contract, whereas the other party failed to perform its duties or obligations. That is called good faith. It is implicit within all contracts that the parties are acting in good faith. In order to be enforceable, a contract cannot violate "public policy." For example, if the subject matter of a contract is illegal, you cannot enforce the contract. A contract for the sale of illegal drugs, for example, violates public policy and is not enforceable.

Multinational Conventions (Accords)

Multinational jurisdiction is an aspect of the sovereignty question. It refers to explicit judicial, legislative, and administrative competence to rule on matters of law. Although jurisdiction is an aspect of sovereignty, it is not exactly the same thing. The laws of a nation may have an extraterritorial impact extending the jurisdiction beyond the sovereign and territorial limits of that nation. This is a big problem with cyberspace since the Internet does not explicitly recognize the sovereignty and territorial limitations, "e.g., the fourth amendment is a local ordinance." There is a conflict of law issue, since there is no uniform, international jurisdictional code.

The main question is… do we treat the Internet as if it were physical space and thus subject to a given jurisdiction, or act as if the Internet is a world unto itself and therefore free of such restraints? Certainly, the frontier idea that the law does not apply in "cyberspace" is not true. In fact, conflicting laws from different jurisdictions may apply, simultaneously, to the same event. But the Internet does not make geographical and jurisdictional boundaries clear. Internet users remain in physical jurisdictions and are subject to laws independent of their presence on the Internet, including the following:

- The laws of the state/nation in which the user resides
- The laws of the state/nation where the server hosting the transaction is located
- The laws of the state/nation which apply to the person or business with whom the transaction takes place.

So, a user in one of the United States conducting a transaction with another user in Britain through a server in Canada could theoretically be subject to the laws of all three countries. Courts in different countries have taken various views on whether they have jurisdiction over items published on the Internet, or business agreements entered into over the Internet.

Cross-Border Privacy and Data Security Laws

In practical terms, a user of the Internet is subject to the laws of the state or nation within which he or she goes online. Thus, numerous users of peer-to-peer file-sharing software have been subject to civil lawsuits for copyright infringement in their state of residence. This system runs into conflicts, however, when these suits are international in nature. Simply put, legal conduct in one nation may be decidedly illegal in another. In fact, even different standards concerning the burden of proof in a civil case can cause jurisdictional problems.

The unique structure of the Internet has raised several judicial concerns. While grounded in physical computers and other electronic devices, the Internet is independent of any geographic location. Yet, real individuals connect to the Internet and interact with others. So, if there are laws that govern the Internet, then it appears that such laws would be fundamentally different from laws that geographic nations use today. The question is exactly how or by whom the law of the Internet will be enforced.

As shown in Figure 10.8, there are four primary modes of regulation of the Internet. Law is the most self-evident of the four primary modes of regulation. As the numerous statutes, evolving case law, and precedents make clear, many actions on the Internet are already

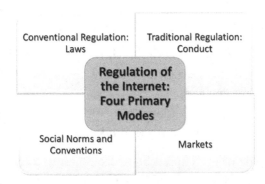

Figure 10.8 Regulation of the Internet: Four primary modes.

subject to conventional legislation. Areas such as gambling, child pornography, and fraud are regulated in very similar ways online as off-line. However, one of the most controversial and unclear areas of evolving laws is the determination of who has subject matter jurisdiction over activity (economic and other) conducted on the Internet, particularly as cross-border transactions affect local jurisdictions. The conclusion is that substantial portions of Internet activity are subject to traditional regulation, and conduct that is unlawful off-line is presumptively unlawful online, and subject to similar laws and regulations. Then, there are norms.

Social norms and conventions regulate conduct in significant ways. Certain activities or kinds of conduct online may not be specifically prohibited by the code architecture of the Internet, or expressly prohibited by applicable law. Nevertheless, these activities or conduct will be invisibly regulated by the inherent standards of the community, in this case the Internet "users." Just as certain patterns of conduct will cause an individual to be ostracized from our real world. So too certain actions will be censored or self-regulated by the norms of whatever community one chooses to associate with on the Internet.

Finally, there are markets. Markets are closely governed by local regulation. By virtue of social norms, markets also regulate certain patterns of conduct on the Internet, while economic markets have limited influence over noncommercial portions of the Internet. The popularity of the Internet as a means for all forms of commercial activity has brought the laws of supply and demand into cyberspace. Though not obvious to most Internet users, every packet of data sent and received by every user on the Internet passes through routers and transmission infrastructure owned by a collection of private and public entities. This is turning into one of the most critical aspects of cyber law and has immediate jurisdictional implications, as laws in force in one jurisdiction have the potential to have dramatic effects in other jurisdictions. Plus, there is the emerging issue of charges for Internet use.

Knowledge Unit Three: Cyber Ethics

The CSEC2017 is a comprehensive model of the body of knowledge for the discipline. Thus, it defines a broad range of essential elements of the cybersecurity function. One critical area of that model involves a discussion related to ethical models and thinking processes as they relate to appropriate behavior in cyberspace. That includes the ethical reactions to various current and emerging societal phenomena that cyberspace uniquely represents for individuals and organizations. The aim of the Cyber Ethics knowledge unit is to make the student aware of the importance of context when it comes to the actions that they take in the virtual environment. Therefore, this CSEC2017 area ensures that students will consider ethics as a whole as they go about their everyday duties, particularly as their work relates to adhering to acceptable cultural and societal norms (Figure 10.9).

In that respect, it must be recognized that the way that an individual, or organization, behaves is not some abstract thing. Ethical behavior is the embodiment of a set of commonly accepted principles and practices that are documented in a formal record of what is considered correct social norms. Because ethics are vital to any profession, organizations such as the Association for Computing Machinery (ACM), the Institute for Electrical and Electronics Engineers (IEEE), and other industry interest groups have promulgated their own set of ethical standards. As might be expected, these codes are specific to their particular professional niche. Still, they communicate the ethical responsibility of cybersecurity professionals in their particular domain. In addition, these codes establish a minimum set of expectations with respect to the level of professional capability required. Finally, they serve as a basis for judging whether that standard of performance has been adequately met.

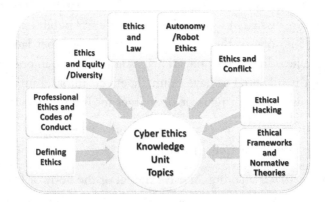

Figure 10.9 The Cyber Ethics knowledge unit topics.

In addition to national societies, a number of professional societies have also taken on the responsibility of stipulating codes of ethical practice. For instance, professional societies such as the Information Systems Audit and Control Association (ISACA), the International Information Systems Security Certifying Consortium (ISC) 2, and the SANS Institute have outlined a detailed requirement for ethical practice for their members, and each has as an ethical code of conduct built into its regulations. Finally, countless proprietary codes of conduct exist, which have been developed by individual organizations for their specific purposes.

A major concern is that, because there is not a single, universally recognized code of conduct promulgated for the cybersecurity profession, it will be difficult to say with certainty what is ethical and what is not in the overall practice. The issue of whether ethical behavior will be enforced by external regulation or whether it will have to rely on internally motivated compliance is also controversial. However, the need for a formally documented point of reference for professional conduct is clearly established.

Defining Ethics

Most cybersecurity professionals are aware of the need to comply with legal mandates. But in order for their behavior to be properly delimited, there also has to be a set of concrete recommendations about what constitutes acceptable personal and professional conduct. In essence, ethics codifies what it takes to comply with a moral precept rather than a legal requirement. Obviously, moral values become legal issues when they are turned into laws, under the specific sanction of a jurisdictive body. But laws are different from morals and society in the sense that they are explicitly stated and have explicit enforcement mechanisms built directly into their structure. Therefore, they are easier to understand and adhere to.

Although they are intangible things, knowledge of the specific requirements for responsible citizenship in cyberspace is an extremely important part of the development of a tangible and comprehensive cybersecurity response. That is because policies that shape how an organization, or an individual, will behave in their everyday life, have to fit with the ethical values and legal constraints of the environment that surrounds them. In essence, the way that a person or business defines its commitment to the confidentiality, integrity, availability, non-repudiation, and authorization of its information is wholly dependent on its ethical perspective, which is dictated by the social environment. It probably goes without saying that in order to ensure substantive and persistent adherence, all of the stakeholders must embody and act on the organization's commonly held social beliefs. Therefore, that organization's ethical point of view has to be wholly and unambiguously defined and understood.

Professional Ethics and Codes of Conduct

An exact specification of the criteria for social responsibility is a critical piece of knowledge for any profession, which is particularly true for a milieu as intangible as the information industry. Nonetheless, due to the abstractness of digital information, it can be difficult for basically honest people to tell when they are violating an ethical rule, or even breaking a law. Thus, it is generally felt that the process for ensuring good ethical decisions starts with the formulation of a commonly accepted, statement of the areas of common concern and the criteria for good decision making within those areas. The generic statement itself would, in effect, establish a formal point of reference that cybersecurity professionals utilize as the approved common basis for guiding their everyday actions.

Consequently, the aim of any formalized model of proper societal conduct is to help every person within a particular context make good day-to-day decisions. Thus, the model serves as a policy-based, fixed point of reference in everybody's decision-making process. In order to be practical and constructive, each individual's choice has to balance what is good for them, against the greater good of the contextual society. That balancing act is always dynamic, in the sense that there is no such thing as an absolutely correct answer. As a consequence, the formulation of a model of proper societal behavior involves the specification of a coherent set of commonly accepted actions for a given setting, which are designed to guide individual and group choices.

It goes without saying that this framework must explicitly embody and document the commonly accepted values and beliefs of the organization as a whole and must be appropriate to the milieu in which it operates. Because they represent the organization's fundamental ethical principles, these recommendations must be formally authorized by the appropriate body within the organization, and then promulgated as a standard statement of suitably correct behavior.

In generic terms, a standard statement of appropriate ethical behavior is customarily called a "professional code of conduct." Professional codes of conduct specify the values and beliefs of that particular organization. Therefore, they are normally referenced to a specific set of shared circumstances, such as job role, or organizational purpose. The code of conduct documents the organization's sanctioned understanding of its values and principles. In that respect, the code dictates the general basis for "right and wrong" as the organization views it.

A formal code is extremely useful as a communal means of ensuring that every aspect of the group decision-making process will properly reflect that organization's shared values and principles within that given context. In addition to its external uses, the code of conduct will also typically specify the appropriate way for the group's members to interrelate with each other and the external environment.

Finally, and most importantly, codes of conduct will define how the overall organization proposes to interact with the society that it is part of. In that respect, formal codes of conduct delineate each of the duties and obligations that every member of the organization owes to the company as well as its societal stakeholders. Thus, in effect, a formal code of conduct becomes the standard point of reference for judging the organization's "citizenship" in its larger environment as well as the adequacy of the behavior of every member of the group. In that respect, the code of conduct documents what the group considers correct and how people should act in reference to that belief.

Specifically, within any given organization, a professional code of conduct documents company's best practices for assurance of confidentiality, integrity, and availability of data assets. In an everyday sense, those practices are normally captured and disseminated by means of a comprehensive statement of formal policies for acceptable use. The acceptable use policy dictates the duties and obligations of individual members in reference to group norms. Acceptable use policies delineate the proper choices for individuals on matters that are dictated by the organization as a whole. Therefore, they reflect the general norms of the group.

Ethics and Equity/Diversity

It's a fact that the shortfall of properly educated cybersecurity professionals is a national crisis. Still, the same narrow set of individuals seem to be the only candidates for those positions. Accordingly, a good bit of the problem rests in the lack of diversity of the workforce. For instance, even though women are in the majority in the United States, the current percent of woman in tech positions is 11% (Hurley, 2017). Thus, cybersecurity is not simply the domain of the white male nerd caricature, which is such an endearing part of popular culture. It is also a place that can benefit from a diverse gender and ethnicity perspective. It is also the place where sustainable solutions require not simply technologists, but a diverse set of disciplines, managers, legal experts, compliance professionals, and human behavior specialists.

The CSEC2017 attests to the fact that cybersecurity extends to every nook and cranny of the organization by including "diversity" as a knowledge item. On the surface, this is an ethical concern. But in the most practical sense, the focus on engineering leaves a lot of easily exploited bases uncovered. In order to address today's multifaceted threats, we need to deploy a diverse set of skills, perspectives, and attitudes. Therefore, in the end, diversity of professional mindset is a simple survival concern. The fact that this is called out as a knowledge unit only serves to highlight the CSEC2017's validity as a conceptual model for the field.

Ethics and Law

As we have said, ethical systems allow members of a profession to make appropriate choices and enforce proper conduct. Ethical systems formalize the foundational principles of proper communal behavior for the group. Ethics is an important area of the body of knowledge because the philosophical frame of reference that we have employed for 2,000 years to define ethical and legally correct behavior is quaintly out of date when it comes to the information industry.

In essence, information technology has extended individual and institutional capabilities beyond any physical horizon ever imagined by traditional moralists and philosophers, and far beyond ideas captured in the precedents and principles of our legal system. Thus, in any discussion about something as abstract as values, it is important to provide a definition of terms. The term "ethical" is frequently used interchangeably with the terms "moral" and "legal." However, that is not correct usage. Ethics benefit cyberspace because they constitute an applied morality. Ethics are logical assumptions about how moral principles should be applied in practice.

Ethical systems represent an organization or an individual's tangible understanding of what is morally correct. Ethical systems become legal systems when the morality they capture is formalized into law. Laws are different from morals and ethics in that they are explicitly stated and have specific enforcement mechanisms and sanctions built into their structure. The distinction between these three terms lies in their degree of formality. Ethics represents the middle ground. Morals encapsulate beliefs. Ethical concepts are practical. They are descriptions of generally desired behavior. Legal frameworks are prescriptive and oriented toward the enforcement of defined standards of behavior. We discussed the legal implications of information assurance in the section on cyber law.

Special Areas of Ethics: Robotics, War, and "Ethical" Hacking

These three knowledge dimensions all derive from the same general condition, which is altered societal reality brought on by the outrageous advance of technology. The prospect of intelligent vehicles and devices like Siri and Alexa, the real threat of cyberwar, and the hacking which pervades every form of media and more importantly serves as a legitimate subculture were unheard of 20 years ago. Now all of that is a reality. The problem lies in the frame of reference we choose to adopt in order to deal with unheard of advancements in artificial intelligence like self-driving cars and manufacturing robots.

This requires a perspective that has yet to be fully realized, let alone formalized. The CSEC2017 raises the issue of what we do about ensuring that advancements in artificial intelligence and digital personhood result in positive societal outcomes. There is no specific legal, or ethical, remedy suggested, only the imperative that we consider these questions within the context of the profession. There are practical implications for all of this since the inevitable popularization of self-driving vehicles will require substantive ethical decision making in the form of decision algorithms built into those machines. For instance, should the self-driving vehicle swerve to miss the little old lady crossing the street and hit the school bus, or vice versa? All of these decisions will eventually have to be captured in the artificial intelligence (AI) and that responsibility implies a healthy dose of ethical thinking.

The same is true with the principles of war and aggression. No bombs will be dropped in the next worldwide conflict. But the effect will still be the same. So, what defines just principles of war and conflict? The same is true with the ubiquitous hacking culture. Cybersecurity professionals will have to make explicit decisions about when lines are crossed and that will require a foundation in moral and ethical thinking. So, in that respect, this knowledge unit is groundbreaking.

Knowledge Unit Four: Cyber Policy

Proper governance of cyberspace is increasingly critical to our national well-being. The reach of digital technology is pervasive and global. Therefore, cyberspace is now a national asset. We now have national infrastructures that deliver basic necessities such as electricity and which support our commercial and financial systems. Those all depend on digital functionality. Moreover, because of the Internet, we have established international social and trade links that are indispensable to our daily lives. Like all critical assets, that milieu must be trusted. Citizens need to be confident that the security and privacy of data, as well as the integrity of the digital domain, are dependable (Figure 10.10).

Underlying the World Wide Web are organizational principles and structures and technical wizardry that has to remain continuously resilient and resistant to arbitrary or malicious behavior. Thus, it is important for us to collectively recognize the challenges that are posed in cyberspace. That recognition is given substance through national and international policies. This is not some abstract exercise. Activities undertaken in cyberspace have consequences in the real world, and so the aim of Societal Security is to establish the rule of law, in order to ensure an open, interoperable, secure, and reliable cyberspace.

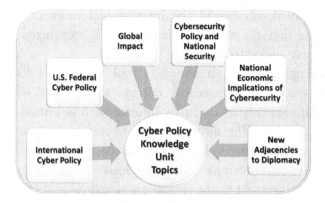

Figure 10.10   The Cyber Policy knowledge unit topics.

This all depends on nations as a whole, recognizing and safeguarding the elements of our increasingly interconnected world. Strategic policies guide the comprehensive conduct of nation-states and organizations. These policies are real-world statements of principle that provide a point of reference for guiding overall behavior based on that group's specific viewpoint. Strategic policies are particularly essential. In the case of cybersecurity, because they state a nation's specific understanding of the suitable response to a broad range of fundamentally abstract challenges.

The issues that are addressed by strategic policies in cyberspace stem from the ever-increasing influence of digital technology on everything from presidential campaigns to national defense. Policy concerns include such significant areas of impact as the effect of modern information technology exploits on the well-being of the national infrastructure, the influence of virtuality on the conduct of international diplomacy, and the proper ethical stance of the international community with respect to the factors that are integral to overall trade and commerce.

Thus, published strategic policy serves as the basis for shaping national behavior in cyberspace, as well as for evolving the behavior of each of the individual members of the international community. In practical application, this means that the overall strategic policy model must encompass every nation's values with respect to correct and reasonable conduct in virtual international relations. Policy must also be capable of ensuring the appropriate everyday interaction of each individual member of the international community, as well as ensuring that any unacceptable behavior is recognized and then appropriately responded to.

Accordingly, in an applied sense, a well-defined and documented strategic policy will underwrite a country's ability to tell whether the various national entities that they interact with in virtual space are behaving correctly. The ability to evaluate everybody's good citizenship in an environment as abstract as cyberspace is defined by evidence of each individual nation's ability to consistently make appropriate decisions with respect to the commonly stated rules of behavior that have been documented in the strategic policies that outline acceptable conduct in virtual space. Although the choices about how to behave are vested in the individual nation-state, the mechanism by which acceptable behavior is either rewarded or punished, is something that is established by the overall policies for acceptable use for the whole.

In order to be fully comprehensive, any CSEC2017 knowledge unit that is meant to guide students in their understanding of societal influences must consider policy in the large. Thus, the purpose of the Cyber Policy knowledge unit is to make students aware of strategic matters that pervade cyberspace. Strategy is a matter of big-picture thinking and analysis. Therefore, this unit has a major helping of discussion related to the shaping of nation-state behavior with respect to general citizenship, which includes the policies that motivate and guide international relations, specifically in matters of trade and also in terms of national defense and national deterrence. The most important element of this is the exploration of the various nuanced applications of economic and political policy as they apply in a virtual environment. That is all captured in the following six knowledge units.

International Cyber Policy

International policy is the basic yardstick by which a government makes decisions. These policies represent the general ends that government as a whole seeks to achieve. At present, there is no commonly accepted, substantive international policy for cyberspace. If acceptance comes, it will have to be through the agency of an international body like the United Nations. That particular body is currently considering a draft policy under the leadership of the International

Telecommunications Union and the U.N. Office on Drugs and Crime (UNODC). The United Nations is also considering the impact of cyberwarfare and has agreed that the assurance of cybersecurity is a global issue that can only be resolved through global partnerships. That consideration includes commonly accepted definitions of what constitutes an act of cyberwar as well as the mechanisms for regulating, enforcing, and auditing compliance with those accords.

U.S. Federal Cyber Policy

Federal government policy in cyberspace is stated in the implementation of the Federal Cybersecurity Modernization Act. This is Title III of the larger E-Government Act (P.L. 107-347), which was signed into law in December 2002. P.L. 107-347 formally recognizes the importance of cybersecurity to the economic and national security interests of the United States. Federal Information Security Management Act (FISMA) requires each federal agency to develop, document, and implement an enterprise-wide program to secure the information and information systems that support the operations and assets of every federal agency, including those provided or managed by another agency contractor, or other source. FISMA also mandates the use of federal standards to categorize impact according to a range of risk levels as well as the security requirements for information and information system in each such category.

The FISMA's standards are specifically applicable to all information within the federal government other than information that has been classified, or the systems designated as national security systems. FIPS Publication 199, Standards for Security Categorization of Federal Information and Information Systems, is the first of two mandatory security standards required by the FISMA legislation. FIPS Publication 200 is the second of the mandatory security standards. FIPS Publication 199 requires agencies to categorize their information systems as low impact, moderate impact, and high impact with respect to the confidentiality, integrity, and availability requirements of the information they contain.

These standards specify minimum-security requirements for federal information and information systems in 17 security-related areas. Federal agencies must meet the minimum-security requirements as defined by FIPS-200 through the use of the security controls specified in NIST Special Publication 800-53, "Recommended Security Controls for Federal Information Systems." NIST Special Publication 800-53 represents the current state of the practice in safeguards and countermeasures.

The minimum-security requirements cover 17 security-related areas. These 17 areas represent a broad-based response that addresses all management, operational, and technical aspects. Policies and procedures play an important role in the effective implementation of enterprise-wide security, as well as the long-term success of the resulting security measures. Thus, organizations must develop and promulgate formal, documented policies and procedures. The organizations must define the minimum-security requirements and must also ensure their effective implementation.

Organizations meet minimum-security requirements by selecting the appropriate security controls, which are obtained from NIST Special Publication 800-53, Recommended Security Controls for Federal Information Systems. The process of selecting the appropriate security controls and assurance requirements is a multifaceted, risk-based activity involving management and operational personnel within the organization. Categorization of the security requirements for every federal system, as required by FIPS Publication 199, is the first step in the risk management process.

The selected set of security controls must include one of three appropriately tailored security control baselines from NIST Special Publication 800-53. The controls are associated with the designated impact levels of the information determined during the security categorization process (e.g., FIPS-199). The resulting set of security controls must be documented in the security plan for the information system.

Global Impact

Globally, cyberspace is full of adversaries. Thus, the CSEC2017 has a specific topic related to the impact of cybersecurity on the global community. The reason why cybersecurity is so critically important is that a major exploit, like a successful cyberattack on the electrical grid, could leave a country or even the world cloaked in darkness, unable to communicate, and without any form of the 21st-century transport. Global threat actors range from state-sponsored groups through criminal enterprises, to any person with an Internet link and their ability to launch a potentially successful cyberattack makes every nation-state, into a potential super power.

There have been efforts to come together on the problem both at the United Nations level (which was mentioned above) and also as a business concern. The World Economic Forum emphasized the need for concerted action to address the problem of international cybercrime in a specific statement of concern after its 2019 worldwide conference in Davos. Thus, there is an awareness that some kind of well-defined and commonly accepted approach is required in order to address the problem of global threat in cyberspace. The concern is that there is no global agreement yet.

Cybersecurity Policy and National Security

Like any other policy initiative, the foundations of international cyber policy are grounded in a set of beliefs. In the case of U.S. international policy, the first of these is the belief that the free flow of information strengthens all societies. The second is the belief that cybersecurity threats endanger international peace and security. U.S. policy is to confront these challenges, while preserving its core principles (White House, 2011). That means that the U.S. international policy for cyberspace is shaped in such a way that it reflects the nation's fundamental commitment to the basic freedom of speech. However, this policy also recognize that exceptions to free speech in cyberspace must exist.

Specific examples cited in the national strategy include child pornography, inciting imminent violence, or organizing an act of terrorism (White House, 2011). Thus, the national strategy ensures expectations for privacy within reason. The strategy also underwrites expectations that data will be protected from fraud, theft, and threats to personal safety. In that respect, the aim of this strategy is to ensure a proper balance between law enforcement and the individual principle of free flow of information. The United States is committed to keeping cyberspace a level playing field. Therefore, it is committed to international initiatives and standards that enhance cybersecurity while safeguarding free trade and the broader free flow of information (White House, 2011).

National Economic Implications of Cybersecurity

From a national standpoint, most of the strategic economic issues center on the long-standing concerns about the overall digital infrastructure and its vulnerability to cyberwarfare and cyberterrorism attacks. The difference between a conventional cybersecurity attack and an attack on critical infrastructure is that the latter type of attack affects the entire. Therefore, we are all in the same boat socially and economically when it comes to attacks on the national infrastructure. Moreover, the diversity and the criticality of the sensors and controllers that comprise a typical infrastructure system make them tempting targets. Thus, besides the normal emphasis on the security of sensitive information, much of national security policy is focused on ensuring the continuing survivability of infrastructure systems.

This is of critical economic importance because a successful attack on an infrastructure system would likely kill many thousands of citizens, perhaps millions, through either civil unrest, failure of public systems, or mass starvation, for instance, when the Northeast (U.S.) blackout occurred. It caused 11 deaths and an estimated $6 billion in economic damages (Trend Micro, 2015). That is the reason why there is increasing interest in a coherent model for defending the critical infrastructure against cyberattack (NIAC, 2018).

New Adjacencies to Diplomacy

This CSEC2017 knowledge unit highlights the growing significance of virtual space in international discourse and diplomacy. That emphasis is important because the Internet has moved normal diplomacy from the exclusive white glove universe of the past into a new and highly dynamic, collaborative dimension, which is inevitably global in nature. Thus, cybersecurity impacts the way that countries interact with each other in the diplomatic arena.

The diplomatic communication process involves a multitude of actors and networks, and it is the key mechanism through which nations foster mutual trust and productive relationships. In that respect, nearly every aspect of human activity has become intertwined with cyberspace; thus, cyber-centered diplomatic actions have become crucial factors in ensuring the security and economic productivity of our global environment.

Much of the activity in the diplomatic area has been centered in three focuses. The first of these is devoted to the strengthening of international bilateral and multilateral international relationships, which can be seen in the cooperative work of the World Economic Congress, the 5I's, and other multinational alliances. The efforts of the United States in this area are expressed in H.R. 3873 (114th): International Cyber Policy Oversight Act of 2015. This Act directs the Secretary of State to conduct bilateral and multilateral activities to define the norms for responsible international behavior in cyberspace, as well as to review the alternative international norms in cyberspace offered by other prominent country actors. It also requires that the Secretary of State provide a detailed description of threats to U.S. national security in cyberspace from other countries, state-sponsored actors, and private actors.

The definition of, and defense against, cybercrime is another leg of the stool. This process is ongoing through the work of commercial agencies like the Business Software Alliance. It is also a major topic in the work of the United Nations and Interpol. The United States has been a major contributor in this effort and development of economic potential. As we have said throughout this section, much of this is driven by the need for a single mutually agreed-on policy for diplomatic cooperation in cyberspace. Much of this is by necessity built around common frameworks. As Americans have seen, cyberspace can be used to exert massive influence on a country's citizens or those of another country. The fact that cybersecurity has the capacity to sway opinions worldwide makes it an important milieu for the conduct of diplomacy.

Knowledge Unit Five: Privacy

This knowledge unit provides students with a specific understanding of privacy and its related challenges. Privacy is a very important and desirable quality in modern life because it underwrites personal freedom. The crux of the issue of privacy for cyberspace is the need to strike the proper balance in this information-driven world between knowing enough about a person, but not too much. That discussion underlies the content of the Privacy knowledge unit within the Societal Security knowledge area (Figure 10.11).

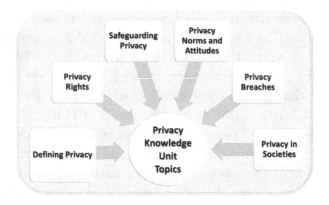

Figure 10.11 The Privacy knowledge unit topics.

Privacy is designed to ensure each individual's reasonable expectation of the confidentiality of their personal data. Fifty years ago, when green eyeshades, pencils, and large ledger books were just going out of style, this wasn't an important issue, because it was not possible to collect and use large quantities of individual information to directly impact an individual person's life. That was then and this is now. Large corporations have developed an insatiable appetite for data. As a result, every business in the Fortune 100 has committed enormous levels of economic and staff resources to developing a better understanding of every person in the United States, which breaches every individual's privacy to some degree.

The degree of knowledge that is generally available about an individual has spawned the data mining industry. That industry provides the capability to get complete, highly aggregated, in-depth, and up-to-date information about anybody and everybody who currently lives a normal life in the United States. This degree of access to each individual's personal information is where the problem lies. In function, data mining simply augments an organization's ability to better understand its customers. This is a benefit in-and-of-itself. Yet at the same time, it also creates a tempting target for abuse because it provides far too much information about everybody's personal life.

If gathering all of the necessary information to invade the private life of a person is not bad enough, the existence of that data raises another concern, which is the accidental, or intentional, violations of its assumed confidentiality. Essentially, the organization that holds the personal data of others has a legal obligation to prevent any harmful viewing or use of it. The consequences of million record losses, which extend back as far as 2003, have never been a major consideration in the study of cybersecurity (Katyama, 2003). Though, the profession stands guard over an inordinate amount of data. Still, this has serious implications for Societal Security, and any competent cybersecurity practitioner must be aware of what those issues are.

The legal test is whether the organization in question took reasonable care to protect the information under its care. If that is not found to be the case, then the custodian of the data is possibly liable for whatever damage ensues. This situation has been illustrated by numerous instances of litigation where the custodial party, a credit reporting agency for instance, was breached and damage ensued for the people whose files were lost. In all of those cases, the liability was found to rest with the keeper of the information.

Defining Privacy

A social system that is founded on the sanctity of individual rights always has to scrutinize the implications of too easy access to too much information, which is because sufficient information about an individual's life, habits, and history can be used to invade their private lives and to whatever extent possible manipulate them. In that respect, this simple distinction also defines the limits of proper use of information.

Because what might be legal is not the same as what is correct from a professional competency standpoint, the competency test is a lot simpler. Anybody whose information is held by an organization has a right to assume that their information will be kept confidential. Thus, any breach of confidentiality violates the reasonable presumption of professional capability. Moreover, that failure to protect an individual's private information is always an infringement of their rights as a citizen no matter what the finding of a court might be.

Privacy Rights

Privacy rights everybody just assumes that their personal privacy is fully protected by legal means; e.g., that no third party can ever acquire, use, or sell information that they have not explicitly authorized. However, as people's Internet surfing habits are captured by third-party cookies and their consumer behavior is recorded in their credit card purchases, it is possible to literally track and monitor every aspect of their daily life, almost as it occurs and "Big Data" has become a monumental hidden industry where most individuals' personal information is bought and sold on the open market like sides of beef. As a result, everybody's assumed right of privacy has been more or less eliminated.

Is Big Data an unethical or illegal enterprise? In an age where Internet exploits are front page news, the correctness of that kind of nakedly commercial behavior is still being debated. But one thing is clear. There ought to be a robust and effective behavioral frame of reference in place to guide organizations in their use of that data, as well as to protect individual privacy in the way the information is used. That is due to the fact that the potential for abuse of personal information is so profound. Hence, the assurance of proper and correct societal behavior is as critical an aspect of the overall consideration of security in cyberspace as are the more tangible technological considerations.

Safeguarding Privacy

The protection of the confidentiality of information, which is one of the prime directives for the field of cybersecurity, has both a safekeeping and a societal aspect to it. And no matter what safekeeping concerns are raised regarding how the breach was carried out, the societal obligation to ensure confidentiality has been violated. These are all matters that a responsible cybersecurity professional needs to understand and it is something that should be a part of every cybersecurity curriculum.

There are many instances where invasion of personal privacy takes place in modern society, for instance, credit monitoring. Credit monitoring agencies collect a lot more than credit history. They also know your legal, marital employment, and medical histories and even what magazines you read. The problem is that the same agencies are subject to the kind of disastrous breaches represented by the Equifax disaster, which exposed the information for 143 million Equifax customers to the Dark Web. There are two things that should be noted here: First, most people would be surprised to find out that Equifax, which is a nameless company to most people, knew so much about them. The second and more important point is that almost none of that information was ever expressly supplied by the individual.

Society's willingness to condone this kind of institutionalized behavior can be excused mainly because the leading edge in cyberspace has progressed so far beyond the bounds of what was conceivable 50 years ago, that most people still do not have sufficient understanding of what those capabilities imply in terms of individual interests and freedoms. And as a result, society hasn't grappled with the essential question, "What is the proper limit to the acquisition and use of knowledge by institutions and organizations?"

Privacy Norms and Attitudes

To make matters infinitely worse, most of the citizens of this country are far too unaware of the impact that knowledge might have on their lives. The problem centers on the fact that profit is the primary impetus for the collection and handling of personally identifiable data. Or in simple terms, businesses make a lot of money buying and selling information about you. Being viewed as livestock by the data mining industry might spark moral outrage, if it weren't for the fact that the workings of the technology mask the actions of the individuals who are gathering that information.

For instance, it is common practice to place third-party tracking cookies on most people's visits to commercial websites. These cookies record the viewing habits of that individual and report that back to their source at odd hours of the night. In that respect, a comparable act in the tangible universe would be to tap a person's home telephone to find out what kind of pizza orders they are placing.

Most people would view this as a violation of their right to privacy because they have seen enough gangster movies to understand that wiretaps are not a legitimate part of everyday business practice. However, there is so little knowledge about how third-party cookies work that the average citizen doesn't quite understand their significance and use. This probably explains why there is nothing like the sort of outcry that would occur if, for instance, the general population found out that their grocery store was following them around recording their every purchase.

Privacy Breaches

The assurance of data confidentiality and integrity is a critical element of trust. Therefore, the breach of privacy resulting from an organization's failure to properly maintain adequate protection is a major violation of trust. That failure can be either intentional or inadvertent; nevertheless, the consequence in both cases is a loss of confidence in the organization as a whole. Since trust is the single quality that every profession requires in order to be considered effectual, that is a serious issue.

One of the primary responsibilities of the field is to make certain that the information that is being safeguarded has a high degree of assurance. In practical terms, this simply means that the certainty exists that the information is confidential, correct, and has not been accidentally or maliciously altered or destroyed. If that occurs, then the cybersecurity professional has failed to satisfy their fundamental professional obligation. The exponential increase in cyberattacks, especially those associated with cybercrime, presents cybersecurity practitioners with an operational challenge. And, since the justification for even having a field of cybersecurity is to ensure the confidentiality and integrity of the data, this aspect of the Societal Security knowledge area is intimately involved with justifying the whole profession.

If gathering all of the necessary information to invade the private life of a person is not bad enough, the existence of that data raises another concern, which is the accidental, or intentional, violations of its assumed confidentiality. Essentially, the organization that holds the personal data of others has a legal obligation to prevent any harmful viewing or use of it. The legal test is whether the organization in question took reasonable care to protect the information under its care. If that is not found to be the case, then the custodian of the data is possibly liable for whatever damage ensues. This situation has been illustrated by numerous instances of litigation where the custodial party, a credit reporting agency for instance, was breached and damage ensued for the people whose files were lost. In all of those cases, the liability was found to rest with the keeper of the information.

Because what might be legal is not the same as what is correct from a professional competency standpoint, the competency test is a lot simpler. Anybody whose information is held by an organization has a right to assume that their information will be kept confidential. Thus, any breach of confidentiality violates the reasonable presumption of professional capability. Moreover, that failure to protect an individual's private information is always an infringement of their rights as a citizen no matter what the finding of a court might be.

Privacy in Societies

Privacy is an identifiable breach of a commonly understood legal principle. The other unique concern associated with the information industry is much harder to pin down, which centers on violations of privacy due to the acquisition and use of personal information as a commercial product. It is a fact that ant individual's personal information is as much a business commodity as manufactured goods and services. A range of institutions, some good and some potentially malicious, have collected and keep most of the vital personal information about everybody in this country, which can include things that people know about themselves, as well as things that they might not know such as the basis of their credit score.

The ability to document a set of detailed expectations about privacy is particularly important in our modern, totally wired virtual universe, since the leading edge continues to evolve at an unprecedented rate. Because of technology's outrageous expansion, the people in the organization are regularly presented with novel and uniquely difficult challenges in their everyday work lives. For example, most companies have access to the credit records of every person who has ever bought, sold, or done business with them. These records are likely to include legal history as well as projections about shopping and credit behavior. The overall implication of that degree of knowledge is that many of the traditional rights to privacy, which the average citizen just assumes is safeguarded because they are protected under older ethical systems, have been totally eliminated and so those records are open to exploitation.

The large amount of accumulated information is harmless as long as there are no threats present. However, it is a serious vulnerability if it is obtained and used for malicious intent. The general security principle that this vast collection of information could potentially violate is confidentiality. However, besides the simple loss of privacy, the misappropriation of personal information can lead to actual financial damage. The fallout from civil litigation over the past decade provides indisputable proof that almost any expense is justified to keep credit data secure.

This is not just a societal issue since the disclosure of private information is also a matter of civil and even criminal liability in some states. As an example, most pharmacies keep the drug history of their customers on file. Generally, most people's purchases at a pharmacy are of interest only to themselves. But if, as has happened in the past, this information is intentionally provided to somebody in order to reveal lurid facts about a political candidate's personal health then that would constitute both an invasion of privacy and a breach of confidentiality, which makes violations of assumed confidentiality a matter for litigation.

Fifty Review Questions: Societal Security

1. What is the most common kind of cybercriminal?
2. What are the behavioral incentives that might lead a person to attack your system?
3. Why are motives used as behavioral signatures? Why are such signatures required?
4. Why is cyberterrorism a critical problem? What does it impact?
5. What is the problem with the collection of evidence in cyberspace?
6. What is chain of custody and why is it important in cybercriminal investigation?
7. Why is cybercrime an economic issue? What aspects of the economy does it impact?
8. What is the specific issue associated with cyberwar? Why is it considered asymmetric?
9. What is the purpose of cyberterrorism? What does it seek to cause?
10. Why is strict attention to detail an essential element of a cyber forensics curriculum?
11. What is the jurisdictional problem associated with cyber law enforcement?

12. Why is it difficult to enforce property rights for digital products?
13. Why is the right to privacy an issue with data mining?
14. Why are contracts difficult to enforce in cyberspace?
15. What are the four primary modes of regulation in cyberspace?
16. Why is chain of custody for virtual evidence important in litigation?
17. Why is it necessary to have cross-border agreements in place for virtual products?
18. How does the issue of sovereignty apply to virtual products in international law?
19. What are the "elements of the contract?" Why must they be explicitly spelled out?
20. What is the problem with drawing up and enforcing privacy protection laws?
21. What is the role of an ethical model of behavior?
22. How is ethical behavior documented – in what form?
23. What is a code of conduct? What is its purpose?
24. Why are codes of conduct essential to businesses?
25. What are codes of conduct used to judge?
26. What is the difference between an ethical principle and the law?
27. How has information technology changed the way we view ethical behavior?
28. What is the reason why ethics has anything to do with AI?
29. How does cyberspace redefine our view of warfare?
30. What is the primary significance of cyber ethics in the effort to control hacking?
31. How is cyber policy different from any other form of policy development?
32. What is policy in-the-large? Why is it an essential part of Societal Security?
33. Why are international bodies critical to the establishment of societal policies for cyber?
34. How does policy relate to national security?
35. What is the definition of "privacy within reason?" Why are these distinctions needed?
36. What are the economic aspects of cybersecurity? Where does infrastructure come in?

37. How is diplomacy tied to Societal Security?
38. What is the International Cyber Policy Oversight Act of 2015?
39. What is the Business Software Alliance? How does it affect diplomacy?
40. What is the role of the United Nations in establishing Societal Security?
41. What does privacy specifically underwrite?
42. Why is privacy particularly important to citizens? What does it prevent?
43. Why are privacy norms important? What causes the lack of norms?
44. Why is data mining potentially a threat to privacy?
45. What is the threat associated with having a large collection of information?
46. What can privacy breaches lead to in terms of real-world consequences?
47. Why is privacy breach a litigation issue? What can cause litigation to happen?
48. What is the role of documented expectations about privacy?
49. What is the economic value of personal information? How does it aid business?
50. How do violations of privacy potentially affect the conduct of public affairs?

You Might Also Like to Read

- Armstrong, Dean, Dan Hyde, and Sam Thomas, *Cyber Security: Law and Practice*, Jordan Publishing, Bristol, 2017.
- Baase, Sarah and Timothy M. Henry, *A Gift of Fire: Social, Legal, and Ethical Issues for Computing Technology*, 5th Edition, Pearson, London, 2017.
- Bayuk, Jennifer L., Jason Healey, and Paul Rohmeyer, *Cyber Security Policy Guidebook*, 1st Edition, Wiley, Hoboken, NJ, 2012.
- Bazzell, Michael, *Hiding from the Internet: Eliminating Personal Online Information*, 4th Edition, Amazon, Seattle, WA, 2018.

- Bazzell, Michael and Justin Carroll, *The Complete Privacy and Security Desk Reference: Volume I: Digital*, Amazon, Seattle, WA, 2016.
- Britz, Marjie, *Computer Forensics and Cyber Crime: An Introduction*, 3rd Edition, Pearson, London, 2013.
- Buchanan, Ben, *The Cybersecurity Dilemma: Hacking, Trust and Fear Between Nations*, 1st Edition, Oxford University Press, Oxford, 2017.
- Clancy, Thomas K., *Cyber Crime and Digital Evidence: Materials and Cases*, 2nd Edition, Lexis-Nexis, New York, 2014.
- Craig, Brian, *Cyberlaw: The Law of the Internet and Information Technology*, 1st Edition, Pearson, London, 2012.
- Dudley, Alfreda, James Braman, and Giovanni Vincenti, *Investigating Cyber Law and Cyber Ethics: Issues, Impacts and Practices*, 1st Edition, IGI Global, Hershey, PA, 2012.
- Guiora, Amos N., *Cybersecurity: Geopolitics, Law, and Policy*, 1st Edition, Routledge, Abingdon, 2017.
- Mitnick, Kevin, *The Art of Invisibility: The World's Most Famous Hacker Teaches You How to Be Safe in the Age of Big Brother and Big Data*, Little-Brown, New York, 2017.
- Schmalleger, Frank and Michael Pittaro, *Crimes of the Internet*, 1st Edition, Pearson, London, 2008.
- Spinello, Richard, *Cyberethics: Morality and Law in Cyberspace*, 6th Edition, Jones and Bartlett, Burlington, MA, 2016.
- Tavani, Herman, *Ethics and Technology: Controversies, Questions, and Strategies for Ethical Computing*, 4th Edition, Wiley, Hoboken, NJ, 2012.

Chapter Summary

- A stable point of reference is required if society is ever going to enforce acceptable individual and/or group behavior. That is the role of CSEC2017 Knowledge Area Seven, Societal Security.
- Ensuring proper behavior of the citizens in an interconnected universe is a critical factor in the assurance of societal interaction.

- Cybersecurity students and practitioners must be able to appreciate, as well as evaluate, the universal conventions, concepts, and concerns of human interactions in a virtual society.
- The presence of a statement of formal principles allows individuals and corporations to formulate an ethical approach to virtual space, as well as to better control their subsequent behavior and interactions.
- The first and most important purpose of the elements of the CSEC2017 Societal Security knowledge area is to formally codify what should be expected in a capable cybersecurity curriculum.
- That formal specification can be used to develop targeted courses and teaching material.
- The Societal Security domain encompasses five large-scale constructs that encompass areas that broadly impact society as a whole, which are as follows:
- *Cybercrime* – all forms of criminal behavior in cyberspace. This knowledge unit provides students with an understanding of the scope, cost, and legal issues relating to cybercriminal activity. Subunits are as follows:
  1. Cybercriminal behavior
  2. Cyberterrorism
  3. Cybercriminal investigation
  4. Economics of cybercrime.
- *Cyber law* – encompasses the current and emerging framework of laws and regulations governing cyberspace. Cyber laws can be classified into five generic categories: governmental regulations, privacy regulations, laws that regulate intellectual property rights, contract and tort law, and laws that regulate computer crime. Subunits are as follows:
  1. Constitutional foundations of cyber law
  2. Intellectual property related to cybersecurity
  3. Privacy laws
  4. Data Security law
  5. Computer hacking laws
  6. Digital evidence

7. Digital contracts
8. Multinational conventions (accords)
9. Cross-border privacy and Data Security laws.

- *Cyber ethics* – fundamental principles that underlie and motivate communal good behavior. That cyber ethics includes the ethical reactions to various current and emerging societal phenomena that cyberspace uniquely represents for individuals and organizations. Subunits are as follows:
  1. Defining ethics
  2. Professional ethics and codes of conduct
  3. Ethics and equity/diversity
  4. Ethics and law
  5. Special areas of ethics – robotics, war, and "ethical" hacking.

- *Cyber policy* – strategic decision making with respect to socially acceptable corporate directions. Strategic policies guide the comprehensive conduct of nation-states and organizations. These policies are real-world statements of principle that provide a point of reference for guiding overall behavior based on that group's specific viewpoint. Subunits are as follows:
  1. International cyber policy
  2. U.S. federal cyber policy
  3. Global impact
  4. Cybersecurity policy and national security
  5. National economic implications of cybersecurity
  6. New adjacencies to diplomacy.

- *Privacy* – assurance of a fundamental right to personal privacy in virtual space. This knowledge unit provides students with a specific understanding of privacy and its related challenges. Subunits are as follows:
  1. Defining privacy
  2. Privacy rights
  3. Safeguarding privacy
  4. Privacy norms and attitudes
  5. Privacy breaches
  6. Privacy in societies.

Learning Objectives for the Human Security Knowledge Area

Mastery of the requisite learning outcomes for the Human Security knowledge area will be established through the student's ability to paraphrase and explicate the key contents of the knowledge units within this knowledge area (Bloom Level Two and Three). In addition, the student will exhibit specific behaviors that demonstrate a capability to utilize these relevant concepts in common practical application. Specifically, the student will be able to paraphrase and explain the following 26 knowledge elements (CSEC, 2019):

1. The various common motives for cybercrime behavior
2. The various common motives for terror activities in cyberspace
3. The various terrorist behaviors geared toward raising societal fear and certainty
4. The methods and practices for investigating both domestic and international crimes
5. The reason why preserving the chain of digital evidence is necessary in prosecuting cybercrimes
6. The constitutional foundations of cyber law
7. The relevant international Data Security and computer hacking laws
8. The relevant laws related to security protection of intellectual property.
9. The relevant laws governing online privacy
10. The difference between virtue ethics, utilitarian ethics, and deontological ethics
11. The professional ethics and codes of conduct of societies, such as ACM, IEEE-CS, AIS, and (ISC) 2.
12. The ways in which decision-making algorithms could be deceptive in setting social policy
13. The impact of international public policy positions on organizations and individuals
14. The nation-specific cybersecurity public policies with respect to protecting sensitive information
15. The nation-specific cybersecurity public policies regarding protection of critical infrastructure
16. The global impact of cybersecurity on a nation's culture

17. The global impact of cybersecurity on a nation's economies
18. The global impact of cybersecurity on a nation's social issues
19. The global impact of cybersecurity on a nation's policies
20. The global impact of cybersecurity on a nation's laws
21. The fundamental concept of privacy
22. The societal definition of what constitutes personally private information
23. The trade-offs between individual privacy and security
24. The trade-off between the rights to privacy by the individual versus the needs of society.
25. The common practices and technologies utilized to safeguard personal privacy
26. The ethics of footprinting in the context of privacy.

Keywords

Behavior – individual personal actions performed that are observable by third parties

Best Use (Policy) – explicit statement of the specific actions required in a given situation

Code of Conduct – documented rules outlining expected behaviors for an organization

Compliance – authenticated actions that indicate that a requirement, rule, or law is followed

Controls – a discrete set of human, or electronic, behaviors set to produce a given outcome

Critical Asset – a function, or object, that is so central to an operation that it cannot be lost

Cybercrime – antisocial acts committed using a computer, typically explicitly illegal acts.

Cyber law – formal legal system for adjudication of acts in cyberspace

Cybersecurity – assurance of confidentiality, integrity, and availability of information

Ethics – a standard for commonly accepted behavior in a given area of practice

Morality – a standard for commonly accepted correct behavior in a given culture

Norms – assurance of consistently correct behavior by individuals in the organization

Infrastructure – a collection of large components arrayed in a logical structure in order to accomplish a given purpose. Commonly used to describe the tangible elements of cyberspace.

Privacy – assurance that personally identifiable data is safeguarded from unauthorized access

Strategic Policy – the process of developing long-term plans of action aimed at furthering and enhancing organizational goals

References

Hurley, Deborah, "Improving Cybersecurity: The Diversity Imperative", Forbes, CIO Network, 7 May 2017, www.forbes.com/sites/ciocentral/2017/05/07/improving-cybersecurity-the-diversity-imperative/#2f9e31c31e30, accessed March 2019.

Joint Task Force (JTF) on Cybersecurity Education, "Cybersecurity Curricula 2017, Curriculum Guidelines for Post-Secondary Degree Programs in Cybersecurity, a Report in the Computing Curricula Series", ACM/IEEE-CS/AIS SIGSEC/IFIP WG 11.8, Version 1.0, 31 December 2019.

Katyama, Fred, "Hacker Hits up to 8M Credit Cards, Secret Service and FBI Probe Security Breach of Visa, MasterCard, Amex and Discover Card Accounts", CNN, 27 February 2003. https://money.cnn.com/2003/02/18/technology/creditcards/, accessed March 2019.

Microsoft Security Team, "The Emerging Era of Cyber Defense and Cybercrime", Microsoft Secure. https://cloudblogs.microsoft.com/microsoftsecure/2016/01/27/the-emerging-era-of-cyber-defense-and-cybercrime/, 27 January 2016.

National Infrastructure Advisory Council (NIAC), "Surviving a Catastrophic Power Outage", Department of Homeland Security, 11 December 2018.

Radware, "2018–2019 Global Application and Network Security Report," 2019. www.radware.com/pleaseregister.aspx?returnurl=7563c321-ce21-4cc9-ae0d-4d75062acf70, accessed March 2019.

The Software Alliance, "Software Management: Security Imperative, Business Opportunity", 2018 BSA Global Software Survey, June 2018. https://gss.bsa.org/wp-content/uploads/2018/05/2018_BSA_GSS_Report_en.pdf, accessed March 2019.

The White House, National Strategy to Secure Cyberspace, February 2011.

Trend Micro, "Report on Cybersecurity and Critical Infrastructure in the Americas", Organization of American States, Trend Micro Incorporated, 2015.

Index

Printed in the United States
by Baker & Taylor Publisher Services